A Henry Adams Reader

A
Henry Adams
Reader

Edited

and with an Introduction

by

Elizabeth Stevenson

Doubleday Anchor Books

Doubleday & Company, Inc.

Garden City, New York

1958

Acknowledgments

"Henry Adams Meets Garibaldi" is reprinted by permission of the American Historical Association from the *American Historical Review* of January 1920, where the selection appeared (with explanatory notes which are omitted) under the title, "Henry Adams and Garibaldi, 1860." The two letters were printed originally in the Boston *Courier* on July 10 and 13, 1860.

Chapter VI of Henry Adams' *Democracy* (to which a title has been given, "Mount Vernon Picnic") is reprinted by permission of Henry Holt and Co., Inc., New York, N.Y.

The following selections are reprinted by permission of Houghton Mifflin Co., Boston, Mass.: three chapters from Henry Adams' *Mont-St.-Michel and Chartres*, II, "La Chanson de Roland," VII, "Roses and Apses," XI, "The Three Queens"; the "Prayer to the Virgin of Chartres," taken from *Letters to a Niece and Prayer to the Virgin of Chartres*, edited by Mabel La Farge; two chapters from Henry Adams' *The Education of Henry Adams*, I, "Quincy," and XXXIV, "A Law of Acceleration, 1904"; Henry Adams' letter of October 9–22, 1890, to Elizabeth Cameron in Volume I, *Letters of Henry Adams*, to which the title, "Samoa, 1890," has been given. Houghton Mifflin also published Henry Adams' *John Randolph*, from which Chapter X, "Eccentricities," is reprinted as "John Randolph's Eccentricities."

The selections from Henry Adams' *The Degradation of the Democratic Dogma*, copyright 1919 by The Macmillan Co. ("The Tendency of History" and "The Rule of Phase Applied to History"), are used with permission of The Macmillan Co.

Acknowledgments

Henry Adams' poem *Buddha and Brahma*, which was published in October 1915 in *The Yale Review*, is reprinted by permission of *The Yale Review*, copyright Yale University Press.

Charles Scribner's Sons published Henry Adams' *The History of the United States*, from which are reprinted four chapters: Volume 1, Chapter XV, "Toussaint Louverture"; Volume 6, Chapter IV, "Harrison and Tecumthe"; Volume 6, Chapter V, "Tippecanoe"; and Volume 7, Chapter XIII, "Privateering." Charles Scribner's Sons also published Henry Adams' *Historical Essays*, from which are reprinted two essays: "Captaine John Smith" and "The New York Gold Conspiracy."

Henry Adams' biography, *The Life of Albert Gallatin*, was published by J. B. Lippincott Co. The selection, "The Importance of Albert Gallatin," comprises the end of Book II and the beginning of Book III.

Henry Adams' novel, *Esther*, was reissued in 1938 in a facsimile reprint by Scholars' Facsimiles and Reprints. Its original publisher was Henry Holt & Co., Inc. The selection, "The American Girl," is a portion of Chapter I.

Contents

[vii]

Contents

Introduction

The man who wrote a curious kind of autobiography in *The Education of Henry Adams* hid more of himself than he revealed in that provocative book. Yet most of Adams' readers come to him through that one book: they are transfixed by it and find its ideas threading a pattern through their ideas for the rest of their lives; but they know not Adams. Taken by itself, the *Education* is an unforgettable statement and challenge. Reading Adams' other writings enriches not only an understanding of the *Education* but a whole period of American life, from the Civil War to World War I. His letters, essays, magazine writings, his novels, biographies, the great unread *History,* and the somewhat neglected first half of his study of unity and multiplicity, the *Mont-St.-Michel and Chartres,* diversify the image of Adams which he purposely narrowed in the *Education.*

Reading the wide range of Adams' writings, one can sense some of the imaginative discoveries made in a long life, a varied life, a life of high pitch and fervor. He was born in Boston, February 16, 1838. He died in Washington, D.C., on March 27, 1918. There is an interest, in following the life through the writings, of seeing a fallible but highly gifted man make matter of his mistakes as well as the good things life threw his way. He came from strongly rational and self-consciously upright New England stock. It was his misfortune, as well as his great good luck, to be endowed with susceptibilities not necessarily linked to rationality, those of the five senses and of the far-ranging imagination. He made a synthesis of his contradictory gifts and created books out of this mingling.

In his own mind the physical scenes were related to the

mental discoveries of his life. The first place to affect his imagination was the old Adams house at Quincy. When he was a small boy, this house was his grandfather's house. Here he was given license all the long summer to read as he liked, lounging on piles of moldering *Congressional Records*, to go swimming down in the bay, to roam the hills behind the town, to live a free boy's life of discovery. The longer he lived away from Quincy and the house, the better he remembered the place, and the more it meant to him. Yet it was only a rambling, unpretentious, clapboarded house, sheltered by the usual local elms. His grandfather had been to him, not the ex-President, but the old man who grew fruit trees, the old man who was always writing, the old man who made him go to school one day when he did not want to go.

The Adams past powerfully affected him. Both his reaction away from family and his reference to family were important. And the house was forever a focal point. It was in that house that he sat one day and wrote the last word of his nine-volume *History*. The grandfather was long dead; the grandson under the roof of the ancestors finished his study of the period in American history in which John Quincy Adams had played no negligible part.

His first childish effort to get out of the local skin of association, meaning, and authority happened to him when he was twelve. His father, Charles Francis Adams, took him on an excursion to see Mount Vernon, the home, not just of the national hero, but of the particular family hero. Here in 1850 the little boy asked himself some puzzling questions, wondering how the beautiful neglected house and its master could have been the product of the abhorred system of slavery. Not at once, but only gradually, he began to doubt certain sectional and family certainties about wickedness. Slavery was the "sum of all wickedness" to a Boston boy, but slavery had produced a George Washington. Many years later, in writing the *Education*, he would think back to that scene to dramatize certain mature doubts as to what constituted the good life: rational choice or a kind of intuitive, organic cohesiveness. New England and the South became two balancing symbols, not of good and evil, but each of a particular kind of irreconcilable good.

After the traditional experience of luxuriating for four years in a small, stagnant Harvard, he made his first voyage away from home. His ostensible purpose was to study law in Germany. His failure in his avowed purpose, his loneliness in Berlin where he practiced preposterous economies, his brave attempt to learn German in a school for little boys, his first try at writing for the newspapers were important in his growing up.

He was venturing to make his own mistakes. Europe was too large an impression to swallow all at once at twenty. Yet living the life of one of Henry James' younger heroes—reading a little German and Latin, studying with a fencing master, looking at pictures he did not understand, almost falling in love—he found something abroad he had not found at home. The rash way he ran off to Sicily to see Garibaldi rounded off his first independent experience before he went home in 1860 to vote for Abraham Lincoln.

The Civil War swept him off his balance as much as it did the citizen soldier who went South from New England to fight. Adams' fight took place in London, but his sequestration from the battlefields had a more damaging effect on him, perhaps, than an active participation in the battles his brother Charles saw. Damaging, but fertilizing, were all these war experiences in London. Loneliness was a forcer of mental growth. He wrote for the Boston and New York papers a column of English impressions; he worked long hours in the Legation office; he read and read; he began to overcome his shyness, to learn to meet people, to take part in the give-and-take of good talk. *John Smith* was the best production of the war years. Doing it late at night set his mind on history, biography, and American destiny. He found out in doing it that he could undertake and complete a job of research. He sold the essay and devoted himself thereafter to the world of writing, although in his predestined complex way he scorned writing and admired only action.

Although he came back to his own country in 1868 out

of step with the national march toward speculation, consolidation, and concentration, he found the arena of bad business practice and bad political practice a brilliant one for his carping pen. He succeeded well enough to annoy certain congressmen and certain capitalists as an intrusive, sharp-witted, and sharp-tongued voice of the Independents. His *New York Gold Conspiracy,* for which he tangled with Jim Fisk in person and traced the national corruption into the White House, was the noisiest success of this period.

Yet his small bright success as a magazine writer seemed to lead to a dead end. He was willing, if not particularly anxious, when asked, to go home to Boston in 1870 to teach history at Harvard and edit the *North American Review.*

He was the quickest of his own students. He had to teach himself, at first, what he taught his students and keep one or two steps ahead of them. To them he was an outrageous, actorish, argumentative, yet genially tolerant gentleman. He flayed their prejudices, astonished their traditions, entranced their interest. In a lighthearted manner, having a horror of seeming to be in earnest, he had again, as he had had in Washington as a free-lance reporter, a great and seemingly effortless success. He transformed the teaching of history in American colleges and universities; he trained a new generation of teachers of history; he conceived for himself the goading ambition of not just teaching but of writing history. He collected the essays of his graduate students, and one of his own, in *Essays in Anglo-Saxon Law.*

As editor of the *North American Review* he controlled an effective outlet for the Independents and had a broad field for his own widening scholarly interests. He edited the magazine just long enough to begin to be bored with it, and broke with its publishers deliberately on a point of politics at the same time he threw up his job at Harvard.

The cruel death of his older sister Louisa by tetanus in 1870, the year of his first going to Harvard, had severed his allegiance to orthodox solutions of existence. He could not accept her death as in any sense meaningful. He held in abeyance all solutions, coming gradually to find understandable only process, flow, evolution, taken in a pessimistic sense. But since he was relatively young when he first worked out these tenets, successful, happily married (to Marian Hooper in 1872), ambitious, his intellectual doubts did not have much effect upon his buoyant emotions.

His removal to Washington from Boston in the fall of 1877 was decisive. He got out of New England forever (except for very agreeable summers at Beverly Farms and Antaeus-like returns to the Old House). His drastic decision was made for the sake of the books in him and for the sake of the more complex and entertaining climate of living in the capital. He wanted to observe politics, he wanted to have leisure to write, he wanted to study a cultivated social world and find out what made it tick. His going south to Washington seemed foolish to some of his friends, but it was very fruitful in happiness and creativeness. He lived in Washington—when not roaming the earth—for the rest of his life. He came to love not only the human comedy of its circles and triangles and long straight avenues, but the dense, dusky life of its surrounding woods.

Private means and private contentment made it possible for him to please himself and to write the books he now felt he must write. But talent, energy, and a fiery persistency were necessary for the high rate of production he maintained during the years that were left to him of personal happiness. Between 1877 and 1885 he wrote two novels, two biographies, planned another biography that was later destroyed or lost, edited the papers of one of his biographical subjects, edited the papers of New England Federalism, and began a nine-volume history: *Democracy, Esther, The Life of Albert Gallatin, John Randolph,* the lost *Aaron Burr,* the papers of Gallatin, *Documents Relating to New England Federalism,* and the *History of the United States during the Administrations of Thomas Jefferson and James Madison.*

After a period of mental depression, Marian Adams killed herself in December 1885 by swallowing some of the chemicals she had used in developing her own photographs. This event cut Adams' life in two. The new house that had been designed by Richardson for Mr. and Mrs. Adams and their discriminating gaieties housed Adams alone now: a small, proud, bitter man. He could not and would not ask for pity, discuss, or even mention, for many years, his dead wife. In enduring pain, and perhaps self-blame, he became not only more keenly intelligent but sharper, harsher, more cruel to himself and to others. He would not be reconciled.

Now began his restless, long-swinging trips across the world and round it: Japan, the South Seas, the islands of the West Indies, the dusty roads of Mexico, the cold frontier of the North Cape, the American West and its accessible wildernesses, Sicily, Russia, the Middle East, and Greece. He set up a routine of restlessness and spent a part of every summer in Paris, a part of every winter in Washington.

He wrote little for publication. He finished the *History*. He wrote the tentative *Tahiti*. He sent home his letters, messages of almost unguarded candor from the far points of his wanderings. His letters were jealously treasured and jealously shared among his friends. He paid a great price to become an interesting man.

Out of the agonies of looking for and not finding solutions, and looking again, came his late works: *Mont-St.-Michel and Chartres* and *The Education of Henry Adams,* the elegiac *Life of George Cabot Lodge,* the speculative essays, *The Rule of Phase Applied to History* and the *Letter to American Teachers of History.* It is necessary to connect the agony with the achievement. His dislocation just after his wife's death was personal and purposeless and might have remained so for the remainder of his life. But he was able at last to trace a relationship between his personal suffering and the general suffering he discerned in the universe.

He did not make out this connection easily or quickly. He wandered first through various archaic societies (the broken-down Latin world of rural Cuba, the gentle, out-of-touch Buddhism of the new Japan, the dying felicities of the island world of the Pacific). He came back to Western civilization in 1892 knowing that he did not like it or belong to it, still not knowing what to prefer. He might have gone through life as a cutting edge, cutting to no purpose, hurting himself, slashing at his friends, and at his age, pointlessly. Two things happened to give a direction to his murderous sharpness.

One was the financial depression of 1893. This general malaise of American society caused him to turn his gaze outward and away from his personal tragedy toward the objective national tragedy. It became important for him to find a necessary artistic, as well as necessary logical, connection between his private hurt and the national hurt. This problem, enlarged to take in his whole experience of life, he gave a shape to, at last, in *The Education*.

In 1895 an accident of travel set him down among the cathedrals of northern France. These buildings gave him his alternative to the prison of his own age. They came to symbolize another kind of life in which all the richness of art, faith, and wealth was poured out in one coherent unity of social effort.

He had at last his two poles of interest; his drama to work out; his studies to make; his books to write. He might have used the Byzantine or classical Greek civilization as his alternative to twentieth-century civilization if he had not at a particularly susceptible moment walked through the door of the cathedral of Coutances.

The age of the cathedrals had virtues his own age lacked. His own age needed an end, an aim, or at least a center to make its remarkable energies mean something. He stated the lack. He stated an alternative. Being a late pessimistic evolutionist, he doubted anything for the future but a continual, rapidly accelerating disintegration through the exercise of purposeless material power.

Out of the movement of his spirit toward unity came *Mont-St.-Michel and Chartres;* out of his movement toward multiplicity and his dread of it came *The Education of Henry Adams.*

A life cannot be explained. Biography and criticism can only track their prey and perhaps get near enough to snap a picture at an interesting angle, but never to capture their victim whole and alive. Reading his books takes one much nearer to the complex typical man of an age who also happened to be a writer. This is still his voice. These works are as flavorful as ever.

Any one selection from a strongly idiosyncratic writer may set the reader off on a personal exploration of the wholes from which these mutilated parts were taken. That is the hope in which these selections from the writings of Henry Adams were made.

E.S.

Journalist

Henry Adams Meets Garibaldi

*Very young, very naïve, trying desperately hard to be so-
phisticated was this young European correspondent who
was Henry Adams at twenty-two. A cat may look at a king,
a young Adams may stare at Garibaldi. He had finished
Harvard. He was rounding off his first experience of Europe
with a lark: an expedition to Sicily to see a guaranteed
hero and a bona fide revolution. For the first time, Henry
Adams could say to himself: "Here I was at last, then, face
to face with one of the great events of our day."*

HENRY ADAMS MEETS GARIBALDI[1]

Palermo, June 9, 1860.

At Naples we knew next to nothing about the state of
things at Palermo, and there was a delicious uncertainty
about having one's head knocked off or losing some of one's
legs, that was gloriously exciting. Here from my room,
looking out over the harbor and the bare old Monte
Pellegrino, it all seems easy and simple enough, and quite
a matter of everyday life, but in Naples the prospect was
like looking down the crater of Vesuvius. There on the
morning of the 5th, I had to fly about from Department
to Department, and never could have taken the first step
towards getting here, if it had not been for the kindness

[1] The two letters appeared first in the Boston *Courier* on
July 10 and 13, 1860. They were reprinted in the *American
Historical Review* in January 1920 under the title "Henry
Adams and Garibaldi, 1860."

of my friends, who pushed me along, and worked like beavers for me. After six hours of driving about in a sun that positively singed me, I got it all straight, and was put on board the steamer *Capri*, bound to Palermo, bearer of despatches to Capt. Palmer of the *Iroquois* and the American Consul.

The *Capri* was originally one of the Neapolitan line of steamers that run from Naples to Marseilles, but is now taken by Government to carry supplies to the garrison at Palermo. We took two brigs in tow, one of them laden with nothing but water. You can form an idea of the management of affairs from that one fact, that even the water for the troops had to be brought from Naples.

Three long hours we had to wait for the Captain, who was at Portici, getting despatches from the King. Unluckily, the King forgot him, and went to dinner, so he had to wait till dinner was over. When he did come aboard, he was as jolly a little fellow as I ever saw, flying about and chatting all the time like a whirligig. He spoke very fair English, too, and as we had the whole ship to ourselves, it was as comfortable as any one could desire.

The weather was exquisite and the sea calm, and as the sun set, we steamed slowly down the bay of Naples with the two vessels in tow. Towards ten o'clock, when I went on deck to take a last look before going to bed, the moon was rising and I could see the island of Capri still on our left, and away behind us the great fiery blotch on the side of Vesuvius.

As we came along into sight of Palermo we heard the reports and saw flashes and smoke of a quick cannonading. I watched it with a feeling of decided discomfort. The idea of being shot, occurred to me with new and unpleasant force. The Captain however consoled me with the assurance that Garibaldi had no cannon, and that this was probably an admiral's salute from the war-ships in the harbor. So we drank a bottle of beer together and told the anxious old gunner that he might have those four precious six-pounders of his unshotted. It was nine o'clock at night when we entered the harbor and, passing a number of great ships of war, we came to anchor near the British admiral and there we lay all night.

The Captain's brother came to take supper with us and give us the latest news, which all parties seemed indifferent to; so when we had finished eating, we sat on deck smoking and talking and listening to a band which was playing waltzes on board the *Hannibal.* There was just moon enough to show how silent and calm and black everything was just as if no Garibaldi were within a thousand miles.

The next morning, the 7th, I went on board our war steamer, the *Iroquois,* and presented the papers I was charged with, and from here to an American merchant vessel, to find our Consul. I found him bearing bravely up, though he had been some three weeks penned up with several other families, on this temporary boarding house, living from hand to mouth. The deck as I saw it was paved to some depth with dogs, chickens, pigs, fleas, babies, trunks and other articles. His spirits were good, however, under all this weight of trials, and he was preparing to return today to his house on shore. The English, by the way, were luckier than the Americans during the troubles, for their line-of-battle ship, the *Hannibal,* was turned into a hotel and baby-house, price nine shillings a day, bed and board. We have no large ships in the Mediterranean now, so paid famine prices for accommodations on board the merchant vessels. Now, however, all was quiet again, and the day I arrived the whole of the refugees were striking for shore.

I took a boat and landed. Numbers of men and boys, nearly all armed and looking very disreputable, were lounging and talking on the quay and round the Porta Felice. Here and there a red-shirt showed itself. They make a very good uniform—rowdy but pugnacious; and now that Garibaldi has made them immortal, all young Sicily is putting them on, and swelling about in them almost as vulgarly, though more excusably, than New York firemen.

Of course you know the whole story of the campaign by this time, and as I am not writing a history of events, but only an account of a flying visit to the city, there is no use in my repeating what everybody has heard. But just to show you how I found affairs, I will note a few of the dates again.

At about three o'clock, the morning of Sunday, May 27th, Garibaldi dismounted from his horse at the Porta Termini, and coolly puffed away at his cigarette while he urged on his fifteen hundred men into the city. All Palermo rose at once. The street fighting and barricading lasted all that day, and that night Garibaldi slept, if he slept at all, in the Senatorial Palace, the very heart of the city, directly cutting in between the royal palace at one end of the straight main street, the Toledo, and the harbor and the castle at the other end, and isolating the royal troops in several separate positions. This was a real Garibaldian move, which ought to have cost him his life and the Sicilians their cause; but as it did not, it put the whole game in his hands. The next day and Tuesday, the barricading and bombarding continued; a good deal of property was destroyed and a good many old people, women and children were killed;—but Garibaldi was the stronger for every bomb that fell. On Wednesday the 30th, the Governor yielded to a cessation of arms, which, on Saturday, was changed into a capitulation and evacuation of the city; a most ludicrously disgraceful proceeding, for which the King would, I think, be justified in blowing the General's brains out with his own royal revolver.

So you see already more than a week had passed since the grand fight, when on the morning of the 7th we watched from the *Iroquois* the long line of Neapolitan troops wind along round the city, with drums beating and colors flying, to their temporary quarters at the Mole. Two hours afterward, when I went on shore, the whole city, except the Castle, was fairly evacuated, and his Majesty's twenty-three thousand troops had shown themselves worthy of their reputation.

So, when I arrived, the lively part of the campaign was over. The shops were still shut and the city still in arms, but there was no more fighting, nor was it likely there would be any more in Palermo. Of course the first explorations were towards the main street, the Toledo which the Royal troops could have raked up and down—from one end from the palace, and at the other from their frigates in the harbor. There were barricades at every five or six rods, higher than my head and mostly cannon-proof. Swarms of people were hurrying about, but no one was doing any work that I saw, except a few Piedmontese on guard at important points. Almost every one had a gun on his shoulder, and the peasants who had come down from the interior in crowds looked about as dirty, as lazy, and as degraded as the best conservative could wish. They were sleeping in the squares, or lounging in groups round the guard-houses, their guns in their hands, and in costumes very suggestive of brigands and cut-throats. It was a strange collection of arms that the insurgents had. There were guns of every shape and length, from the short, fat blunderbuss, suggestive of stage-coaches and highway robberies two centuries ago, up to long-barreled, thin affairs, such as the Arabs might have shot with when Mahomet was a small boy. There were plenty of Neapolitan muskets about, too, which deserters had brought, or cowards had thrown away to run better. All the townspeople seemed to have a rage for cutlasses and dirks, which were half the time tied over their shoulders with twine. Among other armed individuals there was a priest in his black robes, rushing about day after day, with a gun in his hand. A large average of the arms were too old and rusty to be dangerous to any one but the owner. Providence seemed particularly kind to the city, for though every one was carrying his gun loaded and capped and sometimes at full cock, and jamming against the stone barricades in the crowds at the narrow passages, and gesticulating as only these Sicilians and Neapolitans can gesticulate, we heard of no one case of an accident, though it is hardly possible but that there must have been a few. Still to do the Sicilians justice, for all their laziness and brutish look and dirt, it was a peaceable, good-natured crowd, and I have seen in all only one drunken man, and no fighting nor insolence. Perhaps it might not be so well behaved if Garibaldi was not dictator.

I passed barricade after barricade till I came to the Senatorial palace, where the headquarters of the insurgents are. This is not directly on the Toledo, but a little to one side. Before it, there is a small square, and what the naval officers call the improper fountain, improper because there is half Lempriere's Classical Dictionary on it, but a copious insufficiency of costume. There I found a still greater confusion and chaos, and crowds of desperately patriotic Sicilians were sleeping, eating, chattering and howling under the windows of the General-in-Chief. I stopped a minute here to look at fire-cannon of all ages and sizes, mounted on wagon-wheels and looking like the very essence of revolution, rusty, dirty and dangerous to the men that used them. These were new arrivals under Colonel Orsini, for Garibaldi had none in the fight. It is curious how the cannon make their appearance in the city. I met to-day, the 9th, with a splendid new barricade towards the castle, and in it two heavy iron cannon apparently ready for action at any instant for there was a strong guard of red-shirts there, to say nothing of a crowd of armed ragamuffins. Garibaldi must have a dozen now, at the very least, and some are good little field-pieces. They say that these are old cannon buried in 1849, and now dug up again.

A little way above the head-quarters, the other great street of Palermo crosses the Toledo at right angles, and from this spot one can look out of four gates at four quarters of the compass. Can you imagine a General with two thousand foreign troops and twenty-one thousand native troops who would lose a city like this? Still a little way further and I met a high barricade with two heavy cannon, which commanded the Toledo straight up to the royal palace and the city gate. Some red-shirts were on guard there, armed half with muskets and half with rough pikes. Just beyond this I met another guard of Piedmontese who stopped me and turned me back by "Excellency's orders." As they apologized and were deeply pained, as they declared, to have to do it, I felt rather flattered than otherwise, and turning back took the first side street to the left. There is no use describing the looks of the thing, for by this time you probably know more about it than I do myself. It was now comparatively respectable to what it had been, and the dead bodies and disgusting sights had all been cleared away. After a long detour and a very indefinite idea of my whereabouts, I made my way through all the particularly nasty lanes and alleys I could find, back to the Toledo. For dirt Palermo is a city equalled by few. I do not know whether I ran any danger of being robbed; indeed it hardly occurred to me that it was possible. I never dreamed of going armed, was all alone, and looked I suppose a good deal as if I had just stepped out of the Strand in London, so far as dress went, but no one spoke to me or interfered with me in any way. Possibly Garibaldi may have exercised some influence on the robbers and rascals, for he has them shot as they are taken, and the people occasionally amuse themselves by kicking and stoning them to death. I believe about a dozen have kicked their heels at heaven already by the Dictator's orders.

After fairly seeing it all, I came to the conclusion in the first place that Garibaldi was all he was ever said to be. He and his Piedmontese are the whole movement; the rest is not enough to stand by itself now. Put a weaker hand than his here, and see how long these wild brigands would keep order and hold together. I do not pretend to judge of a country where I have only been three days, but my own belief is that Sicily is a bad lot, and it will take many years to make her a good one.

In the second place, let people say what they will, it is utterly inconceivable to me how any sane general, with twenty-three thousand troops, cannon, fortified positions, ships of war, and uncontrolled powers, could have the brazen face to surrender the city. Disaffection in the troops does not account for it. You can depend upon it, that no honest general could submit to such a disgrace as that and live after it. It is one of those things which I could never have believed, and which in any country but Naples would be impossible.

Dreadfully hot and tired, I eat some ice cream and came back to the hotel. Here one's time is agreeably divided between hunting for fleas and watching the fleet in the harbor, which is always firing salutes and making a most hideous noise with them. Almost every nation has its flag here. People are a good deal surprised that we have only one war steamer, and that a small one. We ought to have some line-of-battle ships round Sicily and Naples now.

At dinner we had quite a famous party. The celebrated Colonel Türr sat at the head of the table, next to him the correspondent of the London *Times*, then another of Garibaldi's Colonels, then the correspondent of the London *Illustrated News*, then I think Colonel Orsini, and so on. Brixio is also in the same hotel, and a number of other celebrities.

That same afternoon at six o'clock, I was taken to see the Dictator. The party was five in all, officers and civilians, and the visit was informal; indeed, Garibaldi seems to discourage all formality, and though he has just now all the power of an Emperor, he will not even adopt the state of a General. Europeans are fond of calling him the Washington of Italy, principally because they know nothing about Washington. Catch Washington invading a foreign kingdom on his own hook, in a fireman's shirt! You might as well call Tom Sayers, Sir Charles Grandison.

We walked up the Toledo and found the little square before the palace even rowdier than usual. A band of musicians had been raked together, and they were marching about and making a great noise, and looking very dirty and ragged, with a most varied collection of instruments. Of course the louder they played, the louder the people howled *viva Italia*, and the more chaotic the crowd became. The effect was quite striking, except that it was rather laughable.

We did not stop to look at this long, for the crowd made way to the uniforms, and the sentries at the steps presented arms as we passed. It was nearly the same scene inside the palace as outside. One saw everywhere the head-quarters of revolution pure and simple. On the staircase and in the ante-rooms there was a chaos broken loose, of civilians, peasants, priests, servants, sentries, deserters from the royal army, red-shirts, and the blue-shirts, too, of Orsini's artillery, and all apparently perfectly at home. We had no time to look carefully, however, but passed straight on, every one showing us the greatest respect, until finally the third door opened, and there we were, in the presence of a hero.

Garibaldi had apparently just finished his dinner, and

was sitting at a corner window talking with four or five visitors, gentlemen and ladies of Palermo. He rose as we came in, and came forward shaking hands with each of the party as we were introduced. He had his plain red shirt on, precisely like a fireman, and no mark of authority. His manner is, as you know of course, very kind and off-hand, without being vulgar or demagogic. He talked with each of us, and talked perfectly naturally; no stump oratory and no sham. Just as an instance of his manner, there was one little action of his that struck me. I was seated next him, and as the head of our party remarked that I had come all the way from Naples in order to see him, he turned round and took my hand, thanking me as if I had done him a favor. This is the way he draws people. He talked mostly in French, for his English is not very good. As for what he said, it is of no particular interest to any one, at least as far as it was said to me. The others can report the conversation if they think it worth while to report what was not meant to be reported.

But this was only half the scene. At a round table in the middle of the room, a party of six or eight men were taking dinner. These were real heroes of romance. Two or three had the red shirts on; others were in civil costume; one had a dirty, faded, hussar jacket on; one was a priest in his black robes. They were eating and drinking without regard to us, and as if they were hungry. Especially the priest was punishing his dinner. He is a fine fellow, this priest, a slave to Garibaldi and a glorious specimen of the church militant. I have met him several times, rushing about the streets with a great black cross in his hands. He has a strange, restless face, all passion and impulse. The others were Garibaldi's famous captains—a fine set of heads, full of energy and action.

Here I was at last, then, face to face with one of the great events of our day. It was all perfect; there was Palermo, the insurgent Sicilian city, with its barricades, and its ruined streets with all the marks of war. There was that armed and howling mob in the square below, and the music of the national hymn, and the five revolutionary cannon. There were the guerilla captains who had risked their lives and fortunes for something that the worst envy could not call selfish. And there was the great Dictator, who, when your and my little hopes and ambitions shall have lain in our graves a few centuries with us, will still be honored as a hero, and perhaps half worshipped—who knows!—for a God.

And yet Heaven knows why he, of all men, has been selected for immortality. I, for one, think that Cavour is much the greater man of the two; but practically the future Italy will probably adore Garibaldi's memory, and only respect Cavour's.

As he sat there laughing and chattering and wagging his red-grey beard, and puffing away at his cigar, it seemed to me that one might feel for him all the respect and admiration that his best friends ask, and yet at the same time enter a protest against fate.

As we came away he shook hands with us again, and took leave of us with the greatest kindness. As we made our way through the crowd across the square, we stopped a minute to take a last look at him. He was leaning on the railing of the balcony before his window, quietly smoking his cigar, and watching the restless, yelling crowd below. He seemed hardly to be conscious of the noise and confusion, and looked in his red shirt like the very essence and genius of revolution, as he is.

We walked up the Toledo to see the part which I had been refused admittance to, in the morning. The uniforms opened the way for us everywhere, so that we examined the whole ground at our leisure. I suppose you know all about it, so I shall not waste my time by describing it. Only take care of believing all that the English reporters say; not that they tell lies, but that they are artistic in their work; in other words, they throw a glare of light on their own point of view, and leave the rest of the picture all the darker. The Neapolitans are about the most contemptible nation I ever happened on, and this bombardment was a piece with their character,—but as for a fight between Neapolitans and Sicilians, it seems to me that it is just about nip-and-tuck between the two. Putting principles out of the question, the only sympathy I can feel with any party is with the Piedmontese. The Sicilian common people are famous ever since the Sicilian Vespers, and especially in the cholera troubles of 1837, for being the most brutal and savage crowd known in modern Europe.

So ended my first day in Palermo. The next morning there was still more wandering about the streets. The amount of red, white and green colors displayed is quite astonishing. Every one has a cockade,—or almost every one, except perhaps some of the foreigners. Placards are beginning to make their appearance, just as before the annexation, in the Romagna and Tuscany. "We choose Victor Emanuel the II. for our King." Garibaldi is bound to force that through, if he can, but I think his work here will be of the hardest. However, you are as good a judge of that as we are.

We had quite a funny little "looting" expedition that afternoon, up to the Royal Palace. Some English officers from the *Hannibal* and an American from the *Iroquois*, with some civilians, nine of us in all, went off to walk, and as the only walk is up the Toledo, we brought up finally in the palace. The Neapolitan troops had evacuated it the day before, and it was now held by a guard of fourteen Piedmontese. We had the run of the whole place except the state rooms, and of course made any amount of noise, and satisfied our curiosity, by going everywhere and examining everything. Of course, a building which has had several thousand Neapolitan troops quartered in it for some months keeps little enough of its good looks, and still less of its objects of value, even if there ever were any there, which I doubt. The rooms were full of boxes, beds, scraps of uniforms and soldiers' accoutrements, fragments of manuscripts, books about religion and war, indiscriminate dirt and fleas. It was perhaps as dirty a hole as I ever saw, even in Palermo. Still, plunder is plunder, or "loot," as the Englishmen called it, and the party loaded itself with old woolen epaulets, braid, books, handcuffs, and so on, as mementoes. In the stables we found an army of hungry rats and a dead horse. In the guard-house, a wretched man who was to be shot within twelve hours for an attempt at assassination; this was a sight that I could have spared, for the people had pretty much made the shooting unnecessary. When we came out again on the square we had a grand flea-hunt, for the beasts were all over us by dozens, and they were the biggest and hungriest specimens yet discovered. The *Illustrated News* correspondent, who was one of the party, is to make a sketch representing us dancing about and diving at each other's pantaloons. The officers' white duck showed the game beautifully, but our woolen ones only gave them a shelter, and the consequence is that I am never free nor quiet, for my clothes bagged the most and concealed them the best.

Loaded with the plunder we marched back again, the grinning red-shirts presenting arms to us everywhere. Only one of us could speak Italian, but no one cared for that, and a crowd of the natives had something or other to say to us, good-natured and even liberal. One old brigand whose portrait has already figured in the *News,* insisted on paying for our ices and treating us to Maraschino all round, which was very generous indeed, but the stuff was enough to make one sick, even though it were taken to Garibaldi's health. After it we marched down to the harbor with the romantic old bandit and his gun, in the middle of us.

I had now been two days in the city and had only one object more to detain me here. It is always better and pleasanter to look at more than one side of a question, and I was curious to see how it went with the royal troops, and as I had brought with me from Naples a letter to an officer of the Swiss legion, I did not care to leave the city without presenting it. So, towards evening to-day I walked round the harbor to the quarters of the royal army, perhaps half an hour from the hotel. They still have their barracks and are packed away in a great prison, a cloister and so forth. Three lines of guards stand across the streets towards the city, but I passed without question, and so did every one also, as far as I could see. The troops were just forming for the *rappel* as I crossed the great parade ground, so I delivered my letter to the officer, who was already at the head of his command, and sat down myself before the guard-house to watch the performances. The troops came on the ground with their music and all their equipments, looking as fresh and as effective as any troops I ever saw. There seemed to be no end to the numbers. They poured in, thousands after thousands, and packed the whole great space. I do not think I ever saw so many troops together before; there must have been hard on twenty thousand on the spot, all well-armed, well-dressed and apparently well-drilled.

As they were forming around the square a small guard came in on one side, passing me, and had in charge an old gray-mustachiod Swiss, either drunk or a deserter, or both, who seemed terribly excited, and was talking in a half scream. The Major looked very grave, and disappeared as they brought the man in, but he kept on his screaming as they locked him up, and I could distinguish an endless repetition of "Do with me what you will. Life and death are all one now." Poor old fellow, I wonder whether they shot him. The King is in a bad way when his Swiss desert, for whatever faults the Swiss may have, they have proved themselves faithful, at least.

After about half an hour the troops were marched off again, and my friend came back to me and took me into his quarters. It is a queer place now, this city, for strange sights and scenes. Here was a battalion of foreign troops quartered in a Franciscan monastery, and the cloisters were all alive with busy, chattering German soldiers. We went up the staircase and into my friend's room, a monk's cell, furnished with half-a-dozen chairs, on which a torn and dirty mattress was laid, a table on which there were some lemons and oranges, and a lamp. A couple of glasses of lemonade were ordered, and we sat down and sipped it, and smoked and talked.

It was a strange place for a chance traveller to hit on, and I must say the general effect was gloomy to a degree. The evening was heavy and dull, with the clouds hanging low on the mountains, and as the little white-washed cell got darker and darker, and the hive of soldiers down in the cloisters grew more and more indistinct, while the officer was telling his story, full of bitterness and discontent, I really sympathized with him, and felt almost as gloomy as he.

Of course, one ought to hate a mercenary soldier, and

especially one of the King of Naples. Very likely I should
have hated him if he had been coarse and brutal, but as
he was very handsome, young and well-bred, in fact quite
an extraordinary gentlemanly fellow, the thing was different. His ideas were just about what I had supposed they
would be. He and his division had arrived on the second
day of the fighting, and had not even been in fire. He had
personally nothing to brag of and nothing to be ashamed
at. But he declared solemnly, as his own belief and that of
the whole corps, that the King had been betrayed; that the
city might easily have been held; and that though the
greater part of the Neapolitan troops were cowards rather
than traitors, there were still excellent regiments among
them who would have been more than strong enough under
a capable general. The feeling among these troops was that
they were all sold out, and the commanding officer of the
foreign legion had felt so strongly about it, that when ordered just before the armistice not to stir a step nor to fire
a gun, he had gone to the Commander-in-Chief and with
tears in his eyes, offered him his sword, protesting against
taking any share in such a burning disgrace. The bombardment was just as bad as all the rest of the performance—as
cowardly as it was ill-judged. The soldiers had been badly
treated, and were deserting in crowds; and even the Swiss
and Germans were disgusted with the want of faith kept
with them, in not fulfilling the terms of enlistment, and
were deserting like the rest. He asked me what people said
in the city about Garibaldi's plans, and the immediate
prospect, and I replied that no one knew anything except
the General himself. "Well," said he, "I will tell you the
universal belief among us. It is that the embarcation of our
corps is to be purposely delayed until there is a rising in
Naples, so that we may not be there to put it down. You
will see we shall not get back to Naples till it is all over
there." Do not suppose that I believe all this myself. I only
want to show you what the condition of the royal army is.
Yet he said that even now, demoralized as the troops were,
there were still enough good ones left, with the help of the
eighteen hundred Swiss, to hold their position, and drive
Garibaldi out of the city, in spite of barricades and all. In-

deed, he did not seem to believe much in the Sicilians or their barricades, and called the Piedmontese the only real force that could do any fighting—speaking of them and their General as brave men and honorable enemies.

It was dark when I came away, and he came with me to the shore, to see me on board a boat. We had literally to force our way through the thousands of Neapolitan soldiers who were wandering about, chattering and laughing and playing. We shook hands on parting, and I wished him happily out of the whole affair.

"Yes," said he, "I think indeed the whole matter is now nearly ended; at least for us; and I am not sorry. I am tired both of the people and the service."

A tolerably mournful conclusion of ten years' duty, and a gloomy yielding up of a long struggle against fate. But we liberals may thank God if the battle ends so easily.

H. B. A.

Naples, June 15, 1860.

My last letter, dated from Palermo, the 9th, announced that I should come off as soon as I could. It grew stupid there to one who was only a looker-on and not in the secret course of things. There was little or no society, and still less variety of amusements. Barricades are interesting at first, but one gets very soon angry that they are not taken down. It provoked me to see some fifty thousand men roaming about with guns in their hands, which nine-tenths of them would not dare use against an enemy, unless from behind a wall, and all the time the aqueducts were cut, and no one thought of repairing them, and the communication from street to street was as good as wholly interrupted. Of course, this was all right enough; and it was not to be expected that respectability should get the upper hand again so soon; but I speak naturally as a traveller, not as an insurgent.

From my window I used to watch the ships every day, and the dirty little boys on the quay who were making targets of the marble statues of their kings. Bomba's head was already stoned back again into a rough block of marble, and he had lost all his fingers at the time I left. This was the only wanton destruction I saw, and, under the circumstances, it speaks well for the Sicilians.

Besides, I felt sure that the first act of the melodrama was over, and that the second would not have Palermo for its scene. The most that could be hoped for was a popular vote on the question of annexation to Piedmont, and they seemed to be preparing for this when I was there. But the very idea of this rather hurt my feelings. It is, to be sure, a great compliment to the strength and life of Americanism, that Napoleon and Victor Emanuel and Garibaldi think it necessary to go back to our foundation principle as the source of their authority; but do you know, to my mind these European popular elections have a little too much demonstration in them; they are a sort of continual squatter sovereignty, and very like a satire on our theories. I do not pretend to be a philosopher, but I do know that if I were a conservative I should wish nothing better than these elections for an argument against and a sarcasm on popular governments in their whole length and breadth. It is a sword with two very sharp edges, this, and is apt to cut the wrong way as well as the right.

The *Capri* was still in the harbor on the morning of the 10th, and I took a boat and went off to her. The little captain was flying about in a crowd of officers, busy as could be, but shook hands with me as if I were his dearest friend and we had been separated for years. He was to leave for Naples that same afternoon, and would be most boundlessly delighted to have the pleasure of my company. Perhaps you will appreciate this Italian profusion of politeness better, if I tell you that the captain is a prince, and belongs to an old and famous Neapolitan family.

We were to leave at three o'clock. At four I came on board. Everything was in an Italian confusion. Everybody was screaming and gesticulating, or else lounging and sleeping. Some hundreds of soldiers with their wives, children and baggage, as well as some horses, were being embarked, and of course the scene was much like a pitched battle. On the shore among the soldiers there were a number of the famous policemen, the sbirri, whom the Sicilians have such a love for. These men must feel happy, very; for if they were accidentally caught, the Sicilian mob is not gentle, and they might find themselves skinned alive; or going through some other process of the kind. An officer of the *Iroquois* told me that only the day before I got here, he had seen one of these fellows lying in the middle, his head cut off and put between his legs, and a cigar stuck in his mouth. Whether he deserved his punishment or not, of course we cannot know. But as a matter of pure curiosity I would really like to know how many of the men who served him up in that elegant way would have been policemen themselves if they had been offered money enough for it. There is, to be sure, a great deal that is admirable in this Sicilian revolution, but a great deal, too, that reminds one very much of a servile insurrection. Where is the Sicilian nobility and the gentlemen who ought to take the lead in a movement like this? or is there a single Sicilian competent to sustain Garibaldi or take his place? If not, of course it is the fault of the government they have been under so long, who have crushed out all development; but what sort of a people it must be, if a foreigner, with an army of foreigners, supported by "Native Chiefs" and their clans, make the only great force of the whole movement. One cannot always control his ideas and prejudices. I can never forget, in thinking of Sicily and the kingdom of Naples, that under the Roman government these countries were the great slave-provinces of the empire, and there seems to be a taint of degradation in the people ever since. It is not good stock.

It was past six o'clock before we got off and left Palermo and Sicily behind us. The first cabin was not at all full. A few officers of different ages, and a girl, the daughter of one of them, were all who sat down to supper with us. On deck it was different. The men were wedged together there, and every inch was covered. Among the soldiers were some few Germans, and I talked some time with one of them, a good-natured Viennese, who had served fourteen years in the Austrian army, and altogether had had quite a glorious career: Hungary in '48 and '49; Magenta and Solferino in '59; and now at Palermo. That is a curiously happy list for

any one who seeks the bubble reputation. He told me all
the story of his wrongs; how they had promised him thirty
dollars bonus; cooked meals twice a day, and generally the
life of a prince; and how on coming here he had found himself most outrageously sold; never received a cent of his
money; lived like a dog, and for ten days since he landed
at Palermo had eaten nothing but hard biscuits and raw
pork. He was very good natured under his troubles, though,
abusing Naples and the Neapolitans terribly, but seeming
to think that nothing in the way of bad management had
ever been known in his dear Austria. "They did not do
things so there," he thought; and I did not try to convince
him that they had done things much better. He was on the
sick list, down with fever, and returning to Naples with
some other sick and wounded. He said there had been a
great many desertions in his battalion, which is new and
not wholly formed yet. Indeed, I think he seemed, if anything, rather sorry that he had not deserted too; and though
he scolded loud enough at Neapolitan cowardice, I do not
think he seemed any more eager to storm the barricades
than his betters had been. Such men as these are nothing
to supply the place of the old Swiss regiments. His great
hope now was that the report might be true, of the determined disbanding and dismissal of the whole corps, so that
he might get back to his dear Vienna. Indeed, whether he
stays or not, his military spirit is for the time gone. And
so it must be with the whole army—all demoralized.

The captain was amusing as usual at supper. We drank
the King's health with a proviso for his improvement, and
discussed the political affairs largely. Every one is disgusted, or says he is. Half the army says it is rank treason
that did the business; the other half says it was incompe-
tence. I believe myself that if those generals had been fighting for themselves instead of their King, they would have
done much more than they have done; in other words, as
royal generals they deserve to lose their heads. As men,
their behavior may have been highly praiseworthy, perhaps; though it is at least a question, whether a man does
well in accepting his ruler's favors and rewards, and then
betraying him. To us Americans, all these Italian troubles

reduce themselves simply to a single process, by which one more of the civilized races is forming itself on the ground that we have always stood on, and taking up as its creed the same list of ideas that we have always declared to be the heart and soul of modern civilization. Feeling sure of the result, as we must, we can afford to be a little cooler than other people, and being so strongly prejudiced, we can almost be impartial. So about the King, I feel more pity than pleasure at his troubles. I never heard anything bad of him, except that he is stupid and governed by bad influence; but people who ought to know, have told me that he was a very good sort of a man, as men go. It is the fashion to abuse him, just as it is the fashion to abuse the Pope and the Grand Duke of Tuscany; but you would probably find that these are all good men enough, just as good and very likely a great deal better than you or *I*, or the writers in the London *Times*, who tear a passion to rags so splendidly. We, who are so far ahead on the winning side, can afford to try to be fair to the losers. The King of Naples is probably one of the few men in the Kingdom who has done nothing that he ought to be hung for.

It was curious to see, that night, how people can sleep. At about midnight, after finishing supper and smoking, and while every one was looking up their berths, I went forward to see how the soldiers managed to get along. They were lying all over the deck, tumbled down anywhere, and all snoring like hogs. They lay so thick and it was so dark that I trod on three or four who were in the way, but they did not mind it, and when the engineer, who was passing, kicked them out of the passage, they dragged themselves a few inches on one side, with a groan, but never woke up.

I was not so lucky. Recollecting my last night on board this boat, nothing could persuade me to go down below again, and so I appropriated a sofa in the upper cabin and with gloves on my hands to keep off the fleas, passed the night as well as might be, but little sleep enough came near me.

The next morning all was still, bright and clear. The poor soldiers' wives on deck looked very unhappy, and some, who had fine dark eyes, and pretty olive complexioned faces, looked so pale and patiently sad that they might have made beautiful studies for Magdalens and Madonnas. Certainly sea-sickness is one of the trials of life which brings us all down soonest to our common humanity; these women seemed absolutely refined by it, and their husbands and friends were as careful and gentle towards them as if they were all a set of refined and educated heroes and lovers.

We were crossing the bay of Naples at eight o'clock, and it seemed as though we were coming home, it all looked so pretty and natural. Thanks to the captain's politeness, we, passengers, were put on shore at once, and were not stopped long by the police, whose great curiosity was to know how it all looked in Sicily. Our information made them look all sorts of colors, as we had no particular motive to soften the story.

So my excursion to Palermo ended. Nothing could have been easier or more successful. It is something to have seen the raw elements at work, though one is no element one-self, and though before making a demi-god of Garibaldi one had better wait until it is fairly settled what he is going to make of all this, and whether he is not going to do more harm than good by the whirlwind that he is riding; still, a life has not been wholly uninteresting, even if the only event in it were to have talked with one of the most extraordinary of living men on the scene of his greatest success.

Naples is much as ever. It is the gayest and liveliest place in Italy. The Chiaja is swarming with carriages every after-noon, and the common people lounge about, useless to gods and men, but happy as life is long. Everything is military, but no one now believes in the army, and I have sometimes been dreadfully tempted to whisper "Garibaldi" and "Pa-lermo" in the ears of some of these uniformed rascals, just to see what they would do. I do not believe they have self-respect enough to feel insulted. There have been rumors enough of intended demonstrations, but nothing has hap-pened, and it is better so. They cannot do anything, with-out Garibaldi, and had better not try. There is a great deal of anxiety here; endless rumors of constitutions, insurrec-tions, demonstrations and so forth, and just now the two vessels said to have been captured under American colors, are making a good deal of uneasiness in our part of the city.

This letter is duller than usual. You will excuse it, for it is the last. I've tried to show you Italy as I've seen it, and now I have finished it all. It would be interesting to stay this struggle out here, but it will take a long time, and, after all, the essential points of interest for us Americans are now tolerably secure. Recollect that Garibaldi and the Italians are after two separate objects; one is a Free Italy, and the other is a United Italy. These are two separate things, and though we all sympathize with their struggles for the first, we can afford to hold our own opinions as to the value of the last. That is purely a question of Italian politics, and interests us only as identically the same struggle now going on since fifty years in Germany, interests us; that is, as a minor question of local importance. Of course many people wont agree with this statement of the case, but I am contented to follow on this question the lead of Napoleon the Third. If you prefer to hold to Garibaldi, we can agree to differ amicably.

H. B. A.

Captaine John Smith

Henry Adams spent the years of the Civil War cooped up in the American Legation in London where his father, Charles Francis Adams, as American Minister fought a skillful diplomatic campaign against the British for the benefit of the Union. Henry was his father's secretary and unofficial, unpaid clerk in the understaffed Legation office. In spite of the usefulness of his tedious job, he often thought that he should have been soldiering across Virginia as his brother Charles was, rather than fighting his war in an office.

Dissatisfaction was a goad. He began to think. A whim of interest turned his attention to one of the old American myths. His pursuit of the reality of the John Smith-Pocahontas story through sorely spared hours snatched from the work of the Legation was both an escape and a challenge. He finished the essay only after the war and secured its publication, with some elation, in the North American Review.

This was his first mature piece of work. In it he wrote in his own style for the first time: a fastidious lightness and elegance caressing an irreproachable solidity of fact.

CAPTAINE JOHN SMITH[1]

SOMETIME GOVERNOUR IN VIRGINIA, AND ADMIRALL OF NEW ENGLAND.

Captain John Smith belonged to the extraordinary school of adventurers who gave so much lustre to the reign of

[1] Published first in the *North American Review* for January 1867, later in Adams' *Historical Essays*, Charles Scribner's Sons, 1891.

Elizabeth, and whose most brilliant leader King James brought to the Tower and the block. Like Raleigh, though on a much lower level, Smith sustained many different characters. He was a soldier or a sailor indifferently, a statesman when circumstances gave him power, and an author when occasion required. Born in Lincolnshire in 1579, of what is supposed to have been a good Lancashire family, at a very early age he became a soldier of fortune in the Low Countries, and drifted into the Austrian service, where he took part in the campaign of 1600 against the Turks. Afterward he reappeared as a soldier of the Prince of Transylvania, who gave him a coat-of-arms, which was registered at the Herald's College in London. His extraordinary adventures during the three or four years of his life in Eastern Europe were related in his Autobiography, or "True Travels," a work published in London in 1630, near the close of his life. Dr. Palfrey's *History of New England* contains the earliest critical examination of this portion of Smith's story from an historical and geographical point of view, with a result not on the whole unfavorable to Smith.[2]

In 1604 Smith was again in England, where he soon began to interest himself in the enterprise of colonizing America.

On the 10th of April, 1606, King James conferred a charter upon certain persons in England, who took the title of the Virginia Company, and who proceeded to fit out an expedition of three small vessels, containing, in addition to their crews, one hundred and five colonists headed by a Council, of which Edward Maria Wingfield was chosen President, and Captains Bartholomew Gosnold, John Smith, John Ratcliffe, John Martin, and George Kendall were the other members. After various delays this expedition dropped down the Thames December 20 of the same year, but was kept six weeks in sight of England by unfavorable winds. After a long and difficult voyage, and a further delay of three weeks among the West India Islands, the headlands of Chesapeake Bay were passed April 26, 1607. On

---

[2] Palfrey's *History of New England*, i., pp. 89–92, note.

the 14th of May following, the colonists formally founded Jamestown.

In the mean while trouble had risen between Smith and his colleagues. Smith's story was told in the "Generall Historie" as follows:—

> "Now, Captain Smith, who all this time from their departure from the Canaries was restrained as a prisoner upon the scandalous suggestions of some of the chiefe, (envying his repute), who fained he intended to usurpe the Government, murther the Councell, and make himselfe King; that his confederats were dispersed in all the three ships, and that divers of his confederats that revealed it would affirm it. For this he was committed as a prisoner. Thirteen weeks he remained thus suspected, and by that time the ships should returne, they pretended out of their commisserations to refer him to the Councell in England to receive a check, rather then by particulating his designes make him so odious to the world, as to touch his life, or utterly overthrow his reputation."

Captain Newport, who was about to return to England, exerted his influence so strongly in favor of harmony that Smith was allowed to resume his seat among the Council; but he was not liked by the persons in control of the expedition, and some little light on the causes of their dislike or suspicion may be found in a passage of Wingfield's "Discourse," which said of Smith that "it was proved to his face that he begged in Ireland, like a rogue without a lycence,"—and he adds, "To such I would not my name should be a companyon." If Smith was accused of conspiring to obtain power, the dark events and questionable expedients of his varied and troubled career might well be flung in his face, and produce a considerable influence on the minds of his judges. Harmony was a blessing little known among the unhappy colonists, and before the close of the year, Captain George Kendall, another of the members of the Council, was accused of the same crime with which Smith had been charged, and was tried, convicted, and actually executed.

Newport, who had great influence over the colonists, sailed for England June 22, leaving three months' supplies behind him, and promising to return in seven months with a new company of settlers. His departure was followed by disasters and troubles of every description. The mortality was frightful. More than forty deaths took place before September, some caused by fevers and sickness, some by the Indians, but the larger number by famine. The kindness of the Indians alone, according to the express statement of Percy, who was among the survivors, preserved the remaining colonists from the fate of the lost Roanoke settlement of 1585.

Even this condition of the colony, though during five months together not five able-bodied men could mount the defences, had no effect in quieting the jealousies and dissensions of the leaders. Captain Gosnold died, leaving only Wingfield, Ratcliffe, Smith, and Martin in the Council. The last three combined to depose Wingfield; and this revolution took place September 10, without resistance. Ratcliffe, as the next in order, was chosen President.

"As at this time," said Smith, "were most of our chiefest men either sicke or discontented, the rest being in such dispaire as they would rather starve and rot with idleness then be perswaded to do anything for their owne reliefe without constraint,—our victualles being now within eighteene dayes spent, and the Indians' trade decreasing, I was sent to the mouth of ye river to trade for Corne, and try the River for Fish; but our fishing we could not effect by reason of the stormy weather." Fortunately the Indians were found willing to trade for corn, and by means of their supplies the lives of the settlers were saved. On the 9th of November, Smith made a longer excursion, partially exploring the Chickahominy, and was received with much kindness by the Indians, who supplied him with corn enough to have "laded a ship." Elated by his success and encouraged by the friendly attitude of the savages,—or, according to his own account, eager "to discharge the imputation of malicious tungs, that halfe suspected I durst not, for so long delaying,"—he determined to carry on his exploration of the Chickahominy to its source. On the 10th of December he started in the pinnace, which he left at a place he called Apocant, forty miles above the mouth of the Chickahominy, and continued his journey in a barge. Finally, rather than endanger the barge, he hired a canoe and two Indians to row it, and with two of his own company, named Robinson and Emry, went twenty miles higher. "Though some wise men may condemn this too bould attempt of too much indiscretion, yet if they well consider the friendship of the Indians in conducting me, the desolatenes of the country, the propabilitie of [discovering] some lacke, and the malicious judges of my actions at home, as also to have some matters of worth to incourage our adventurers in England, might well have caused any honest minde to have done the like, as wel for his own discharge as for the publike good."

At length they landed to prepare their dinner, and Smith with one Indian walked on along the course of the river, while Robinson and Emry with the other Indian remained to guard the canoe. Within a quarter of an hour he heard a hallooing of Indians and a loud cry, and fearing treachery, he seized his guide, whose arm he bound fast to his own hand, while he prepared his pistol for immediate use. As they "went discoursing," an arrow struck him on the right thigh, but without harm. He soon found himself attacked by some two hundred savages, against whose arrows he used his guide as a shield, discharging his pistol three or four times. The Indian chief, Opechankanough, then called upon him to surrender, and the savages laid their bows on the ground, ceasing to shoot.

"My hinde treated betwixt them and me of conditions of peace; he discovered me to be the Captaine. My request was to retire to ye boate; they demaunded my armes; the rest they saide were slaine, only me they would reserve; the Indian importuned me not to shoot. In retiring, being in the midst of a low quagmire, and minding them more then my steps, I stept fast into the quagmire, and also the Indian in drawing me forth. Thus surprised, I resolved to trie their mercies; my armes I caste from me, till which none durst approach me. Being ceazed on me, they drew me out and led me to the King."

Thus far, to avoid confusion, the account has followed the "True Relation," written by Smith, and published in London in 1608, the year after the events described.[3] In 1624 Smith published in London his "Generall Historie," which contained a version of the story varying essentially from that of the "True Relation." In continuing the account of his captivity, the two narratives will be placed side by side, for convenience of comparison, and the principal variations will be printed in Italics.

After describing the circumstances of his capture, which took place far up the Chickahominy River, Smith continued in his double narrative:—

A TRUE RELATION.
1608.

"They drew me out and led me to the King. I presented him with a compasse diall. . . . With kinde speeches and bread he requited me, conducting me where the Canow lay, and John Robinson slaine, with 20 or 30 arrowes in him. Emry I saw not. I perceived by the aboundance of fires all over the woods, *at each place I expected when they would execute me, yet they used me with what kindnes they could.* Approaching their Towne, which was within 6 miles where I was taken, . . . the Captaine conducting me to his lodging, a quarter of venison and some ten pound of bread I had for supper; what I left was reserved for me, and sent with me to my lodging. Each morning 3 women presented me

THE GENERALL HISTORIE.
1624.

"Then according to their composition they drew him forth and led him to the fire where his men were slaine. Diligently they chafed his benumbed limbs. He demanding for their Captaine they showed him Opechankanough king of Pamaunkee, to whom he gave a round ivory double-compass Dyall. Much they marvailed at the playing of the Fly and Needle. . . . *Notwithstanding, within an houre after they tied him to a tree, and as many as could stand about him prepared to shoot him,* but the King holding up the Compass in his hand, they all laid down their bowes and arrowes, and in a triumphant manner led him to Orapaks, where he was after their manner kindly feasted and well used. . . .

[3] *A True Relation of Virginia*, by Captain John Smith. With an Introduction and Notes by Charles Deane. Boston, 1866.

three great platters of fine bread; *more venison than ten men could devour I had;* my gowne, points and garters, my compas and a tablet they gave me again; though 8 ordinarily guarded me, I wanted not what they could devise to content me; and still our longer acquaintance increased our better affection. . . . I desired he [the King] would send a messenger to Paspahegh [Jamestown] with a letter I would write, by which they should understand how kindly they used me, and that I was well, least they should revenge my death; this he granted, and sent three men, in such weather as in reason were unpossible by any naked to be endured. . . . The next day after my letter came a salvage to my lodging with his sword to have slaine me. . . . This was the father of him I had slayne, whose fury to prevent, the King presently conducted me to another Kingdome, upon the top of the next northerly river, called Youghtanan. Having feasted me, he further led me to another branch of the river called Mattapament; to two other hunting townes they led me, and to each of these countries a house of the great Emperor of Pewhakan, whom as yet I supposed to bee at the Fals; *to him I told him I must goe, and so returne to Paspahegh.* After this foure or five dayes march, we returned to Rasawrack, the first towne they brought me too, where binding the Mats, in

Smith they conducted to a long house where *thirtie or fortie tall fellowes did guard him,* and ere long *more bread and venison was brought him than would have served twentie men.* I think his stomach at that time was not very good; what he left they put in baskets and tyed over his head; about midnight they set the meat again before him. All this time not one of them would eat a bit with him, till the next morning they brought him as much more, and then did they eate all the olde, and reserved the newe as they had done the other; which made him think they would fat him to eate him. Yet in this desperate estate to defend him from the cold, one Maocassater brought him his gowne in requitall of some beads and toyes Smith had given him at his first arrival in Virginia.

"Two dayes after, a man would have slaine him (but that the guard prevented it) for the death of his sonne, to whom they conducted him to recover the poore man then breathing his last. . . . In part of a Table booke he writ his minde to them at the Fort, and . . . the messengers . . . according to his request went to Jamestowne in as bitter weather as could be of frost and snow, and within three dayes returned with an answer. "Then they led him to the Youthtanunds, the Mattaponients, the Payankatanks, the Nantaughtacunds, and Omaw-

bundles, they marched two dayes journey and crossed the river of Youghtanan where it was as broad as Thames; so conducting me to a place called Menapacute in Pamaunke, where yᵉ King inhabited. . . .

"From hence this kind King conducted mee to a place called Topahanocke, a kingdome upon another River northward. The cause of this was, that the yeare before, a shippe had beene in the River of Pamaunke, who having been kindly entertained by Powhatan their Emperour, they returned thence, and discovered the River of Topahanocke, where being received with like kindnesse, yet he slue the King and tooke of his people; and they supposed I were hee, but the people reported him a great man that was Captaine, and using mee kindly, the next day we departed. . . .

"The next night I lodged at a hunting town of Powhatams, and the next day arrived at Waranacomoco upon the river of Pamauncke, where the great king is resident. . . .

"Arriving at Weramocomoco, their Emperour . . . kindly welcomed me with good wordes and great Platters of sundrie Victuals, *assuring mee his friendship, and my libertie within foure dayes.* . . . Hee desired mee to forsake Paspahegh, and to live with him upon his River,—a Countrie called Capa Howasicke; hee promised to give me Corne, Venison, or what I wanted to

maniments upon the rivers of Rapahannock and *Patawomeck, over all those rivers* and back againe by divers other severall nations to the King's habitation at Pamaunkee, where they entertained him with most strange and fearfull Conjurations. . . .

"At last they brought him to Meronocomoco, where was Powhatan their Emperor. Here more than two hundred of those grim Courtiers stood wondering at him, as he had been a monster; till Powhatan and his trayne had put themselves in their greatest braveries. . . . At his entrance before the King, all the people gave a great shout. The Queene of Appamatuck was appointed to bring him water to wash his hands, and another brought him a bunch of feathers, instead of a Towell to dry them. *Having feasted him after their best barbarous manner they could, a long consultation was held; but the conclusion was, two great stones were brought before Powhatan; then as many as could lay their hands on him dragged him to them, and thereon laid his head; and being ready with their clubs to beate out his braines, Pocahontas the King's dearest daughter, when no intreaty could prevaile, got his head in her armes, and laid her owne upon his to save him from death; whereat the Emperour was contented he should live to make him hatchets, and her bells, beads, and copper.* . . .

A TRUE RELATION
(*Continued*).

feede us; Hatchets and Copper
wee should make him, and
none should disturbe us. This
request I promised to performe;
and thus having with all the
kindnes hee could devise,
sought to content me, hee sent
me home *with 4 men*, one that
usually carried my Gowne and
Knapsacke after me, two other
loded with bread, and one to
accompanie me. . . .

"From Weramocomoco is
but 12 miles, yet the Indians
trifled away that day, and
would not goe to our Forte by
any perswasions; but in cer-
taine olde hunting houses of
Paspahegh we lodged all night.
The next morning ere Sunne
rise, we set forward for our
Fort, where we arrived within
an houre, where each man with
truest signes of joy they could
expresse welcomed mee, except
M. Archer, and some 2 or 3 of
his, who was then in my absence sworne Counsellour,
though not with the consent of
Captaine Martin. Great blame
and imputation was laide upon
mee by them for the losse of
our two men which the Indian
slew; insomuch that they pur-
posed to depose me; but *in the
midst of my miseries it pleased
God to send Captaine Nuport,
who arriving there the same
night so tripled our joy as for a
while these plots against me
were deferred*, though with
much malice against me,
which Captain Newport in a
short time did plainly see."

THE GENERALL HISTORIE
(*Continued*).

"Two dayes after, Powhatan
having disguised himselfe in
the most fearfullest manner he
could . . . more like a devil
than a man, with some two
hundred more as black as himselfe, came unto him and told
him now they were friends,
and presently he should goe to
Jamestowne, to send him two
great gunnes and a gryndstone,
for which he would give him
the Country of Capahowosick,
and for ever esteeme him as his
sonne Nantaquoud. So to
Jamestowne *with 12 guides*
Powhatan sent him, *he still expecting (as he had done all
this long time of his imprisonment) every houre to be put to
one death or other, for all their
feasting*. But almightie God
(by his divine providence) had
mollified the hearts of those
sterne Barbarians with compassion. The next morning betimes
they came to the Forte. . . .
"*Now in Jamestowne they
were all in combustion, the
strongest preparing once more
to run away with the Pinnace;
which with the hazzard of his
life, with Sabre, falcon, and
musket shot, Smith forced now
the third time to stay or sinke.*
Some, no better than they
should be, had plotted with
the President the next day to
have put him to death by the
Leviticall law, for the lives of
Robinson and Emry, pretend-
ing the fault was his that had
led them to their ends: but *he
quickly tooke such order with
such lawyers, that he layd them
by the heeles till he sent some*

THE GENERALL HISTORIE
(*Continued*).

of them prisoners for Eng-
land. . . .
"Newport got in and arrived
at James Towne not long after
the redemption of Captaine
Smith. . . .

"Written by Thomas Stud-
ley, the first Cape Merchant in
Virginia, Robert Fenton, Edward Harrington, and J. S."

Comparison of the two narratives thus for the first time
placed side by side, betrays a tone of exaggeration in the
later story. Eight guards, which had been sufficient in 1608,
were multiplied into thirty or forty tall fellows in 1624.
What was enough for ten men at the earlier time would
feed twenty according to the later version. In 1608 four
guides were an ample escort to conduct Smith to Jamestown, but they were reinforced to the number of twelve
sixteen years afterward. With the best disposition toward
Smith, one cannot forget that he belonged to the time when
Falstaff and his misbegotten knaves in Kendal Green appeared upon the stage. The execution wrought upon the
lawyers who wished to try Smith for his life on his return
to Jamestown was prompt and decisive according to the
story of 1624, but in 1608 "in the midst of my miseries it
pleased God to send" Captain Newport to defer the plots
of Smith's enemies. With sabre, falcon, and musket-shot he
forced the mutinous crew of the pinnace to stay or sink,
according to the "Generall Historie," while the "True Relation" was silent as to any feat of arms, but simply said
that Captain Newport arrived the same evening.

The same exaggeration marked the account of Smith's
treatment among the savages. According to the story written a few months after the event, a people was described,
savage, but neither cruel nor bloodthirsty; reckless perhaps
of life in battle, but kind and even magnanimous toward
their captive. The "True Relation" implied that no demonstration was made against Smith's life, such as he described

in 1624 as occurring within an hour after his capture. Only a few days after he was taken prisoner, he directed Opechankanough to take him to Powhatan, and even then he knew that he was to be allowed to return to Jamestown. "To him I told him I must go, and so return to Paspahegh." Powhatan received him with cordiality, and having sought to content him with all the kindness he could devise, sent him with a guard of honor back to his friends. In the "True Relation," the behavior of the Indians toward Smith was more humane than he would have received at the hands of civilized peoples. He found no cause to fear for his life, except from a savage whose son he had killed, and from whom Opechankanough protected him. One line indeed alluded to a fear that they fed him so fat as to make him much doubt they meant to sacrifice him; but this evidence of the kindness of the Indians implied that he believed himself to have been mistaken in having entertained the suspicion. Yet in 1624, throughout his long imprisonment, he was still expecting every hour to be put to one death or another.

These variations would not concern the ordinary reader of colonial history, if they stopped at trifling inconsistencies. They would merely prove the earlier narrative to be the safer authority for historians to follow, which is an established law of historical criticism. The serious divergence occurred in Smith's account of his visit to Powhatan, which in 1608 was free from the suspicion of danger to his life, but in 1624 introduced Pocahontas as his savior from a cruel execution. The absence of Pocahontas, and of any allusion to her interference, or of reference to the occasion on which she interfered, makes the chief characteristic of the earlier story, and if the law of evidence is sound, requires the rejection of the latter version as spurious.

Smith's silence in 1608 about his intended execution and his preservation by Pocahontas was the more remarkable, because the "True Relation" elsewhere mentioned Pocahontas, with every appearance of telling the whole share she had in Smith's affairs. Smith's captivity occurred in December. In the following month of May, Smith imprisoned at

Jamestown some Indians whom he suspected of treachery. The "True Relation" continued:—

> "Powhatan, understanding we detained certaine Salvages, sent his daughter, a child of tenne yeares old, which not only for feature, countenance, and proportion much exceedeth any of the rest of his people, but for wit and spirit the only Nonpareil of his Country: this he sent by his most trustie messenger, called Rawhunt, as much exceeding in deformitie of person, but of a subtill wit and crafty understanding. He with a long circumstance told me how well Powhatan loved and respected mee, and in that I should not doubt any way of his kindnesse he had sent his child, which he most esteemed, to see me: . . . his little daughter he had taught this lesson also."

Smith regarded Pocahontas as a person so much worth winning to his interests that he surrendered the prisoners to her.

> "We guarded them as before to the Church, and after prayer gave them to Pocahontas, the King's Daughter, in regard of her father's kindnesse in sending her. . . . Pocahontas also we requited, with such trifles as contented her, to tel that we had used the Paspaheyans very kindly in so releasing them."

Had Pocahontas saved Smith's life four months before, Smith would have been likely to surrender the prisoners out of gratitude to her, rather than "in regard of her father's kindnesse in sending" his favorite child to ask a return for his own hospitality.

No American needs to learn that Pocahontas is the most romantic character in the history of his country. Her name and story are familiar to every schoolboy, and families of the highest claim to merit trace their descent from the Emperor's daughter that saved the life of Captain John Smith. In the general enthusiasm, language and perhaps commonsense have been strained to describe her attributes. Her beauty and wild grace, her compassion and disinterestedness, her Christian life and pure character, have been dwelt upon with warmth the more natural as the childhood of the nation furnished little latitude to imagination. One after another, American historians have contented themselves with repeating the words of the "Generall Historie," heaping praises which no critics were cynical enough to gainsay, now on the virtues of Pocahontas, and now on the courage and constancy of Smith.

The exclusive share of the later narrative in shaping popular impressions was well shown by the standard authority for American history. In the early editions of Bancroft's "History of the United States," the following version of Smith's adventure was given:—

"The gentle feelings of humanity are the same in every race, and in every period of life; they bloom, though unconsciously, even in the bosom of a child. Smith had easily won the confiding fondness of the Indian maiden; and now, the impulse of mercy awakened within her breast, she clung firmly to his neck, as his head was bowed to receive the strokes of the tomahawk. Did the childlike superstition of her kindred reverence her interference as a token from a superior power? Her fearlessness and her entreaties persuaded the council to spare the agreeable stranger, who might make hatchets for her father, and rattles and strings of beads for herself, the favorite child. The barbarians, whose decision had long been held in suspense by the mysterious awe which Smith had inspired, now resolved to receive him as a friend, and to make him a partner of their councils. They tempted him to join their bands, and lend assistance in an attack upon the white men at Jamestown; and when his decision of character succeeded in changing the current of their thoughts, they dismissed him with mutual promises of friendship and benevolence."

In a note appended to these paragraphs the author quoted:—

"Smith, I. 158–162, and II. 29–33. The account is fully contained in the oldest book printed on Virginia, in our Cambridge library. It is a thin quarto, in black-letter, by John Smith, printed in 1608,—A True Relation, etc."

The story, in passing through the medium of Mr. Bancroft's mind, gained something which did not belong to the original, or belonged to it only in a modified degree. The spirit of Smith infused itself into the modern historian, as it had already infused itself into the works of his predecessors. The lights were intensified; the shadows deepened; the gradations softened. The copy surpassed its model. This tendency went so far that the author quoted the "True Relation" as the full authority for what was to be found only in the "Generall Historie," if indeed it was all to be found even there. When Mr. Bancroft collated his version of the story with the black-letter pamphlet in the Cambridge library, the popular reputation of Smith had already created an illusion in his mind resembling the optical effect of refracted light. He saw something which did not exist, —the exaggerated image of a figure beyond.

The labors of Charles Deane have made necessary a thorough examination into the evidence bearing on Smith's story; and Deane's notes make such an inquiry less laborious than the mass of material seemed to threaten. With that aid, an analysis of the evidence can be brought within narrow compass.

The first President of the colony was Edward Maria Wingfield, who in September, 1607, was deprived of his office, and placed in confinement by Smith and the other members of the Council. When Newport—who with a new company of settlers arrived at Jamestown Jan. 8, 1608, immediately after Smith's release—began his second return voyage to London, he took the deposed President Wingfield with him, and they arrived safely at Blackwall on the 21st of May. Wingfield kept a diary during his stay in Virginia, and after his return he wrote with its assistance a defence of himself and his administration, privately circulated in manuscript, and at a later period used by Purchas, but afterward forgotten and hidden in the dust of the Lambeth Library. From this obscurity it was drawn by Mr. Deane, who published it with notes in the fourth

volume of the Archæologia Americana in 1860.[4] Excepting a few papers of little consequence, this is the earliest
known writing which came directly from the colony. The
manuscript of Smith's "True Relation," its only possible
rival, could not have reached England before the month
of July, while Wingfield's manuscript was intended for
immediate circulation in May or June. Wingfield's work,
which was called "A Discourse of Virginia," is therefore
new authority on the early history of the colony, and has
peculiar value as a test for the correctness of the "True Relation." Its account of Smith's captivity could only have
been gained from his own mouth, or from those to whom
he told the story, and its accuracy can be tested by the
degree of its coincidence with the "True Relation."

A number of passages in this short pamphlet would be
worth extracting; but the inquiry had best be narrowed to
the evidence in regard to Pocahontas. The passage from
Wingfield, telling of Smith's adventures among the Indians,
ran as follows:—

> "*Dec.* The 10th of December Mr. Smith went up the
> ryver of the Chechohomynies to trade for corne. He was
> desirous to see the heade of that river; and when it was
> not passible with the shallop, he hired a cannow and an
> Indian to carry him up further. The river the higher grew
> worse and worse. Then he went on shoare with his guide,
> and left Robinson and Emmery, twoe of our men in the
> cannow, which were presently slaine by the Indians,
> Pamaonke's men, and he himself taken prysoner; and by
> the means of his guide his lief was saved. And Pama-
> onché haveing him prisoner, carried him to his neybors
> wyroances to see if any of them knewe him for one of
> those which had bene, some two or three yeres before
> us, in a river amongst them Northward, and taken awaie
> some Indians from them by force. At last he brought
> him to the great Powaton (of whome before wee had

[4] *A Discourse of Virginia*, by Edward Maria Wingfield, the
First President of the Colony. Edited by Charles Deane, Member of the American Antiquarian Society, and of the Massachusetts Historical Society. Boston: Privately printed, 1860.

no knowledg), who sent him home to our towne the viii[th] of January. . . .

"Mr. Archer sought how to call Mr. Smith's lief in question, and had indited him upon a chapter in Leviticus for the death of his twoe men. He had had his tryall the same daie of his retorne, and I believe his hanging the same or the next daie, so speedie is our law there; but it pleased God to send Captn. Newport unto us the same evening to our unspeakable comfort, whose arrivall saved Mr. Smyth's life and mine."

Deane, in editing Wingfield in 1860, furnished a note upon this passage, in which for the first time a doubt was thrown upon the story of Pocahontas's intervention. Yet the discovery of Wingfield's narrative added little to the evidence contained in the "True Relation,"—always a well-known work. The "Discourse" supplied precise dates, fixing Smith's departure on the 10th of December, and his return on the 8th of January, his absence being exactly four weeks in length; it said that Smith's guide saved his life, which might be a variation from the story of the "True Relation;" it dwelt on the danger Smith ran, from the enmity of Archer, which might be only the result of Wingfield's dislike of that person. In general, this new evidence, though clearly independent of the "True Relation," confirmed it in essentials, and especially in the omission of reference to Pocahontas. So remarkable an incident as her protection of Smith, if known to Wingfield, would scarcely have been omitted in this narrative, which must have contained the version of Smith's adventures current among the colonists after his return to Jamestown.

These two works are the only contemporaneous authority for the first year of the colonial history. A wide gap intervenes between them and the next work; and the strength of Deane's case rests so largely on the negative evidence offered by the "True Relation" and the "Discourse," that for his purpose further search was useless. Every one, whether believing or disbelieving the "Generall Historie," must agree that Pocahontas was not mentioned, either by name or by implication, as the preserver of Smith's

life either by Smith in the "True Relation" or by Wingfield in his "Discourse." The inquiry might stop here, and
each reader might be left to form his own opinion as to
the relative value of the conflicting narratives; but the
growth of a legend is as interesting as the question of its
truth.

Newport returned to England April 10, 1608, carrying
Wingfield with him, and leaving Ratcliffe President of the
Colony, with Martin, Smith, and Archer in the Council, together with a new member, Matthew Scrivener, who had
arrived with Newport. Smith in June explored successfully
a part of Chesapeake Bay, and returning July 21, found,
according to the "Generall Historie," the colonists in a miserable condition, unable to do anything but complain of
Ratcliffe, whose principal offence appears to have been his
obliging the colonists to build him "an unnecessary building for his pleasure in the woods." Ratcliffe, whose real
name was Sicklemore, was a poor creature, if the evidence
in regard to him can be believed. He was deposed, and
Scrivener, Smith's "deare friend," though then exceedingly
ill, succeeded him as President. This revolution was rapidly
effected; for three days later, July 24, Smith again set out
with twelve men, to finish his explorations, and made a
complete tour round the bay, which supplied his materials
for the map published at Oxford in 1612. He did not return to Jamestown till the 7th of September, and on the
10th he assumed the Presidency, "by the Election of the
Councell and request of the Company." Scrivener appears
merely to have held the office during Smith's pleasure, and
voluntarily resigned it into his hands.

The history of Smith's administration of the colony from
Sept. 10, 1608, till the end of September, 1609, is given
in the "Generall Historie," and may be studied with advantage as an example of Smith's style. Whatever may
have been the merits of his government, he had no better success than his predecessors, and he not only failed
to command obedience, but was left almost or quite without a friend. He was ultimately deposed and sent to England under articles of complaint. The precise tenor of these
articles is unknown; but Mr. Deane has found in the Co-

lonial Office a letter of Ratcliffe, alias Sicklemore, dated
Oct. 4, 1609, in which he announced to the Lord Treasurer that "this man [Smith] is sent home to answere some
misdemeanors whereof I perswade me he can scarcely clear
himselfe from great imputation of blame." Beyond a doubt
the difficulties of the situation were very great, and the
men Smith had to control were originally poor material,
and were made desperate by their trials; but certainly his
career in Virginia terminated disastrously, both for himself
and for the settlement. The Virginia Company, notwithstanding his applications, never employed him again.

The colony went from bad to worse. George Percy, a
brother of the Earl of Northumberland, succeeded Smith
in the Presidency. The condition of the colonists between
Smith's departure in October, 1609, and the arrival of Sir
Thomas Gates in May, 1610, was terrible. Percy was so
"sicke hee could neither goe nor stand." Ratcliffe, with a
number of others, was killed by Indians. The remainder
fed on roots, acorns, fish, and actually on the savages whom
they killed, and on each other,—one man murdering his
wife and eating her. Out of the whole number, said to have
been five hundred, not more than sixty were living when
Gates arrived; and he immediately took them on board
ship, and abandoning Jamestown, set sail for England.
Only by accident they met a new expedition under Lord
Delaware, at the mouth of the river, which brought a
year's provisions, and restored the fortunes of the settlement. In spite of the discouragement produced in England
by these disasters, the Company renewed its efforts, and
again sent out Sir Thomas Gates with six vessels and three
hundred men, who arrived in August, 1611. The government was then in the hands of Sir Thomas Dale, who assumed it in May, 1611, and retained it till 1616. If the ultimate success of the colony was due to any single man,
the merit appears to belong to Dale; for his severe and despotic rule crushed the insubordination that had been the
curse of the State, compelled the idle to work, and maintained order between the colonists and the Indians.

In the mean while Smith, who had taken final leave of
the colony, appears to have led a quiet life in London dur-

ing several years. Lost from sight during the years 1610
and 1611, he appeared again in 1612 busied in the same
direction as before. In that year he published at Oxford a
short work called "A Map of Virginia. With a Description
of the Countrey, the Commodities, People, Government,
and Religion. Written by Captaine Smith, sometimes Gov-
ernour of the Countrey. Whereunto is annexed the proceedings of those Colonies, &c., by W. S." The latter part of
the publication, which purported to be drawn from the
writings of certain colonists, was afterward reprinted, with
alterations, as the Third Book of the "Generall Historie,"
from the title of which it appears that "W. S." stood for
the initials of William Simons, Doctor of Divinity.

In this tract only one passage bore upon Smith's story
of Pocahontas. Among the customs described as peculiar
to the Indians was the form of execution practised against
criminals. Their heads, Smith said, were placed upon an
altar, or sacrificing-stone, while "one with clubbes beates
out their braines." During his captivity Smith added, not
indeed that he had actually seen this mode of execution,
but that an Indian had been beaten in his presence till he
fell senseless, without a cry or complaint. The passage is
remarkable for more than one reason. In the first place, the
mode of execution there described was uncommon, if not
unknown, among the Indians of the sea-coast; in the second place, the passage contained the germ of Smith's later
story. Practised lawyers may decide whether, under the
ordinary rules of evidence, this passage implies that Smith
had himself not been placed in the position described, and
future students may explain why Smith should have suppressed his own story, supposing it to have been true. The
inference is strong that if anything of the sort had occurred,
it would have been mentioned here; and this argument is
strengthened by a short narration of his imprisonment given
in the second part of the pamphlet, for which Dr. Simons
was the nominal authority. This version ran as follows:—

"A month those barbarians kept him prisoner. Many
strange triumphs and conjurations they made of him;
yet he so demeened himself amongst them as he not only

diverted them from surprising the fort, but procured his own liberty, and got himself and his company such estimation among them that those savages admired him as a Demi God. So returning safe to the Fort, once more stayed the pinnace her flight for England."

This work was, as above mentioned, afterward reprinted, under the author's name, as the Third Book of the "Generall Historie." The passage just quoted was there reproduced with the evidently intentional substitution of "six or seven weekes" for "a month," as in the original. In the "Generall Historie" the concluding paragraph was omitted, and in its place stood, "The manner how they used and delivered him is as followeth." Then, breaking abruptly into the middle of the old narrative, the story which has been quoted was interpolated.

The narrative in the second part of the "Map of Virginia," of which the above extract forms a part, was signed by the name of Thomas Studley alone, while in the "Generall Historie" the enlarged account bore also the signatures of Edward Harrington, Robert Fenton, and Smith himself. A question may arise as to the extent to which these persons should be considered as dividing with Smith the responsibility for the story. Thomas Studley died on the 28th of August, 1607. Both he and Edward Harrington had lain four months in their graves before Smith ever heard of Powhatan or Pocahontas. The date of Robert Fenton's death is not so clear, but there is no reason to suppose that he had any share in the narration of events which Smith alone witnessed.

The argument so far as the Oxford tract is concerned would be strong enough, if it went no further; but it becomes irresistible when this tract not only mentions Pocahontas, but introduces her as the savior of Smith's life, although it says no word of her most famous act in this character. The allusion occurred toward the end of the pamphlet, where the assumed writer took occasion to defend Smith against certain charges, one of them being an alleged scheme on his part of marrying Powhatan's daughter Pocahontas in order to acquire a claim to the throne. The writer denied the charge, and added:—

> "It is true she was the very nonparell of his kingdome, and at most not past 13 or 14 yeares of age. Very often shee came to our fort with what shee could get for Captaine Smith, that ever loved and used all the countrie well, but her especially he ever much respected; and she so well requited it that when her father intended to have surprised him, shee, by stealth in the darke night, came through the wild woods and told him of it."

The Oxford tract of 1612 may be considered decisive that down to that date the story of Pocahontas had not been made public. Here we take leave of Smith as an authority for a period of some ten years, during which he published but one work, not relating to the present subject. An entirely new class of colonists had in 1610–1611 taken the place of the first settlers, almost exterminated by the disasters of 1609–1610. Among the new-comers in the train of Lord Delaware, in 1610, was William Strachey, who held the office of Secretary of the Colony. Little is known of Strachey, except that after his return to England he compiled a work called the "Historie of Travaile into Virginia," never completed in its original plan, but still extant in two neatly written manuscripts, printed by the Hakluyt Society in 1849. The date of its composition was probably about the year 1615. It consisted largely of extracts from Smith's previous works, though without acknowledgment of their origin; it also contained original matter, and especially some curious references to Pocahontas,[5] but no reference, direct or indirect, to her agency in saving Smith's life, and no trace of the high esteem which such an act would have won for her.

Next in order after Strachey's manuscript comes a work which is quite original, and gives perhaps the best account of the colony ever made public by an eye-witness. This is a small volume in quarto, printed in London in 1615, and called "A True Discourse of the Present Estate of Virginia

[5] See Deane's edition of the "True Relation," p. 72.

. . . till the 18th of June, 1614, together with . . . the Christening of Powhatan's daughter and her Marriage with an Englishman. Written by Raphe Hamor, late Secretarie in the Colonie." It contains a minute and graphic story how "Pocahuntas, King Powhatan's daughter, whose fame has spread even to England, under the name of Non Parella," while staying with some tribe, subject to her father, on the Potomac, was seized and carried away by Captain Argol, who had sailed up that river on a trading expedition. Her imprisonment as a hostage at Jamestown, her visit to her father's residence with Sir Thomas Dale and a strong force of English, Powhatan's failure to redeem her, and her subsequent marriage to John Rolfe April 5, 1613, are all circumstantially narrated; and finally an extremely interesting account is given of a visit which Hamor made to Powhatan, and of the conversation he had with that extraordinary savage. Besides this work of Hamor, the volume also contains several letters from persons in Virginia, one of which is by John Rolfe, written with the object of justifying his marriage. Afterward, when the arrival of Pocahontas in England had excited an interest throughout Europe in her story, Hamor's book was translated and published in Germany.

Although repeated allusions to Pocahontas occur in the works already mentioned, in Hamor she makes, for the first time, her appearance as a person of political importance. In the "True Relation" Smith represented her as a pretty and clever child ten years old, once sent with a trusted messenger by Powhatan to the fort to entreat the liberation of some Indians whom Smith had seized. The Oxford tract mentioned her as a friend of Smith, but a mere child. Strachey gave a curious description of her intimate relations with the colony during his residence there:—

"Pocahuntas, a well featured but wanton yong girle, Powhatan's daughter, sometymes resorting to our fort, of the age then of eleven or twelve yeares, would get the boyes forth with her into the markett place, and make them wheele, falling on their hands, turning up their heeles upwards, whome she would followe and wheele so her self, naked as she was, all the fort over."

Pocahontas was then apparently considered as a child like any other; but from the time when Argol treacherously seized her she took an important position,—in the first place, as the guaranty of a peace which Powhatan promised, and preserved during the remainder of her life and of his own; in the second place, as a person calculated to excite interest in England in behalf of the colony; and finally, as an eminent convert to the English Church, through whom a religious influence might be exercised among her father's subjects. Hamor's book was filled with her history, and Rolfe's letter showed much anxiety to prove the propriety of his course in marrying her. Both writers were interested in exciting as much sympathy for her as could be roused. Yet neither the one nor the other alluded to the act which has since become her first claim to praise, and which has almost thrown the rest of her story out of sight. There is no reason to suppose that in Virginia in 1614 the persons best informed were yet aware that Pocahontas had saved Smith's life.

In the month of June, 1616, Sir Thomas Dale arrived at Plymouth on his return home, bringing with him among his suite the baptized Pocahontas, then called Rebecca Rolfe, who with her husband and child came at the charge of the Company to visit England, and to prove to the world the success of the colony. She became at once the object of extraordinary attention, and in the following winter she was the most distinguished person in society. Her portrait taken at that time still exists, and shows a somewhat hard-featured figure, with a tall hat and ruff, appearing ill at ease in the stiff and ungraceful fashions of the day. Gentlemen of the court sent the engraving, as the curiosity of the season, in their letters to correspondents abroad. The Church received her with great honor, and the Bishop of London gave her an entertainment, celebrated in enthusiastic terms by Purchas. At the court masque in January, 1617, Pocahontas was among the most conspicuous guests. The King and Queen received her in special audiences; and to crown all, tradition reports, with reasonable foundation, that King James, in his zeal for the high principles of divine right and the sacred character of royalty, expressed his serious displeasure that Rolfe, who was at best a simple gentleman, should have ventured so far beyond his position as to ally himself with one who was of imperial blood.

Just at that time, when the influence of London society had set its stamp of fashion on the name of the Indian girl, and when King James had adopted her as rightfully belonging within the pale of the divinity that hedges a king, Samuel Purchas, "Parson of St. Martin's by Ludgate," published the third edition of his "Pilgrimage." Purchas, although not himself an explorer, was an enthusiast on the subject of travels and adventures; and in compiling the collection now so eagerly sought and so highly valued by collectors of books, he had, so far as related to Virginia, the direct assistance of personal witnesses, and also of manuscripts now unhappily lost except for his extracts. He was well acquainted with Smith, who "gently communicated" his notes to him, and who was in London, and visited Pocahontas at Brentford. Purchas himself saw Pocahontas. He was present when "my Honble. and Rev^d. Patron the Lord Bishop of London, D^r. King, entertained her with festivall state and pompe beyond what I have seen in his great hospitalitie afforded to other ladies," in his "hopefull zeale by her to advance Christianitie." He knew Tomocomo, an Indian of Powhatan's tribe, who came with her to England. "With this savage I have often conversed at my good friend's Master Doctor Goldstone, where he was a frequent guest; and where I have both seen him sing and dance his diabolicall measures, and heard him discourse of his countrey and religion, Sir Thomas Dale's man being the interpretour." He knew Rolfe also, who lent him his manuscript Discourse on Virginia. Yet Purchas's book contained no allusion to the heroic intervention on behalf of Smith, the story of whose captivity is simply copied from Simons's quarto of 1612; the diffuse comments on men and manners in Virginia contain no trace of what would have been correctly regarded as the most extraordinary incident in colonial history.

Silence in a single instance, as in Wingfield or in Strachey, might be accounted for, or at all events might be overlooked; but silence during a long period of years and under the most improbable circumstances, cannot be ignored. Wingfield, Smith himself, Simons, Strachey, Hamor, Rolfe, and Purchas, all the authorities without exception known to exist, are equally dumb when questioned as to a circumstance which since 1624 has become the most famous part of colonial history. The field is exhausted. No other sources exist from which to draw authentic information. Nothing remains but to return to Smith, and to inquire when it was that this extraordinary story first made its appearance, and how it obtained authority.

The blaze of fashionable success that surrounded Pocahontas in London lighted the closing scene of her life. She was obliged, against her will as was believed, to set out on her return to Virginia, but she never actually left the shores of England. Detained in the Thames by several weeks of contrary winds, her failing strength altogether gave way; and in March, 1617, in the word-play of Purchas, "she came at Gravesend to her end and grave." Her father, Powhatan, survived her less than a year.

Smith in the mean while was busied with projects in regard to New England and the fisheries. His efforts to form a colony there and to create a regular system of trade had little success; but to spread a knowledge of the new country among the people of England, he printed, in 1616, a small quarto, called "A Description of New England," and in 1620 he published another pamphlet, entitled "New England's Trials," a second and enlarged edition of which appeared in 1622. There at last, in 1622, the long-sought allusion to his captivity occurred in the following words:—

"For wronging a soldier but the value of a penny I have caused Powhatan send his own men to Jamestowne to receive their punishment at my discretion. It is true in our greatest extremitie they shot me, slue three of my men, and by the folly of them that fled took me prisoner; yet God made Pocahontas the King's daughter the means to deliver me; and thereby taught me to know their treacheries to preserve the rest."

The first appearance of this famous story can therefore be fixed within five years,—between 1617 and 1622,—although the complete account is only to be found in the "Generall Historie," printed in 1624, from which copious extracts have already been quoted. Only one point of difficulty still requires attention.

Smith there said (pp. 121–123) that when Pocahontas came to England he wrote for her a sort of letter of introduction to the Queen, or, in his own words, "a little booke to this effect to the Queen, an abstract whereof followeth."

"Some ten yeeres agoe, being in Virginia and taken prisoner by the power of Powhatan their chiefe King, . . . I cannot say I felt the least occasion of want that was in the power of those my mortall foes to prevent, notwithstanding al their threats. After some six weeks fatting amongst those Salvage Courtiers, at the minute of my execution, she hazarded the beating out of her owne braines to save mine, and not onely that, but so prevailed with her father that I was safely conducted to Jamestowne."

This letter rests on the authority of the "Generall Historie," and has neither more nor less weight than that work gives it. Smith's "abstract of the effect" of the little book was as liable to interpolations as the text of the "Generall Historie" elsewhere. At the time it was published, in 1624, not only had Pocahontas long been dead, but Queen Anne herself had in 1619 followed her to the grave, and Smith remained alone to vouch for his own accuracy. The Virginia Company had no interest in denying the truth of a story so well calculated to draw popular sympathy toward the colony.

Smith's character was always a matter of doubt. Thomas Fuller, one of Smith's contemporaries, published the "Worthies of England" some thirty years after Smith's death, when the civil wars had intervened to obliterate the recollection of personal jealousies, and when Smith must have been little remembered. Fuller devoted a page to Smith's history in the following vein:—

> "From the Turks in Europe he passed to the Pagans in America, where, towards the latter end of the reign of Queen Elizabeth, such his perils, preservations, dangers, deliverances, they seem to most men above belief, to some beyond truth. Yet have we two witnesses to attest them, the prose and the pictures, both in his own book; and it soundeth much to the diminution of his deeds that he alone is the herald to publish and proclaim them."

The essential evidence on each side of this curious question has now been exhausted, although it would be easy to argue indefinitely in regard to Smith's general character. This must be done by the first historian who attempts again to deal with the history of the Virginia Colony. The argument may be left for future and final judgment, but some reasonable theory is still required to explain the existence of the story assumed to be false. Deane, like Palfrey, hints that Smith in the latter part of his life fell into the hands of hack-writers, who adapted his story for popular effect. Perhaps the truth may be somewhat as follows.

The examination of Smith's works has shown that his final narrative was the result of gradual additions. The influence exercised by Pocahontas on the affairs of the colony, according to the account given in 1608, was slight. In 1612 she first appeared in her heroic character. Her capture and her marriage to Rolfe gave her importance. Her visit to England made her the most conspicuous figure in Virginia, and romantic incidents in her life were likely to be created, if they did not already exist, by the exercise of the popular imagination, attracted by a wild and vigorous picture of savage life.

The history of the emperor's daughter became, as Smith implied, a subject for the stage. Nothing was more natural or more probable. It is not even necessary to assume that Smith invented the additions to his own story. He may have merely accepted them after they had obtained a hold on the minds of his contemporaries.

In the mean while Smith's own career had failed, and his ventures ended disastrously, while in most cases he did not obtain the employment which he continued to seek with unrelaxed energy. In 1622 a disaster occurred in Virginia which roused the greatest interest and sympathy in England, and gave occasion for renewed efforts in behalf of the colony. The Indians rose against the English, and in the month of May a massacre took place around Jamestown. The opportunity was one not to be lost by a man who like Smith, while burning to act, was still smarting under what he considered undeserved neglect, and he hastened to offer his services to the Company, with a plan for restoring peace; but his plan and his offer of services were again declined. Still, the resource which he had frequently used remained, and by publishing the "Generall Historie" he made a more ambitious appeal to the public than any he had yet attempted. In this work he embodied everything that could tend to the increase of his own reputation, and drew material from every source that could illustrate the history of English colonization. Pocahontas was made to appear in it on every possible occasion, and his own share in the affairs of the colony was magnified at the expense of his companions. None of those whose reputations he treated with harshness appeared to vindicate their own characters, far less to assert their knowledge in regard to Pocahontas. The effort indeed failed of its object, for he remained unemployed and without mark of distinction. "He led his old age in London, where his having a Prince's mind imprisoned in a poor man's purse rendered him to the contempt of such who were not ingenuous. Yet he efforted his spirits with the remembrance and relation of what formerly he had been and what he had done." So Fuller wrote, who might have known him in his later years. Smith died quietly in his bed, in London, in June, 1631. His will has been published by Deane, but furnishes little new information. In the absence of criticism, his book survived to become the standard authority on Virginian history. The readiness with which it was received is scarcely so remarkable as the credulity which has left it unquestioned almost to the present day.

The New York Gold Conspiracy

Home from a long siege in London, Adams came back to
America to transfix a gaudy moment of national corruption
in such articles as his Sessions, The Legal Tender Act, *and*
The New York Gold Conspiracy. *For two years, 1868 to*
1870, he lived and wrote in the Washington, D.C., of Ulys-
ses S. Grant. After an absence of eight years he found his
native land full of an alarming interest and energy. He
seized upon the badness of the national scene as his sub-
ject. In sharp critical dissent from the way things were
tending, he enjoyed the sensation of making a telling com-
ment. He wrote his articles with zestful care, sent them off
to successful publication in various magazines, and talked,
reacted, and enjoyed himself as one of the insurgent Inde-
pendents and as a very busy young party-goer, with the
reputation of being one of the best dancers in the capital.

THE NEW YORK GOLD CONSPIRACY[1]

The Civil War in America, with its enormous issues of de-
preciating currency and its reckless waste of money and
credit by the government, created a speculative mania such
as the United States, with all its experience in this respect,
had never before known. Not only in Broad Street, the centre of New York speculation, but far and wide throughout
the Northern States, almost every man who had money em-

[1] Appeared first in the English *Westminster Review* for October, 1870, and was included in Adams' *Historical Essays,* Charles
Scribner's Sons, 1891.

ployed a part of his capital in the purchase of stocks or of gold, of copper, of petroleum, or of domestic produce, in the hope of a rise in prices, or staked money on the expectation of a fall. To use the jargon of the street, every farmer and every shop-keeper in the country seemed to be engaged in "carrying" some favorite security "on a margin." Whoever could obtain a hundred dollars sent it to a broker with orders to buy whatever amount of stocks the broker would consent to purchase. If the stock rose, the speculator prospered; if it fell until the deposit or margin was lost, the broker demanded a new deposit, or sold the stock to protect himself. By means of this simple and smooth machinery, which differs in no essential respect from the processes of *roulette* or *rouge-et-noir*, the nation flung itself into the Stock Exchange, until the "outsiders," as they were called, in opposition to the regular brokers of Broad Street, represented the entire population of the American Republic. Every one speculated, and for a time successfully.

The inevitable reaction began when the government, about a year after the close of the war, stopped its issues and ceased borrowing. The greenback currency had for a moment sunk to a value of only 37 cents to the dollar. On the worst day of all, the 11th of July, 1864, one sale of $100,000 in gold was actually made at 310, equivalent to about 33 cents in the dollar.[2] At that point the depreciation stopped, and the paper which had come so near falling into entire discredit steadily rose in value, first to 50 cents, then to 60 and 70, until in the summer of 1869 it stood at about 73½ cents.

So soon as the industrious part of the public felt the touch of solid values, the fabric of fictitious wealth began to melt away under their eyes. Before long the so-called "outsiders," the men who speculated on their own account, and could not act in agreement or combination, began to suffer. One by one, or in masses, they were made the prey of larger operators; their last margins were consumed, and they dropped to the solid level of slow, productive industry.

[2] See *Men and Mysteries of Wall Street,* by James K. Medbery, pp. 250, 251.

Some lost everything, many lost still more than they had; and few families of ordinary connection and standing in the United States cannot tell, if they choose, some story of embezzlement or breach of trust committed in those days. Some men who had courage and a sense of honor, found life too heavy for them: others went mad. The greater part turned in silence to their regular pursuits, and accepted their losses as they could. Almost every rich American could produce from some pigeon-hole a bundle of worthless securities, and could show checkbooks representing the only remaining trace of margin after margin consumed in attempts to satisfy the insatiable broker. A year or two of incessant losses swept the weaker gamblers from the street.

Even those who continued to speculate found it necessary to change their mode of operations. Chance no longer ruled over the Stock Exchange and the gold market. The fate of a battle, the capture of a city, or the murder of a President had hitherto broken the plans of the strongest combinations, and put all speculators, whether great or small, on fairly even ground; but as the period of sudden and uncontrollable disturbing elements passed away, the market fell more and more completely into the hands of cliques which found a point of adhesion in some great mass of incorporated capital. Three distinct railways, with their enormous resources, became the property of Cornelius Vanderbilt, who by means of their credit and capital again and again swept millions of dollars into his pocket by a process curiously similar to gambling with loaded dice. Vanderbilt was one of the most respectable of these great operators. The Erie Railway was controlled by Daniel Drew, and while Vanderbilt at least acted in the interests of his corporations, Drew cheated equally his corporation and the public. Between these two men and the immense incorporated power they swayed, smaller operators one after another were crushed, until the survivors learned to seek shelter within some clique sufficiently strong to afford protection. Speculation in this manner began to consume itself, and the largest combination of capital was destined to swallow every weaker combination which ventured to appear in the market.

The New York Gold Conspiracy

Between the inevitable effect of a healthy currency and the omnipotence of capital in the stock market, a sounder state of society began. The public, which had been robbed with cynical indifference by Drew and Vanderbilt, could feel no sincere regret when they saw these two cormorants reduced to tearing each other. In the year 1867 Vanderbilt undertook to gain possession of the Erie Road, as he had already obtained possession of the New York Central, the second trunk-line between New York and the West. Vanderbilt was supposed to own property to the value of some $50,000,000, which might all be made directly available for stock operations. He bought the greater part of the Erie stock. Drew sold him all he could take, and then issued as much more as was required to defeat Vanderbilt's purpose. After a violent struggle, which overthrew the guaranties of social order, Drew triumphed, and Vanderbilt abandoned the contest. The Erie corporation paid him a large sum to reimburse his alleged losses. At the same time it agreed that Drew's accounts should be passed, and he obtained a release in full, and retired from the direction. The Erie Road, almost exhausted by such systematic plundering, was left in the undisturbed, if not peaceful, control of Mr. Jay Gould and Mr. James Fisk, Jr., whose reign began in the month of July, 1868.

Jay Gould was a partner in the firm of Smith, Gould, & Martin, brokers in Wall Street. He had been before engaged in railway enterprises, and his operations had not been of a nature likely to encourage public confidence in his ideas of fiduciary relations. He was a broker, and a broker is almost by nature a gambler,—perhaps the last profession suitable for a railway manager. In character he was marked by a disposition for silent intrigue. He preferred to operate on his own account, without admitting other persons into his confidence. His nature suggested survival from the family of spiders: he spun webs, in corners and in the dark. His disposition to subtlety and elaboration of intrigue was irresistible. He had not a conception of a moral principle. The class of men to whom he belonged understood no distinction between right and wrong in matters of speculation, so long as the daily settlements were

[55]

punctually effected. In this respect Gould was probably as honest as the mass of his fellows, according to the moral standard of the street; but he was an uncommonly fine and unscrupulous intriguer, skilled in the processes of stock-gambling, and passably indifferent to the praise or censure of society.

James Fisk, Jr., was still more original in character. He was not yet forty years of age, and had the instincts of fourteen. He came originally from Vermont, probably the most respectable and correct State in the Union, and his father had been a pedler who sold goods from town to town in his native valley of the Connecticut. The son followed his father's calling with boldness and success. He drove his huge wagon, made resplendent with paint and varnish, with four or six horses, through the towns of Vermont and Western Massachusetts; and when his father remonstrated at his reckless management, the young man, with his usual bravado, took his father into his service at a fixed salary, with the warning that he was not to put on airs on the strength of his new dignity. A large Boston firm which had supplied young Fisk with goods on credit, attracted by his energy, took him into the house. The war broke out; his influence drew the firm into some bold speculations which were successful. In a few years he retired with some $100,-000, which he subsequently lost. He formed a connection with Daniel Drew in New York, and a new sign, ominous of future trouble, was raised in Wall Street, bearing the names of Fisk & Belden, brokers.

Personally Fisk was coarse, noisy, boastful, ignorant, the type of a young butcher in appearance and mind. Nothing could be more striking than the contrast between him and his future associate Gould. One was small and slight in person, dark, sallow, reticent, and stealthy, with a trace of Jewish origin; the other was large, florid, gross, talkative, and obstreperous. Fisk's redeeming point was his humor, which had a flavor of American nationality. His mind was extraordinarily fertile in ideas and expedients, while his conversation was filled with unusual images and strange forms of speech, quickly caught up and made popular by the New York press. In respect to honesty as between

Gould and Fisk, the latter was perhaps, if possible, less deserving of trust than the former. A story not without a stroke of satirical wit was told by him to illustrate his estimate of abstract truth. An old woman who had bought of the elder Fisk a handkerchief which cost ninepence in the New England currency, where six shillings are reckoned to the dollar, complained to Mr. Fisk, Jr., that his father had cheated her. Mr. Fisk considered the case maturely, and gave a decision based on *a priori* principles. "No!" said he, "the old man wouldn't have told a lie for ninepence;" and then, as if this assertion needed some reasonable qualification, he added, "though he would have told eight of them for a dollar!" The distinction as regarded the father may have been just, since the father held old-fashioned ideas as to wholesale and retail trade; but in regard to the son this relative degree of truth cannot be predicated with confidence, since, if the investigating committee of Congress and its evidence are to be believed, Mr. Fisk seldom or never speaks truth at all.[3]

An intrigue equally successful and disreputable brought these two men into the Erie board of directors, whence they speedily drove their more timid predecessor Drew. In July, 1868, Gould made himself president and treasurer of the corporation. Fisk became comptroller. A young lawyer named Lane became counsel. These three directors made a majority of the executive committee, and were masters of Erie. The board of directors held no meetings. The executive committee was never called together, and the three men—Fisk, Gould, and Lane—became from that time the absolute, irresponsible owners of the Erie Railway, not less than if it had been their personal property and plaything.

This property was in effect, like all the great railway corporations, an empire within a republic. It consisted of

[3] House of Representatives. Report, No. 31. Forty-first Congress, Second Session. Report of the Committee on Banking and Currency, in response to a Resolution of the House of Representatives, passed Dec. 13, 1869, directing the Committee "to investigate the causes that led to the unusual and extraordinary fluctuations of Gold in the City of New York, from the 21st to the 27th of September, 1869," accompanied by the testimony collected by the Committee.

a trunk-line of road four hundred and fifty-nine miles in length, with branches three hundred and fourteen miles in extent, or seven hundred and seventy-three miles of road in all. Its capital stock amounted to about $35,000,000. Its gross receipts exceeded $15,000,000 per annum. It employed not less than fifteen thousand men, and supported their families. Over this wealth and influence,—greater than that directly swayed by any private citizen, greater than is absolutely and personally controlled by most kings, and far too great for public safety either in a democracy or in any other form of society,—the vicissitudes of a troubled time placed two men in irresponsible authority; and both these men belonged to a low moral and social type. Such an elevation has been rarely seen in modern history. The most dramatic of modern authors, Balzac himself, who loved to deal with similar violent alternations of fortune, or Alexandre Dumas, with all his extravagance of imagination, never reached a conception bolder or more melodramatic than this, or conceived a plot so enormous, or a catastrophe so original, as was to be developed.

One of the earliest acts of the new rulers was such as Balzac or Dumas might have predicted and delighted in. They established themselves in a palace. The old offices of the Erie Railway were in the lower part of the city, among the wharves and warehouses,—a situation no doubt convenient for business, but not agreeable as a residence; and the new proprietors naturally wished to reside on their property. Mr. Fisk and Mr. Gould accordingly bought a building of white marble, not unlike a European palace, situated about two miles from the business quarter, and containing a large theatre, or opera-house. They also purchased several smaller houses adjoining it. The opera-house cost about $700,000, and a large part of the building was at once leased by the two purchasers to themselves as the Erie corporation, to serve as offices. This suite of apartments was then furnished by themselves, as representing the corporation, at an expense of some $300,000, and in a style which, though called vulgar, was not more vulgar than that of almost any palace in Europe. The adjoining houses were connected with the main building; and in one of these

Mr. Fisk had his private apartments, with a private passage to his opera-box. He also assumed direction of the theatre, of which he became manager-in-chief. To these royal arrangements he brought tastes commonly charged as the worst results of royal license. The atmosphere of the Erie offices was not disturbed with moral prejudices; and as the opera supplied Mr. Fisk's mind with amusement, so the opera *troupe* supplied him with a permanent harem. Whatever Mr. Fisk did was done on an extraordinary scale.

These arrangements regarded only the pleasures of the American Aladdin. In the conduct of their interests, the new directors showed a capacity for large conceptions and a vigor in the execution of their schemes that alarmed the entire community. At the annual election in 1868, when Gould, Fisk, and Lane, having borrowed or bought proxies for the greater part of the stock, caused themselves to be elected for the ensuing year, the respectable portion of the public throughout the country was astonished and shocked to learn that the new board of directors contained two names peculiarly notorious and obnoxious to honest men, —William M. Tweed and Peter B. Sweeney. To every honest American they conveyed a peculiar sense of terror and disgust. The State of New York in its politics was much influenced, if not controlled, by the city of New York. The city politics were so entirely in the hands of the Democratic party as to preclude even the existence of a strong minority. The party organization centred in a political club, held together by its patronage and by a system of jobbery unequalled elsewhere in the world. The Tammany Club, thus swaying the power of a small nation of several million souls, was itself ruled by William M. Tweed and Peter B. Sweeney, absolute masters of this system of theft and fraud, and to American eyes the incarnation of political immorality.

The effect of this alliance was felt in the ensuing winter in the passage of a bill through the State legislature, and its signature by the governor, abolishing the former system of annual elections of the entire board of Erie directors, and authorizing the board to classify itself in such a manner that only a portion should be changed each year. The prin-

ciple of the bill was correct; but its practical effect enabled
Gould and Fisk to make themselves directors for five years
in spite of any attempt on the part of the stockholders
to remove them. The formality of annual re-election was
spared them; and so far as the stockholders were concerned,
there was no great injustice in the act. The Erie Road was
in the peculiar position of being without an owner. There
was no *cestui que trust,* unless the English stockholders
could be called such. In America the stock was almost exclusively held for speculation, not for investment; and in
the morals of Wall Street, speculation had almost come to
mean disregard of intrinsic value. In this case society at
large was the injured party, and society knew its risk.

This step was only a beginning. The Tammany ring exercised a power beyond politics. Under the existing Constitution of the State, the judges of the State courts are
elected by the people. Thirty-three such judges formed the
State judiciary, and each of the thirty-three was clothed
with equity powers running through the whole State. Of
these judges Tammany Hall elected several, and the Erie
Railway controlled others in country districts. Each of these
judges might forbid proceedings before any and all the
other judges, or stay proceedings in suits already com-
menced. Thus the lives and the property of the public were
in the power of the new combination; and two of the city
judges, Barnard and Cardozo, had already acquired a peculiarly infamous reputation as so-called "slaves to the
ring," which left no question as to the depths to which their
prostitution of justice would descend.

The alliance between Tammany and Erie was thus
equivalent to investing Gould and Fisk with the attributes
of sovereignty; but in order to avail themselves to the utmost of their judicial powers, they also required the ablest
legal assistance. The degradation of the bench had been
rapidly followed by the degradation of the bar. Prominent
and learned lawyers were already accustomed to avail
themselves of social or business relations with judges to forward private purposes. One whose partner might be ele-
vated to the bench was certain to be generally retained in
cases brought before this special judge; and litigants were

taught by experience that a retainer in such cases was profitably bestowed. Others found a similar advantage resulting from known social relations with the court. The debasement of tone was not confined to the lower ranks of advocates; and probably this steady demoralization of the bar made it possible for the Erie ring to obtain the services of Mr. David Dudley Field as its legal adviser. Mr. Field, a gentleman of European reputation, in regard to which he was understood to be peculiarly solicitous, was an eminent law reformer, author of the New York Code, delegate of the American Social Science Association to the European International Congress, and asserted by his partner, Mr. Shearman, in evidence before a committee of the New York legislature, to be a man of quixotic sense of honor. Mr. Shearman himself, a gentleman of English parentage, had earned public gratitude by arraigning and deploring with unsurpassed courage and point the condition of the New York judiciary, in an admirable essay in the "North American Review" for July, 1867. The value of Mr. Field's services to Messrs. Fisk and Gould was not to be measured even by the enormous fees their generosity paid him. His power over certain judges became so absolute as to impress the popular imagination; and the gossip of Wall Street insisted that he had a silken halter round the neck of Judge Barnard and a hempen one round that of Cardozo. He who had a year before threatened Barnard on his own bench with impeachment next appeared in the character of Barnard's master, and issued as a matter of course the edicts of his court.

One other combination was made by the Erie managers to extend their power. They bought a joint-stock bank in New York City, with a capital of $1,000,000. The assistance thus gained was purchased at a moderate price, since it was by no means represented by the capital. The great cliques and so-called "operators" of Wall Street and Broad Street carry on their transactions by a system of credits and clearing-houses with little use of money. The banks certify their checks, and the certified checks settle balances. Nominally and by law the banks only certified to the extent of *bona fide* deposits, but in reality the custom of disregarding the strict letter of the law was not unknown; and in case of the bank in question, the Comptroller of the Currency, an officer of the national Treasury, testified that on an examination of its affairs in April, 1869, out of fifteen checks deposited in its hands as security for certifications made by it, selected at hazard for inquiry, and representing a nominal value of $1,500,000, three only were good. The rest represented accommodation extended to brokers and speculators without security. This bank on Thursday, Sept. 24, 1869, certified checks to the amount of nearly $7,500,000 for Gould alone. What sound security Gould deposited against this mass of credit may be left to the imagination. His operations were not confined to this bank alone, although this was the only one owned by the ring.

Thus Gould and Fisk created a combination more powerful than any that has been controlled by mere private citizens in America or in Europe since society for self-protection established the supreme authority of the judicial name. They exercised the legislative and the judicial powers of the State; they possessed almost unlimited credit, and society was at their mercy. One authority alone stood above them, beyond their control; and this was the distant but threatening figure of the national government.

Powerful as they were, the Erie managers were seldom in funds. The marble palace in which they lived, the theatre they supported, the bribery and profusion of management by which they could alone maintain their defiance of public opinion, the enormous schemes for extending their operations into which they rushed, all required greater resources than could be furnished even by the wholesale plunder of the Erie Road. They were obliged from time to time to issue from their castle, and harry the industrious public or their brother freebooters. The process was different from that known to the dark ages, but the objects and the results were the same. At one time Fisk is said to have ordered heavy speculative sales of stock in an express company which held a contract with the Erie Railway. The sales being effected, the contract was declared annulled. The stock naturally fell, and Fisk realized the difference. He then ordered heavy purchases, and having renewed the contract the stock rose again, and Fisk a second time swept the street.[4] In the summer and autumn of 1869 the two managers issued and sold two hundred and thirty-five thousand new shares of Erie stock, or nearly as much as its entire capital when they assumed power in July, 1868. With the aid of the money thus obtained, they succeeded in withdrawing about $12,500,000 in currency from circulation at the very moment of the year when currency was most in demand in order to harvest the crops. For weeks the nation writhed and quivered under the torture of this modern rack, until the national government itself was obliged to interfere and threaten a sudden opening of the Treasury. Whether the Erie speculators operated for a rise or for a fall, whether they bought or sold, and whether they were engaged in manipulating stocks or locking up currency or cornering gold, they were always a nuisance and scandal.

In order to understand a so-called corner in gold, readers must bear in mind that the supply of gold immediately available for transfers was limited within distinct bounds. New York and the country behind it contained an amount usually estimated at about $20,000,000. The national government commonly held from $75,000,000 to $100,000,-000, which might be thrown bodily on the market if the President ordered it. To obtain gold from Europe or other sources required time.

In the second place, gold was a commodity bought and sold like stocks, in a special market or gold-room situated next the Stock Exchange in Broad Street and practically a part of it. In gold as in stocks, the transactions were both real and speculative. The real transactions were mostly purchases or loans made by importers who required coin to pay customs-duties on their imports. This legitimate business was supposed to require from $5,000,000 to $7,500,000 per day. The speculative transactions were wagers on the rise or fall of price, and neither required any transfer of gold nor implied its existence, although in times of excitement hundreds of millions were nominally bought, sold, and loaned.

Under the late Administration, Mr. McCulloch, then Sec-

[4] *Men and Mysteries of Wall Street*, p. 168.

retary of the Treasury, had thought it his duty to guarantee
a stable currency, although Congress forbade him to restore the gold standard. During four years gold had fluctu-
ated little, and principally from natural causes, and the
danger of attempting to create an artificial scarcity had prevented the operators from trying an experiment sure to irritate the government. The financial policy of the new Administration was not so definitely fixed, and the success of
a speculation would depend on the action of Mr. Boutwell,
the new secretary, whose direction was understood to have
begun by a marked censure on the course pursued by his
predecessor.

Of all financial operations, cornering gold is the most brilliant and the most dangerous, and possibly the hazard and
splendor of the attempt were the reasons of its fascination
to Jay Gould's fancy. He dwelt upon it for months, and
played with it like a pet toy. His fertile mind discovered
that it would prove a blessing to the community; and on
this theory, half honest and half fraudulent, he stretched
the widely extended fabric of the web in which mankind
was to be caught. The theory was partially sound. Starting
from the principle that the price of grain in New York was
regulated by the price in London, and was not affected by
currency fluctuations, Gould argued that if the premium on
gold could be raised from thirty to forty cents at harvest-
time, the farmers' grain would be worth $1.40 instead of
$1.30; and as a consequence the farmer would hasten to
send his crop to New York over the Erie Railway, which
was sorely in need of freights. With the assistance of another gentleman, Gould calculated the exact premium at
which the Western farmer would consent to dispose of his
grain, and thus distance the three hundred sail then hasten-
ing from the Danube to supply the English market. Gold,
which was then heavy at 134, must be raised to 145.

This clever idea, like the other ideas of the gentlemen of
Erie, had the single fault of requiring that some one somewhere should be swindled. The scheme was probably feasi-
ble; but sooner or later the reaction from such an artificial
stimulant must have come, and whenever it came some one
must suffer. Nevertheless, Gould probably argued that so

long as the farmer got his money, the Erie Railway its freights, and he his small profits on the gold he bought, he need not ask who else might be injured; and indeed by the time the reaction came and gold was ready to fall as he expected, Gould would probably have been ready to assist the process by speculative sales in order to enable the Western farmer to buy his spring goods cheap as he had sold his autumn crops dear. Gould was equally ready to buy gold cheap and sell it dear on his private account; and as he proposed to bleed New York merchants for the benefit of the Western farmer, so he was willing to bleed Broad Street for his own. The patriotic object was the one which for obvious reasons Gould preferred to put forward, and on which he hoped to rest his ambitious structure.

The operation of raising the price of gold from 133 to 145 offered no great difficulty to men who controlled the resources of the Erie Railway. Credit alone was needed, and of credit Gould had an unlimited supply. The only serious danger lay in the possible action of the national government, which had not taken the philanthropic view of the public good peculiar to the managers of Erie. Secretary Boutwell, who should have assisted Gould in "bulling" gold, was gravely suspected of being a bear, and of wishing to depress the premium to nothing. If the Secretary of the Treasury were determined to stand in Gould's path, even the combined forces of Erie and Tammany dared not jostle against him; and therefore Gould must control the government, whether by fair means or foul, by persuasion or by purchase. He undertook the task; and after his proceedings in both directions have been thoroughly drawn into light, the public can see how dramatic and artistic a conspiracy in real life may be when slowly elaborated from the subtle mind of a clever intriguer, and carried into execution by a band of unshrinking scoundrels.

The first requisite for Gould's purpose was a channel of direct communication with the President; and here he was peculiarly favored by chance. Mr. Abel Rathbone Corbin, formerly lawyer, editor, speculator, lobby-agent, familiar, as he claims, with everything, had succeeded during his varied career in accumulating from one or another of his hazardous pursuits a comfortable fortune, and had crowned his success, at the age of sixty-seven or thereabout, by contracting a marriage with General Grant's sister at the moment when General Grant was on the point of reaching the highest eminence possible to an American citizen. To say that Corbin's moral dignity had passed absolutely pure through the somewhat tainted atmosphere in which his life had been spent would be flattering him too highly; but at least he was no longer engaged in active occupation, and he lived quietly in New York watching the course of public affairs, and remarkable for respectability becoming to a President's brother-in-law. Gould enjoyed a slight acquaintance with Corbin, and proceeded to improve it. He assumed and asserts that he felt a respect for Corbin's shrewdness and sagacity. Corbin claims to have first impressed the crop theory on Gould's mind; while Gould testifies that he indoctrinated Corbin with this idea, which became a sort of monomania with the President's brother-in-law, who soon began to preach it to the President himself. On the 15th of June, 1869, the President came to New York, and was there the guest of Corbin, who urged Gould to call and pay his respects to the Chief Magistrate. Gould had probably aimed at this result. He called; and the President of the United States not only listened to the president of Erie, but accepted an invitation to Fisk's theatre, sat in Fisk's private box, and the next evening became the guest of these two gentlemen on their Newport steamer,—while Fisk, arrayed, as the newspapers reported, "in a blue uniform, with a broad gilt cap-band, three silver stars on his coat-sleeve, lavender gloves, and a diamond breast-pin as large as a cherry, stood at the gangway, surrounded by his aids, bestarred and bestriped like himself," and welcomed his distinguished friend.

The Erie managers had already arranged that the President should on this occasion be sounded in regard to his financial policy; and when the selected guests—among whom were Gould, Fisk, and others—sat down at nine o'clock to supper, the conversation was directed to the subject of finance. "Some one," says Gould, "asked the President what his view was." The "some one" in question was

of course Fisk, who alone had the impudence to put such
an inquiry. The President bluntly replied that there was a
certain amount of fictitiousness about the prosperity of the
country, and that the bubble might as well be tapped in
one way as another. The remark was fatal to Gould's plans,
and he felt it, in his own words, as "a wet blanket."

Meanwhile the post of assistant-treasurer at New York
had become vacant, and it was a matter of interest to Gould
that some person friendly to himself should occupy this position, which in its relations to the public is second in importance only to the Secretaryship of the Treasury itself.
Gould consulted Corbin, and Corbin suggested the name of
General Butterfield,—a former officer in the volunteer army.
The appointment was not a wise one; nor does it appear
in evidence by what means Corbin succeeded in bringing
it about. He was supposed to have used A. T. Stewart, the
wealthy importer, as his instrument for the purpose; but
whatever the influence may have been, Corbin appears to
have set it in action, and General Butterfield entered upon
his duties toward the 1st of July.

The preparations thus made show that some large
scheme was never absent from Gould's mind, although between the months of May and August he made no attempt
to act upon the markets. Between August 20 and September 1, in company with Messrs. Woodward and Kimber,
two large speculators, he made what is known as a pool or
combination to raise the premium on gold, and some ten
or fifteen millions were bought, but with very little effect
on the price. The tendency of the market was downward,
and was not easily counteracted. Perhaps under ordinary
circumstances he might have abandoned his project; but
an incident suddenly occurred which drew him headlong
into the operation.

Whether the appointment of General Butterfield
strengthened Gould's faith in Corbin's secret powers does
not appear in evidence, though it may readily be assumed
as probable; but the next event seemed to authorize an unlimited faith in Corbin, as well as to justify the implicit belief of an Erie treasurer in the corruptibility of all mankind.
The unsuspicious President again passed through New

York, and came to breakfast at Corbin's house on the 2d of
September. He saw no one but Corbin while there, and the
same evening at ten o'clock departed for Saratoga. Gould
was immediately informed by Corbin that the President,
in discussing the financial situation, had shown himself a
convert to the Erie theory about marketing the crops, and
had "stopped in the middle of a conversation in which he
had expressed his views and written a letter" to Secretary
Boutwell. This letter was not produced before the investigating committee; but Secretary Boutwell testified as follows in regard to it:—

> "I think on the evening of the 4th of September I re-
> ceived a letter from the President dated at New York,
> as I recollect it: I am not sure where it is dated. I have
> not seen the letter since the night I received it. I think
> it is now in my residence in Groton. In that letter he
> expressed an opinion that it was undesirable to force
> down the price of gold. He spoke of the importance to
> the West of being able to move their crops. His idea was
> that if gold should fall, the West would suffer and the
> movement of the crops would be retarded. The impres-
> sion made on my mind by the letter was that he had
> rather a strong opinion to that effect. . . . Upon the re-
> ceipt of the President's letter on the evening of the 4th of
> September, I telegraphed to Judge Richardson [Assist-
> ant Secretary at Washington] this despatch: 'Send no or-
> der to Butterfield as to sales of gold until you hear from
> me.'"

Gould had succeeded in reversing the policy of the national government; but this was not all. He knew what the
government would do before any officer of the government
knew it. Gould was at Corbin's house on the 2d of September; and although the evidence of both these gentlemen
was very confused on the point, the inference is inevitable
that Gould saw Corbin privately within an hour or two
after the letter to Boutwell was written; and that at this
interview, while the President was still in the house, Corbin
gave information to Gould about the President's letter,—
perhaps showed him the letter itself. Then followed a

transaction worthy of the French stage. Corbin's evidence gives his own account of it:—

"On the 2d of September (referring to memoranda) Mr. Gould offered to let me have some of the gold he then possessed. . . . He spoke to me, as he had repeatedly done before, about taking a certain amount of gold owned by him. I finally told Mr. Gould that for the sake of a lady, my wife, I would accept $500,000 of gold for her benefit, as I shared his confidence that gold would rise. . . . He afterward insisted that I should take a million more, and I did so on the same condition for my wife. He then sent me this paper."

The paper in question was as follows:—

> Smith, Gould, Martin, & Co., Bankers.
> 11 Broad Street, New York, Sept. 2, 1869.

Mr. ——

> Dear Sir,—We have bought for your account and risk,—
> 500,000, gold, 132, R.
> 1,000,000, gold, 133⅝, R.
> which we will carry on demand with the right to use.
> Smith, Gould, Martin, & Co.

The memorandum meant that for every rise of one per cent in the price of gold Corbin was to receive $15,000, and his name nowhere to appear. If Gould saw Corbin in the morning and learned from him what the President had written, he must have made his bargain on the spot, and then going directly to the city he must in one breath have ordered this memorandum to be made out and large quantities of gold to be purchased before the President's letter left Corbin's house.

No time was lost. The same afternoon Gould's brokers bought large amounts in gold. One testifies to buying $1,315,000 at 134⅛. September 3 the premium was forced up to 36; September 4, when Boutwell received his letter, it had risen to 37. There Gould met a check, as he described his position in nervous Americanisms:—

"I did not want to buy so much gold. In the spring I put gold up from 32 to 38 and 40, with only about seven millions. But all these fellows went in and sold short, so that in order to keep it up I had to buy or else to back down and show the white feather. They would sell it to you all the time. I never intended to buy more than four or five millions of gold, but these fellows kept purchasing it on, and I made up my mind that I would put it up to 40 at one time. . . . We went into it as a commercial transaction, and did not intend to buy such an amount of gold. I was forced into it by the bears selling out. They were bound to put it down. I got into the contest. All these other fellows deserted me like rats from a ship. Kimber sold out and got short. . . . He sold out at 37. He got short of it, and went up" (or, in English, he failed).

The bears would not consent to lie still and be flayed. They had the great operators for once at a disadvantage, and were bent on revenge. Gould's position was hazardous. When Kimber sold out at 37, which was probably on the 7th of September, the market broke; and on the 8th the price fell back to 35. At the same moment, when the "pool" was ended by Kimber's desertion, Corbin, with his eminent shrewdness and respectability, told Gould "that gold had gone up to 37," and that he "should like to have this matter realized,"—which was equivalent to saying that he wished to be paid something on account. This was said September 6; and Gould was obliged the same day to bring him a check for $25,000, drawn to the order of Jay Gould, and indorsed in blank by him with a proper regard for Corbin's modest desire not to have his name appear. The transaction did credit to Corbin's sagacity, and showed at least that he was acquainted with the men he dealt with. Undoubtedly it placed Gould in a difficult position; but as Gould already held some fifteen millions of gold and needed Corbin's support, he preferred to pay $25,000 outright rather than allow Corbin to throw his gold on the market. Yet the fabric of Gould's web had been so seriously injured that for a week—from the 8th to the 15th of September—

he was unable to advance and equally unable to retreat without severe losses. He sat at his desk in the opera-house, silent as usual, tearing little slips of paper which he threw on the floor in his abstraction, while he revolved new combinations in his mind.

Down to this moment James Fisk, Jr., had not appeared in the affair. Gould had not taken him into his confidence; and not until after September 10 did Gould decide that nothing else could be done. Fisk was not a safe ally in so delicate an affair; but apparently no other aid offered itself. Gould approached him; and as usual Gould's touch was like magic. Fisk's evidence begins here, and may be believed when very strongly corroborated:—

"Gold having settled down to 35, and I not having cared to touch it, he was a little sensitive on the subject, feeling as if he would rather take his losses without saying anything about it. . . . One day he said to me, 'Don't you think gold has got to the bottom?' I replied that I did not see the profit in buying gold unless you have got into a position where you can command the market. He then said he had bought quite a large amount of gold, and I judged from his conversation that he wanted me to go into the movement and help strengthen the market. Upon that I went into the market and bought. I should say that was about the 15th or 16th of September. I bought at that time about seven or eight millions, I think."

The market responded slowly to these enormous purchases; and on the 16th the clique was still struggling to recover its lost ground.

Meanwhile Gould placed a million and a half of gold to the account of General Butterfield, as he had done to the account of Corbin, and notified him of the purchase; so Gould swears, in spite of General Butterfield's denial. The date of this purchase is not fixed. Through Corbin a notice was also sent by Gould about the middle of September to the President's private secretary, General Porter, informing him that half a million was placed to his credit. Porter repudiated the purchase, but Butterfield took no apparent

notice of Gould's transaction on his account. On the 10th
of September the President again came to New York, where
he remained his brother-in-law's guest till the 13th; and
during this visit Gould again saw him, although Corbin
avers that the President then intimated his wish to the
servant that this should be the last time Gould obtained
admission. "Gould was always trying to get something out
of him," he said; and if he had known how much Gould
had succeeded in getting out of him, he would have admired the man's genius, even while shutting the door in his
face.

On the morning of September 13 the President set out
on a journey to the little town of Washington, situated
among the mountains of western Pennsylvania, where he
was to remain a few days. Gould, who consulted Corbin
regularly every morning and evening, was still extremely
nervous in regard to the President's policy; and as the crisis
approached, his nervousness led him into the blunder of doing too much. Probably the bribe offered to Porter was a
mistake, but a greater mistake was made by pressing Corbin's influence too far. Gould induced Corbin to write an
official article for the New York press on the financial policy
of the government,—an article afterward inserted in the
"New York Times" through the kind offices of Mr. James
McHenry; and he also persuaded or encouraged Corbin to
write a letter directly to the President. This letter, written
September 17 under the influence of Gould's anxiety, was
instantly sent by a special messenger of Fisk to reach the
President before he returned to the capital. The messenger
carried also a letter of introduction to General Porter, the
private secretary, in order to secure the personal delivery
of this important despatch.

On Monday, September 20, gold again rose. Throughout Tuesday and Wednesday Fisk continued to purchase
without limit, and forced the price up to 40. At that time
Gould's firm of Smith, Gould, & Martin, through which the
operation was conducted, had purchased some $50,000,-
000; yet the bears went on selling, although they could
continue the contest only by borrowing Gould's own gold.
Gould, on the other hand, could no longer sell and clear

himself, for the reason that the sale of $50,000,000 would have broken the market. The struggle became intense. The whole country watched with astonishment the battle between the bulls and the bears. Business was deranged, and values were unsettled. There were indications of a panic in the stock market; and the bears in their emergency vehemently pressed the government to intervene. Gould wrote to Boutwell a letter so impudent as to indicate desperation and loss of his ordinary coolness. He began:—

"Sir,—There is a panic in Wall Street, engineered by a bear combination. They have withdrawn currency to such an extent that it is impossible to do ordinary business. The Erie Company requires eight hundred thousand dollars to disburse,— . . . much of it in Ohio, where an exciting political contest is going on, and where we have about ten thousand employed; and the trouble is charged on the Administration. . . . Cannot you, consistently, increase your line of currency?"

From a friend such a letter would have been an outrage; but from a member of the Tammany ring, the principal object of detestation to the government, such a threat or bribe—whichever it may be called—was incredible. Gould was, in fact, at his wits' end. He dreaded a panic, and he felt that it could no longer be avoided.

The scene next shifts for a moment to the distant town of Washington, among the hills of western Pennsylvania. On the morning of September 19, President Grant and his private secretary General Porter were playing croquet on the lawn, when Fisk's messenger, after twenty-four hours of travel by rail and carriage, arrived at the house, and sent in to ask for General Porter. When the President's game was ended, Porter came, received his own letter from Corbin, and called the President, who entered the room and took his brother-in-law's despatch. He then left the room, and after some ten or fifteen minutes' absence returned. The messenger, tired of waiting, then asked, "Is it all right?" "All right," replied the President; and the messenger hastened to the nearest telegraph station, and sent word to Fisk, "Delivered; all right."

The messenger was altogether mistaken. Not only was all not right, but all was going hopelessly wrong. The President had at the outset supposed the man to be an ordinary post-office agent, and the letter an ordinary letter which had arrived through the post-office. Not until Porter asked some curious question as to the man, did the President learn that he had been sent by Corbin merely to carry this apparently unimportant letter of advice. The President's suspicions were excited; and the same evening, at his request, Mrs. Grant wrote a hurried note to Mrs. Corbin, telling her how greatly the President was distressed at the rumor that Mr. Corbin was speculating in Wall Street, and how much he hoped that Mr. Corbin would "instantly disconnect himself with anything of that sort."

This letter, subsequently destroyed—or said to have been destroyed—by Mrs. Corbin, arrived in New York on the morning of Wednesday, September 22, the day when Gould and his enemies the bears were making simultaneous appeals to Secretary Boutwell. Mrs. Corbin was greatly excited and distressed by her sister-in-law's language. She carried the letter to her husband, and insisted that he should instantly abandon his interest in the gold speculation. Corbin, although considering the scruples of his wife and her family highly absurd, assented to her wish; and when Gould came that evening as usual, with $50,000,000 of gold on his hands and extreme anxiety on his mind, Corbin read to him two letters,—the first, written by Mrs. Grant to Mrs. Corbin; the second, written by Mr. Corbin to President Grant, assuring him that he had not a dollar of interest in gold. The assurance of this second letter was, at any sacrifice, to be made good.

Corbin proposed that Gould should give him a check for $100,000, and take his $1,500,000 off his hands. A proposition more impudent than this could scarcely be imagined. Gould had already paid Corbin $25,000, and Corbin asked for $100,000 more at the moment when it was clear that the $25,000 he had received had been given him under a misunderstanding of his services. He even represented himself as doing Gould a favor by letting him have a million and a half more gold at the highest market price, at a time when Gould had fifty millions which he must sell or be ruined. What Gould might under ordinary circumstances have replied, may be imagined; but for the moment he could say nothing. Corbin had but to show this note to a single broker in Wall Street, and the fabric of Gould's speculation would fall to pieces. Gould asked for time, and went away. He consulted no one; he gave Fisk no hint of what had happened. The next morning he returned to Corbin, and made him the following offer:—

"'Mr. Corbin, I cannot give you anything if you will go out. If you will remain in, and take the chances of the market, I will give you my check [for $100,000].' 'And then,' says Corbin, 'I did what I think it would have troubled almost any other business man to consent to do, —refuse one hundred thousand dollars on a rising market. If I had not been an old man married to a middle-aged woman, I should have done it (of course with her consent) just as sure as the offer was made. I said, "Mr. Gould, my wife says *no!* Ulysses thinks it wrong, and that it ought to end." So I gave it up. . . . He looked at me with an air of severe distrust, as if he was afraid of treachery in the camp. He remarked, "Mr. Corbin, I am undone if that letter gets out." . . . He stood there for a little while looking very thoughtful, exceedingly thoughtful. He then left and went into Wall Street; . . . and my impression is that he it was, and not the government, that broke that market.'"

Corbin was right; throughout all these transactions his insight into Gould's character was marvellous.

It was the morning of Thursday, September 23. Gould and Fisk went to Broad Street together; but as usual Gould was silent and secret, while Fisk was noisy and communicative. Their movements were completely separate. Gould acted through his own firm of Smith, Gould, & Martin, while Fisk operated principally through his old partner, Belden. One of Smith's principal brokers testifies:—

" 'Fisk never could do business with Smith, Gould, &
Martin very comfortably. They would not do business
for him. It was a very uncertain thing of course where
Fisk might be. He is an erratic sort of genius. I don't
think anybody would want to follow him very long. I
am satisfied that Smith, Gould, & Martin controlled their
own gold, and were ready to do as they pleased with it
without consulting Fisk. I do not think there was any
general agreement. . . . None of us who knew him cared
to do business with him. I would not have taken an order from him nor had anything to do with him.' " Belden
was considered a very low fellow. " 'I never had anything
to do with him or his party,' said one broker employed
by Gould. 'They were men I had a perfect detestation
of; they were no company for me. I should not have
spoken to them at all under any ordinary circumstances.' "
Another says, " 'Belden is a man in whom I never had
any confidence in any way. For months before that, I
would not have taken him for a gold transaction.' "

Yet Belden bought millions upon millions of gold. He
himself swore that he had bought twenty millions by
Thursday evening, without capital or credit except that of
his brokers. Meanwhile Gould, on reaching the city, had at
once given secret orders to sell. From the moment he left
Corbin he had but one idea, which was to get rid of his
gold as quietly as possible. "I purchased merely enough to
make believe I was a bull," says Gould. This double process continued all that afternoon. Fisk's wild purchases carried the price to 144, and the panic in the street became
more and more serious as the bears realized the extremity
of their danger. No one can tell how much gold which did
not exist they had contracted to deliver or pay the difference in price. One of the clique brokers swears that by
Thursday evening the street had sold the clique one hundred and eighteen millions of gold; and every rise of one
per cent of this sum implied a loss of more than $1,000,000
to the bears. Naturally the terror was extreme, for half
Broad Street and thousands of speculators would have been

ruined if compelled to settle gold at 150 which they had sold at 140. By that time nothing more was heard in regard to philanthropic theories of benefit to the Western farmer.

Gould's feelings may easily be imagined. He knew that Fisk's reckless management would bring the government upon his shoulders, and he knew that unless he could sell his gold before the order came from Washington he would be a ruined man. He knew, too, that Fisk's contracts must inevitably be repudiated. This Thursday evening he sat at his desk in the Erie offices at the opera-house, while Fisk and Fisk's brokers chattered about him.

> "I was transacting my railway business. I had my own views about the market, and my own fish to fry. I was all alone, so to speak, in what I did, and I did not let any of those people know exactly how I stood. I got no ideas from anything that was said there. I had been selling gold from 35 up all the time, and I did not know till the next morning that there would probably come an order about twelve o'clock to sell gold."

Gould had not told Fisk of Corbin's retreat, or of his own orders to sell.

Friday morning Gould and Fisk went together to Broad Street and took possession of the private back-office of a principal broker, "without asking the privilege of doing so," as the broker observes in his evidence. The first news brought to Gould was a disaster. The government had sent three men from Washington to examine the bank which Gould owned; and the bank sent word to Gould that it feared to certify for him as usual, and was itself in danger of a panic, caused by the presence of officers, which created distrust of the bank. It barely managed to save itself. Gould took the information silently, and his firm redoubled sales of gold. His partner, Smith, gave the orders to one broker after another,—"Sell ten millions!" "The order was given as quick as a flash, and away he went," says one of these men. "I sold only eight millions." "Sell, sell, sell! do nothing but sell! only don't sell to Fisk's brokers," were the orders which Smith himself acknowledges. In the gold-room Fisk's brokers were shouting their rising bids, and the packed crowd grew frantic with terror and rage as each successive rise showed their increasing losses. The wide streets outside were thronged with excited people; the telegraph offices were overwhelmed with messages ordering sales or purchases of gold or stocks; and the whole nation was watching eagerly to see what the result of this convulsion was to be. Trade was stopped, and even the President felt that it was time to raise his hand. No one who has not seen the New York gold-room can understand the spectacle it presented, —now a pandemonium, now silent as the grave. Fisk, in his dark back-office across the street, with his coat off, swaggered up and down, "a big cane in his hand," and called himself the Napoleon of Wall Street. He believed that he directed the movement, and while the street outside imagined that he and Gould were one family, and that his purchases were made for the clique, Gould was silently flinging away his gold at any price he could get for it.

Whether Fisk expected to carry out his contract and force the bears to settle, or not, is doubtful; but the evidence seems to show that he was in earnest, and felt sure of success. His orders were unlimited. "Put it up to 150!" was one which he sent to the gold-room. Gold rose to 150. At length the bid was made, "160 for any part of five millions!" and no one any longer dared take it. "161 for five millions!" "162 for five millions!" No answer was made, and the offer was repeated, "162 for any part of five millions!" A voice replied, "Sold one million at 62!" The bubble suddenly burst; and within fifteen minutes, amid an excitement without parallel even in the wildest excitements of the war, the clique brokers were literally swept away and left struggling by themselves, bidding still 160 for gold in millions which no one would any longer take their word for, while the premium sank rapidly to 135. A moment later the telegraph brought from Washington the government order to sell, and the result was no longer possible to dispute. Fisk had gone too far, while Gould had secretly weakened the ground under his feet.

Gould was saved. His fifty millions were sold; and although no one knows what his gains or losses may have been, his firm was able to meet its contracts and protect its brokers. Fisk was in a very different situation. So soon as it became evident that his brokers would be unable to carry out their contracts, every one who had sold gold to them turned in wrath to Fisk's office. Fortunately for him it was protected by armed men whom he had brought with him from his castle of Erie; but the excitement was so great that both Fisk and Gould thought best to retire as rapidly as possible by a back entrance leading into another street, and to seek the protection of the opera-house. There nothing but an army could disturb them; no civil mandate was likely to be served without their permission within those walls, and few men cared to face Fisk's ruffians in order to force an entrance.

The winding up of this famous conspiracy may be told in few words; but no account could be complete which failed to reproduce in full the story of Fisk's last interview with Corbin, as told by Fisk himself:—

"I went down to the neighborhood of Wall Street Friday morning, and the history of that morning you know. When I got back to our office, you can imagine I was in no enviable state of mind, and the moment I got up street that afternoon I started right round to old Corbin's to rake him out. I went into the room, and sent word that Mr. Fisk wanted to see him in the dining-room. I was too mad to say anything civil, and when he came into the room, said I, 'You damned old scoundrel, do you know what you have done here, you and your people?' He began to wring his hands, and, 'Oh,' he says, 'this is a horrible position! Are you ruined?' I said I didn't know whether I was or not; and I asked him again if he knew what had happened. He had been crying, and said he had just heard; that he had been sure everything was all right; but that something had occurred entirely different from what he had anticipated. Said I, 'That don't amount to anything; we know that gold ought not to be at 31, and that it would not be but for such performances as you have had this last week; you know damned well

it would not if you had not failed.' I knew that some-
body had run a saw right into us, and said I, 'This whole
damned thing has turned out just as I told you it would.'
I considered the whole party a pack of cowards, and I
expected that when we came to clear our hands they
would sock it right into us. I said to him, 'I don't know
whether you have lied or not, and I don't know what
ought to be done with you.' He was on the other side of
the table, weeping and wailing, and I was gnashing my
teeth. 'Now,' he says, 'you must quiet yourself.' I told
him I didn't want to be quiet. I had no desire to ever
be quiet again, and probably never should be quiet
again. He says, 'But, my dear sir, you will lose your reason.' Says I, 'Speyers [a broker employed by him that
day] has already lost his reason; reason has gone out of
everybody but me.' I continued, 'Now, what are you going to do? You have got us into this thing, and what are
you going to do to get us out of it?' He says, 'I don't
know. I will go and get my wife.' I said, 'Get her down
here!' The soft talk was all over. He went upstairs, and
they returned tottling into the room, looking older than
Stephen Hopkins. His wife and he both looked like death.
He was tottling just like that. [Illustrated by a trembling
movement of his body.] I have never seen him from that
day to this."

This is sworn evidence before a committee of Congress;
and its humor is the more conspicuous, because the story
probably contained from beginning to end not a word of
truth. No such interview ever occurred, except in the un-
confined apartments of Fisk's imagination. His own previous
statements make it certain that he was not at Corbin's house
at all that day, and that Corbin did come to the Erie offices
that evening, and again the next morning. Corbin denies
the truth of the account without limitation; and adds that
when he entered the Erie offices the next morning, Fisk was
there. "I asked him how Mr. Gould felt after the great
calamity of the day before." He remarked, "Oh, he has no
courage at all. He has sunk right down. There is nothing
left of him but a heap of clothes and a pair of eyes." The

internal evidence of truth in this anecdote would support Mr. Corbin against the world.[5]

In regard to Gould, Fisk's graphic description was probably again inaccurate. Undoubtedly the noise and scandal of the moment were extremely unpleasant to this silent and impenetrable intriguer. The city was in a ferment, and the whole country pointing at him with wrath. The machinery

[5] Mr. Fisk to the Editor of the Sun:—

Erie Railway Company, Comptroller's Office,
New York, Oct. 4, 1869.

To the Editor of the Sun,

Dear Sir,— . . . Mr. Corbin has constantly associated with me; . . . *he spent more than an hour with me in the Erie Railway Office on the afternoon of Saturday, September 25, the day after the gold panic.* . . . I enclose you a few affidavits which will give you futher information concerning this matter.

I remain your obedient servant,
James Fisk, Jr.

Affidavit of Charles W. Pollard.

State of New York, City and County of New York, ss.

C. W. Pollard being duly sworn, says: "I have frequently been the bearer of messages between Mr. James Fisk, Jr., and Mr. Abel R. Corbin, brother-in-law of President Grant. . . . Mr. Corbin called on me at the Erie building on Thursday, 23d September, 1869, telling me he came to see how Messrs. Fisk and Gould were getting along. . . . He called again on Friday, the following day, at about noon; appeared to be greatly excited, and said he feared *we* should lose a great deal of money. The following morning, Saturday, September 25, Mr. Fisk told me to take his carriage and call upon Mr. Corbin and say to him that he and Mr. Gould would like to see him (Corbin) at their office. I called and saw Mr. Corbin. He remarked upon greeting me: 'How does Mr. Fisk bear his losses?' and added, *'It is terrible for us.'* He then asked me to bring Mr. Fisk up to his house immediately, as he was indisposed, and did not feel able to go down to his (Fisk's) office. I went after Mr. Fisk, who returned immediately with me to Mr. Corbin's residence, but shortly after came out with Mr. Corbin, who accompanied him to Mr. Fisk's office, where he was closeted with him and Mr. Gould for about two hours. . . ."

There are obvious inconsistencies among these different accounts, which it is useless to attempt to explain. The fact of Saturday's interview appears to be beyond dispute.

of the gold exchange had broken down, and he alone could extricate the business community from the pressing danger of a general panic. He had saved himself, but in a manner that could not have been to his taste. Yet his course from this point must have been almost self-evident to his mind, and there is no reason to suppose that he hesitated.

Gould's contracts were all fulfilled. Fisk's contracts, all except one, in respect to which the broker was able to compel a settlement, were repudiated. Gould probably suggested to Fisk that it was better to let Belden fail, and to settle a handsome fortune on him, than to sacrifice something more than $5,000,000 in sustaining him. Fisk therefore threw Belden over, and swore that he had acted only under Belden's order; in support of which statement he produced a paper to the following effect:—

September 24.

Dear Sir,—I hereby authorize you to order the purchase and sale of gold on my account during this day to the extent you may deem advisable, and to report the same to me as early as possible. It is to be understood that the profits of such order are to belong entirely to me, and I will, of course, bear any losses resulting.

Yours,

William Belden.

James Fisk, Jr.

This document was not produced in the original, and certainly never existed. Belden himself could not be induced to acknowledge the order; and no one would have believed him had he done so. Meanwhile the matter is before the national courts, and Fisk may probably be held to his contracts; but it will be difficult to execute judgment upon him, or to discover his assets.

One of the first acts of the Erie gentlemen after the crisis was to summon their lawyers and set in action their judicial powers. The object was to prevent the panic-stricken brokers from using legal process to force settlements, and so render the entanglement inextricable. Messrs. Field and Shearman came, and instantly prepared a considerable number of injunctions, which were sent to their judges, signed at once, and immediately served. Gould then was able to dictate the terms of settlement; and after a week of paralysis, Broad Street began to show signs of returning life. As a legal curiosity, one of these documents issued three months after the crisis may be reproduced in order to show the powers wielded by the Erie managers:—

Supreme Court.

H. N. Smith, Jay Gould, H. H. Martin,
and J. B. Bach, Plaintiffs,
against   Injunction
John Bonner and Arthur L. Sewell,   by order.
Defendants.

It appearing satisfactorily to me by the complaint duly verified by the plaintiffs that sufficient grounds for an order of injunction exist, I do hereby order and enjoin . . . that the defendants, John Bonner and Arthur L. Sewell, their agents, attorneys, and servants, refrain from pressing their pretended claims against the plaintiffs, or either of them, before the Arbitration Committee of the New York Stock Exchange, or from taking any proceedings thereon, or in relation thereto, except in this action.

George G. Barnard, J. S. C.

New York, Dec. 29, 1869.

Bonner had practically been robbed with violence by Gould, and instead of his being able to bring the robber into court as the criminal, the robber brought him into court as criminal, and the judge forbade him to appear in any other character. Of all Mr. Field's distinguished legal reforms and philanthropic projects, this injunction is beyond a doubt the most brilliant and the most successful.[6]

[6] These remarks on Mr. Field's professional conduct as counsel of the Erie Railway excited a somewhat intemperate controversy, and Mr. Field's partisans in the press made against the authors of the "Chapters of Erie" a charge that these writers "indelicately interfered in a matter alien to them in every way," —the administration of justice in New York being, in this point of view, a matter in which Mr. Field and the Erie Railway were

The fate of the conspirators was not severe. Corbin went to Washington, where he was snubbed by the President, and disappeared from public view, only coming to light again before the Congressional committee. General Butterfield, whose share in the transaction is least understood, was permitted to resign his office without an investigation. Speculation for the next six months was at an end. Every person involved in the affair seemed to have lost money, and dozens of brokers were swept from the street. But Jay

alone concerned. Mr. Field himself published a letter in the "Westminster Review" for April, 1871, in which, after the general assertion that the passages in the "New York Gold Conspiracy" which related to him "cover about as much untruth as could be crowded into so many lines," he made the following corrections:

First, he denied, what was never suggested, that he was in any way a party to the origin or progress of the Gold Conspiracy, until (secondly) he was consulted on the 28th of September, when (thirdly) he gave an opinion as to the powers of the members of the Gold and Stock Exchanges. Fourthly, he denied that he had relations of any sort with any judge in New York, or any power over these judges, other than such as English counsel have in respect to English judges. Fifthly, he asserted that among twenty-eight injunctions growing out of the gold transactions his partners obtained only ten, and only one of these ten, the one quoted above, from Justice Barnard. Sixthly, that this injunction was proper to be sought and granted. Seventhly, that Mr. Bonner was not himself the person who had been "robbed with violence," but the assignee of the parties.

On the other hand, Mr. Field did not deny that the injunction as quoted was genuine, or that he was responsible for it, or that it did, as asserted, shut the defendants out of the courts as well as out of the Gold Exchange Arbitration Committee, or that it compelled them to appear only as defendants in a case where they were the injured parties.

In regard to the power which Mr. Field, whether as a private individual or as Erie counsel, exercised over the New York bench, his correction affected the story but little. In regard to Mr. Bonner, the fact of his being principal or representative scarcely altered the character of Mr. Field's injunction. Finally, so far as the text is concerned, after allowing full weight to all Mr. Field's corrections, the public can decide for itself how many untruths it contained. The subject ceased to be one of consequence even to Mr. Field after the subsequent violent controversy which arose in March, 1871, in regard to other points of Mr. Field's professional conduct.

Gould and James Fisk, Jr., continued to reign over Erie, and no one can say that their power or their credit was sensibly diminished by a shock which for the time prostrated the interests of the country.

Nevertheless, sooner or later the last traces of the disturbing influence of war and paper money will disappear in America, as they have sooner or later disappeared in every other country which has passed through the same evils. The result of this convulsion itself has been in the main good. It indicates the approaching end of a troubled time. Messrs. Gould and Fisk will at last be obliged to yield to the force of moral and economical laws. The Erie Railway will be rescued, and its history will perhaps rival that of the great speculative manias of the last century. The United States will restore a sound basis to its currency, and will learn to deal with the political reforms it requires. Yet though the regular process of development may be depended upon, in its ordinary and established course, to purge American society of the worst agents of an exceptionally corrupt time, the history of the Erie corporation offers one point in regard to which modern society everywhere is directly interested. For the first time since the creation of these enormous corporate bodies, one of them has shown its power for mischief, and has proved itself able to override and trample on law, custom, decency, and every restraint known to society, without scruple, and as yet without check. The belief is common in America that the day is at hand when corporations far greater than the Erie—swaying power such as has never in the world's history been trusted in the hands of private citizens, controlled by single men like Vanderbilt, or by combinations of men like Fisk, Gould, and Lane, after having created a system of quiet but irresistible corruption —will ultimately succeed in directing government itself. Under the American form of society no authority exists capable of effective resistance. The national government, in order to deal with the corporations, must assume powers refused to it by its fundamental law,—and even then is exposed to the chance of forming an absolute central government which sooner or later is likely to fall into the hands it is struggling to escape, and thus destroy the limits of its power only in order to make corruption omnipotent. Nor is this danger confined to America alone. The corporation is in its nature a threat against the popular institutions spreading so rapidly over the whole world. Wherever a popular and limited government exists this difficulty will be found in its path; and unless some satisfactory solution of the problem can be reached, popular institutions may yet find their existence endangered.

Novelist

Mount Vernon Picnic

Gone was the Washington correspondent, gone the bachelor professor and editor of Harvard. Married, on the track of writing instead of teaching history, Henry was a contented householder on H Street, contemplating the universe as well as the scene before him: Lafayette Square, the White House, the embassies, and their amusing denizens.

Out of an excess of energy spared from his studies in biography and history grew the novel Democracy. It is a book with a giddy surface, gay manners, and below the bright satiric texture a troubled questioning about the malfunctioning of the democratic process.

The selection given below is the whole of Chapter VI, a digression in which Adams sent his characters down the Potomac to Mount Vernon to hold a picnic with the ghost of George Washington. It constitutes a rapid sketch for a life that may have been contemplated but was never written.

MOUNT VERNON PICNIC[1]

In February the weather became warmer and summer-like. In Virginia there comes often at this season a deceptive gleam of summer, slipping in between heavy storm-clouds of sleet and snow; days and sometimes weeks when the

[1] From *Democracy* by Henry Adams. Reprinted by permission of Henry Holt and Co., Inc., New York, N.Y. *Democracy* was published anonymously in 1880. This selection comprises the whole of Chapter VI.

temperature is like June; when the earliest plants begin to show their hardy flowers, and when the bare branches of the forest trees alone protest against the conduct of the seasons. Then men and women are languid; life seems, as in Italy, sensuous and glowing with colour; one is conscious of walking in an atmosphere that is warm, palpable, radiant with possibilities; a delicate haze hangs over Arlington, and softens even the harsh white glare of the Capitol; the struggle of existence seems to abate; Lent throws its calm shadow over society; and youthful diplomatists, unconscious of their danger, are lured into asking foolish girls to marry them; the blood thaws in the heart and flows out into the veins, like the rills of sparkling water that trickle from every lump of ice or snow, as though all the ice and snow on earth, and all the hardness of heart, all the heresy and schism, all the works of the devil, had yielded to the force of love and to the fresh warmth of innocent, lamb-like, confiding virtue. In such a world there should be no guile—but there is a great deal of it notwithstanding. Indeed, at no other season is there so much. This is the moment when the two whited sepulchres at either end of the Avenue reek with the thick atmosphere of bargain and sale. The old is going; the new is coming. Wealth, office, power are at auction. Who bids highest? who hates with most venom? who intrigues with most skill? who has done the dirtiest, the meanest, the darkest, and the most, political work? He shall have his reward.

Senator Ratcliffe was absorbed and ill at ease. A swarm of applicants for office dogged his steps and beleaguered his rooms in quest of his endorsement of their paper characters. The new President was to arrive on Monday. Intrigues and combinations, of which the Senator was the soul, were all alive, awaiting this arrival. Newspaper correspondents pestered him with questions. Brother senators called him to conferences. His mind was pre-occupied with his own interests. One might have supposed that, at this instant, nothing could have drawn him away from the political gaming-table, and yet when Mrs. Lee remarked that she was going to Mount Vernon on Saturday with a little party, including the British Minister and an Irish gentleman staying as a guest at the British Legation, the Senator surprised her by expressing a strong wish to join them. He explained that, as the political lead was no longer in his hands, the chances were nine in ten that if he stirred at all he should make a blunder; that his friends expected him to do something when, in fact, nothing could be done; that every preparation had already been made, and that for him to go on an excursion to Mount Vernon, at this moment, with the British Minister, was, on the whole, about the best use he could make of his time, since it would hide him for one day at least.

Lord Skye had fallen into the habit of consulting Mrs. Lee when his own social resources were low, and it was she who had suggested this party to Mount Vernon, with Carrington for a guide and Mr. Gore for variety, to occupy the time of the Irish friend whom Lord Skye was bravely entertaining. This gentleman, who bore the title of Dunbeg, was a dilapidated peer, neither wealthy nor famous. Lord Skye brought him to call on Mrs. Lee, and in some sort put him under her care. He was young, not ill-looking, quite intelligent, rather too fond of facts, and not quick at humour. He was given to smiling in a deprecatory way, and when he talked, he was either absent or excited; he made vague blunders, and then smiled in deprecation of offence, or his words blocked their own path in their rush. Perhaps his manner was a little ridiculous, but he had a good heart, a good head, and a title. He found favour in the eyes of Sybil and Victoria Dare, who declined to admit other women to the party, although they offered no objection to Mr. Ratcliffe's admission. As for Lord Dunbeg, he was an enthusiastic admirer of General Washington, and, as he privately intimated, eager to study phases of American society. He was delighted to go with a small party, and Miss Dare secretly promised herself that she would show him a phase.

The morning was warm, the sky soft, the little steamer lay at the quiet wharf with a few negroes lazily watching her preparations for departure. Carrington, with Mrs. Lee and the young ladies, arrived first, and stood leaning against the rail, waiting the arrival of their companions. Then came Mr. Gore, neatly attired and gloved, with a light spring overcoat; for Mr. Gore was very careful of his personal appearance, and not a little vain of his good looks. Then a pretty woman, with blue eyes and blonde hair, dressed in black, and leading a little girl by the hand, came on board, and Carrington went to shake hands with her. On his return to Mrs. Lee's side, she asked about his new acquaintance, and he replied with a half-laugh, as though he were not proud of her, that she was a client, a pretty widow, well known in Washington. "Any one at the Capitol would tell you all about her. She was the wife of a noted lobbyist, who died about two years ago. Congressmen can refuse nothing to a pretty face, and she was their idea of feminine perfection. Yet she is a silly little woman, too. Her husband died after a very short illness, and, to my great surprise, made me executor under his will. I think he had an idea that he could trust me with his papers, which were important and compromising, for he seems to have had no time to go over them and destroy what were best out of the way. So, you see, I am left with his widow and child to look after. Luckily, they are well provided for."

"Still you have not told me her name."

"Her name is Baker—Mrs. Sam Baker. But they are casting off, and Mr. Ratcliffe will be left behind. I'll ask the captain to wait."

About a dozen passengers had arrived, among them the two Earls, with a footman carrying a promising lunch-basket, and the planks were actually hauled in when a carriage dashed up to the wharf, and Mr. Ratcliffe leaped out and hurried on board. "Off with you as quick as you can!" said he to the negro-hands, and in another moment the little steamer had begun her journey, pounding the muddy waters of the Potomac and sending up its small column of smoke as though it were a newly invented incense-burner approaching the temple of the national deity. Ratcliffe explained in great glee how he had barely managed to escape his visitors by telling them that the British Minister was waiting for him, and that he would be back again presently. "If they had known where I was going," said he, "you would have seen the boat swamped with office-seekers. Illinois alone would have brought you to a watery grave." He was in high spirits, bent upon enjoying his holiday, and as they passed the arsenal with its solitary sentry, and the navy-yard, with its one unseaworthy wooden war-steamer, he pointed out these evidences of national grandeur to Lord Skye, threatening, as the last terror of diplomacy, to send him home in an American frigate. They were thus indulging in senatorial humour on one side of the boat, while Sybil and Victoria, with the aid of Mr. Gore and Carrington, were improving Lord Dunbeg's mind on the other.

Miss Dare, finding for herself at last a convenient seat where she could repose and be mistress of the situation, put on a more than usually demure expression and waited with gravity until her noble neighbour should give her an opportunity to show those powers which, as she believed, would supply a phase in his existence. Miss Dare was one of those young persons, sometimes to be found in America, who seem to have no object in life, and while apparently devoted to men, care nothing about them, but find happiness only in violating rules; she made no parade of whatever virtues she had, and her chief pleasure was to make fun of all the world and herself.

"What a noble river!" remarked Lord Dunbeg, as the boat passed out upon the wide stream; "I suppose you often sail on it?"

"I never was here in my life till now," replied the untruthful Miss Dare; "we don't think much of it; it's too small; we're used to so much larger rivers."

"I am afraid you would not like our English rivers then; they are mere brooks compared with this."

"Are they indeed?" said Victoria, with an appearance of vague surprise; "how curious! I don't think I care to be an Englishwoman then. I could not live without big rivers."

Lord Dunbeg stared, and hinted that this was almost unreasonable.

"Unless I were a Countess!" continued Victoria, meditatively, looking at Alexandria, and paying no attention to his lordship; "I think I could manage if I were a C-c-countess. It is such a pretty title!"

"Duchess is commonly thought a prettier one," stam-

mered Dunbeg, much embarrassed. The young man was
not used to chaff from women.

"I should be satisfied with Countess. It sounds well. I am
surprised that you don't like it." Dunbeg looked about him
uneasily for some means of escape but he was barred in.
"I should think you would feel an awful responsibility in
selecting a Countess. How do you do it?"

Lord Dunbeg nervously joined in the general laughter as
Sybil ejaculated: "Oh, Victoria!" but Miss Dare continued
without a smile or any elevation of her monotonous voice:

"Now, Sybil, don't interrupt me, please. I am deeply interested in Lord Dunbeg's conversation. He understands
that my interest is purely scientific, but my happiness requires that I should know how Countesses are selected.
Lord Dunbeg, how would you recommend a friend to
choose a Countess?"

Lord Dunbeg began to be amused by her impudence,
and he even tried to lay down for her satisfaction one or
two rules for selecting Countesses, but long before he had
invented his first rule, Victoria had darted off to a new
subject.

"Which would you rather be, Lord Dunbeg? an Earl or
George Washington?"

"George Washington, certainly," was the Earl's courteous though rather bewildered reply.

"Really?" she asked with a languid affectation of surprise; "it is awfully kind of you to say so, but of course you
can't mean it."

"Indeed I do mean it."

"Is it possible? I never should have thought it."

"Why not, Miss Dare?"

"You have not the air of wishing to be George Washington."

"May I again ask, why not?"

"Certainly. Did you ever see George Washington?"

"Of course not. He died fifty years before I was born."

"I thought so. You see you don't know him. Now, will
you give us an idea of what you imagine General Washington to have looked like?"

Dunbeg gave accordingly a flattering description of

General Washington, compounded of Stuart's portrait and Greenough's statue of Olympian Jove with Washington's features, in the Capitol Square. Miss Dare listened with an expression of superiority not unmixed with patience, and then she enlightened him as follows:

"All you have been saying is perfect stuff—excuse the vulgarity of the expression. When I am a Countess I will correct my language. The truth is that General Washington was a raw-boned country farmer, very hard-featured, very awkward, very illiterate and very dull; very bad tempered, very profane, and generally tipsy after dinner."

"You shock me, Miss Dare!" exclaimed Dunbeg.

"Oh! I know all about General Washington. My grandfather knew him intimately, and often stayed at Mount Vernon for weeks together. You must not believe what you read, and not a word of what Mr. Carrington will say. He is a Virginian and will tell you no end of fine stories and not a syllable of truth in one of them. We are all patriotic about Washington and like to hide his faults. If I weren't quite sure you would never repeat it, I would not tell you this. The truth is that even when George Washington was a small boy, his temper was so violent that no one could do anything with him. He once cut down all his father's fruit-trees in a fit of passion, and then, just because they wanted to flog him, he threatened to brain his father with the hatchet. His aged wife suffered agonies from him. My grandfather often told me how he had seen the General pinch and swear at her till the poor creature left the room in tears; and how once at Mount Vernon he saw Washington, when quite an old man, suddenly rush at an un-offending visitor, and chase him off the place, beating him all the time over the head with a great stick with knots in it, and all just because he heard the poor man stammer; he never could abide s-s-stammering."

Carrington and Gore burst into shouts of laughter over this description of the Father of his country, but Victoria continued in her gentle drawl to enlighten Lord Dunbeg in regard to other subjects with information equally mendacious, until he decided that she was quite the most eccentric person he had ever met. The boat arrived at

Mount Vernon while she was still engaged in a description of the society and manners of America, and especially of the rules which made an offer of marriage necessary. According to her, Lord Dunbeg was in imminent peril; gentlemen, and especially foreigners, were expected, in all the States south of the Potomac, to offer themselves to at least one young lady in every city: "and I had only yesterday," said Victoria, "a letter from a lovely girl in North Carolina, a dear friend of mine, who wrote me that she was right put out because her brothers had called on a young English visitor with shot guns, and she was afraid he wouldn't recover, and, after all, she says she should have refused him."

Meanwhile Madeleine, on the other side of the boat, undisturbed by the laughter that surrounded Miss Dare, chatted soberly and seriously with Lord Skye and Senator Ratcliffe. Lord Skye, too, a little intoxicated by the brilliancy of the morning, broke out into admiration of the noble river, and accused Americans of not appreciating the beauties of their own country.

"Your national mind," said he, "has no eyelids. It requires a broad glare and a beaten road. It prefers shadows which you can cut out with a knife. It doesn't know the beauty of this Virginia winter softness."

Mrs. Lee resented the charge. America, she maintained, had not worn her feelings threadbare like Europe. She had still her story to tell; she was waiting for her Burns and Scott, her Wordsworth and Byron, her Hogarth and Turner. "You want peaches in spring," said she. "Give us our thousand years of summer, and then complain, if you please, that our peach is not as mellow as yours. Even our voices may be soft then," she added, with a significant look at Lord Skye.

"We are at a disadvantage in arguing with Mrs. Lee," said he to Ratcliffe; "when she ends as counsel, she begins as witness. The famous Duchess of Devonshire's lips were not half as convincing as Mrs. Lee's voice."

Ratcliffe listened carefully, assenting whenever he saw that Mrs. Lee wished it. He wished he understood precisely what tones and half-tones, colours and harmonies, were.

They arrived and strolled up the sunny path. At the tomb they halted, as all good Americans do, and Mr. Gore, in a tone of subdued sorrow, delivered a short address—

"It might be much worse if they improved it," he said, surveying its proportions with the æsthetic eye of a cultured Bostonian. "As it stands, this tomb is a simple misfortune which might befall any of us; we should not grieve over it too much. What would our feelings be if a Congressional committee reconstructed it of white marble with Gothic pepper-pots, and gilded it inside on machine-moulded stucco!"

Madeleine, however, insisted that the tomb, as it stood, was the only restless spot about the quiet landscape, and that it contradicted all her ideas about repose in the grave. Ratcliffe wondered what she meant.

They passed on, wandering across the lawn, and through the house. Their eyes, weary of the harsh colours and forms of the city, took pleasure in the worn wainscots and the stained walls. Some of the rooms were still occupied; fires were burning in the wide fireplaces. All were tolerably furnished, and there was no uncomfortable sense of repair or newness. They mounted the stairs, and Mrs. Lee fairly laughed when she was shown the room in which General Washington slept, and where he died.

Carrington smiled too. "Our old Virginia houses were mostly like this," said he; "suites of great halls below, and these gaunt barracks above. The Virginia house was a sort of hotel. When there was a race or a wedding, or a dance, and the house was full, they thought nothing of packing half a dozen people in one room, and if the room was large, they stretched a sheet across to separate the men from the women. As for toilet, those were not the mornings of cold baths. With our ancestors a little washing went a long way."

"Do you still live so in Virginia?" asked Madeleine.

"Oh no, it is quite gone. We live now like other country people, and try to pay our debts, which that generation never did. They lived from hand to mouth. They kept a stable-full of horses. The young men were always riding about the country, betting on horse-races, gambling, drinking, fighting, and making love. No one knew exactly what he was worth until the crash came about fifty years ago, and the whole thing ran out."

"Just what happened in Ireland!" said Lord Dunbeg, much interested and full of his article in the *Quarterly;* "the resemblance is perfect, even down to the houses."

Mrs. Lee asked Carrington bluntly whether he regretted the destruction of this old social arrangement.

"One can't help regretting," said he, "whatever it was that produced George Washington, and a crowd of other men like him. But I think we might produce the men still if we had the same field for them."

"And would you bring the old society back again if you could?" asked she.

"What for? It could not hold itself up. General Washington himself could not save it. Before he died he had lost his hold on Virginia, and his power was gone."

The party for a while separated, and Mrs. Lee found herself alone in the great drawing-room. Presently the blonde Mrs. Baker entered, with her child, who ran about making more noise than Mrs. Washington would have permitted. Madeleine, who had the usual feminine love of children, called the girl to her and pointed out the shepherds and shepherdesses carved on the white Italian marble of the fireplace; she invented a little story about them to amuse the child, while the mother stood by and at the end thanked the story-teller with more enthusiasm than seemed called for. Mrs. Lee did not fancy her effusive manner, or her complexion, and was glad when Dunbeg appeared at the doorway.

"How do you like General Washington at home?" asked she.

"Really, I assure you I feel quite at home myself," replied Dunbeg, with a more beaming smile than ever. "I am sure General Washington was an Irishman. I know it from the look of the place. I mean to look it up and write an article about it."

"Then if you have disposed of him," said Madeleine, "I think we will have luncheon, and I have taken the liberty to order it to be served outside."

There a table had been improvised, and Miss Dare was inspecting the lunch, and making comments upon Lord Skye's cuisine and cellar.

"I hope it is very dry champagne," said she, "the taste for sweet champagne is quite awfully shocking."

The young woman knew no more about dry and sweet champagne than of the wine of Ulysses, except that she drank both with equal satisfaction, but she was mimicking a Secretary of the British Legation who had provided her with supper at her last evening party. Lord Skye begged her to try it, which she did, and with great gravity remarked that it was about five per cent. she presumed. This, too, was caught from her Secretary, though she knew no more what it meant than if she had been a parrot.

The luncheon was very lively and very good. When it was over, the gentlemen were allowed to smoke, and conversation fell into a sober strain, which at last threatened to become serious.

"You want half-tones!" said Madeleine to Lord Skye: "are there not half-tones enough to suit you on the walls of this house?"

Lord Skye suggested that this was probably owing to the fact that Washington, belonging, as he did, to the universe, was in his taste an exception to local rules.

"Is not the sense of rest here captivating?" she continued. "Look at that quaint garden, and this ragged lawn, and the great river in front, and the superannuated fort beyond the river! Everything is peaceful, even down to the poor old General's little bedroom. One would like to lie down in it and sleep a century or two. And yet that dreadful Capitol and its office-seekers are only ten miles off."

"No! that is more than I can bear!" broke in Miss Victoria in a stage whisper, "that dreadful Capitol! Why, not one of us would be here without that dreadful Capitol! except, perhaps, myself."

"You would appear very well as Mrs. Washington, Victoria."

"Miss Dare has been so very obliging as to give us her views of General Washington's character this morning," said

Dunbeg, "but I have not yet had time to ask Mr. Carrington for his."

"Whatever Miss Dare says is valuable," replied Carrington, "but her strong point is facts."

"Never flatter! Mr. Carrington," drawled Miss Dare; "I do not need it, and it does not become your style. Tell me, Lord Dunbeg, is not Mr. Carrington a little your idea of General Washington restored to us in his prime?"

"After your account of General Washington, Miss Dare, how can I agree with you?"

"After all," said Lord Skye, "I think we must agree that Miss Dare is in the main right about the charms of Mount Vernon. Even Mrs. Lee, on the way up, agreed that the General, who is the only permanent resident here, has the air of being confoundedly bored in his tomb. I don't myself love your dreadful Capitol yonder, but I prefer it to a bucolic life here. And I account in this way for my want of enthusiasm for your great General. He liked no kind of life but this. He seems to have been greater in the character of a home-sick Virginia planter than as General or President. I forgive him his inordinate dulness, for he was not a diplomatist and it was not his business to lie, but he might once in a way have forgotten Mount Vernon."

Dunbeg here burst in with an excited protest; all his words seemed to shove each other aside in their haste to escape first. "All our greatest Englishmen have been home-sick country squires. I am a home-sick country squire myself."

"How interesting!" said Miss Dare under her breath.

Mr. Gore here joined in: "It is all very well for you gentlemen to measure General Washington according to your own private twelve-inch carpenter's rule. But what will you say to us New Englanders who never were country gentlemen at all, and never had any liking for Virginia? What did Washington ever do for us? He never even pretended to like us. He never was more than barely civil to us. I'm not finding fault with him; everybody knows that he never cared for anything but Mount Vernon. For all that, we idolize him. To us he is Morality, Justice, Duty, Truth; half a dozen Roman gods with capital letters. He is austere, solitary, grand; he ought to be deified. I hardly feel easy, eating, drinking, smoking here on his portico without his permission, taking liberties with his house, criticising his bedrooms in his absence. Suppose I heard his horse now trotting up on the other side, and he suddenly appeared at this door and looked at us. I should abandon you to his indignation. I should run away and hide myself on the steamer. The mere thought unmans me."

Ratcliffe seemed amused at Gore's half-serious notions. "You recall to me," said he, "my own feelings when I was a boy and was made by my father to learn the Farewell Address by heart. In those days General Washington was a sort of American Jehovah. But the West is a poor school for Reverence. Since coming to Congress I have learned more about General Washington, and have been surprised to find what a narrow base his reputation rests on. A fair military officer, who made many blunders, and who never had more men than would make a full army-corps under his command, he got an enormous reputation in Europe because he did not make himself king, as though he ever had a chance of doing it. A respectable, painstaking President, he was treated by the Opposition with an amount of deference that would have made government easy to a baby, but it worried him to death. His official papers are fairly done, and contain good average sense such as a hundred thousand men in the United States would now write. I suspect that half of his attachment to this spot rose from his consciousness of inferior powers and his dread of responsibility. This government can show to-day a dozen men of equal abilities, but we don't deify them. What I most wonder at in him is not his military or political genius at all, for I doubt whether he had much, but a curious Yankee shrewdness in money matters. He thought himself a very rich man, yet he never spent a dollar foolishly. He was almost the only Virginian I ever heard of, in public life, who did not die insolvent."

During this long speech, Carrington glanced across at Madeleine, and caught her eye. Ratcliffe's criticism was not to her taste. Carrington could see that she thought it unworthy of him, and he knew that it would irritate her. "I will lay a little trap for Mr. Ratcliffe," thought he to himself; "we will see whether he gets out of it." So Carrington began, and all listened closely, for, as a Virginian, he was supposed to know much about the subject, and his family had been deep in the confidence of Washington himself.

"The neighbours hereabout had for many years, and may have still, some curious stories about General Washington's closeness in money matters. They said he never bought anything by weight but he had it weighed over again, nor by tale but he had it counted, and if the weight or number were not exact, he sent it back. Once, during his absence, his steward had a room plastered, and paid the plasterer's bill. On the General's return, he measured the room, and found that the plasterer had charged fifteen shillings too much. Meanwhile the man had died, and the General made a claim of fifteen shillings on his estate, which was paid. Again, one of his tenants brought him the rent. The exact change of fourpence was required. The man tendered a dollar, and asked the General to credit him with the balance against the next year's rent. The General refused and made him ride nine miles to Alexandria and back for the fourpence. On the other hand, he sent to a shoemaker in Alexandria to come and measure him for shoes. The man returned word that he did not go to any one's house to take measures, and the General mounted his horse and rode the nine miles to him. One of his rules was to pay at taverns the same sum for his servants' meals as for his own. An innkeeper brought him a bill of three-and-ninepence for his own breakfast, and three shillings for his servant. He insisted upon adding the extra ninepence, as he did not doubt that the servant had eaten as much as he. What do you say to these anecdotes? Was this meanness or not?"

Ratcliffe was amused. "The stories are new to me," he said. "It is just as I thought. These are signs of a man who thinks much of trifles; one who fusses over small matters. We don't do things in that way now that we no longer have to get crops from granite, as they used to do in New Hampshire when I was a boy."

Carrington replied that it was unlucky for Virginians that

they had not done things in that way then: if they had, they would not have gone to the dogs.

Gore shook his head seriously; "Did I not tell you so?" said he. "Was not this man an abstract virtue? I give you my word I stand in awe before him, and I feel ashamed to pry into these details of his life. What is it to us how he thought proper to apply his principles to nightcaps and feather dusters? We are not his body servants, and we care nothing about his infirmities. It is enough for us to know that he carried his rules of virtue down to a pin's point, and that we ought, one and all, to be on our knees before his tomb."

Dunbeg, pondering deeply, at length asked Carrington whether all this did not make rather a clumsy politician of the father of his country.

"Mr. Ratcliffe knows more about politics than I. Ask him," said Carrington.

"Washington was no politician at all, as we understand the word," replied Ratcliffe abruptly. "He stood outside of politics. The thing couldn't be done to-day. The people don't like that sort of royal airs."

"I don't understand!" said Mrs. Lee. "Why could you not do it now?"

"Because I should make a fool of myself," replied Ratcliffe, pleased to think that Mrs. Lee should put him on a level with Washington. She had only meant to ask why the thing could not be done, and this little touch of Ratcliffe's vanity was inimitable.

"Mr. Ratcliffe means that Washington was too respectable for our time," interposed Carrington.

This was deliberately meant to irritate Ratcliffe, and it did so all the more because Mrs. Lee turned to Carrington, and said, with some bitterness: "Was he then the only honest public man we ever had?"

"Oh no!" replied Carrington cheerfully; "there have been one or two others."

"If the rest of our Presidents had been like him," said Gore, "we should have had fewer ugly blots on our short history."

Ratcliffe was exasperated at Carrington's habit of drawing discussion to this point. He felt the remark as a personal insult, and he knew it to be intended. "Public men," he broke out, "cannot be dressing themselves to-day in Washington's old clothes. If Washington were President now, he would have to learn our ways or lose his next election. Only fools and theorists imagine that our society can be handled with gloves or long poles. One must make one's self a part of it. If virtue won't answer our purpose, we must use vice, or our opponents will put us out of office, and this was as true in Washington's day as it is now, and always will be."

"Come," said Lord Skye, who was beginning to fear an open quarrel; "the conversation verges on treason, and I am accredited to this government. Why not examine the grounds?"

A kind of natural sympathy led Lord Dunbeg to wander by the side of Miss Dare through the quaint old garden. His mind being much occupied by the effort of stowing away the impressions he had just received, he was more than usually absent in his manner, and this want of attention irritated the young lady. She made some comments on flowers; she invented some new species with startling names; she asked whether these were known in Ireland; but Lord Dunbeg was for the moment so vague in his answers that she saw her case was perilous.

"Here is an old sun-dial. Do you have sun-dials in Ireland, Lord Dunbeg?"

"Yes; oh, certainly! What! sun-dials? Oh, yes! I assure you there are a great many sun-dials in Ireland, Miss Dare."

"I am so glad. But I suppose they are only for ornament. Here it is just the other way. Look at this one! they all behave like that. The wear and tear of our sun is too much for them; they don't last. My uncle, who has a place at Long Branch, had five sun-dials in ten years."

"How very odd! But really now, Miss Dare, I don't see how a sun-dial could wear out."

"Don't you? How strange! Don't you see, they get soaked with sunshine so that they can't hold shadow. It's like me, you know. I have such a good time all the time that I can't be unhappy. Do you ever read the *Burlington Hawkeye*, Lord Dunbeg?"

"I don't remember; I think not. Is it an American serial?" gasped Dunbeg, trying hard to keep pace with Miss Dare in her reckless dashes across country.

"No, not serial at all!" replied Virginia; "but I am afraid you would find it very hard reading. I shouldn't try."

"Do you read it much, Miss Dare?"

"Oh, always! I am not really as light as I seem. But then I have an advantage over you because I know the language."

By this time Dunbeg was awake again, and Miss Dare, satisfied with her success, allowed herself to become more reasonable, until a slight shade of sentiment began to flicker about their path.

The scattered party, however, soon had to unite again. The boat rang its bell for return, they filed down the paths and settled themselves in their old places. As they steamed away, Mrs. Lee watched the sunny hill-side and the peaceful house above, until she could see them no more, and the longer she looked, the less she was pleased with herself. Was it true, as Victoria Dare said, that she could not live in so pure an air? Did she really need the denser fumes of the city? Was she, unknown to herself, gradually becoming tainted with the life about her? or was Ratcliffe right in accepting the good and the bad together, and in being of his time since he was in it? Why was it, she said bitterly to herself, that everything Washington touched, he purified, even down to the associations of his house? and why is it that everything we touch seems soiled? Why do I feel unclean when I look at Mount Vernon? In spite of Mr. Ratcliffe, is it not better to be a child and to cry for the moon and stars?

The little Baker girl came up to her where she stood, and began playing with her parasol.

"Who is your little friend?" asked Ratcliffe.

Mrs. Lee rather vaguely replied that she was the daughter of that pretty woman in black; she believed her name was Baker.

"Baker, did you say?" repeated Ratcliffe.

"Baker—Mrs. Sam Baker; at least so Mr. Carrington told me; he said she was a client of his."

In fact Ratcliffe soon saw Carrington go up to her and remain by her side during the rest of the trip. Ratcliffe watched them sharply and grew more and more absorbed in his own thoughts as the boat drew nearer and nearer the shore.

Carrington was in high spirits. He thought he had played his cards with unusual success. Even Miss Dare deigned to acknowledge his charms that day. She declared herself to be the moral image of Martha Washington, and she started a discussion whether Carrington or Lord Dunbeg would best suit her in the *rôle* of the General.

"Mr. Carrington is exemplary," she said, "but oh, what joy to be Martha Washington and a Countess too!"

The American Girl

This excerpt from Adams' second novel, Esther, torn out of context, may echo a little the leisurely, life-long conversation that Adams and such friends as King, Hay, St. Gaudens, La Farge, Richardson, Spring-Rice, and others picked up and set going again whenever they chanced to meet, whether in London, Papeete, or Washington, D.C. These particular paragraphs concern a favorite topic which had a way of insinuating itself into Adams' serious writing—appearing variously in his History, Mont-St.-Michel, and Education—as well as in his unguarded letters and talk: woman in general, the American woman in particular, and, most privately, Marian Adams.

Esther's bright talk is the best part of the book, which is generally more somber and serious than Democracy. Adams' friends stand as shadows, slightly askew, behind the leading characters of the novel. George Strong is easily Clarence King; Stephen Hazard is partially Adams' cousin, the minister of Trinity Church, Boston, Phillips Brooks; Wharton resembles both La Farge and St. Gaudens. The heroine, who is asked by her pastoral fiancé to give up a brave and individualistic unbelief, is Marian Adams in character if not in act. (Adams' wife very probably never saw the manuscript or the finished book. It was Adams' most private and secret production.)

THE AMERICAN GIRL[1]

"I saw you had Miss Dudley with you at church this morning," said Wharton, still absorbed in study of his enamel, and quite unconscious of his host's evident restlessness.

"Ah! then you could see Miss Dudley!" cried the clergyman, who could not forgive the abrupt dismissal of his own affairs by the two men, and was eager to bring the talk back to his church.

"I can always see Miss Dudley," said Wharton quietly.

"Why?" asked Hazard.

"She is interesting," replied the painter. "She has a style of her own, and I never can quite make up my mind whether to like it or not."

"It is the first time I ever knew you to hesitate before a style," said Hazard.

"I hesitate before every thing American," replied Wharton, beginning to show a shade of interest in what he was talking of. "I don't know—you don't know—and I never yet met any man who could tell me, whether American types are going to supplant the old ones, or whether they are to come to nothing for want of ideas. Miss Dudley is one of the most marked American types I ever saw."

"What are the signs of the most marked American type you ever saw?" asked Hazard.

"In the first place, she has a bad figure, which she makes answer for a good one. She is too slight, too thin; she looks fragile, willowy, as the cheap novels call it, as though you could break her in halves like a switch. She dresses to suit her figure and sometimes overdoes it. Her features are imperfect. Except her ears, her voice, and her eyes which have a sort of brown depth like a trout brook, she has no very good points."

"Then why do you hesitate?" asked Strong, who was not entirely pleased with this cool estimate of his cousin's person.

[1] From *Esther*, published in 1884 by Henry Holt and Co., Inc. Adams used a pseudonym, Frances Snow Compton. Reissued in 1938 by Scholars' Facsimiles and Reprints. The selection is lifted out of Chapter I.

"There is the point where the subtlety comes in," replied the painter. "Miss Dudley interests me. I want to know what she can make of life. She gives one the idea of a lightly-sparred yacht in mid-ocean; unexpected; you ask yourself what the devil she is doing there. She sails gayly along, though there is no land in sight and plenty of rough weather coming. She never read a book, I believe, in her life. She tries to paint, but she is only a second rate amateur and will never be any thing more, though she has done one or two things which I give you my word I would like to have done myself. She picks up all she knows without an effort and knows nothing well, yet she seems to understand whatever is said. Her mind is as irregular as her face, and both have the same peculiarity. I notice that the lines of her eyebrows, nose and mouth all end with a slight upward curve like a yacht's sails, which gives a kind of hopefulness and self-confidence to her expression. Mind and face have the same curves."

"Is that your idea of our national type?" asked Strong. "Why don't you put it into one of your saints in the church, and show what you mean by American art?"

"I wish I could," said the artist. "I have passed weeks trying to catch it. The thing is too subtle, and it is not a grand type, like what we are used to in the academies. But besides the riddle, I like Miss Dudley for herself. The way she takes my brutal criticisms of her painting makes my heart bleed. I mean to go down on my knees one of these days, and confess to her that I know nothing about it; only if her style is right, my art is wrong."

"What sort of a world does this new deity of yours belong to?" asked the clergyman.

"Not to yours," replied Wharton quickly. "There is nothing medieval about her. If she belongs to any besides the present, it is to the next world which artists want to see, when paganism will come again and we can give a divinity to every waterfall."

Biographer

The Importance of Albert Gallatin

If I had been born in Geneva when Gallatin was, instead
of in Boston; if I had come to colonial America when he
did; if I had served under the early Presidents as he did;
then I might have been such a man as he: *so Adams, half
consciously seems to have ruminated as he worked at the
writing of his biography,* The Life of Albert Gallatin.

*Adams had a profound sense of identification with Albert
Gallatin as well as a candid admiration for his acts and
outlook. This clever Swiss who was Jefferson's and Madison's good right hand was Adams' own idea of the best
statesman and the best man of his time.*

The Gallatin *is a little read book, but it is a first rate life
of a neglected man, and it reveals many of its author's most
basic biases.*

THE IMPORTANCE OF ALBERT GALLATIN[1]

The struggle was completely over. All the dangers, real and
imaginary, had vanished. The great Federal party which
had created, organized, and for twelve years administered
the government, and whose chief now handed it, safe and
undisturbed, to Mr. Jefferson and his friends, was prostrate,
broken and torn by dying convulsions. The new political
force of which Mr. Jefferson was the guide had no word
of sympathy for the vanquished. Full of hope and self-

[1] From *The Life of Albert Gallatin*, published by J. B. Lippincott Co., in 1879. The selection comprises the end of Book II
and the beginning of Book III.

confidence, he took the helm and promised that "now the ship was put on her Republican tack she would show by the beauty of her motion the skill of her builders." Even Mr. Gallatin's cooler head felt the power of the strong wine, success. He too believed that human nature was to show itself in new aspects, and that the failures of the past were due to the faults of the past. "Every man, from John Adams to John Hewitt, who undertakes to do what he does not understand deserves a whipping," he wrote to his wife a year later, when his tailor had spoiled a coat for him. He had yet to pass through his twelve years of struggle and disappointment in order to learn how his own followers and his own President were to answer his ideal, when the same insolence of foreign dictation and the same violence of a recalcitrant party presented to their and to his own lips the cup of which John Adams was now draining the dregs.

In governments, as in households, he who holds the purse holds the power. The Treasury is the natural point of control to be occupied by any statesman who aims at organization or reform, and conversely no organization or reform is likely to succeed that does not begin with and is not guided by the Treasury. The highest type of practical statesmanship must always take this direction. Washington and Jefferson doubtless stand pre-eminent as the representatives of what is best in our national character or its aspirations, but Washington depended mainly upon Hamilton, and without Gallatin Mr. Jefferson would have been helpless. The mere financial duties of the Treasury, serious as they are, were the least of the burdens these men had to carry; their keenest anxieties were not connected most nearly with their own department, but resulted from that effort to control the whole machinery and policy of government which is necessarily forced upon the holder of the purse. Possibly it may be said with truth that a majority of financial ministers have not so understood their duties, but, on the other hand, the ministers who composed this majority have hardly left great reputations behind them. Perhaps, too, the very magnitude and overshadowing influence of the Treasury have tended to rouse a certain jealousy in the minds of successive Presidents, and have worked to dwarf an authority legitimate in itself, but certainly dangerous to the Executive head. Be this as it may, there are, to the present time, in all American history only two examples of practical statesmanship which can serve as perfect models, not perhaps in all respects for imitation, but for study, to persons who wish to understand what practical statesmanship has been under an American system. Public men in considerable numbers and of high merit have run their careers in national politics, but only two have had at once the breadth of mind to grapple with the machine of government as a whole, and the authority necessary to make it work efficiently for a given object; the practical knowledge of affairs and of politics that enabled them to foresee every movement; the long apprenticeship which had allowed them to educate and discipline their parties; and finally, the good fortune to enjoy power when government was still plastic and capable of receiving a new impulse. The conditions of the highest practical statesmanship require that its models should be financiers; the conditions of our history have hitherto limited their appearance and activity to its earlier days.

The vigor and capacity of Hamilton's mind are seen at their best not in his organization of the Treasury Department, which was a task within the powers of a moderate intellect, nor yet in the essays which, under the name of reports, instilled much sound knowledge, besides some that was not so sound, into the minds of legislature and people; still less are they shown in the arts of political management, —a field into which his admirers can follow him only with regret and some sense of shame. The true ground of Hamilton's great reputation is to be found in the mass and variety of legislation and organization which characterized the first Administration of Washington, and which were permeated and controlled by Hamilton's spirit. That this work was not wholly his own is of small consequence. Whoever did it was acting under his leadership, was guided consciously or unconsciously by his influence, was inspired by the activity which centred in his department, and sooner or later the work was subject to his approval. The results—legislative and administrative—were stupendous and can never be repeated. A government is organized once for all, and until that of the United States fairly goes to pieces no man can do more than alter or improve the work accomplished by Hamilton and his party.

What Hamilton was to Washington, Gallatin was to Jefferson, with only such difference as circumstances required. It is true that the powerful influence of Mr. Madison entered largely into the plan of Jefferson's Administration, uniting and modifying its other elements, and that this was an influence the want of which was painfully felt by Washington and caused his most serious difficulties; it is true, too, that Mr. Jefferson reserved to himself a far more active initiative than had been in Washington's character, and that Mr. Gallatin asserted his own individuality much less conspicuously than was done by Mr. Hamilton; but the parallel is nevertheless sufficiently exact to convey a true idea of Mr. Gallatin's position. The government was in fact a triumvirate almost as clearly defined as any triumvirate of Rome. During eight years the country was governed by these three men,—Jefferson, Madison, and Gallatin,—among whom Gallatin not only represented the whole political influence of the great Middle States, not only held and effectively wielded the power of the purse, but also was avowedly charged with the task of carrying into effect the main principles on which the party had sought and attained power.

In so far as Mr. Jefferson's Administration was a mere protest against the conduct of his predecessor, the object desired was attained by the election itself. In so far as it represented a change of system, its positive characteristics were financial. The philanthropic or humanitarian doctrines which had been the theme of Mr. Jefferson's philosophy, and which, in a somewhat more tangible form, had been put into shape by Mr. Gallatin in his great speech on foreign intercourse and in his other writings, when reduced to their simplest elements amount merely to this: that America, standing outside the political movement of Europe, could afford to follow a political development of her own; that she might safely disregard remote dangers; that her armaments might be reduced to a point little above mere police necessities; that she might rely on natural self-interest for her foreign commerce; that she might depend on average common sense for her internal prosperity and order; and that her capital was safest in the hands of her own citizens. To establish these doctrines beyond the chance of overthrow was to make democratic government a success, while to defer the establishment of these doctrines was to incur the risk, if not the certainty, of following the career of England in "debt, corruption, and rottenness."

In this political scheme, whatever its merits or its originality, everything was made to depend upon financial management, and, since the temptation to borrow money was the great danger, payment of the debt was the great dogma of the Democratic principle. "The discharge of the debt is vital to the destinies of our government," wrote Mr. Jefferson to Mr. Gallatin in October, 1809, when the latter was desperately struggling to maintain his grasp on the Administration; "we shall never see another President and Secretary of the Treasury *making all other objects subordinate to this.*" And Mr. Gallatin replied: "The reduction of the debt was certainly the principal object in bringing me into office." With the reduction of debt, by parity of reasoning, reduction of taxation went hand in hand. On this subject Mr. Gallatin's own words at the outset of his term of office give the clearest idea of his views. On the 16th November, 1801, he wrote to Mr. Jefferson:

"If we cannot, with the probable amount of impost and sale of lands, pay the debt at the rate proposed and support the establishments on the proposed plans, one of three things must be done; either to continue the internal taxes, or to reduce the expenditure still more, or to discharge the debt with less rapidity. The last recourse to me is the most objectionable, not only because I am firmly of opinion that if the present Administration and Congress do not take the most effective measures for that object, the debt will be entailed on us and the ensuing generations, together with all the systems which support it and which it supports, but also, any sinking fund operating in an increased ratio as it progresses, a very small deduction from an appropriation for that object would make a considerable difference in the ultimate term of redemption which, provided we can in some shape manage the three per cents. without redeeming them at their nominal value, I think may be paid at fourteen or fifteen years.

"On the other hand, if this Administration shall not reduce taxes, they never will be permanently reduced. To strike at the root of the evil and avert the danger of increasing taxes, encroaching government, temptations to offensive wars, &c., nothing can be more effectual than a repeal of *all* internal taxes; but let them all go and not one remain on which sister taxes may be hereafter engrafted. I agree most fully with you that pretended tax-preparations, treasure-preparations, and army-preparations against contingent wars tend only to encourage wars. If the United States shall unavoidably be drawn into a war, the people will submit to any necessary tax, and the system of internal taxation which then shall be thought best adapted to the then situation of the country may be created instead of engrafted on the old or present plan. If there shall be no real necessity for them, their abolition by this Administration will most powerfully deter any other from reviving them."

To these purposes, in the words of Mr. Jefferson, all other objects were made subordinate, and to carry these purposes into effect was the peculiar task of Mr. Gallatin. No one else appears even to have been thought of; no one else possessed any of the requisites for the place in such a degree as made him even a possible rival. The whole political situation dictated the selection of Mr. Gallatin for the Treasury as distinctly as it did that of Mr. Jefferson for the Presidency.

But the condition on which alone the principles of the Republicans could be carried out was that of peace. To use again Mr. Gallatin's own words, written in 1835: "No nation can, any more than any individual, pay its debts unless its annual receipts exceed its expenditures, and the two necessary ingredients for that purpose, which are common to all nations, are frugality and peace. The United States have enjoyed the last blessing in a far greater degree than any of the great European powers. And they have had another peculiar advantage, that of an unexampled increase of population and corresponding wealth. We are indebted almost exclusively for both to our geographical and internal situation, the only share which any Administration or individual can claim being its efforts to preserve peace and to check expenses either improper in themselves or of subordinate importance to the payment of the public debt. In that respect I may be entitled to some public credit, as nearly the whole of my public life, from 1795, when I took my seat in Congress, till 1812, when the war took place, was almost exclusively devoted with entire singleness of purpose to those objects."[2]

To preserve peace, therefore, in order that the beneficent influence of an enlightened internal policy might have free course, was the special task of Mr. Madison. How much Mr. Gallatin's active counsel and assistance had to do with the foreign policy of the government will be seen in the narrative. Here, however, lay the danger, and here came the ultimate shipwreck. It is obvious at the outset that the weak point of what may be called the Jeffersonian system lay in its rigidity of rule. That system was, it must be confessed, a system of doctrinaires, and had the virtues and faults of *a priori* reasoning. Far in advance, as it was, of any other political effort of its time, and representing, as it doubtless did, all that was most philanthropic and all that most boldly appealed to the best instincts of mankind, it made too little allowance for human passions and vices; it relied too absolutely on the power of interest and reason as opposed to prejudice and habit; it proclaimed too openly to the world that the sword was not one of its arguments, and that peace was essential to its existence. When narrowed down to a precise issue, and after eliminating from the problem the mere dogmas of the extreme Hamiltonian Federalists, the real difference between Mr. Jefferson and moderate Federalists like Rufus King, who represented four-fifths of the Federal party, lay in the question how far a government could safely disregard the use of force as an element in politics. Mr. Jefferson and Mr. Gallatin maintained that every interest should be subordinated to the

[2] Letter to Gales & Seaton, 5th February, 1835, *Writings*, ii. 535.

necessity of fixing beyond peradventure the cardinal principles of true republican government in the public mind, and that after this was accomplished, a result to be marked by extinction of the debt, the task of government would be changed and a new class of duties would arise. Mr. King maintained that republican principles would take care of themselves, and that the government could only escape war and ruin by holding ever the drawn sword in its hand. Mr. Gallatin, his eyes fixed on the country of his adoption, and loathing the violence, the extravagance, and the corruption of Europe, clung with what in a less calm mind would seem passionate vehemence to the ideal he had formed of a great and pure society in the New World, which was to offer to the human race the first example of man in his best condition, free from all the evils which infected Europe, and intent only on his own improvement. To realize this ideal might well, even to men of a coarser fibre than Mr. Gallatin, compensate for many insults and much wrong, borne with dignity and calm remonstrance. True, Mr. Gallatin always looked forward to the time when the American people might safely increase its armaments; but he well knew that, as the time approached, the need would in all probability diminish: meanwhile, he would gladly have turned his back on all the politics of Europe, and have found compensation for foreign outrage in domestic prosperity. The interests of the United States were too serious to be put to the hazard of war; government must be ruled by principles; to which the Federalists answered that government must be ruled by circumstances.

The moment when Mr. Jefferson assumed power was peculiarly favorable for the trial of his experiment. Whatever the original faults and vices of his party might have been, ten years of incessant schooling and education had corrected many of its failings and supplied most of its deficiencies. It was thoroughly trained, obedient, and settled in its party doctrines. And while the new administration thus profited by the experience of its adversity, it was still more happy in the inheritance it received from its predecessor. Whatever faults the Federalists may have committed, and no one now disputes that their faults and blunders were many, they had at least the merit of success; their processes may have been clumsy, their tempers were under decidedly too little control, and their philosophy of government was both defective and inconsistent; but it is an indisputable fact, for which they have a right to receive full credit, that when they surrendered the government to Mr. Jefferson in March, 1801, they surrendered it in excellent condition. The ground was clear for Mr. Jefferson to build upon. Friendly relations had been restored with France without offending England; for the first time since the government existed there was not a serious difficulty in all our foreign relations, the chronic question of impressment alone excepted; the army and navy were already reduced to the lowest possible point; the civil service had never been increased beyond very humble proportions; the debt, it is true, had been somewhat increased, but in nothing like proportion to the increase of population and wealth; and through all their troubles the Federalists had so carefully managed taxation that there was absolutely nothing for Mr. Gallatin to do, and he attempted nothing, in regard to the tariff of impost duties, which were uniformly moderate and unexceptionable, while even in regard to the excise and other internal taxes he hesitated to interfere. This almost entire absence of grievances to correct extended even to purely political legislation. The alien and sedition laws expired by limitation before the accession of Mr. Jefferson, and only the new organization of the judiciary offered material for legislative attack. Add to all this that Europe was again about to recover peace.

On the other hand, the difficulties with which Mr. Jefferson had to deal were no greater than always must exist under any condition of party politics. From the Federalists he had nothing to fear; they were divided and helpless. The prejudices and discords of his own followers were his only real danger, and principally the pressure for office which threatened to blind the party to the higher importance of its principles. In proportion as he could maintain some efficient barrier against this and similar excesses and fix the attention of his followers on points of high policy, his Administration could rise to the level of purity which

was undoubtedly his ideal. What influence was exerted by
Mr. Gallatin in this respect will be shown in the course of
the narrative.

The assertion that Jefferson, Madison, and Gallatin were
a triumvirate which governed the country during eight
years takes no account of the other members of Mr. Jefferson's Cabinet, but in point of fact the other members
added little to its strength.

John Randolph's Eccentricities

Adams' biography, John Randolph, *is an example of the full force of his style and rather terrible attention turned upon a subject of which he was contemptuous. Yet that subject, the falsely glittering career of John Randolph of Roanoke, exercised an unwarranted fascination upon Adams. It pierced both prejudice and disapproval.*

He never resolved for himself the inconsistencies of John Randolph's conduct: to be so bad and succeed so well; to be so careless and yet so true; to be so arrogant, proud, cruel, and almost traitorous, and yet honest, plain, and more consistent than Thomas Jefferson. The ghost of John Randolph which his imagination had conjured up from the known facts bothered him, teased him, bedeviled him until he had to write the book.

The stripped-down leanness of its style and the fierceness of its emotions make it more readable than the worthier Gallatin.

JOHN RANDOLPH'S ECCENTRICITIES[1]

If disappointment and sorrow could soften a human heart, Randolph had enough to make him tender as the gentlest. From the first, some private trouble weighed on his mind, and since he chose to make a mystery of its cause a biographer is bound to respect his wish. The following letter

[1] Chapter X of Adams' biography, *John Randolph,* published by Houghton Mifflin Co., in 1882 in the American Statesmen Series.

to his friend Nicholson, written probably in the year 1805, shows his feeling on this point:—

"*Monday, 4 March*. Dear Nicholson,—By *you* I would be understood; whether the herd of mankind comprehend me or not, I care not. Yourself, the Speaker, and Bryan are, of all the world, alone acquainted with my real situation. On that subject I have only to ask that you will preserve the same reserve that I have done. Do not misunderstand me, my good friend. I do not doubt your honor or discretion. Far from it. But on this subject I am, perhaps, foolishly fastidious. God bless you, my noble fellow. I shall ever hold you most dear to my heart."

From such expressions not much can be safely inferred. Doubtless he imagined his character and career to be greatly influenced by one event or another in his life, but in reality both he and his brother Richard seem to have had from the first the same vehement, ill-regulated minds, and the imagination counted for more with them than the reality, whatever it was. His was a nature that would have made for itself a hell even though fate had put a heaven about it. Quarrelling with his brother's widow, he left Bizarre to bury himself in a poor corner among his overseers and slaves at Roanoke. "I might be now living at Bizarre," he wrote afterwards, "if the reunion of his [Richard's] widow with the [traducers?] of her husband had not driven me to Roanoke;" "a savage solitude," he called it, "into which I have been driven to seek shelter." This was in 1810. He had already quarrelled with his step-father, Judge Tucker, as kind-hearted a man as ever lived, and of this one-sided quarrel we have an account which, even if untrue, is curious. It seems that Randolph had been talking violently against the justice and policy of the law which passed estates, in failure of direct heirs, to brothers of half-blood; whereupon Judge Tucker made the indiscreet remark, "Why, Jack, you ought not to be against that law, for you know if you were to die without issue you would wish your half-brothers to have your estate." "I'll be damned, sir, if I do know it," said Randolph, according to the story, and from that day broke off relations with his step-father. In 1810 he was only with the utmost difficulty dissuaded by his counsel from bringing suit against Judge Tucker for fraudulent management of his estate during that guardianship which had ended more than fifteen years before. He knew that the charge was false, but he was possessed by it. Two passions, besides that for drink, were growing on him with age,—avarice and family pride; taken together, three furies worse than the cruelest disease or the most crushing disasters. Yet disaster, too, was not wanting. His nephew St. George, Richard's eldest son, deaf and dumb from his birth, became quite irrational in 1813, and closed his days in an asylum. The younger nephew, Tudor, whom he had loved as much as it was in his nature to love any one, and who was to be the representative of his race, fell into a hopeless consumption the next year, and, being sent abroad, died at Cheltenham in 1815. Thus Randolph, after falling out with his step-father and half-brothers, after quitting Bizarre and quarrelling with his brother's widow, lost his nephews, failed in public life, and was driven from his seat in Congress. Had he been an Italian he would have passed for one possessed of the evil eye, one who brought destruction on all he loved, and every peasant would have secretly made the sign of the cross on meeting him. His defeat by Eppes in the spring of 1813 disgusted him with politics, and he visited his mortification on his old friends. Macon wrote to Nicholson February 1, 1815:—

"Jonathan did not love David more than I have Randolph, and I still have that same feeling towards him, but somehow or other I am constrained from saying [anything] about it or him, unless now and then to defend him against false accusations, or what I believe to be such. There is hardly any evil that afflicts one more than the loss of a friend, especially when not conscious of having given any cause for it. I cannot account for the coldness with which you say he treated you, or his not staying at your house while in Baltimore. Stanford now and then comes to where I sit in the House, and shows me a letter from R. to him, which is all I see from him. He has not wrote to me since he left Congress [in March, 1813], nor I but once to him, which was to inclose him a book of his that I found in the city when I came to the next session. I have said thus much in answer to your letter, and it is more than has been said or written to any other person."

The sudden and happy close of the war in January, 1815, brought about a curious revolution in the world of politics. Everything that had happened before that convulsion seemed now wiped from memory. Men once famous and powerful were forgotten; men whose political sins had been dark and manifold were forgiven and received back into the fold. Among the rest was Randolph. He recovered his seat in the spring of 1815, and returned to Congress with a great reputation for bold and sarcastic oratory. He came back to a new world, to a government which had been strengthened and nationalized by foreign war beyond the utmost hopes of Washington or John Adams. Mr. Jefferson's party was still in power, but not a thread was left of the principles with which Mr. Jefferson had started on his career in 1801. The country had a debt compared with which that of the federalist administrations was light; it had a navy which was now more popular than ever Mr. Jefferson had been in his palmiest days, and an army which Randolph dared no longer call "ragamuffin;" the people had faced the awful idea of conscription, at the bidding of James Madison and James Monroe, two men who had nearly broken up the Union, in 1798, at the mere suggestion of raising half a dozen regiments; at the same command the national bank was to be reëstablished;—in every direction states' rights were trampled on;—and all this had been done by Randolph's old friends and his own party. During his absence, Congress, like school-boys whose monitor has left the room, had passed the bill for the Yazoo compromise. This was not the whole. Chief Justice Marshall and the Supreme Court were at work. Their decisions were rapidly riveting these results into something more than mere political precedents or statute law. State sovereignty was crumbling under their assaults, and the nation was already too powerful for the safety of Virginia.

Mr. Jefferson, in his old age, took the alarm, and began to preach a new crusade against the Supreme Court and the heresies of federal principles. He rallied about him the "old republicans" of 1798. Mr. Madison and Mr. Monroe, Mr. Gallatin and the northern democrats, were little disposed to betake themselves again to that uncomfortable boat which they had gladly abandoned for the broader and stauncher deck of the national ship of state; but William B. Giles was ready to answer any bugle-call that could summon him back to the Senate, or give him another chance for that cabinet office which had been the ambition of his life; and John Randolph was at all times ready to clap on again his helmet of Mambrino and have a new tilt at the windmill which had once already demolished him. If Virginia hesitated, South Carolina might be made strong in the faith, and Georgia was undaunted by the Yazoo experience. If the northern democrats no longer knew what states' rights meant, the slave power, which had grown with the national growth, could be organized to teach them.

Into this movement Randolph flung himself headlong, and in such a party he was a formidable ally. Doubtless there was much about him that seemed ridiculous to bystanders, and still more that not only seemed, but was, irrational. Neither his oratory nor his wit would have been tolerated in a northern State. To the cold-blooded New Englander who did not love extravagance or eccentricity, and had no fancy for plantation manners, Randolph was an obnoxious being. Those traits of character and person of which he was proud as evidence of his Pocahontas and Powhatan ancestry, they instinctively attributed to an ancestral type of a different kind. It was not the Indian whom they saw in this lean, forked figure, with its elongated arms and long, bony forefinger, pointing at the objects of his aversion as with a stick; it was not an Indian countenance they recognized in this parchment face, prematurely old and seamed with a thousand small wrinkles; in that bright, sharply sparkling eye; in the flattering, caressing tone and manner, which suddenly, with or without provocation, changed into wanton brutality. The Indian owns no such person or such temperament, which, if derived from any ancestry, belongs to an order of animated beings still nearer than the Indian to the jealous and predacious instincts of dawning intelligence.

There is no question that such an antagonist was formidable. The mode of political warfare at first adopted by instinct, he had now by long experience developed into a science. Terror was the favorite resource of his art, and he had so practised as to have reached a high degree of success in using it. He began by completely mastering his congressional district. At best, it is not easy for remote, sparsely settled communities to shake off a political leader who has no prominent rival in his own party, and no strong outside opposition, but when that leader has Randolph's advantages it becomes impossible to contest the field. His constituents revolted once, but never again. His peculiarities were too well known and too much in the natural order of things to excite surprise or scandal among them. They liked his long stump speeches and sharp, epigrammatic phrases, desultory style and melodramatic affectations of manner, and they were used to coarseness that would have sickened a Connecticut peddler. They liked to be flattered by him, for flattery was one of the instruments he used with most lavishness. "In conversing with old men in Charlotte County," says a native of the spot, writing in 1878, "they will talk a long time about how Mr. Randolph flattered this one to carry his point; how he drove men clean out of the country who offended him; how ridiculous he sometimes made his acquaintances appear: they will entertain you a long time in this way before they will mention one word about his friendship for anybody or anybody's for him."

He was simple enough in his methods, and as they were all intended to lead up to terror in the end, there was every reason for simplifying them to suit the cases.

"How do you do, Mr. L.? I am a candidate for Congress, and should be pleased to have your vote."

"Unfortunately, I have no vote, Mr. Randolph."

"Good-morning, Mr. L."

He never forgave a vote given to his opponent, and he worked his district over to root out the influences which defeated him in 1813. One example of his method is told in regard to a Mr. S., a plain farmer, who had carried his precinct almost unanimously for Eppes. Randolph is said to have sought him out one court day in the most public place he could find, and, addressing him with great courtesy, presently put to him a rather abstruse question of politics. Passing from one puzzling and confusing inquiry to another, raising his voice, attracting a crowd by every artifice in his power, he drew the unfortunate man farther and farther into the most awkward embarrassment, continually repeating his expressions of astonishment at the ignorance to which his victim confessed. The scene exposed the man to ridicule and contempt, and is said to have destroyed his influence.

He sometimes acted a generous, sometimes a brutal, part; the one, perhaps, not less sincere than the other while it lasted, but neither of them in any sense simple expressions of emotion. Although he professed vindictiveness as a part of his Powhatan inheritance, and although he proclaimed himself to be one who never forsook a friend or forgave a foe, it is evident that his vindictiveness was often assumed merely in order to terrify; there was usually a method and a motive in his madness, noble at first in the dawn of young hope, but far from noble at last in the gloom of disappointment and despair. "He did things," says Mr. Henry Carrington, "which nobody else could do, and made others do things which they never did before, and of which they repented all the days of their lives; and on some occasions he was totally regardless of private rights, and not held amenable to the laws of the land."

This trait of his character gave rise to a mass of local stories, many of which have found their way into print, but which are for the most part so distorted in passing through the mouths of overseers and neighbors as to be quite worthless for biography. Another mass of legend has collected itself about his life in Washington and his travels. The less credit we give to the more extravagant of these stories, the nearer we shall come to the true man. At times he was violent or outrageous from the mere effect of drink, but to do him justice, his brutality was commonly directed against what he supposed, or chose to think, presumption, ignorance, dishonesty, cant, or some other trait of a low and grovelling mind. He rarely insulted any man whom he believed to be respectable, and he was always kind and affectionate to those he loved; but although he controlled himself thus far in society, he carried terrorism in politics to an extreme. He could be gentle when he pleased, but he often preferred to be arrogant. Only a few months before his death, in February, 1833, he forced some states'-rights resolutions through a meeting of the county of Charlotte. A certain Captain Watkins, who was at the meeting, declined to follow him, and avowed himself a supporter of President Jackson. Randolph, while his resolutions were under discussion, addressed himself to Captain Watkins, saying that he did not expect "an old Yazoo speculator" to approve of them. Captain Watkins rose and denied the charge. At this, Randolph looked him steadily in the face, and pointing his finger at him said,—

"You are a Yazoo man, Mr. Watkins."

Mr. Watkins, much agitated and embarrassed, rose again and made an explanation. Randolph, with the same deliberation, simply repeated,—

"You are a Yazoo man, Mr. Watkins."

A third time Mr. Watkins rose, and was met again by the same cold assertion, "You are a Yazoo man;" until at last he left the room, completely broken down.

Mr. Watkins had, in fact, once owned some of the Yazoo land warrants. He was, of course, no admirer of Randolph, who rode rough-shod over him in return. If it be asked why a man who treated his neighbors thus was not fifty times shot down where he stood by exasperated victims, the answer is that he knew those with whom he was dealing. He never pressed a quarrel to the end, or resented an insult further than was necessary to repel it. He was notorious for threatening to use his weapons on every occasion of a tavern quarrel, but at such times he was probably excited by drink; when quite himself he never used them if it was possible to avoid it. In 1807 he even refused to fight General Wilkinson, and allowed the general to post him as a coward; and he did this on the ground that the general had no right to hold him accountable for his expressions: "I cannot descend to your level." Indeed, with all Randolph's quarrelsome temper and vindictive spirit, he had but one duel during his public life. His insulting language and manner came not from the heart, but from the head: they were part of his system, a method of controlling society as he controlled his negroes. His object was to rule, not to revenge, and it would have been folly to let himself be shot unless his situation required it. Randolph had an ugly temper and a strong will; but he had no passions that disturbed his head.

In what is called polite society these tactics were usually unnecessary, and then bad manners were a mere habit, controllable at will. In such society, therefore, Randolph was seen at his best. The cultivated Virginian, with wit and memory, varied experience, audacious temper, and above all a genuine flavor of his native soil; the Virginian, in his extremest form, such as any one might well be curious once to see,—this was the attraction in Randolph which led strangers to endure and even to seek his acquaintance. Thus, as extremes meet, Massachusetts men were apt to be favorites with this Ishmaelite; they were so thoroughly hostile to all his favorite prejudices that they could make a tacit agreement to disagree in peace. Josiah Quincy was one of his friends; Elijah Mills, the Massachusetts senator, another. In a letter dated January 19, 1816, Mr. Mills thus describes him:—

"He is really a most singular and interesting man; regardless entirely of form and ceremony in some things, and punctilious to an extreme in others. He, yesterday, dined with us. He was dressed in a rough, coarse, short hunting-coat, with small-clothes and boots, and over his boots a pair of coarse cotton leggins, tied with strings round his legs. He engrossed almost the whole conversation, and was exceedingly amusing as well as eloquent and instructive."

Again on January 14, 1822:—

"Our Massachusetts people, and I among the number, have grown great favorites with Mr. Randolph. He has invited me to dine with him twice, and he has dined with us as often. He is now what he used to be in his best days, in good spirits, with fine manners and the most fascinating conversation. . . . For the last two years he has been in a state of great perturbation, and has indulged himself in the ebullitions of littleness and acerbity, in which he exceeds almost any man living. He is now in better humor, and is capable of making himself exceedingly interesting and agreeable. How long this state of things may continue may depend upon accident or caprice. He is, therefore, not a desirable inmate or a safe friend, but under proper restrictions a most entertaining and instructive companion."

In 1826 Mr. Mills was ill, and Randolph insisted on acting as his doctor.

"He now lives within a few doors of me, and has called almost every evening and morning to see me. This has been very kind of him, but is no earnest of continued friendship. In his likings and dislikings, as in everything else, he is the most eccentric being upon the face of the earth, and is as likely to abuse friend as foe. Hence, among all those with whom he has been associated during the last thirty years, there is scarcely an individual whom he can call his friend. At times he is the most entertaining and amusing man alive, with manners the most pleasant and agreeable; and at other times he is sour, morose, crabbed, ill-natured, and sarcastic, rude in manners, and repulsive to everybody. Indeed, I think he is partially deranged, and seldom in the full possession of his reason."

The respectable senator from Massachusetts, "poor little

Mills," as Randolph calls him, seems to have snatched but a fearful joy in this ill-assorted friendship.

The system of terrorism, which was so effective in the politics of Charlotte, was not equally well suited to the politics of Washington; to overawe a congressional district was possible, but when Randolph tried to crush Mr. Jefferson and Mr. Madison by these tactics, the experiment not only failed, but reacted so violently as to drive him out of public life. Nevertheless, within the walls of the House of Representatives his success was considerable; he inspired terror, and to oppose him required no little nerve, and, perhaps, a brutality as reckless as his own. He made it his business to break in young members as he would break a colt, bearing down on them with superciliousness and sarcasm. In later life he had a way of entering the House, booted and spurred, with whip in hand, after the business had begun, and loudly saluting his friends to attract attention; but if any one whom he disliked was speaking, he would abruptly turn on his heel and go out. Mr. S. G. Goodrich describes him in 1820, during the Missouri debate, as rising and crying out in a shrill voice, which pierced every nook and corner of the hall, "Mr. Speaker, I have but one word to say,—one word, sir; and that is to state a fact. The measure to which the gentleman has just alluded originated in a dirty trick." Under some circumstances he even ventured on physical attacks, but this was very rare. He had a standing feud with Willis Alston of North Carolina, and they insulted each other without serious consequences for many years. Once, in 1811, as the members were leaving the House, Alston, in his hearing, made some offensive remark about a puppy. Randolph described the scene to Nicholson in a letter dated January 28, 1811:—

"This poor wretch, after I had prevailed upon the House to adjourn, uttered *at* me some very offensive language, which I was not bound to overhear; but he took care to throw himself in my way on the staircase, and repeat his foul language to another in my hearing. Whereupon I said, 'Alston, if it were worth while, I would cane you,—and I believe I will cane you!' and caned him accordingly, with all the nonchalance of Sir Harry Wildair himself."

The affair, however, got no farther than the police court, and Randolph very justly added in his letter, "For Macon's sake (although he despises him) I regret it, and for my own, for in such cases victory is defeat." He called himself an Ishmael: his hand was against everybody, and everybody's hand was against him. His political career had now long ended so far as party promotion was concerned, and there remained only an overpowering egotism, a consuming rage for notoriety, contemptible even in his own eyes, but overmastering him like the passion for money or drink.

Of all his eccentricities, the most pitiful and yet the most absurd were not those which sprang from his lower but from his higher instincts. The better part of his nature made a spasmodic struggle against the passions and appetites that degraded it. Half his rudeness and savagery was due to pride which would allow no one to see the full extent of his weakness. At times he turned violently on himself. So in the spring of 1815 he snatched at religion and for an instant felt a serious hope that through the church he might purify his nature; yet even in his most tender moments there was something almost humorous in his childlike incapacity to practice for two consecutive instants the habit of self-control or the simplest instincts of Christianity. "I am no disciple of Calvin or Wesley," he wrote in one of these moods; "but I feel the necessity of a changed nature; of a new life; of an altered heart. I feel my stubborn and rebellious nature to be softened, and that it is essential to my comfort here as well as to my future welfare, to cultivate and cherish feelings of good-will towards all mankind; to strive against envy, malice, and all uncharitableness. I think I have succeeded in forgiving all my enemies. There is not a human being that I would hurt if it were in my power; not even Bonaparte."

If in his moments of utmost Christian exaltation he could only think he had forgiven his enemies and would hurt no human being if he had the power, what must have been his passion for inflicting pain when the devil within his breast held unchecked dominion!

Historian

The four chapters selected from the nine-volume History
of the United States during the Administrations of Thomas
Jefferson and James Madison *represent the multiplicity of
Adams' interests rather than the unity of his theme. The
whole* History *must be read to appreciate that unity; a few
scattered chapters will serve to give an idea of the variety
of tone, treatment, and matter which Adams, at the height
of his powers, could bring together under the one subject
of America's coming of age.*

*Adams cast a wide net. Here, chosen almost at random
from the long, complex, but perfectly orchestrated* History
*are three episodes: Toussaint Louverture's revolution in
Haiti, Tecumthe's valiant attempt to throw back the settler's invasion of the Indian lands of the old Northwest, and
a lyrical tribute to Yankee seamanship. Each selection has
a small unity of its own, but fits into a subordinate place
in the large pattern of the* History. *In that whole, each part
contributes something to Adams' exhibition of the tragi-
comic achievement of an American nationality in the years
1800 to 1816.*

Toussaint Louverture[1]

Fortunately for the Prince of Peace, the world contained at that moment one man for whom Bonaparte entertained more hatred and contempt, and whom he was in still more haste to crush. The policy which Talleyrand had planned, and into which he had drawn the First Consul, could not be laid aside in order to punish Spain. On the contrary, every day rendered peace with England more necessary, and such a peace was inconsistent with a Spanish war. That Bonaparte felt no strong sympathy with Talleyrand's policy of peace in Europe and peaceful development abroad, is more than probable; but he was not yet so confident of his strength as to rely wholly on himself,—he had gone too far in the path of pacification to quit it suddenly for one of European conquest and dynastic power. He left Godoy and Spain untouched, in order to rebuild the empire of France in her colonies. Six weeks after he had threatened war on Charles IV., his agent at London, Oct. 1, 1801, signed with Lord Hawkesbury preliminary articles of peace which put an end to hostilities on the ocean. No sooner did Bonaparte receive the news[2] than he summoned his brother-in-law Leclerc to Paris. Leclerc was a general of high reputation, who had married the beautiful Pauline Bonaparte and was then perhaps the most promising member of the family next to Napoleon himself. To him, October 23, Napoleon entrusted the command of an immense expedition already ordered to collect at Brest, to destroy the power

[1] Chapter XV of Volume 1 of Adams' *History of the United States*, published by Charles Scribner's Sons between 1889 and 1891.

[2] *Correspondance*, vii. 279; Bonaparte to Berthier, 16 Vendémiaire, An x. (Oct. 8, 1801).

of Toussaint Louverture and re-establish slavery in the Island of St. Domingo.[3]

The story of Toussaint Louverture has been told almost as often as that of Napoleon, but not in connection with the history of the United States, although Toussaint exercised on their history an influence as decisive as that of any European ruler. His fate placed him at a point where Bonaparte needed absolute control. St. Domingo was the only centre from which the measures needed for rebuilding the French colonial system could radiate. Before Bonaparte could reach Louisiana he was obliged to crush the power of Toussaint.

The magnificent Island of St. Domingo was chiefly Spanish. Only its western end belonged by language as well as by history to France; but this small part of the island, in the old days of Bourbon royalty, had been the most valuable of French possessions. Neither Martinique nor Guadeloupe compared with it. In 1789, before the French Revolution began, nearly two thirds of the commercial interests of France centred in St. Domingo;[4] its combined exports and imports were valued at more than one hundred and forty million dollars; its sugar, coffee, indigo, and cotton supplied the home market, and employed in prosperous years more than seven hundred ocean-going vessels, with seamen to the number, it was said, of eighty thousand. Paris swarmed with creole families who drew their incomes from the island, among whom were many whose political influence was great; while, in the island itself, society enjoyed semi-Parisian ease and elegance, the natural product of an exaggerated slave-system combined with the manners, ideas, and amusements of a French proprietary caste.

In 1789 the colony contained about six hundred thousand inhabitants, five sixths of whom were full-blooded negroes held in rigid slavery. Of the eighty or hundred thousand free citizens, about half were mulattoes, or had some infusion of negro blood which disqualified them from holding political power. All social or political privileges were

---

[3] Ibid., vii. 298. Bonaparte to Berthier, 1 Brumaire, An x. (Oct. 23, 1801).

[4] *Pamphile de Lacroix, Mémoires,* ii. 277.

held by forty or fifty thousand French creoles, represented by the few hundred planters and officials who formed the aristocracy of the island. Between the creoles and the mulattoes, or mixed-breeds, existed the jealousy sure to result from narrow distinctions of blood marking broad differences in privilege. These were not the only jealousies which raged in the colony; for the creoles were uneasy under the despotism of the colonial system, and claimed political rights which the home government denied. Like all colonists of that day, in the quiet of their plantations they talked of independence, and thought with envy of their neighbors in South Carolina, who could buy and sell where they pleased.

When in 1789 France burst into a flame of universal liberty, the creoles of St. Domingo shared the enthusiasm so far as they hoped to gain by it a relaxation of the despotic colonial system; but they were alarmed at finding that the mulattoes, who claimed to own a third of the land and a fourth of the personalty in the colony, offered to make the Republic a free gift of one fifth of their possessions on condition of being no longer subjected to the creole tyranny of caste. The white and mulatto populations were thus brought into collision. The National Assembly of France supported the mulattoes. The creoles replied that they preferred death to sharing power with what they considered a bastard and despicable race. They turned royalists. Both parties took up arms, and in their struggle with each other they at length dropped a match into the immense powder-magazine upon which they both lived. One August night in the year 1791 the whole plain of the north was swept with fire and drenched with blood. Five hundred thousand negro slaves in the depths of barbarism revolted, and the horrors of the massacre made Europe and America shudder.

For several years afterward the colony was torn by convulsions; and to add another element of confusion, the Spaniards and English came in, hoping to effect its conquest. Feb. 4, 1794, the National Assembly of France took the only sensible measure in its power by proclaiming the abolition of slavery; but for the moment this step only embroiled matters the more. Among its immediate results was one of great importance, though little noticed at the time.

[139]

A negro chief, who since the outbreak had become head of a royalist band in Spanish pay, returned, in April, 1794, within French jurisdiction and took service under the Republic. This was Toussaint Louverture, whose father, the son of a negro chief on the slave-coast of Africa, had been brought to St. Domingo as a slave. Toussaint was born in 1746. When he deserted the Spanish service, and with some four thousand men made the sudden attack which resulted in clearing the French colony of Spanish troops, he was already forty-eight years old.

Although Toussaint was received at once into the French service, not until more than a year later, July 23, 1795, did the National Convention recognize his merits by giving him the commission of brigadier-general. Within less than two years, in May, 1797, he was made General-in-Chief, with military command over the whole colony. The services he rendered to France were great, and were highly rewarded. His character was an enigma. Hated by the mulattoes with such vindictiveness as mutual antipathies and crimes could cause, he was liked by the whites rather because he protected and flattered them at the expense of the mulattoes than because they felt any love for him or his race. In return they flattered and betrayed him. Their praise or blame was equally worthless; yet to this rule there were exceptions. One of the best among the French officers in St. Domingo, Colonel Vincent, was deep in Toussaint's confidence, and injured his own career by obstinate attempts to intervene between Bonaparte and Bonaparte's victim. Vincent described Toussaint, in colors apparently unexaggerated, as the most active and indefatigable man that could be imagined,—one who was present everywhere, but especially where his presence was most needed; while his great sobriety, his peculiar faculty of never resting, of tiring out a half-dozen horses and as many secretaries every day; and, more than all, his art of amusing and deceiving all the world,—an art pushed to the limits of imposture,— made him so superior to his surroundings that respect and submission to him were carried to fanaticism.[5]

[5] *Vie de Toussaint,* par Saint-Remy, p. 322.

Gentle and well-meaning in his ordinary relations, vehement in his passions, and splendid in his ambition, Toussaint was a wise, though a severe, ruler so long as he was undisturbed; but where his own safety or power was in question he could be as ferocious as Dessalines and as treacherous as Bonaparte. In more respects than one his character had a curious resemblance to that of Napoleon, —the same abnormal energy of body and mind; the same morbid lust for power, and indifference to means; the same craft and vehemence of temper; the same fatalism, love of display, reckless personal courage, and, what was much more remarkable, the same occasional acts of moral cowardice. One might suppose that Toussaint had inherited from his Dahomey grandfather the qualities of primitive society; but if this was the case, the conditions of life in Corsica must have borne some strong resemblance to barbarism, because the rule of inheritance which applied to Toussaint should hold good for Bonaparte. The problem was the more interesting because the parallelism roused Napoleon's anger, and precipitated a conflict which had vast influence on human affairs. Both Bonaparte and Louverture were the products of a revolution which gave its highest rewards to qualities of energy and audacity. So nearly identical were the steps in their career, that after the 18th Brumaire Toussaint seemed naturally to ape every action which Bonaparte wished to make heroic in the world's eyes. There was reason to fear that Toussaint would end in making Bonaparte ridiculous; for his conduct was, as it seemed to the First Consul, a sort of negro travesty on the consular *régime*.

When the difficulties between France and America became serious, after Talleyrand's demand for money and sweeping attacks upon American commerce, Congress passed an Act of June 13, 1798, suspending commercial relations with France and her dependencies. At that time Toussaint, although in title only General-in-Chief, was in reality absolute ruler of St. Domingo. He recognized a general allegiance to the French Republic, and allowed the Directory to keep a civil agent—the Citizen Roume—as a check on his power; but in fact Roume was helpless in his hands. Toussaint's only rival was Rigaud, a mulatto, who commanded the southern part of the colony, where Jacmel and other ports were situated. Rigaud was a perpetual danger to Louverture, whose safety depended on tolerating no rival. The Act of Congress threatened to create distress among the blacks and endanger the quiet of the colony; while Rigaud and the French authority would be strengthened by whatever weakened Louverture. Spurred both by fear and ambition, Toussaint took the character of an independent ruler. The United States government, counting on such a result, had instructed its consul to invite an advance; and, acting on the consul's suggestion, Toussaint sent to the United States an agent with a letter to the President[6] containing the emphatic assurance that if commercial intercourse were renewed between the United States and St. Domingo it should be protected by every means in his power. The trade was profitable, the political advantages of neutralizing Toussaint were great; and accordingly the President obtained from Congress a new Act, approved Feb. 9, 1799, which was intended to meet the case. He also sent a very able man—Edward Stevens—to St. Domingo, with the title of Consul-General, and with diplomatic powers. At the same time the British Ministry despatched General Maitland to the same place, with orders to stop at Philadelphia and arrange a general policy in regard to Toussaint. This was rapidly done. Maitland hurried to the island, which he reached May 15, 1799, within a month after the arrival of Stevens. Negotiations followed, which resulted, June 13, in a secret treaty[7] between Toussaint and Maitland, by which Toussaint abandoned all privateering and shipping, receiving in return free access to those supplies from the United States which were needed to content his people, fill his treasury, and equip his troops.

To this treaty Stevens was not openly a party; but in Toussaint's eyes he was the real negotiator, and his influence had more to do with the result than all the ships and soldiers at Maitland's disposal. Under this informal tripar-

[6] Toussaint to President Adams, 16 Brumaire, An vii. (Nov. 6, 1798); MSS. State Department Archives.
[7] Treaty of June 13, 1799; MSS. State Department Archives.

tite agreement, Toussaint threw himself into the arms of the United States, and took an enormous stride toward the goal of his ambition,—a crown.

Louverture had waited only to complete this arrangement before attacking Rigaud. Then the fruits of his foreign policy ripened. Supplies of every kind flowed from the United States into St. Domingo; but supplies were not enough. Toussaint began the siege of Jacmel,—a siege famous in Haytian history. His position was hazardous. A difficult war in a remote province, for which he could not bring the necessary supplies and materials by land; a suspicious or hostile French agent and government; a population easily affected by rumors and intrigues; finally, the seizure by English cruisers of a flotilla which, after his promise to abandon all shipping, was bringing his munitions of war along the coast for the siege,—made Toussaint tremble for the result of his civil war. He wrote once more to the President,[8] requesting him to send some frigates to enforce the treaty by putting an end to all trade with the island except such as the treaty permitted. Stevens again came to his assistance. The United States frigate, "General Greene," was sent to cruise off Jacmel in February and March, 1800, and was followed by other vessels of war. Rigaud's garrison was starved out; Jacmel was abandoned; and Rigaud himself, July 29, 1800, consented to quit the country.

Toussaint's gratitude was great, and his confidence in Stevens unbounded. Even before the fall of Jacmel, Stevens was able to inform Secretary Pickering that Toussaint was taking his measures slowly but certainly to break connection with France.[9] "If he is not disturbed, he will preserve appearances a little longer; but as soon as France interferes with this colony, he will throw off the mask and declare it independent." Hardly was Rigaud crushed, when the first overt act of independence followed. Toussaint imprisoned Roume, and on an invitation from the municipalities assumed the civil as well as military authority, under the

[8] Toussaint to President Adams, Aug. 14, 1799; MSS. State Department Archives.
[9] Stevens to Pickering, Feb. 13, 1800; MSS. State Department Archives.

title of governor. In announcing to his Government that this step was to be taken, Stevens added:[10] "From that moment the colony may be considered as forever separated from France. Policy perhaps may induce him to make no open declaration of independence before he is compelled." A few days afterward Toussaint took the Napoleonic measure of seizing by force the Spanish part of the island, which had been ceded to France by the treaty of Bâle five years before, but had not yet been actually transferred. In thus making war on the ally of France, Toussaint had no other motive, as Stevens explained,[11] than to prevent the French government from getting a footing there. Bonaparte had given a new Constitution to France after the 18th Brumaire. Toussaint, after the deposition of Roume, which was his *coup d'état* and 18th Brumaire, gave a new Constitution to St. Domingo in the month of May, 1801, by which he not only assumed all political power for life, but also ascribed to himself the right of naming his own successor. Bonaparte had not yet dared to go so far, although he waited only another year, and meanwhile chafed under the idea of being imitated by one whom he called a "gilded African."

Perhaps audacity was Louverture's best policy; yet no wise man would intentionally aggravate his own dangers by unnecessary rashness, such as he showed in Bonaparte's face. He was like a rat defying a ferret; his safety lay not in his own strength, but in the nature of his hole. Power turned his head, and his regular army of twenty thousand disciplined and well-equipped men was his ruin. All his acts, and much of his open conversation, during the years 1800 and 1801, showed defiance to the First Consul. He prided himself upon being "First of the Blacks" and "Bonaparte of the Antilles." Warning and remonstrance from the Minister of Marine in France excited only his violent anger.[12] He insisted upon dealing directly with sovereigns, and not with their ministers, and was deeply irritated with Bonaparte for answering his letters through the Minister of Ma-

[10] Ibid., April 19, 1800; MSS. State Department Archives.
[11] Ibid.
[12] Ibid., May 24, 1800; MSS. State Department Archives.

rine. Throwing one of these despatches aside unopened, he was heard to mutter before all his company the words, "*Ministre!* . . . *valet!* . . ."[13] He was right in the instinct of self-assertion, for his single hope lay in Bonaparte's consent to his independent power; but the attack on Spanish St. Domingo, and the proclamation of his new Constitution, were unnecessary acts of defiance.

When Jefferson became President of the United States and the Senate confirmed the treaty of Morfontaine, had Louverture not lost his balance he would have seen that Bonaparte and Talleyrand had out-manœuvred him, and that even if Jefferson were not as French in policy as his predecessor had been hostile to France, yet henceforth the United States must disregard sympathies, treat St. Domingo as a French colony, and leave the negro chief to his fate. England alone, after the month of February, 1801, stood between Toussaint and Bonaparte. Edward Stevens, who felt the storm that was in the air, pleaded ill-health and resigned his post of consul-general. Jefferson sent Tobias Lear to Cap Français in Stevens's place, and Lear's first interview showed that Toussaint was beginning to feel Talleyrand's restraints. The freedom he had enjoyed was disappearing, and he chafed at the unaccustomed limitations. He complained bitterly that Lear had brought him no personal letter from the President; and Lear in vain explained the custom of the Government, which warranted no such practice in the case of consuls. "It is because of my color!" cried Toussaint.[14] Justice to President Jefferson and a keener sense of the diplomatic situation would have shown him that such a letter could not be written by the President consistently with his new relations of friendship toward France; and in fact almost the first act of Pichon, on taking charge of the French Legation in Washington after the treaty, was to remonstrate against any recognition of Tous-

[13] *Pamphile de Lacroix, Mémoires,* ii. 52.
[14] Lear to Madison, July, 1801; MSS. State Department Archives.

saint, and to cause Lear's want of diplomatic character which offended Louverture.[15]

Rarely has diplomacy been used with more skill and energy than by Bonaparte, who knew where force and craft should converge. That in this skill mendacity played a chief part, need hardly be repeated. Toussaint was flattered, cajoled, and held in a mist of ignorance, while one by one the necessary preparations were made to prevent his escape; and then, with scarcely a word of warning, at the First Consul's order the mist rolled away, and the unhappy negro found himself face to face with destruction. The same ships that brought news of the preliminary treaty signed at London brought also the rumor of a great expedition fitting at Brest and the gossip of creole society in Paris, which made no longer a secret that Bonaparte meant to crush Toussaint and restore slavery at St. Domingo. Nowhere in the world had Toussaint a friend or a hope except in himself. Two continents looked on with folded arms, more and more interested in the result, as Bonaparte's ripening schemes began to show their character. As yet President Jefferson had no inkling of their meaning. The British government was somewhat better informed, and perhaps Godoy knew more than all the rest; but none of them grasped the whole truth, or felt their own dependence on Toussaint's courage. If he and his blacks should succumb easily to their fate, the wave of French empire would roll on to Louisiana and sweep far up the Mississippi; if St. Domingo should resist, and succeed in resistance, the recoil would spend its force on Europe, while America would be left to pursue her democratic destiny in peace.

Bonaparte hurried his preparations. The month of October, 1801, saw vast activity in French and Spanish ports, for a Spanish squadron accompanied the French fleet. Not a chance was to be left for Toussaint's resistance or escape. To quiet English uneasiness, Bonaparte dictated to Talleyrand a despatch explaining to the British government the

[15] Pichon to Decrès, 18 Fructidor, An ix. (Sept. 5, 1801); Archives de la Marine, MSS.

nature of the expedition.[16] "In the course which I have taken of annihilating the black government at St. Domingo," he said, "I have been less guided by considerations of commerce and finance than by the necessity of stifling in every part of the world every kind of germ of disquiet and trouble; but it could not escape me that St. Domingo, even after being reconquered by the whites, would be for many years a weak point which would need the support of peace and of the mother country; . . . that one of the principal benefits of peace, at the actual moment, for England was its conclusion at a time when the French government had not yet recognized the organization of St. Domingo, and in consequence the power of the blacks; and if it had done so, the sceptre of the new world would sooner or later have fallen into the hands of the blacks."

No such explanations were given to the United States, perhaps because no American minister asked for them. Livingston landed at Lorient November 12, the day before Bonaparte wrote these words; Leclerc's expedition sailed from Brest November 22; and Livingston was presented to the First Consul in the diplomatic audience of December 6. Caring nothing for Toussaint and much for France, Livingston did not come prepared to find that his own interests were the same with those of Toussaint, but already by December 30 he wrote to Rufus King: "I know that the armament, destined in the first instance for Hispaniola, is to proceed to Louisiana provided Toussaint makes no opposition."

While the First Consul claimed credit with England for intending to annihilate the black government and restore slavery at St. Domingo, he proclaimed to Toussaint and the negroes intentions of a different kind. He wrote at last a letter to Toussaint, and drew up a proclamation to the inhabitants of the island, which Leclerc was to publish. "If you are told," said this famous proclamation,[17] "that these forces are destined to ravish your liberty, answer: The Republic has given us liberty, the Republic will not suffer it to

[16] *Correspondance*, vii. 319; Bonaparte to Talleyrand, 22 Brumaire, An x. (Nov. 13, 1801).

[17] Ibid., vii. 315; Proclamation, 17 Brumaire, An x. (Nov. 8, 1801).

be taken from us!" The letter to Toussaint was even more curious, when considered as a supplement to that which had been written to the British government only five days before. "We have conceived esteem for you," wrote Bonaparte to the man he meant to destroy,[18] "and we take pleasure in recognizing and proclaiming the great services you have rendered to the French people. If their flag floats over St. Domingo, it is to you and to the brave blacks that they owe it." Then, after mildly disapproving certain of Toussaint's acts, and hinting at the fatal consequences of disobedience, the letter continued: "Assist the Captain-General [Leclerc] with your counsels, your influence, and your talents. What can you desire?—the liberty of the blacks? You know that in all the countries where we have been, we have given it to the peoples who had it not." In order to quiet all alarms of the negroes on the subject of their freedom, a pledge still more absolute was given in what Americans might call the Annual Message sent to the French Legislature a week afterward. "At St. Domingo and at Guadeloupe there are no more slaves. All is free there; all will there remain free."[19]

A few days afterward Leclerc's expedition sailed; and the immense fleet, with an army of ten thousand men and all their equipments, arrived in sight of St. Domingo at the close of January, 1802. Toussaint was believed to have watched them from a look-out in the mountains while they lay for a day making their preparations for combined action. Then Leclerc sailed for Cap Français, where Christophe commanded. After a vain attempt to obtain possession of the town as a friend, he was obliged to attack. February 5 Christophe set the place in flames, and the war of races broke out.

The story of this war, interesting though it was, cannot be told here. Toussaint's resistance broke the force of Bonaparte's attack. Although it lasted less than three months, it swept away one French army, and ruined the industry of

[18] Ibid., vii. 322; Bonaparte to Toussaint, 27 Brumaire, An x. (Nov. 18, 1801).

[19] Ibid., 327; Exposé de la situation de la République, 1 Frimaire, An x. (Nov. 22, 1801).

the colony to an extent that required years of repair. Had
Toussaint not been betrayed by his own generals, and had
he been less attached than he was to civilization and
despotic theories of military rule, he would have achieved
a personal triumph greater than was won by any other man
of his time. His own choice was to accept the war of races,
to avoid open battle where his troops were unequal to their
opponents, and to harass instead of fighting in line. He
would have made a war of guerillas, stirred up the terror
and fanaticism of the negro laborers, put arms into their
hands, and relied on their courage rather than on that of
his army. He let himself be overruled. "Old Toussaint," said
Christophe afterward, "never ceased saying this, but no one
would believe him. We had arms; pride in using them destroyed us."[20] Christophe, for good reasons, told but half
the story. Toussaint was not ruined by a few lost battles, but
by the treachery of Christophe himself and of the other
negro generals. Jealous of Toussaint's domination, and perhaps afraid of being sent to execution like Moyse—the best
general officer in their service—for want of loyalty to his
chief, Christophe, after one campaign, April 26, 1802, surrendered his posts and forces to Leclerc without the knowledge and against the orders of Toussaint. Then Louverture
himself committed the fatal mistake of his life, which he of
all men seemed least likely to commit,—he trusted the word
of Bonaparte. May 1, 1802, he put himself in Leclerc's
hands in reliance on Leclerc's honor.

Surprising as such weakness was in one who had the sen-
sitiveness of a wild animal to danger,—Leclerc himself
seemed to be as much surprised that the word of honor of
a French soldier should be believed as any bystander at
seeing the negro believe it,—the act had a parallel in the
weakness which led Bonaparte, twelve years afterward, to
mount the deck of the "Bellerophon," and without even the
guaranty of a pledge surrender himself to England. The
same vacillations and fears, the same instinct of the desperate political gambler, the same cowering in the face of
fate, closed the active lives of both these extraordinary men.

[20] *Pamphile de Lacroix, Mémoires,* ii. 228.

Such beings should have known how to die when their lives were ended. Toussaint should have fought on, even though only to perish under the last cactus on his mountains, rather than trust himself in the hands of Bonaparte.

The First Consul's orders to Leclerc were positive, precise, and repeated.[21] "Follow exactly your instructions," said he, "and the moment you have rid yourself of Toussaint, Christophe, Dessalines, and the principal brigands, and the masses of the blacks shall be disarmed, send over to the continent all the blacks and mulattoes who have played a *rôle* in the civil troubles. . . . Rid us of these gilded Africans, and we shall have nothing more to wish."[22] With the connivance and at the recommendation of Christophe, by a stratagem such as Bonaparte used afterward in the case of the Duc d'Enghien and of Don Carlos IV., Toussaint was suddenly arrested, June 10, 1802, and hurried on ship-board. Some weeks later he was landed at Brest; then he disappeared. Except a few men who were in the secret, no one ever again saw him. Plunged into a damp dungeon in the fortress of Joux, high in the Jura Mountains on the Swiss frontier, the cold and solitude of a single winter closed this tropical existence. April 7, 1803, he died forgotten, and his work died with him. Not by Toussaint, and still less by Christophe or Dessalines, was the liberty of the blacks finally established in Hayti, and the entrance of the Mississippi barred to Bonaparte.

The news of Leclerc's success reached Paris early in June,[23] and set Bonaparte again in motion. Imagining that the blacks were at his mercy, orders were at once issued to provide for restoring them to slavery. The truth relating to this part of the subject, habitually falsified or concealed by Bonaparte and his admirers,[24] remained hidden among the manuscript records of the Empire; but the order to restore slavery at Guadeloupe was given, June 14, by the

[21] *Correspondance*, vii. 413; Bonaparte to Leclerc, 25 Ventôse, An x. (March 16, 1802).

[22] Ibid., 503, 504; Bonaparte to Leclerc, 12 Messidor, An x. (July 1, 1802).

[23] *Moniteur*, 24 Prairial, An x. (June 13, 1802).

[24] *Correspondance*, xxx. 535; Notes sur St. Domingue.

Minister of the Marine to General Richepanse, who commanded there, and on the same day a similar instruction was sent to General Leclerc at St. Domingo, in each case leaving the general to act according to his discretion in the time and manner of proceeding.

"As regards the return of the blacks to the old *régime*," wrote the Minister to General Leclerc,[25] "the bloody struggle out of which you have just come victorious with glory commands us to use the utmost caution. Perhaps we should only entangle ourselves in it anew if we wished precipitately to break that idol of liberty in whose name so much blood has flowed till now. For some time yet vigilance, order, a discipline at once rural and military, must take the place of the positive and pronounced slavery of the colored people of your colony. Especially the master's good usage must reattach them to his rule. When they shall have felt by comparison the difference between a usurping and tyrannical yoke and that of the legitimate proprietor interested in their preservation, then the moment will have arrived for making them return to their original condition, from which it has been so disastrous to have drawn them."

[25] *Decrès to Leclerc,* 25 Prairial, An x. (June 14, 1802); Archives de la Marine, MSS. Cf. *Revue Historique,* "Napoléon Premier et Saint Domingue," Janvier-Février, 1884.

Harrison and Tecumthe[1]

Although no one doubted that the year 1812 was to witness a new convulsion of society, if signs of panic occurred they were less marked in crowded countries where vast interests were at stake, than in remote regions which might have been thought as safe from Napoleon's wars as from those of Genghis Khan. As in the year 1754 a petty fight between two French and English scouting parties on the banks of the Youghiogheny River, far in the American wilderness, began a war that changed the balance of the world, so in 1811 an encounter in the Indian country, on the banks of the Wabash, began a fresh convulsion which ended only with the fall of Napoleon. The battle of Tippecanoe was a premature outbreak of the great wars of 1812.

Governor William Henry Harrison, of the Indiana Territory, often said he could tell by the conduct of his Indians, as by a thermometer, the chances of war and peace for the United States as estimated in the Cabinet at London. The remark was curious, but not surprising. Uneasiness would naturally be greatest where least control and most irritation existed. Such a region was the Northwestern Territory. Even the spot where violence would break out might be predicted as somewhere on the waterline of the Maumee and the Wabash, between Detroit at one extremity and Vincennes at the other. If a guess had been ventured that the most probable point would be found on that line, about half way between Lake Erie and the Ohio River, the map would have shown that Tippecanoe Creek, where it flowed into the Wabash, corresponded with the rough suggestion.

[1] Chapter IV of Volume 6 of the *History*.

The Indiana Territory was created in 1800; and the former delegate of the whole Northwestern Territory, William Henry Harrison, was then appointed governor of the new division. Until the year 1809, Illinois formed part of the Indiana Territory; but its single settlement at Kaskaskia was remote. The Indiana settlement consisted mainly of two tracts,—one on the Ohio, opposite Louisville in Kentucky, at the falls, consisting of about one hundred and fifty thousand acres, called Clark's Grant; the other, at Vincennes on the Wabash, where the French had held a post, without a definite grant of lands, under an old Indian treaty, and where the Americans took whatever rights the French enjoyed. One hundred miles of wilderness separated these two tracts. In 1800, their population numbered about twenty-five hundred persons; in 1810, nearly twenty-five thousand.

Northward and westward, from the bounds of these districts the Indian country stretched to the Lakes and the Mississippi, unbroken except by military posts at Fort Wayne and Fort Dearborn, or Chicago, and a considerable settlement of white people in the neighborhood of the fortress at Detroit. Some five thousand Indian warriors held this vast region, and were abundantly able to expel every white man from Indiana if their organization had been as strong as their numbers. The whites were equally eager to expel the Indians, and showed the wish openly.

Governor Harrison was the highest authority on matters connected with the northwestern Indians. During eight years of Harrison's government Jefferson guided the Indian policy; and as long as Jefferson insisted on the philanthropic principles which were his pride, Harrison, whose genius lay in ready adaptation, took his tone from the President, and wrote in a different spirit from that which he would have taken had he represented an aggressive chief. His account of Indian affairs offered an illustration of the law accepted by all historians in theory, but adopted by none in practice; which former ages called "fate," and metaphysicians called "necessity," but which modern science has refined into the "survival of the fittest." No acid ever worked more mechanically on a vegetable fibre than the white man acted on the Indian. As the line of American settlements approached, the nearest Indian tribes withered away.

Harrison reported conscientiously the incurable evils which attended the contact of the two hostile forms of society. The first, but not the most serious, was that the white man, though not allowed to settle beyond the Indian border, could not be prevented from trespassing far and wide on Indian territory in search of game. The practice of hunting on Indian lands, in violation of law and existing treaties, had grown into a monstrous abuse. The Kentucky settlers crossed the Ohio River every autumn to kill deer, bear, and buffalo for their skins, which they had no more right to take than they had to cross the Alleghanies, and shoot or trap the cows and sheep in the farm-yards of Bucks County. Many parts of the Northwestern Territory which as late as 1795 abounded in game, ten years afterward contained not game enough to support the small Indian parties passing through them, and had become worthless for Indian purposes except as a barrier to further encroachment.[2]

The tribes that owned these lands were forced either to remove elsewhere, or to sell their old hunting-grounds to the government for supplies or for an annuity. The tribes that sold, remaining near the settlements to enjoy their annuity, were more to be pitied than those that removed, which were destined to destruction by war. Harrison reported that contact with white settlements never failed to ruin them. "I can tell at once," he wrote in 1801,[3] "upon looking at an Indian whom I may chance to meet, whether he belongs to a neighboring or to a more distant tribe. The latter is generally well-clothed, healthy, and vigorous; the former half-naked, filthy, and enfeebled by intoxication, and many of them without arms excepting a knife, which they carry for the most villanous purposes." Harrison estimated the number of Indian warriors then in the whole valley of the Wabash as not exceeding six hundred; the sale of whiskey was unlawful, yet they were supposed to consume six thousand gallons of whiskey a year, and their

[2] Dawson's *Harrison*, p. 8.
[3] Ibid., p. 11.

drunkenness so often ended in murder that among three of the tribes scarcely a chief survived.

"I have had much difficulty," wrote Harrison in the same letter from Vincennes, "with the small tribes in this immediate neighborhood; namely the Piankeshaws, the Weas, and the Eel River Miamis. These three tribes form a body of the most depraved wretches on earth. They are daily in this town in considerable numbers, and are frequently intoxicated to the number of thirty or forty at once, when they commit the greatest disorders, drawing their knives and stabbing every one they meet with; breaking open the houses of the citizens, killing their cattle and hogs, and breaking down their fences. But in all their frolics they generally suffer the most themselves. They kill each other without mercy. Some years ago as many as four were found dead in a morning; and although those murders were actually committed in the streets of the town, yet no attempt to punish them has ever been made."

The Piankeshaws were reduced to twenty-five or thirty warriors; the Weas and Eel River Indians were mere remnants. The more powerful tribes at a distance saw with growing alarm the steady destruction of the border warriors; and the intelligent Indians everywhere forbade the introduction of whiskey, and tried to create a central authority to control the degraded tribes.

A third evil was much noticed by Harrison. By treaty, if an Indian killed a white man the tribe was bound to surrender the murderer for trial by American law; while if a white man killed an Indian, the murderer was also to be tried by a white jury. The Indians surrendered their murderers, and white juries at Vincennes hung them without scruple; but no jury in the territory ever convicted a white man of murdering an Indian. Harrison complained to the President of the wanton and atrocious murders committed by white men on Indians, and the impossibility of punishing them in a society where witnesses would not appear, criminals broke jail, and juries refused to convict. Throughout the territory the people avowed the opinion that a white man ought not in justice to suffer for killing an Indian;[4] and many of them, like the uncle of Abraham Lincoln,[5] thought it a virtuous act to shoot an Indian at sight. Harrison could combat this code of popular law only by proclamations offering rewards for the arrest of murderers, who were never punished when arrested. In 1801 the Delawares alone complained of six unatoned murders committed on their tribe since the Treaty of Greenville, and every year increased the score.

> "All these injuries," reported Harrison in 1801, "the Indians have hitherto borne with astonishing patience; but though they discover no disposition to make war on the United States at present, I am confident that most of the tribes would eagerly seize any favorable opportunity for that purpose; and should the United States be at war with any of the European nations who are known to the Indians, there would probably be a combination of more than nine tenths of the Northern tribes against us, unless some means are used to conciliate them."

So warmly were the French remembered by the Indians, that if Napoleon had carried out his Louisiana scheme of 1802 he could have counted on the active support of nearly every Indian tribe on the Mississippi and the Lakes; from Pensacola to Detroit his orders would have been obeyed. Toward England the Indians felt no such sentimental attachment; but interest took the place of sentiment. Their natural line of trade was with the Lakes, and their relations with the British trading-post at Malden, opposite Detroit, became more and more close with every new quarrel between Washington and London.

President Jefferson earnestly urged the Indians to become industrious cultivators of the soil; but even for that reform one condition was indispensable. The Indians must be protected from contact with the whites; and during the change in their mode of life, they must not be drugged, murdered, or defrauded. Trespasses on Indian land and purchases of tribal territory must for a time cease, until the

[4] Ibid., pp. 7, 31, 32.
[5] *Life of Lincoln*, by Hay and Nicolay, chap. i.

[156]

Indian tribes should all be induced to adopt a new system. Even then the reform would be difficult, for Indian warriors thought death less irksome than daily labor; and men who did not fear death were not easily driven to toil.

There President Jefferson's philanthropy stopped. His greed for land equalled that of any settler on the border, and his humanity to the Indian suffered the suspicion of having among its motives the purpose of gaining the Indian lands for the whites. Jefferson's policy in practice offered a reward for Indian extinction, since he not only claimed the territory of every extinct tribe on the doctrine of paramount sovereignty, but deliberately ordered[6] his Indian agents to tempt the tribal chiefs into debt in order to oblige them to sell the tribal lands, which did not belong to them, but to their tribes:—

> "To promote this disposition to exchange lands which they have to spare and we want, for necessaries which we have to spare and they want, we shall push our trading-houses, and be glad to see the good and influential individuals among them in debt; because we observe that when these debts get beyond what the individuals can pay, they become willing to lop them off by a cession of lands."

No one would have felt more astonishment than Jefferson had some friend told him that this policy, which he believed to be virtuous, was a conspiracy to induce trustees to betray their trusts; and that in morals it was as improper as though it were not virtuously intended. Shocked as he would have been at such a method of obtaining the neighboring estate of any Virginia family, he not only suggested but vigorously carried out the system toward the Indians.

In 1804 and 1805, Governor Harrison made treaties with the Miamis, Eel Rivers, Weas, Piankeshaws, and Delawares,—chiefly the tribes he called "a body of the most depraved wretches upon earth,"—by which he obtained the strip of country, fifty miles wide, between the Ohio and the White rivers, thus carrying the boundary back toward the Wabash. The treaty excited deep feeling among the

[6] Jefferson to Harrison, Feb. 27, 1803; Works, iv. 471.

better Indians throughout the territory, who held long debates on their means of preventing its execution.

Among the settlers in Indiana, an internal dispute mingled with the dangers of Indian relations. For this misfortune Harrison himself was partially to blame. A Virginian by birth, naturally inclined toward Southern influences, he shared the feelings of the Kentucky and Virginia slave-owners who wanted the right of bringing their slaves with them into the Territory, contrary to the Ordinance of 1787. The men who stood nearest the governor were earnest and active in the effort to repeal or evade the prohibition of slavery, and they received from Harrison all the support he could give them. With his approval, successive appeals were made to Congress. Perhaps the weightiest act of John Randolph's career as leader of the Republican majority in the House was to report, March 2, 1803, that the extension of slavery into Indiana was "highly dangerous and inexpedient," and that the people of Indiana "would at no distant day find ample remuneration for a temporary privation of labor and immigration" in the beneficence of a free society. Cæsar Rodney, of Delaware, in March, 1804, made a report to a contrary effect, recommending a suspension for ten years of the anti-slavery clause in the Ordinance; but the House did not act upon it.

The advocates of a slave system, with Harrison's co-operation, then decided that the Territory should pass into the second grade, which under the Ordinance of 1787 could be done when the population should number five thousand male whites of full age. The change was effected in the winter of 1804–1805, by means open to grave objection.[7] Thenceforward Harrison shared his power with a Legislative Council and a House of Representatives; while the legislature chose a territorial delegate to Congress. The first territorial legislature, in 1805, which was wholly under Harrison's influence, passed an Act, subsequently revised and approved Sept. 17, 1807, permitting owners of slaves to bring them into the Territory and keep them there for a number of days, during which time the slave might be

---

[7] Dunn's *Indiana* (American Commonwealths), p. 324.

emancipated on condition of binding himself to service for a term of years to which the law set no limit.[8]

The overpowering influence and energy of the governor and his Southern friends gave them during these years undisputed control. Yet the anti-slavery sentiment was so strong as to make the governor uncomfortable, and almost to endanger his personal safety; until at last, in 1808, the issue was fairly brought before the people in the elections. Both in that and in the following year the opponents of slavery outvoted and defeated the governor's party. Feelings became exceedingly bitter, and the Territory was distracted by feuds which had no small influence on matters of administration, and on the Indian troubles most of all. Between the difficulties of introducing negroes and expelling Indians, Harrison found that his popularity had been lessened, if not lost.[9] He could not fail to see that a military exploit was perhaps his only hope of recovering it; and for such an exploit he had excuses enough.

The treaties of 1804–1805, which threatened the Indians with immediate loss of their hunting-grounds in the Wabash valley, caused a fermentation peculiarly alarming because altogether new. Early in 1806 Harrison learned that a Shawanee Indian, claiming to be a prophet, had gathered a number of warriors about him at Greenville, in Ohio, and was preaching doctrines that threatened trouble. Harrison attributed the mischief to the Prophet; but he learned in time that the Prophet's brother Tecumseh—or more properly Tecumthe—gave the movement its chief strength.

Indians and whites soon recognized Tecumthe as a phenomenon. His father was a Shawanee warrior, in no way distinguished; his mother, a Creek or Cherokee Indian, captured and adopted by the Shawanee,—and of these parents three children at one birth were born about the year 1780, a few miles from Springfield, Ohio. The third brother lived and died obscure; Tecumthe and the Prophet became famous, although they were not chiefs of their tribe, and had

[8] Dillon's *History of Indiana,* App. G., p. 617.
[9] Dunn, p. 397.

no authority of office or birth. Such of the chiefs as were
in the pay or under the power of the United States government were jealous of their influence, and had every reason for wishing to suppress the leaders of a movement
avowedly designed to overthrow the system of tribal independence. From the first, Tecumthe aimed at limiting the
authority of the tribes and their chiefs in order to build
up an Indian confederacy, embracing not the chiefs but the
warriors of all the tribes, who should act as an Indian Congress and assume joint ownership of Indian lands.

This scheme was hostile to the plans though not to the
professions of President Jefferson. Its object was to prevent
the piecemeal sale of Indian lands by petty tribal chiefs,
under pressure of government agents. No one could hon-
estly deny that the object was lawful and even regular; for
in the Treaty of Greenville in 1795, which was the only
decisive authority or precedent, the United States had admitted and acted on the principle for which Tecumthe con-
tended,—of accepting its cessions of land, not from single
tribes, but from the whole body of northwestern Indians,
without entering on the subject of local ownership.[10] Governor Harrison and President Jefferson were of course aware
of the precedent, and decided to disregard it[11] in order to
act on the rule better suited to their purposes; but their
decision was in no way binding on Tecumthe or the tribes
who were parties to the Treaty of Greenville.

During the year 1807 Tecumthe's influence was increased by the "Chesapeake" excitement, which caused the
Governor-general of Canada to intrigue among the Indians
for aid in case of war. Probably their increase of influence
led the Prophet and his brother, in May or June, 1808, to
establish themselves on Tippecanoe Creek, the central point
of Indian strategy and politics. Vincennes lay one hundred
and fifty miles below, barely four-and-twenty hours down
the stream of the Wabash; Fort Dearborn, or Chicago, was
a hundred miles to the northwest; Fort Wayne the same
distance to the northeast; and excepting a short portage,

[10] Treaty of Greenville; State Papers, Indian Affairs, p. 562.
[11] Harrison to the Secretary of War, March 22, 1814; Drake's
Tecumseh, p. 161.

the Tippecanoe Indians could paddle their canoes to Malden and Detroit in one direction, or to any part of the waters of the Ohio and Mississippi in the other. At the mouth of Tippecanoe Creek the reformers laid out a village that realized Jefferson's wish, for the Indians there drank no whiskey, and avowed themselves to be tillers of the soil. Their professions seemed honest. In August, 1808, the Prophet came to Vincennes and passed two weeks with Governor Harrison, who was surprised to find that no temptation could overcome the temperance of the Prophet's followers. The speech then made in the public talk with the governor remains the only record of the Prophet's words, and of the character he wished to pretend, if not to adopt.

"I told all the redskins," he said to Harrison, "that the way they were in was not good, and that they ought to abandon it; that we ought to consider ourselves as one man, but we ought to live agreeable to our several customs,—the red people after their mode, and the white people after theirs; particularly that they should not drink whiskey; that it was not made for them, but the white people, who alone know how to use it; and that it is the cause of all the mischiefs which the Indians suffer. . . . Determine to listen to nothing that is bad; do not take up the tomahawk, should it be offered by the British or by the Long-knives; do not meddle with anything that does not belong to you, but mind your own business, and cultivate the ground, that your women and your children may have enough to live on. I now inform you that it is our intention to live in peace with our father and his children forever."

Whatever want of confidence Harrison felt in these professions of peace, he recorded his great surprise at finding the temperance to be real; and every one who visited the settlement at Tippecanoe bore witness to the tillage, which seemed to guarantee a peaceful intent; for if war had been in Tecumthe's mind, he would not have placed town, crops, and stock within easy reach of destruction.

Nothing could be more embarrassing to Jefferson than to see the Indians follow his advice; for however well-disposed he might be, he could not want the Indians to become civilized, educated, or competent to protect themselves,—yet he was powerless to protect them. The Prophet asked that the sale of liquor should be stopped; but the President could no more prevent white settlers from selling liquor to the Indians than he could prevent the Wabash from flowing. The tribes asked that white men who murdered Indians should be punished; but the President could no more execute such malefactors than he could execute the smugglers who defied his embargo. The Indians had rights recognized by law, by treaty, and by custom, on which their existence depended; but these rights required force to maintain them, and on the Wabash President Jefferson had less police power than the Prophet himself controlled.

Wide separation could alone protect the Indians from the whites, and Tecumthe's scheme depended for its only chance of success on holding the white settlements at a distance. The Prophet said nothing to Harrison on that point, but his silence covered no secret. So notorious was the Indian hostility to land-cessions, that when Governor Hull of Michigan Territory, in November, 1807, negotiated another such cession at Detroit,[12] the Indian agent at Fort Wayne not only doubted its policy, but insinuated that it might have been dictated by the British in order to irritate the Indians; and he reported that the Northern Indians talked of punishing with death the chiefs who signed it.[13]

Aware of the danger, Harrison decided to challenge it. The people of his Territory wanted the lands of the Wabash, even at the risk of war. The settlement at Tippecanoe was supposed to contain no more than eighty or a hundred warriors, with four or five times that number within a radius of fifty miles. No immediate outbreak was to be feared; and Harrison, "conceiving that a favorable opportunity then offered"[14] for carrying the boundary from the White River to the Wabash, asked authority to make a new purchase. Secretary Eustis, July 15, 1809, wrote

[12] Treaty of Nov. 7, 1807; State Papers, Indian Affairs, p. 747.
[13] Dawson's *Harrison*, p. 106.
[14] Ibid., p. 129.

him a cautious letter,[15] giving the required permission, but insisting that, "to prevent any future dissatisfaction, the chiefs of all the nations who had or pretended right to these lands" were to be present as consenting parties to the treaty. On this authority Harrison once more summoned together "the most depraved wretches upon earth,"—Miamis, Eel Rivers, Delawares, Pottawatomies, and Kickapoos,—and obtained from them, Sept. 30, 1809, several enormous cessions of territory which cut into the heart of the Indian country for nearly a hundred miles up both banks of the Wabash valley. These transfers included about three million acres.

Harrison knew that this transaction would carry despair to the heart of every Indian in his Territory. The Wabash valley alone still contained game. Deprived of their last resource, these Indians must fall back to perish in the country of the Chippewas and Sioux, their enemies.[16] Already impoverished by the decrees of Napoleon, the Orders in Council, and the embargo, which combined to render their peltry valueless, so that they could scarcely buy the powder and shot to kill their game,[17] the Indians had thenceforward no choice but to depend on British assistance. Harrison's treaty immediately strengthened the influence of Tecumthe and the Prophet. The Wyandots, or Hurons, regarded by all the Indian tribes in the Territory as first in dignity and influence, joined Tecumthe's league, and united in a declaration that the late cessions were void, and would not be recognized by the tribes. The winter of 1809–1810 passed quietly; but toward May, 1810, alarming reports reached Vincennes of gatherings at the Prophet's town, and of violence to be expected. When the salt, which was part of the usual annuity, reached Tippecanoe, Tecumthe refused to accept it, and drove the boatmen away. He charged the American government with deceiving the Indians; and he insisted, as the foundation of future peace,

15 Eustis to Harrison, July 15, 1809. Indian Affairs, p. 761.

16 Harrison to the Secretary of War, March 22, 1814; Drake's *Tecumseh*, p. 162.

17 Dawson, p. 142.

that the cessions of 1809 should be annulled, and no future cession should be good unless made by all the tribes.

Harrison knew that his treaties of 1809 opened an aggressive policy, which must naturally end in an Indian war. Some of the best citizens in the Territory thought that the blame for the consequences ought not to rest on the Indians.[18] Since the election of Madison to the Presidency in November, 1808, war with England had been so imminent, and its effect on the Indians so marked, that Harrison could not help seeing the opportunity of a military career, and he had given much study to military matters.[19] His plans, if they accorded with his acts, included an Indian war, in which he should take the initiative. His treaties of 1809 left him no choice, for after making such a war inevitable, his only safety lay in crushing the Indians before the British could openly aid them. Unfortunately, neither Madison nor Eustis understood his purpose, or would have liked it. They approved his land-purchases, which no Administration and no citizen would have dared reject; but they were very unwilling to be drawn into an Indian war, however natural might be such a consequence of the purchases.

So it happened that as early as the summer of 1810 war was imminent in the Wabash and Maumee valleys, and perhaps only British influence delayed it. British interests imperatively required that Tecumthe's confederacy should be made strong, and should not be wrecked prematurely in an unequal war. From Malden, opposite Detroit, the British traders loaded the American Indians with gifts and weapons; urged Tecumthe to widen his confederacy, to unite all the tribes, but not to begin war till he received the signal from Canada. All this was duly reported at Washington.[20] On the other hand, Harrison sent for Tecumthe; and August 12, 1810, the Indian chief came for

[18] Harrison to Eustis, July 4, 1810; Dawson, p. 149. Harrison to Governor Scott, Dec. 13, 1811; Dawson, p. 244. Badollet's Letters to Gallatin; Gallatin MSS. Dillon's *Indiana*, p. 455.

[19] Harrison to Governor Scott of Kentucky, March 10, 1809; Dawson, p. 119.

[20] State Papers, Indian Affairs, p. 799.

a conference to Vincennes. Indians and whites, in considerable numbers, armed and alert, fearing treachery on both sides, witnessed the interview.

Tecumthe took, as his right, the position he felt himself to occupy as the most powerful American then living,—who, a warrior himself, with five thousand warriors behind him, held in one hand an alliance with Great Britain, in the other an alliance with the Indians of the southwest. Representatives of the Wyandots, Kickapoos, Pottawatomies, Ottawas, and Winnebagoes announced the adhesion of their tribes to the Shawanee Confederacy and the election of Tecumthe as their chief. In this character he avowed to Harrison, in the broadest and boldest language, the scope of his policy:[21]—

"Brother, since the peace was made in 1795 you have killed some of the Shawanee, Winnebagoes, Delawares, and Miamis, and you have taken our land from us; and I do not see how we can remain at peace with you if you continue to do so. . . . You try to force the red people to do some injury; it is you that are pushing them on to do mischief. You endeavor to make distinctions; you wish to prevent the Indians from doing as we wish them,—from uniting and considering their land as the common property of the whole. You take tribes aside and advise them not to come into this measure. . . . The reason, I tell you, is this: You want, by your distinctions of Indian tribes, in allotting to each a particular tract of land, to make them to war with each other. You never see an Indian come and endeavor to make the white people do so. You are continually driving the red people; and at last you will drive them into the great lake, where they cannot either stand or work.

"Since my residence at Tippecanoe we have endeavored to level all distinctions, to destroy village chiefs by whom all mischief is done: it is they who sell our lands to the Americans. Our object is to let all our affairs be transacted by warriors. This land that was sold, and the goods that were given for it, was only done by a few.

[21] War Department Archives, MSS.

The treaty was afterward brought here, and the Weas were induced to give their consent because of their small numbers. . . . In future we are prepared to punish those chiefs who may come forward to propose to sell their land. If you continue to purchase of them, it will produce war among the different tribes, and at last I do not know what will be the consequence to the white people."

Earnestly denying the intention of making war, Tecumthe still declared that any attempt on Harrison's part to enter into possession of the land lately ceded would be resisted by force. In the vehemence of discussion he used language in regard to the United States which caused great excitement, and broke up the meeting for that day; but he lost no time in correcting the mistake. After the conference closed, he had a private interview with Harrison, and repeated his official ultimatum. He should only with great reluctance make war on the United States, against whom he had no other complaint than their land-purchases; he was extremely anxious to be their friend, and if the governor would prevail upon the President to give up the lands lately purchased, and agree never to make another treaty without the consent of all the tribes, Tecumthe pledged himself to be a faithful ally to the United States, and to assist them in all their wars with the English; otherwise he would be obliged to enter into an English alliance.

Harrison told him that no such condition had the least chance of finding favor with the Government. "Well," rejoined Tecumthe, as though he had expected the answer, "as the great chief is to decide the matter, I hope the Great Spirit will put sense enough into his head to induce him to direct you to give up this land. It is true, he is so far off he will not be injured by the war; he may sit still in his town and drink his wine, while you and I will have to fight it out."

Therewith Tecumthe and Harrison parted, each to carry on his preparations for the conflict. The Secretary of War wrote to Harrison in November instructing him to defer the military occupation of the new purchase on the Wabash, but giving no orders as to the policy intended to be taken by the Government. Wanting peace, he threw on Harrison the responsibility for war.[22]

"It has indeed occurred to me," wrote the secretary, "that the surest means of securing good behavior from this conspicuous personage [Tecumthe] and his brother, would be to make them prisoners; but at this time more particularly, it is desirable that peace with all the Indian tribes should be preserved; and I am instructed by the President to express to your Excellency his expectation and confidence that in all your arrangements this may be considered (as I am confident it ever has been) a primary object with you."

[22] Dawson, pp. 173, 174.

Tippecanoe[1]

Notwithstanding the hostile spirit on both sides, the winter of 1810–1811 passed without serious disturbance on the Wabash, and the summer of 1811 arrived before Harrison thought proper to take the next step. Then, June 24, he sent to Tecumthe and the Prophet a letter, or speech, intended to force an issue.

"Brothers," he wrote,[2] "this is the third year that all the white people in this country have been alarmed at your proceedings. You threaten us with war; you invite all the tribes to the north and west of us to join against us. Brothers, your warriors who have lately been here deny this, but I have received the information from every direction. The tribes on the Mississippi have sent me word that you intended to murder me, and then to commence a war upon our people. I have also received the speech that you sent to the Pottawatomies and others to join you for that purpose; but if I had no other evidence of your hostility to us, your seizing the salt which I lately sent up the Wabash is sufficient."

Except the seizure of five barrels of salt intended for other Indians, in June, 1811, no overt act yet showed the intention to begin a war, and certainly no such immediate intention existed; but two white men were at that moment murdered in the Illinois Territory, a drunken Indian was murdered at Vincennes, and these acts of violence, together with the general sense of insecurity, caused the government officials to write from all quarters to the War Department

[1] Chapter V of Volume 6 of the *History*.
[2] Dawson's *Harrison,* p. 179.

that Tecumthe must be suppressed. Tecumthe himself seemed disposed to avoid cause for attack. July 4 he sent word that he would come to Vincennes; and to Harrison's alarm he appeared there, July 27, with two or three hundred warriors for an interview with the governor. The act proved courage, if not rashness. Harrison's instructions hinted advice to seize the two Indian leaders, if it could be done without producing a war, and Harrison had ample time to prepare his measures.

Tecumthe came and remained two days at Vincennes, explaining, with childlike candor, his plans and wishes. As soon as the council was over, he said, he should visit the Southern tribes to unite them with those of the North in a peaceful confederacy; and he hoped no attempt would be made to settle the disputed territory till his return in the spring. A great number of Indians were to come in the autumn to live at Tippecanoe; they must use the disputed region for hunting-ground. He wished everything to remain in its present situation till his return; he would then go and see the President and settle everything with him. The affairs of all the tribes in that quarter were in his own hands, and he would despatch messengers in every direction to prevent the Indians from doing further mischief.

Tecumthe seemed to think that his wish would prevent Harrison from further aggression for the time. A few days afterward he passed down the Wabash, with some twenty warriors, on his diplomatic errand to the Creeks; but before he was fairly out of sight, July 31, a number of citizens met at Vincennes, and adopted resolutions demanding that the settlement at Tippecanoe should be broken up. Immediate action, before Tecumthe should return, was urged by Harrison's party, and by many frightened settlers. Harrison's personal wish could not be doubted.

The Secretary of War had already ordered the Fourth Regiment of U. S. Infantry, under Colonel Boyd, with a company of riflemen,—making in the whole a force of five hundred regular troops,—to descend the Ohio from Pittsburgh as rapidly as possible, and place themselves under

Harrison's orders; but Eustis added instructions not easily followed or understood. July 17 he wrote to Harrison,[3]—

"In case circumstances shall occur which may render it necessary or expedient to attack the Prophet and his followers, the force should be such as to insure the most complete success. This force will consist of the militia and regular troops. . . . If the Prophet should commence or seriously threaten hostilities, he ought to be attacked."

Under these instructions, Harrison was warranted in doing what he pleased. Not even Tecumthe denied the seriousness of his hostile threats, and Harrison had every reason to begin the war at once, if war must be; but although Eustis spoke his own mind clearly, he failed to reckon upon the President, and this neglect was the cause of another letter to Harrison, written three days later:[4]—

"Since my letter of the 17th instant, I have been particularly instructed by the President to communicate to your Excellency his earnest desire that peace may, if possible, be preserved with the Indians, and that to this end every proper means may be adopted. . . . Circumstances conspire at this particular juncture to render it peculiarly desirable that hostilities of any kind or to any degree, not indispensably required, should be avoided. The force under Colonel Boyd has been ordered to descend the Ohio, . . . and although the force is at the disposal of your Excellency, I am instructed to inform you that the President indulges the hope and expectation that your exertions and measures with the Indians will be such as may render their march to the Indian Territory unnecessary, and that they may remain liable to another disposition."

Without paying attention to the President's wishes emphatically expressed in these orders of July 20, Harrison passed the next month in raising forces for an expedition to satisfy the wishes of the Western people. No doubt was

[3] Ibid., p. 190.
[4] Ibid., p. 191.

felt on the Ohio that Harrison meant to attack the Indians at Tippecanoe; and so serious a campaign was expected that Kentucky became eager to share it. Among other Kentuckians, Joseph H. Daveiss, Aaron Burr's persecutor, wrote,[5] August 24, to Harrison, offering himself as a volunteer: "Under all the privacy of a letter," said he, "I make free to tell you that I have imagined there were two men in the West who had military talents; and you, sir, were the first of the two. It is thus an opportunity of service much valued by me." Daveiss doubted only whether the army was to attack at once, or to provoke attack.

Harrison accepted Daveiss's services, and gave him command of the dragoons, a mounted force of about one hundred and thirty men from Indiana and Kentucky. The Fourth U. S. Infantry, three hundred strong according to Colonel Boyd who commanded it,[6] arrived in the Territory at the beginning of September. As rapidly as possible Harrison collected his forces, and sent them up the river to a point in the new purchase about sixty-five miles above Vincennes. The exact force was afterward much disputed.[7] Harrison reported his effectives as a few more than nine hundred men. Some sixty Kentucky volunteers were of the number.

The last instructions from the Department, dated August 29,[8] made no change in the tenor of the President's orders. When Harrison joined his army, October 6, at the camp above Vincennes, he wrote to Eustis,[9]—

"I sincerely wish that my instructions were such as to authorize me to march up immediately to the Prophet's town. The troops which I command are a fine body of men, and the proportion of regulars, irregulars, infantry, and dragoons such as I could wish it. I have no reason to doubt the issue of a contest with the savages, and I

[5] Ibid., p. 200.
[6] Boyd to Eustis, Dec. 10, 1811; MSS. War Department Records.
[7] Marshall's *Kentucky*, ii. 509.
[8] Dawson, p. 195. Cf. McAffee, p. 18.
[9] Harrison to Eustis, Oct. 6, 1811; MSS. War Department Archives.

am much deceived if the greater part of both officers and men are not desirous of coming in contact with them."

In doubt what to do next, Harrison waited while his army built a small wooden fort, to which he gave his own name, and which was intended to establish formal possession of the new purchase. While the army was engaged in this work, one of the sentinels was fired at and wounded in the night of October 10 by some person or persons unseen and unknown. Harrison regarded this as a beginning of hostilities by the Prophet, and decided to act as though war was declared. October 12 he received from Secretary Eustis a letter dated September 18, never published though often referred to,[10] which is not found in the records of the government. Harrison replied the next day:[11]—

"Your letter of the 18th ult. I had the honor to receive yesterday. My views have hitherto been limited to the erection of the fort which we are now building, and to a march, by way of feint, in the direction of the Prophet's town, as high, perhaps, as the Vermilion River. But the powers given me in your last letter, and circumstances which have occurred here at the very moment on which it was received, call for measures of a more energetic kind."

With this despatch Harrison enclosed a return of the soldiers present under his command. "You will observe," he said, "that our effectives are but little over nine hundred." The rank-and-file consisted of seven hundred and forty-two men fit for duty. Harrison thought this force too small, and sent back to Vincennes for four companies of mounted riflemen. Two of the four companies joined him,[12] but their strength was not reported. These returns showed that the army, with the two additional companies, numbered at

[10] Dawson, p. 253.
[11] Harrison to Eustis, Oct. 13, 1811; MSS. War Department Archives.
[12] Harrison to Eustis, Nov. 2, 1811; MSS. War Department Archives.

least one thousand effectives. One of the officers of the Fourth U. S. Infantry, writing November 21, said that the force was a little upward of eleven hundred men.[13]

While the Americans were determined not to return without a battle, the Indians had been strictly ordered by Tecumthe to keep the peace, and showed the intention to avoid Harrison's attack. As early as September 25, the Prophet sent a number of Indians to Vincennes to protest his peaceful intentions, and to promise that Harrison's demands should be complied with.[14] Harrison returned no answer and sent no demands. October 28 he broke up his camp at Fort Harrison, and the army began its march up the river. The governor remained one day longer at the fort, and from there, October 29, sent some friendly Indians to the Prophet with a message requiring that the Winnebagoes, Pottawatomies, and Kickapoos, at Tippecanoe, should return to their tribes; that all stolen horses should be given up, and that murderers should be surrendered. He intended at a later time to add a demand for hostages,[15] in case the Prophet should accede to these preliminary terms.

Harrison did not inform the friendly Indians where they would find him, or where they were to bring their answer.[16] Crossing to the west bank of the Wabash to avoid the woods, the troops marched over a level prairie to the mouth of the Vermilion River, where they erected a blockhouse to protect their boats. The Vermilion River was the extreme boundary of the recent land-cession; and to cross it, under such circumstances, was war. Harrison looked for resistance; but not an Indian was seen, and November 3 the army resumed its march, keeping in the open country, until on the evening of November 5 it arrived, still unmolested, within eleven miles of the Prophet's town. From the Vermilion River to Tippecanoe was fifty miles.

The next morning, November 6, the army advanced to-

[13] Letter in New England Palladium, Dec. 24, 1811.
[14] Dawson, p. 196.
[15] Ibid., p. 196.
[16] Speech of Captain Charley, July 10, 1814; State Papers, Indian Affairs, i. 830.

ward the town, and as the column approached, Indians were frequently seen in front and on the flanks. Interpreters tried to parley with them, but they returned no answer except insulting or threatening gestures. Two miles from the town the army unexpectedly entered a difficult country, thick with wood and cut by deep ravines, where Harrison was greatly alarmed, seeing himself at the mercy of an attack; but no attack was made. When clear of the woods, within a mile and a half of the town, he halted his troops and declared his intention to encamp. Daveiss and all the other officers urged him to attack the town at once; but he replied that his instructions would not justify his attacking the Indians unless they refused his demands, and he still hoped to hear something in the course of the evening from the friendly Indians sent from Fort Harrison. Daveiss remonstrated, and every officer in the army supported him. Harrison then pleaded the danger of further advance. "The experience of the last two days," he said,[17] "ought to convince every officer that no reliance ought to be placed upon the guides as to the topography of the country; that, relying on their information, the troops had been led into a situation so unfavorable that but for the celerity with which they changed their position a few Indians might have destroyed them; he was therefore determined not to advance to the town until he had previously reconnoitred."

The candor of this admission did not prove the military advantages of the halt; and neither of Harrison's reasons was strengthened by a third, which he gave a month afterward in a letter to the Governor of Kentucky. "The success of an attack upon the town by day," he said,[18] "was very problematical. I expected that they would have met me the next day to hear my terms; but I did not believe that they would accede to them, and it was my determination to attack and burn the town the following night." Daveiss and the other officers, looking at the matter only as soldiers, became more urgent, until Harrison at last yielded, and resolving no longer to hesitate in treating the Indians as en-

[17] Dawson, p. 206.
[18] Harrison to Governor Scott, Dec. 13, 1811; Dawson, p. 244.

emies,[19] ordered an advance, with the determination to attack. "I yielded to what appeared the general wish," he said in his official report,[20] "and directed the troops to advance." They advanced about four hundred yards, when three Indians sent by the Prophet came to meet them, bringing a pacific message, and urging that hostilities should if possible be avoided. Harrison's conscience, already heavy-ladened, again gave way at this entreaty.[21] "I answered that I had no intention of attacking them until I discovered that they would not comply with the demands that I had made; that I would go on and encamp at the Wabash, and in the morning would have an interview with the Prophet and his chiefs, and explain to them the determination of the President; that in the mean time no hostilities should be committed."

Had Harrison's vacillation been due to consciousness of strength, his officers would have had no just reason for remonstrance; but he estimated his force at about eight hundred effective men, and the Indians at more than six hundred.[22] He knew that no victory over the Northern Indians had ever been won where the numbers were anything like equal.[23] Before him was an unknown wilderness; behind him was a line of retreat, one hundred and fifty miles long, and he had supplies for very few days. He could not trust the Indians; and certainly they could not trust him, for he meant in any case to surprise their town the next night. Delay was dangerous only to the whites,—advantageous only to the Indians. Daveiss felt so strongly the governor's hesitation that he made no secret of his discontent, and said openly not only that the army ought to attack,[24] but also that it would be attacked before morning, or would march home with nothing accomplished.[25] Indeed, if Harrison

[19] McAffee, p. 25. Dawson, p. 206.
[20] Harrison to Eustis, Nov. 18, 1811; State Papers, Indian Affairs, p. 776.
[21] Ibid.
[22] Dawson, p. 216.
[23] Ibid., pp. 216, 250.
[24] Ibid., p. 211.
[25] McAffee, p. 28.

had not come there to destroy the town, he had no sufficient military reason for being there at all.

Having decided to wait, Harrison had next to choose a
camping-ground. The army marched on, looking for some
spot on the river where wood as well as water could be
obtained, until they came within one hundred and fifty
yards of the town, when the Indians, becoming alarmed,
called on them to stop. Harrison halted his men and asked
the Indians to show him a place suitable for his purpose,
which they did;[26] and the troops filed off in front of the
town, at right angles to the Wabash, till they reached a
creek less than a mile to the northwest. Next to the town
was a marshy prairie; beyond the marsh the ground rose
about ten feet to a level covered with oaks; and then about
a hundred yards farther it suddenly dropped to the creek
behind, where the banks were thick with willow and brush-
wood. No spot in the neighborhood was better suited for
a camp than this saddle-back between the marsh and the
brook, but Harrison saw that it offered serious disadvantages. "I found the ground destined for the encampment,"
he reported, "not altogether such as I could wish it. It was,
indeed, admirably calculated for regular troops that were
opposed to regulars, but it afforded great facility to the
approach of the savages."

There Harrison camped. The troops were stationed in a
sort of triangle, following the shape of the high land,[27]—
the base toward the northeast, the blunt apex toward the
southwest; but at no part of the line was any attempt made
to intrench, or palisade, or in any way to cover the troops.
Harrison afterward explained that he had barely axes
enough to procure firewood. The want of axes had been
discovered at Fort Harrison, and hardly excused the neglect to intrench at Tippecanoe, for it had not prevented
building the fort. The army pitched its tents and lighted
its fires for the night, with no other protection than a single
line of sentries, although the creek in the rear gave cover to
an attack within a few yards of the camp.

[26] Harrison to Eustis, Nov. 18, 1811; State Papers, Indian
Affairs, p. 776.
[27] See Plan of Camp. Lossing, p. 205.

The night was dark, with light rain at intervals; the troops slept on their arms, and their rest was disturbed by no sound. Many accounts have been given of what passed in the Prophet's town,[28] but none of them deserve attention. During the night neither Harrison nor his sentinels heard or saw anything that roused their suspicions. Harrison, in a brief report of the next day,[29] said that the first alarm was given at half-past four o'clock in the morning. His full report of November 18 corrected the time to a few minutes before four. Still another account, on the day after the battle, named five o'clock as the moment.[30] Harrison himself was about to leave his tent, before calling the men to parade, when a sentinel at the farthest angle of the camp above the creek fired a shot. In an instant the Indian yell was raised, and before the soldiers at that end of the camp could leave their tents, the Indians had pierced the line, and were shooting the men by the light of the camp-fires. Within a few moments, firing began along the whole line, until the camp, except for a space next the creek, was encircled by it. Fortunately for Harrison, the attacking party at the broken angle had not strength to follow up its advantage, and the American line was soon re-formed in the rear. Harrison rode to the point, and at the northeast angle met Daveiss and his dismounted dragoons. Daveiss reported that the Indians, under cover of the trees, were annoying the troops severely, and asked leave to dislodge them. The order was given; and Daveiss, followed by only a few men, rushed forward among the trees, where he soon fell, mortally wounded. The troops, after forming, held their position without further disaster till daybreak, when they advanced and drove the Indians into the swamp. With this success the battle ended, having lasted two hours.

For the moment the army was saved, but only at great cost. Daveiss, who held an anomalous position almost as prominent as that of Harrison himself, died in the after-

[28] Ibid., p. 203.

[29] Harrison to Eustis, Nov. 8, 1811; National Intelligencer, Nov. 30, 1811. Niles, i. 255.

[30] William Taylor to ———, Nov. 8, 1811; National Intelligencer, Dec. 7, 1811.

noon. Captain Baen, acting major of the Fourth Regiment, two lieutenants, and an ensign of the same regiment, were killed or wounded; two lieutenant-colonels, four captains, and several lieutenants of the Indiana militia were on the same list, and the general's aid-de-camp was killed. One hundred and fifty-four privates were returned among the casualties, fifty-two of whom were killed or mortally wounded. The total loss was one hundred and eighty-eight, of whom sixty-one were killed or mortally wounded.[31] The bodies of thirty-eight Indians were found on the field.

If the army had cause for anxiety before the battle, it had double reason for alarm when it realized its position on November 7. If Harrison's own account was correct, he had with him only eight hundred men. Sixty-one had been killed or mortally wounded, and he had near a hundred and fifty wounded to carry with him in his retreat. His effective force was diminished more than one fourth, according to his biographer;[32] his camp contained very little flour and no meat, for the few beeves brought with the army were either driven away by the Indians or stampeded by the noise of the battle; and his only base of supplies was at Vincennes, one hundred and seventy miles away. The Indians could return in greater numbers, but his own force must steadily grow weaker. Harrison was naturally a cautious man; he felt strongly the dangers that surrounded him, and his army felt them not less.[33]

The number of Indian warriors engaged in the night attack was estimated by Harrison at six hundred.[34] The law of exaggeration, almost invariable in battle, warrants belief that not more than four hundred Indians were concerned in the attack. The Prophet's Indians were few. Tecumthe afterward spoke of the attack as an "unfortunate transaction that took place between the white people and a few of our young men at our village,"[35]—as though it was an affair in which the young warriors had engaged against the

[31] General Return; State Papers, Indian Affairs, i. 779.
[32] Dawson, p. 233.
[33] Ibid., p. 233. Lossing, p. 206, *note*.
[34] Report of Nov. 18, 1811; Niles, i. 304.
[35] Dawson, p. 267.

will of the older chiefs. Tecumthe commonly told the truth, even with indiscretion; and nothing in the American account contradicted his version of the affair at Tippecanoe. Harrison's ablest military manœuvre had been the availing himself of Tecumthe's over-confidence in quitting the country at so critical a moment.

Although Harrison did not venture to send out a scout for twenty-four hours, but remained in camp waiting attack, no further sign of hostilities was given. "Night," said one of the army,[36] "found every man mounting guard, without food, fire, or light, and in a drizzling rain. The Indian dogs, during the dark hours, produced frequent alarms by prowling in search of carrion about the sentinels." On the morning of November 8, the dragoons and mounted riflemen approached the town and found it deserted. Apparently the Indians had fled in haste, leaving everything, even a few new English guns and powder. The army took what supplies were needed, and set fire to the village. Meanwhile every preparation had been made for rapid retreat. The wagons could scarcely carry all the wounded, and Harrison abandoned the camp furniture and private baggage. "We managed, however, to bring off the public property," he reported. At noon of November 9 the train started, and by night-fall had passed the dangerous woods and broken country where a few enemies could have stopped it. No Indians appeared; the march was undisturbed; and after leaving a company of the U. S. Fourth Regiment at Fort Harrison, the rest of the force arrived, November 18, at Vincennes.

The battle of Tippecanoe at once became a point of pride throughout the Western country, and Harrison received the official applause and thanks of Kentucky, Indiana, and Illinois; but Harrison's account of his victory was not received without criticism, and the battle was fought again in the press and in private. The Fourth Regiment more than hinted that had it not been for their steadiness the whole party would have been massacred. At Vincennes, Harrison was severely attacked. In Kentucky criticism was

[36] Lossing, p. 206, *note*.

open, for the family and friends of Joseph Daveiss were old Federalists, who had no interest in the military triumphs of a Republican official. Humphrey Marshall, Daveiss's brother-in-law, published a sharp review of Harrison's report, and hinted plainly that Daveiss had fallen a victim to the General's blunders. With characteristic vigor of language, Marshall called Harrison "a little, selfish, intriguing busybody," and charged him with having made the war without just cause, for personal objects.[37] These attacks caused the Western Republicans to sustain with the more ardor their faith in Harrison's military genius, and their enthusiasm for the victory of Tippecanoe; but President Madison and Secretary Eustis guarded themselves with some care from expressing an opinion on the subject.

Whatever his critics might say, Harrison gained his object, and established himself in the West as the necessary leader of any future campaign. That result, as far as it was good, seemed to be the only advantage gained at Tippecanoe. Harrison believed that the battle had broken the Prophet's influence, and saved the frontier from further alarm; he thought that in the event of a British war, the Indians would remain neutral having "witnessed the inefficacy of British assistance;"[38] he expected the tribes to seek peace as a consequence of what he considered the severest defeat they had ever received since their acquaintance with the white people;[39] and the expectation was general that they would deliver the Prophet and Tecumthe into the hands of the American government. For a time these impressions seemed reasonable. The Prophet lost influence, and the peace was not further disturbed; but presently the Western people learned that the Prophet had returned to Tippecanoe, and that all things had resumed their old aspect, except that no one could foresee when the Indians would choose to retaliate for Harrison's invasion.

Toward January, Tecumthe returned from the South, and sent word that he was ready to go to Washington.

[37] Marshall's *Kentucky*, ii. 507, 521.
[38] Harrison to J. M. Scott, Dec. 2, 1811. Niles, i. 311.
[39] Harrison to Eustis, Dec. 4, 1811; State Papers, Indian Affairs, p. 779.

March 1, 1812, a deputation of some eighty Indians visited Vincennes, and told Harrison that the whole winter had been passed in sending messages to the different villages to consult on their future course, and that all agreed to ask for peace. They blamed the Prophet for the affair at Tippecanoe, and asked leave to visit Washington to obtain peace from the President. Harrison gladly assented, for a delegation of Indians sent to Washington was a guaranty of peace during the time of their absence. He expected them to appear at Fort Wayne in April, ready for the journey.

The Indian hesitation was probably due to doubt whether war would take place between the United States and England. The whole influence of the British agents was exerted to unite the Indians and to arm them, but to prevent a premature outbreak. The British Indian agent at Amherstburg sent Tecumthe a message blaming the attack on Harrison. Tecumthe replied:[40]—

> "You tell us to retreat or turn to one side should the Big Knives come against us. Had I been at home in the late unfortunate affair I should have done so; but those I left at home were (I cannot call them men) a poor set of people, and their scuffle with the Big Knives I compared to a struggle between little children who only scratch each other's faces. The Kickapoos, Winnebagoes have since been at Post Vincennes and settled the matter amicably."

The situation was well understood. "If we have a British war, we shall have an Indian war," wrote the commandant from Fort Wayne.[41] "From the best information I can get, I have every reason to believe we shall have an Indian war this spring, whether we have a British war or not." Harrison must himself have felt that the campaign to Tippecanoe could only add to his dangers unless it was followed up. After April 1, 1812, illusions vanished; for Indian hostilities began all along the border. April 6 two settlers were

[40] MSS. Canadian Archives. C. 676, p. 147.
[41] J. Rhea to Eustis, March 14, 1812; State Papers, Indian Affairs, p. 806.

murdered within three miles of Fort Dearborn, at Chicago; several murders were committed near Fort Madison, above St. Louis, on the Mississippi; but the warning which spread wild alarm throughout Indiana was the murder of a whole family early in April within five miles of Vincennes, and April 14 that of a settler within a few miles of the Ohio River. Another murder a few weeks afterward, on the White River, completed the work of terror.

Then a general panic seized the people. The militia dared not turn out; for while they collected at one spot, the Indians might attack their isolated cabins. Even Vincennes was thought to be in danger, and the stream of fugitives passed through it as rapidly as possible on their way southward, until depopulation threatened the Territory.[42] "Most of the citizens in this country," reported Harrison, May 6,[43] "have abandoned their farms, and taken refuge in such temporary forts as they have been able to construct. Nothing can exhibit more distress than those wretched people crowded together in places almost destitute of every necessary accommodation." Misled by the previous peaceful reports, the Government had sent the Fourth Regiment to Detroit; not even a company of militia could be procured nearer than the falls of the Ohio; and Harrison called for help in vain.

Fortunately, Tecumthe was not yet ready for war. Six weeks after the hostilities began he appeared at a grand council, May 16, at Massassinway on the Wabash, between Tippecanoe and Fort Wayne. His speech to the tribes assembled there was more temperate than ever.[44]

"Governor Harrison made war on my people in my absence," he said. "It was the will of God that he should do so. We hope it will please God that the white people may let us live in peace; we will not disturb them, neither have we done it, except when they came to our village with the intention of destroying us. We are happy to state to our brothers present that the unfortunate trans-

[42] Dawson, p. 263.
[43] State Papers, Indian Affairs, p. 808.
[44] Dawson, p. 266.

action that took place between the white people and a few of our young men of our village has been settled between us and Governor Harrison; and I will further state, had I been at home there would have been no bloodshed at that time."

He added that the recent murders had been committed by Pottawatomies not under his control, and he offered no excuse for them.

"Should the bad acts of our brothers the Pottawatomies draw on us the ill-will of our white brothers, and they should come again and make an unprovoked attack on us at our village, we will die like men; but we will never strike the first blow. . . . We defy a living creature to say we ever advised any one, directly or indirectly, to make war on our white brothers. It has constantly been our misfortune to have our views misrepresented to our white brethren. This has been done by pretended chiefs of the Pottawatomies and others that have been in the habit of selling land to the white people that did not belong to them."

This was the situation on the Wabash in May and June, 1812. Not only was Tecumthe unwilling to strike the first blow, but he would not even retaliate Harrison's invasion and seizure of the disputed territory. He waited for Congress to act, but every one knew that whenever Congress should declare war against England, war must also be waged with the Indians; and no one could doubt that after provoking the Indian war, Americans ought to be prepared to wage it with effect, and without complaint of its horrors.

Privateering[1]

The people of the Atlantic coast felt the loss of the "Chesapeake" none too keenly. Other nations had a history to support them in moments of mortification, or had learned by centuries of experience to accept turns of fortune as the fate of war. The American of the sea-coast was not only sensitive and anxious, but he also saw with singular clearness the bearing of every disaster, and did not see with equal distinctness the general drift of success. The loss of the "Chesapeake" was a terrible disaster, not merely because it announced the quick recovery of England's pride and power from a momentary shock, but also because it threatened to take away the single object of American enthusiasm which redeemed shortcomings elsewhere. After the loss of the "Chesapeake," no American frigate was allowed the opportunity to fight with an equal enemy. The British frigates, ordered to cruise in company, gave the Americans no chance to renew their triumphs of 1812.

Indeed, the experience of 1813 tended to show that the frigate was no longer the class of vessel best suited to American wants. Excessively expensive compared with their efficiency, the "Constitution," "President," and "United States" could only with difficulty obtain crews; and when after much delay they were ready for sea, they could not easily evade a blockading squadron. The original cost of a frigate varied from two hundred thousand dollars to three hundred thousand; that of a sloop-of-war, like the "Hornet," "Wasp," or "Argus," varied between forty and fifty thousand dollars. The frigate required a crew of about four hundred men; the sloop carried about one hundred and

[1] Chapter XIII of Volume 7 of the *History*.

fifty. The annual expense of a frigate in active service was about one hundred and thirty-four thousand dollars; that of the brig was sixty thousand. The frigate required much time and heavy timber in her construction; the sloop could be built quickly and of ordinary material. The loss of a frigate was a severe national disaster; the loss of a sloop was not a serious event.

For defensive purposes neither the frigate nor the brig counted heavily against a nation which employed ships-of-the-line by dozens; but even for offensive objects the frigate was hardly so useful as the sloop-of-war. The record of the frigates for 1813 showed no results equivalent to their cost. Their cruises were soon told. The "President," leaving Boston April 30, ran across to the Azores, thence to the North Sea, and during June and July haunted the shores of Norway, Scotland, and Ireland, returning to Newport September 27, having taken thirteen prizes. The "Congress," which left Boston with the "President," cruised nearly eight months in the Atlantic, and returned to Boston December 14, having captured but four merchantmen. The "Chesapeake," which sailed from Boston Dec. 13, 1812, cruised four months in the track of British commerce, past Madeira and Cape de Verde, across the equator, and round through the West Indies, returning to Boston April 9, having taken six prizes; at the beginning of her next cruise, June 1, the "Chesapeake" was herself captured. The adventures of the "Essex" in the Pacific were such as might have been equally well performed by a sloop-of-war, and belonged rather to the comparative freedom with which the frigates moved in 1812 than to the difficult situation that followed. No other frigates succeeded in getting to sea till December 4, when the "President" sailed again. The injury inflicted by the frigates on the Atlantic was therefore the capture of twenty-three merchantmen in a year. At the close of 1813, the "President" and the "Essex" were the only frigates at sea; the "Constitution" sailed from Boston only Jan. 1, 1814; the "United States" and "Macedonian" were blockaded at New London; the "Constellation" was still at Norfolk; the "Adams" was at Washington, and the "Congress" at Boston.

When this record was compared with that of the sloops-of-war, the frigates were seen to be luxuries. The sloop-of-war was a single-decked vessel, rigged sometimes as a ship, sometimes as a brig, but never as a sloop, measuring about one hundred and ten feet in length by thirty in breadth, and carrying usually eighteen thirty-two-pound carronades and two long twelve-pounders. Of this class the American navy possessed in 1812 only four examples,—the "Hornet," the "Wasp," the "Argus," and the "Syren." The "Wasp" was lost Oct. 18, 1812, after capturing the "Frolic." The "Syren" remained at New Orleans during the first year of the war, and then came to Boston, but saw no ocean service of importance during 1813. The "Hornet" made three prizes, including the sloop-of-war "Peacock," and was then blockaded with the "United States" and "Macedonian;" but the smaller vessel could do what the frigates could not, and in November the "Hornet" slipped out of New London and made her way to New York, where she waited an opportunity to escape to sea. The story will show her success. Finally, the "Argus" cruised for a month in the British Channel, and made twenty-one prizes before she was captured by the "Pelican."

The three frigates, "President," "Congress," and "Chesapeake," captured twenty-three prizes in the course of the year, and lost the "Chesapeake." The two sloops, the "Hornet" and "Argus," captured twenty-four prizes, including the sloop-of-war "Peacock," and lost the "Argus."

The government at the beginning of the war owned four smaller vessels,—the "Nautilus" and "Vixen" of fourteen guns, and the "Enterprise" and "Viper" of twelve. Another brig, the "Rattlesnake," sixteen, was bought. Experience seemed to prove that these were of little use. The "Nautilus" fell into the hands of Broke's squadron July 16, 1812, within a month after the declaration of war. The "Vixen" was captured Nov. 22, 1812, by Sir James Yeo. The "Viper," Jan. 17, 1813, became prize to Captain Lumley in the British frigate "Narcissus." The "Enterprise" distinguished itself by capturing the "Boxer," and was regarded as a lucky vessel, but was never a good or fast one.[2] The

[2] Lieutenant Creighton to Secretary Jones, March 9, 1814; Niles, vi. 69.

"Rattlesnake," though fast, was at last caught on a lee shore by the frigate "Leander," July 11, 1814, and carried into Halifax.[3]

In the enthusiasm over the frigates in 1812, Congress voted that six forty-fours should be built, besides four ships-of-the-line. The Act was approved Jan. 2, 1813. Not until March 3 did Congress pass an Act for building six new sloops-of-war. The loss of two months was not the only misfortune in this legislation. Had the sloops been begun in January, they might have gone to sea by the close of the year. The six sloops were all launched within eleven months from the passage of the bill, and the first of them, the "Frolic," got to sea within that time, while none of the frigates or line-of-battle ships could get to sea within two years of the passage of the law. A more remarkable oversight was the building of only six sloops, when an equal number of forty-fours and four seventy-fours were ordered. Had Congress voted twenty-four sloops, the proportion would not have been improper; but perhaps the best policy would have been to build fifty such sloops, and to prohibit privateering. The reasons for such a course were best seen in the experiences of the privateers.

The history of the privateers was never satisfactorily written. Neither their number, their measurements, their force, their captures, nor their losses were accurately known. Little ground could be given for an opinion in regard to their economy. Only with grave doubt could any judgment be reached even in regard to their relative efficiency compared with government vessels of the same class. Yet their experience was valuable, and their services were very great.

In the summer of 1812 any craft that could keep the sea in fine weather set out as a privateer to intercept vessels approaching the coast. The typical privateer of the first few months was the pilot-boat, armed with one or two long-nine or twelve-pound guns. Of twenty-six privateers sent from New York in the first four months of war, fifteen carried crews of eighty men or less. These small vessels es-

[3] Niles, vi. 391.

pecially infested the West Indies, where fine weather and light breezes suited their qualities. After the seas had been cleared of such prey as these petty marauders could manage, they were found to be unprofitable,—too small to fight and too light to escape. The typical privateer of 1813 was a larger vessel,—a brig or schooner of two or three hundred tons, armed with one long pivot-gun, and six or eight lighter guns in broadside; carrying crews which varied in number from one hundred and twenty to one hundred and sixty men; swift enough to escape under most circumstances even a frigate, and strong enough to capture any armed merchantman.

After the war was fairly begun, the British mercantile shipping always sailed either under convoy or as armed "running ships" that did not wait for the slow and comparatively rare opportunities of convoy, but trusted to their guns for defence. The new American privateer was adapted to meet both chances. Two or three such craft hanging about a convoy could commonly cut off some merchantman, no matter how careful the convoying man-of-war might be. By night they could run directly into the fleet and cut out vessels without even giving an alarm, and by day they could pick up any craft that lagged behind or happened to stray too far away. Yet the "running ships" were the chief objects of their search, for these were the richest prizes; and the capture of a single such vessel, if it reached an American port in safety, insured success to the cruise. The loss of these vessels caused peculiar annoyance to the British, for they sometimes carried considerable amounts of specie, and usually were charged with a mail which was always sunk and lost in case of capture.

As the war continued, experience taught the owners of privateers the same lesson that was taught to the government. The most efficient vessel of war corresponded in size with the "Hornet" or the new sloops-of-war building in 1813. Tonnage was so arbitrary a mode of measurement that little could be learned from the dimensions of five hundred tons commonly given for these vessels; but in a general way they might be regarded as about one hundred and fifteen or one hundred and twenty feet long on the spardeck and thirty-one feet in extreme breadth. Unless such vessels were swift sailers, particularly handy in working to windward, they were worse than useless; and for that reason the utmost effort was made both by the public and private constructors to obtain speed. At the close of the war the most efficient vessel afloat was probably the American sloop-of-war, or privateer, of four or five hundred tons, rigged as a ship or brig, and carrying one hundred and fifty or sixty men, with a battery varying according to the ideas of the captain and owners, but in the case of privateers almost invariably including one "long Tom," or pivot-gun.

Yet for privateering purposes the smaller craft competed closely with the larger. For ordinary service no vessel could do more effective work in a more economical way than was done by Joshua Barney's "Rossie" of Baltimore, or Boyle's "Comet" of the same port, or Champlin's "General Armstrong" of New York,—schooners or brigs of two or three hundred tons, uncomfortable to their officers and crews, but most dangerous enemies to merchantmen. Vessels of this class came into favor long before the war, because of their speed, quickness in handling, and economy during the experience of twenty years in blockade-running and evasion of cruisers. Such schooners could be built in any Northern sea-port in six weeks or two months at half the cost of a government cruiser.

The government sloop-of-war was not built for privateering purposes. Every government vessel was intended chiefly to fight, and required strength in every part and solidity throughout. The frame needed to be heavy to support the heavier structure; the quarters needed to be thick to protect the men at the guns from grape and musketry; the armament was as weighty as the frame would bear. So strong were the sides of American frigates that even thirty-two-pound shot fired at forty or fifty feet distance sometimes failed to penetrate, and the British complained as a grievance that the sides of an American forty-four were thicker than those of a British seventy-four.[4] The American ship-builders spared no pains to make all their vessels in

[4] James, p. 18.

every respect—in size, strength, and speed—superior to the vessels with which they were to compete; but the government ship-carpenter had a harder task than the private ship-builder, for he was obliged to obtain greater speed at the same time that he used heavier material than the British constructors. As far as the navy carpenters succeeded in their double object, they did so by improving the model and increasing the proportions of the spars.

The privateer was built for no such object. The last purpose of a privateer was to fight at close range, and owners much preferred that their vessels, being built to make money, should not fight at all unless much money could be made. The private armed vessel was built rather to fly than to fight, and its value depended far more on its ability to escape than on its capacity to attack. If the privateer could sail close to the wind, and wear or tack in the twinkling of an eye; if she could spread an immense amount of canvas and run off as fast as a frigate before the wind; if she had sweeps to use in a calm, and one long-range gun pivoted amidships, with plenty of men in case boarding became necessary,—she was perfect. To obtain these results the builders and sailors ran excessive risks. Too lightly built and too heavily sparred, the privateer was never a comfortable or a safe vessel. Beautiful beyond anything then known in naval construction, such vessels roused boundless admiration, but defied imitators. British constructors could not build them, even when they had the models; British captains could not sail them; and when British admirals, fascinated by their beauty and tempted by the marvellous qualities of their model, ordered such a prize to be taken into the service, the first act of the carpenters in the British navy-yards was to reduce to their own standard the long masts, and to strengthen the hull and sides till the vessel should be safe in a battle or a gale. Perhaps an American navy-carpenter must have done the same; but though not a line in the model might be altered, she never sailed again as she sailed before. She could not bear conventional restraints.

Americans were proud of their privateers, as they well might be; for this was the first time when in competition with the world, on an element open to all, they proved their capacity to excel, and produced a creation as beautiful as it was practical. The British navy took a new tone in regard to these vessels. Deeply as the American frigates and sloops-of-war had wounded the pride of the British navy, they never had reduced that fine service to admitted inferiority. Under one pretext or another, every defeat was excused. Even the superiority of American gunnery was met by the proud explanation that the British navy, since Trafalgar, had enjoyed no opportunity to use their guns. Nothing could convince a British admiral that Americans were better fighters than Englishmen; but when he looked at the American schooner he frankly said that England could show no such models, and could not sail them if she had them. In truth, the schooner was a wonderful invention. Not her battles, but her escapes won for her the open-mouthed admiration of the British captains, who saw their prize double like a hare and slip through their fingers at the moment when capture was sure. Under any ordinary condition of wind and weather, with an open sea, the schooner, if only she could get to windward, laughed at a frigate.

As the sailing rather than the fighting qualities of the privateer were the chief object of her construction, those were the points best worth recording; but the newspapers of the time were so much absorbed in proving that Americans could fight, as to cause almost total neglect of the more important question whether Americans could sail better than their rivals. All great nations had fought, and at one time or another every great nation in Europe had been victorious over every other; but no people, in the course of a thousand years of rivalry on the ocean, had invented or had known how to sail a Yankee schooner. Whether ship, brig, schooner, or sloop, the American vessel was believed to outsail any other craft on the ocean, and the proof of this superiority was incumbent on the Americans to furnish. They neglected to do so. No clear evidence was ever recorded of the precise capacities of their favorite vessels. Neither the lines of the hull, the dimensions of the spars, the rates of sailing by the log in different weather, the points of sailing,—nothing precise was ever set down.

Of the superiority no doubts could be entertained. The best proof of the American claim was the British admission. Hardly an English writer on marine affairs—whether in newspapers, histories, or novels—failed to make some allusion to the beauty and speed of American vessels. The naval literature of Great Britain from 1812 to 1860 was full of such material. The praise of the invention was still commonly accompanied by some expression of dislike for the inventor, but even in that respect a marked change followed the experiences of 1812–1814. Among the Englishmen living on the island of Jamaica, and familiar with the course of events in the West Indies from 1806 to 1817, was one Michael Scott, born in Glasgow in 1789, and in the prime of his youth at the time of the American war. In the year 1829, at the age of forty, he began the publication in "Blackwood's Magazine" of a series of sketches which rapidly became popular as "Tom Cringle's Log." Scott was the best narrator and probably the best informed man who wrote on the West Indies at that period; and his frequent allusions to the United States and the war threw more light on the social side of history than could be obtained from all official sources ever printed.

"I don't like Americans," Scott said; "I never did and never shall like them. I have seldom met an American gentleman in the large and complete sense of the term. I have no wish to eat with them, drink with them, deal with or consort with them in any way; but let me tell the whole truth,—*nor fight* with them, were it not for the laurels to be acquired by overcoming an enemy so brave, determined, and alert, and every way so worthy of one's steel as they have always proved."

The Americans did not fight the War of 1812 in order to make themselves loved. According to Scott's testimony they gained the object for which they did fight. "In gunnery and small-arm practice we were as thoroughly weathered on by the Americans during the war as we overtopped them in the bull-dog courage with which our boarders handled those genuine English weapons,—the cutlass and the pike." Superiority in the intellectual branches of warfare was conceded to the Americans; but even in regard to physical qualities, the British were not inclined to boast.

> "In the field," said Scott, "or grappling in mortal combat on the blood-slippery quarter-deck of an enemy's vessel, a British soldier or sailor is the bravest of the brave. No soldier or sailor of any other country, saving and excepting those damned Yankees, can stand against them."

Had English society known so much of Americans in 1807, war would have been unnecessary.

Yet neither equality in physical courage nor superiority in the higher branches of gunnery and small-arms was the chief success of Americans in the war. Beyond question the schooner was the most conclusive triumph. Readers of Michael Scott could not forget the best of his sketches,—the escape of the little American schooner "Wave" from two British cruisers, by running to windward under the broad-side of a man-of-war. With keen appreciation Scott detailed every motion of the vessels, and dwelt with peculiar emphasis on the apparent desperation of the attempt. Again and again the thirty-two-pound shot, as he described the scene, tore through the slight vessel as the two crafts raced through the heavy seas within musket-shot of one another, until at last the firing from the corvette ceased. "The breeze had taken off, and the 'Wave,' resuming her superiority in light winds, had escaped." Yet this was not the most significant part of "Tom Cringle's" experience. The "Wave," being afterward captured at anchor, was taken into the royal service and fitted as a ship-of-war. Cringle was ordered by the vice-admiral to command her, and as she came to report he took a look at her:—

> "When I had last seen her she was a most beautiful little craft, both in hull and rigging, as ever delighted the eye of a sailor; but the dock-yard riggers and carpenters had fairly bedevilled her, at least so far as appearances went. First they had replaced the light rail on her gun-wale by heavy solid bulwarks four feet high, surmounted by hammock nettings at least another foot; so that the symmetrical little vessel that formerly floated on the foam

light as a sea-gull now looked like a clumsy, dish-shaped Dutch dogger. Her long, slender wands of masts which used to swing about as if there were neither shrouds nor stays to support them were now as taut and stiff as church-steeples, with four heavy shrouds of a side, and stays and back-stays, and the Devil knows what all."

"If them heave-'emtaughts at the yard have not taken the speed out of the little beauty I am a Dutchman" was the natural comment,—as obvious as it was sound.

The reports of privateer captains to their owners were rarely published, and the logs were never printed or deposited in any public office. Occasionally, in the case of a battle or the loss of guns or spars or cargo in a close pursuit, the privateer captain described the causes of his loss in a letter which found its way into print; and from such letters some idea could be drawn of the qualities held in highest regard, both in their vessels and in themselves. The first and commonest remark was that privateers of any merit never seemed to feel anxious for their own safety so long as they could get to windward a couple of gunshots from their enemy. They would risk a broadside in the process without very great anxiety. They chiefly feared lest they might be obliged to run before the wind in heavy weather. The little craft which could turn on itself like a flash and dart away under a frigate's guns into the wind's eye long before the heavy ship could come about, had little to fear on that point of sailing; but when she was obliged to run to leeward, the chances were more nearly equal. Sometimes, especially in light breezes or in a stronger wind, by throwing guns and weighty articles overboard privateers could escape; but in heavy weather the ship-of-war could commonly outcarry them, and more often could drive them on a coast or into the clutches of some other man-of-war.

Of being forced to fly to leeward almost every privateer could tell interesting stories. A fair example of such tales was an adventure of Captain George Coggeshall, who afterward compiled, chiefly from newspapers, an account of the privateers, among which he preserved a few stories that would otherwise have been lost.[5] Coggeshall commanded a two-hundred-ton schooner, the "David Porter," in which he made the run to France with a cargo and a letter-of-marque. The schooner was at Bordeaux in March, 1814, when Wellington's army approached. Afraid of seizure by the British if he remained at Bordeaux, Coggeshall sailed from Bordeaux for La Rochelle with a light wind from the eastward, when at daylight March 15, 1814, he found a large ship about two miles to windward. Coggeshall tried to draw his enemy down to leeward, but only lost ground until the ship was not more than two gunshots away. The schooner could then not run to windward without taking the enemy's fire within pistol-shot, and dared not return to Bordeaux. Nothing remained but to run before the wind. Coggeshall got out his square-sail and studding-sails ready to set, and when everything was prepared he changed his course and bore off suddenly, gaining a mile in the six or eight minutes lost by the ship in spreading her studding-sails. He then started his water-casks, threw out ballast, and drew away from his pursuer, till in a few hours the ship became a speck on the horizon.

Apparently a similar but narrower escape was made by Captain Champlin of the "Warrior," a famous privateer-brig of four hundred and thirty tons, mounting twenty-one guns and carrying one hundred and fifty men.[6] Standing for the harbor of Fayal, Dec. 15, 1814, he was seen by a British man-of-war lying there at anchor. The enemy slipped her cables and made sail in chase. The weather was very fresh and squally, and at eight o'clock in the evening the ship was only three miles distant. After a run of about sixty miles, the man-of-war came within grape-shot distance and opened fire from her two bow-guns. Champlin luffed a little, got his long pivot-gun to bear, and ran out his starboard guns as though to fight, which caused the ship to shorten sail for battle. Then Champlin at two o'clock in the morning threw overboard eleven guns, and escaped. The British ship was in sight the next morning, but did not pursue farther.

[5] Coggeshall's *History of American Privateers*, p. 188.
[6] Extract of letter from Captain Champlin; Niles, viii. 110.

Often the privateers were obliged to throw everything overboard at the risk of capsizing, or escaped capture only by means of their sweeps. In 1813 Champlin commanded the "General Armstrong," a brig of two hundred and forty-six tons and one hundred and forty men. Off Surinam, March 11, 1813, he fell in with the British sloop-of-war "Coquette," which he mistook for a letter-of-marque, and approached with the intention of boarding. Having come within pistol-shot and fired his broadsides, he discovered his error. The wind was light, the two vessels had no headway, and for three quarters of an hour, if Champlin's account could be believed, he lay within pistol-shot of the man-of-war. He was struck by a musket-ball in the left shoulder; six of his crew were killed and fourteen wounded; his rigging was cut to pieces; his foremast and bowsprit injured, and several shots entered the brig between wind and water, causing her to leak; but at last he succeeded in making sail forward, and with the aid of his sweeps crept out of range. The sloop-of-war was unable to cripple or follow him.[7]

Sometimes the very perfection of the privateer led to dangers as great as though perfection were a fault. Captain Shaler of the "Governor Tompkins," a schooner, companion to the "General Armstrong," chased three sail Dec. 25, 1812, and on near approach found them to be two ships and a brig. The larger ship had the appearance of a government transport; she had boarding-nettings almost up to her tops, but her ports appeared to be painted, and she seemed prepared for running away as she fought. Shaler drew nearer, and came to the conclusion that the ship was too heavy for him; but while his first officer went forward with the glass to take another look, a sudden squall struck the schooner without reaching the ship, and in a moment, before the light sails could be taken in, "and almost before I could turn round, I was under the guns, not of a transport, but of a large frigate, and not more than a quarter of a mile from her." With impudence that warranted punishment, Shaler fired his little broadside of nine or twelve pounders into

[7] Extract from log, March 11, 1813; Niles, iv. 133.

the enemy, who replied with a broadside of twenty-four-pounders, killing three men, wounding five, and causing an explosion on deck that threw confusion into the crew; but the broadside did no serious injury to the rigging. The schooner was then just abaft the ship's beam, a quarter of a mile away, holding the same course and to windward. She could not tack without exposing her stern to a raking fire, and any failure to come about would have been certain destruction. Shaler stood on, taking the ship's fire, on the chance of outsailing his enemy before a shot could disable the schooner. Side by side the two vessels raced for half an hour, while twenty-four-pound shot fell in foam about the schooner, but never struck her, and at last she drew ahead beyond range. Even then her dangers were not at an end. A calm followed; the ship put out boats; and only by throwing deck-lumber and shot overboard, and putting all hands at the sweeps, did Shaler "get clear of one of the most quarrelsome companions that I ever met with."[8]

The capacities of the American privateer could to some extent be inferred from its mishaps. Notwithstanding speed, skill, and caution, the privateer was frequently and perhaps usually captured in the end. The modes of capture were numerous. April 3, 1813, Admiral Warren's squadron in the Chesapeake captured by boats, after a sharp action, the privateer "Dolphin" of Baltimore, which had taken refuge in the Rappahannock River. April 27 the "Tom" of Baltimore, a schooner of nearly three hundred tons, carrying fourteen guns, was captured by his Majesty's ships "Surveillante" and "Lyra" after a smart chase. Captain Collier of the "Surveillante" reported: "She is a remarkably fine vessel of her class, and from her superior sailing has already escaped from eighteen of his Majesty's cruisers." May 11, the "Holkar" of New York was driven ashore off Rhode Island and destroyed by the "Orpheus" frigate. May 19, Captain Gordon of the British man-of-war "Ratler," in company with the schooner "Bream," drove ashore and captured the "Alexander" of Salem, off Kennebunk, "considered the fastest sailing privateer out of the United States," according to

[8] Shaler's Report of Jan. 1, 1813; Niles, v. 429.

Captain Gordon's report.[9] May 21, Captain Hyde Parker
of the frigate "Tenedos," in company with the brig "Cur-
lew," captured the "Enterprise" of Salem, pierced for
eighteen guns. May 23, the "Paul Jones," of sixteen guns
and one hundred and twenty men, fell in with a frigate in
a thick fog off the coast of Ireland, and being crippled by
her fire surrendered. July 13, Admiral Cockburn captured
by boats at Ocracoke Inlet the fine privateer-brig "Ana-
conda" of New York, with a smaller letter-of-marque. July
17, at sea, three British men-of-war, after a chase of four
hours, captured the "Yorktown" of twenty guns and one
hundred and forty men. The schooner "Orders in Council"
of New York, carrying sixteen guns and one hundred and
twenty men, was captured during the summer, after a long
chase of five days, by three British cutters that drove her
under the guns of a frigate. The "Matilda," privateer of
eleven guns and one hundred and four men, was captured
off San Salvador by attempting to board the British letter-
of-marque "Lyon" under the impression that she was the
weaker ship.

In these ten instances of large privateers captured or destroyed in 1813, the mode of capture happened to be recorded; and in none of them was the privateer declared
to have been outsailed and caught by any single British vessel on the open seas. Modes of disaster were many, and
doubtless among the rest a privateer might occasionally be
fairly beaten in speed, but few such cases were recorded,
although British naval officers were quick to mention these
unusual victories. Unless the weather gave to the heavier
British vessel-of-war the advantage of carrying more sail in
a rough sea, the privateer was rarely outsailed.

The number of privateers at sea in 1813 was not recorded. The list of all private armed vessels during the
entire war included somewhat more than five hundred
names.[10] Most of these were small craft, withdrawn after a
single cruise. Not two hundred were so large as to carry
crews of fifty men. Nearly two hundred and fifty, or nearly
half the whole number of privateers, fell into British hands.

[9] *London Gazette* for 1813, p. 1574.
[10] Emmons's *Navy of the United States*, pp. 170–197.

Probably at no single moment were more than fifty sea-going vessels on the ocean as privateers, and the number was usually very much less; while the large privateer-brigs or ships that rivalled sloops-of-war in size were hardly more numerous than the sloops themselves.

The total number of prizes captured from the British in 1813 exceeded four hundred, four fifths of which were probably captured by privateers, national cruisers taking only seventy-nine. If the privateers succeeded in taking three hundred and fifty prizes, the whole number of privateers could scarcely have exceeded one hundred. The government cruisers "President," "Congress," "Chesapeake," "Hornet," and "Argus" averaged nearly ten prizes apiece. Privateers averaged much less; but they were ten times as numerous as the government cruisers, and inflicted four times as much injury.

Such an addition to the naval force of the United States was very important. Doubtless the privateers contributed more than the regular navy to bring about a disposition for peace in the British classes most responsible for the war. The colonial and shipping interests, whose influence produced the Orders in Council, suffered the chief penalty. The West India colonies were kept in constant discomfort and starvation by swarms of semi-piratical craft darting in and out of every channel among their islands; but the people of England could have borne with patience the punishment of the West Indies had not the American cruisers inflicted equally severe retribution nearer home.

Great Britain was blockaded. No one could deny that manifest danger existed to any merchant-vessel that entered or left British waters. During the summer the blockade was continuous. Toward the close of 1812 an American named Preble, living in Paris, bought a small vessel, said to have belonged in turn to the British and French navy, which he fitted as a privateer-brig, carrying sixteen guns and one hundred and sixty men. The "True-Blooded Yankee," commanded by Captain Hailey, sailed from Brest March 1, 1813, and cruised thirty-seven days on the coasts of Ireland and Scotland, capturing twenty-seven valuable vessels; sinking coasters in the very bay of Dublin; landing and taking possession of an island off the coast of Ireland, and of a town in Scotland, where she burned seven vessels in the harbor. She returned safely to Brest, and soon made another cruise. At the same time the schooner "Fox" of Portsmouth burned or sunk vessel after vessel in the Irish Sea, as they plied between Liverpool and Cork. In May, the schooner "Paul Jones" of New York, carrying sixteen guns and one hundred and twenty men, took or destroyed a dozen vessels off the Irish coast, until she was herself caught in a fog by the frigate "Leonidas," and captured May 23 after a chase in which five of her crew were wounded.

While these vessels were thus engaged, the brig "Rattlesnake" of Philadelphia, carrying sixteen guns and one hundred and twenty men, and the brig "Scourge" of New York, carrying nine guns and one hundred and ten men, crossed the ocean and cruised all the year in the northern seas off the coasts of Scotland and Norway, capturing some forty British vessels, and costing the British merchants and shipowners losses to the amount of at least two million dollars. In July the "Scourge" fell in with Commodore Rodgers in the "President," and the two vessels remained several days in company off the North Cape, while the British admiralty sent three or four squadrons in search of them without success. July 19, after Rodgers had been nearly a month in British waters, one of these squadrons drove him away, and he then made a circuit round Ireland before he turned homeward. At the same time, from July 14 to August 14, the "Argus" was destroying vessels in the British Channel at the rate of nearly one a day. After the capture of the "Argus," August 14, the "Grand Turk" of Salem, a brig carrying sixteen guns and one hundred and five men, cruised for twenty days in the mouth of the British Channel without being disturbed. Besides these vessels, others dashed into British waters from time to time as they sailed forward and back across the ocean in the track of British commerce.

No one disputed that the privateers were a very important branch of the American navy; but they suffered under serious drawbacks, which left doubtful the balance of merits and defects. Perhaps their chief advantage compared with government vessels was their lightness,—a quality which no government would have carried to the same extent. The long-range pivot-gun was another invention of the privateer, peculiarly successful and easily adapted for government vessels. In other respects, the same number or even half the number of sloops-of-war would have probably inflicted greater injury at less cost. The "Argus" showed how this result could have been attained. The privateer's first object was to save prizes; and in the effort to send captured vessels into port the privateer lost a large proportion by recapture. Down to the moment when Admiral Warren established his blockade of the American coast from New York southward, most of the prizes got to port. After that time the New England ports alone offered reasonable chance of safety, and privateering received a check.[11] During the war about twenty-five hundred vessels all told were captured from the British. Many were destroyed; many released as cartels; and of the remainder not less than seven hundred and fifty, probably one half the number sent to port, were recaptured by the British navy. Most of these were the prizes of privateers, and would have been destroyed had they been taken by government vessels. They were usually the most valuable prizes, so that the injury that might have been inflicted on British commerce was diminished nearly one half by the system which encouraged private war as a money-making speculation.

Another objection was equally serious. Like all gambling ventures, privateering was not profitable. In the list of five hundred privateers furnished by the Navy Department,[12] three hundred were recorded as having never made a prize. Of the remainder, few made their expenses. One of the most successful cruises of the war was that of Joshua Barney on the Baltimore schooner "Rossie" at the outbreak of hostilities, when every prize reached port. Barney sent in prizes supposed to be worth fifteen hundred thousand dollars; but after paying charges and duties and selling the goods, he

[11] Memorial of Baltimore merchants, Feb. 19, 1814; State Papers, Naval Affairs, p. 300.
[12] Emmons.

found that the profits were not sufficient to counterbalance the discomforts, and he refused to repeat the experiment. His experience was common. As early as November, 1812, the owners of twenty-four New York privateers sent to Congress a memorial declaring that the profits of private naval war were by no means equal to the hazards, and that the spirit of privateering stood in danger of extinction unless the government would consent in some manner to grant a bounty for the capture or destruction of the enemy's property.

If private enterprise was to fail at the critical moment, and if the government must supply the deficiency, the government would have done better to undertake the whole task. In effect, the government in the end did so. The merchants asked chiefly for a reduction of duties on prize-goods. Gallatin pointed out the serious objections to such legislation, and the little probability that the measure would increase the profits of privateering or the number of privateers. The actual privateers, he said, were more than enough for the food offered by the enemy's trade, and privateering, like every other form of gambling, would always continue to attract more adventurers than it could support.[13]

Congress for the time followed Gallatin's advice, and did nothing; but in the summer session of 1813, after Gallatin's departure for Europe, the privateer owners renewed their appeal, and the acting Secretary of the Treasury, Jones, wrote to the chairman of the Naval Committee July 21, 1813,[14]—

"The fact is that . . . privateering is nearly at an end: and from the best observation I have been enabled to make, it is more from the deficiency of remuneration in the net proceeds of their prizes than from the vigilance and success of the enemy in recapturing."

In deference to Jones's opinion, Congress passed an Act, approved Aug. 2, 1813, reducing one third the duties on prize-goods. Another Act, approved August 3, granted a

[13] Gallatin to Langdon Cheves, Dec. 8, 1812; Annals, 1812–1813, p. 434.
[14] Annals, 1813–1814, i. 473.

bounty of twenty-five dollars for every prisoner captured and delivered to a United States agent by a private armed vessel. A third Act, approved August 2, authorized the Secretary of the Navy to place on the pension list any privateersman who should be wounded or disabled in the line of his duty.

These complaints and palliations tended to show that the privateer cost the public more than the equivalent government vessel would have cost. If instead of five hundred privateers of all sizes and efficiency, the government had kept twenty sloops-of-war constantly at sea destroying the enemy's commerce, the result would have been about the same as far as concerned injury to the enemy, while in another respect the government would have escaped one of its chief difficulties. Nothing injured the navy so much as privateering. Seamen commonly preferred the harder but more profitable and shorter cruise in a privateer, where fighting was not expected or wished, to the strict discipline and murderous battles of government ships, where wages were low and prize-money scarce. Of all towns in the United States, Marblehead was probably the most devoted to the sea; but of nine hundred men from Marblehead who took part in the war, fifty-seven served as soldiers, one hundred and twenty entered the navy, while seven hundred and twenty-six went as privateersmen.[15] Only after much delay and difficulty could the frigates obtain crews. The "Constitution" was nearly lost by this cause at the beginning of the war; and the loss of the "Chesapeake" was supposed to be chiefly due to the determination of the old crew to quit the government service for that of the privateers.

Such drawbacks raised reasonable doubts as to the balance of advantages and disadvantages offered by the privateer system. Perhaps more careful inquiry might show that, valuable as the privateers were, the government would have done better to retain all military and naval functions in its own hands, and to cover the seas with small cruisers capable of pursuing a system of thorough destruction against the shipping and colonial interests of England.

[15] Roads's *Marblehead*, p. 255.

Letter Writer

Samoa, 1890

"*No future experience, short of being eaten, will ever make us feel so new again.*" *So wrote Adams upon first landing on the island of Tutuila in the company of his friend John La Farge. In 1890 he began at last to come to life again. He had known only numbness and apathy since the hour of his wife's suicide in December 1885. Samoa woke him again. The hurt mind looked out and saw—with unnatural keenness—peoples, places, and ideas, embodied and full-colored. In such letters as this one to Elizabeth Cameron, the best of his private contemporary readers, he wrote with new sharpness, vigor, and idiosyncratic strength. In such letters he poured out fresh insights, convictions, forebodings, prejudices.*

This is one letter only of the hundreds he wrote: better one, as a stimulus to reading straight through the thick collections of his correspondence, than a small selection, necessarily crippled in representing a mind that changed and grew with each decade of its life.

SAMOA, 1890[1]

TO ELIZABETH CAMERON

Apia, October 9, 1890.

Well we are here, and I am sitting in the early morning on the verandah of a rough cottage, in a grove of cocoa-nut

[1] This letter is taken from Volume I of the *Letters of Henry Adams,* published by Houghton Mifflin Co., in 1930 and 1938.

palms, with native huts all about me, and across the grass, fifty yards away, I can see and hear the sea with its distant line of surf on the coral reef beyond. Natives clothed mostly in a waist-cloth, but sometimes their toilet completed by a hybiscus or other flower in their hair, pass every moment or two before my cabin, often handsome as Greek gods. I am the guest of Consul Sewall,[2] whose consulate is within the same grove, near the beach. . . .

Sunday morning at nine o'clock or thereabouts, the "Alameda" turned a corner of Tutuila, and I saw the little schooner knocking about in the open sea beyond. The day was overcast, threatening rain. From the shore, half a dozen large boats, filled with naked savages, were paddling down with the wind, singing a curiously wild chant to their paddles. La Farge and I felt that we were to be captured and probably eaten, but the cruise of sixty miles in a forty-ton schooner, beating to windward in tropical squalls, was worse than being eaten. We dropt into the boat among scores of naked Samoans, half of them swimming, or clambering over our backs, with war clubs to sell, and when we reached our schooner, we stood in the rain and watched the "Alameda" steam away. That was our first joy. Whatever fate was in store, we had escaped from the steamer, and might die before another would come.

The cutter was commanded by Captain Peter, a huge captain, but little skilled in the languages with which I am more or less acquainted. His six sailors were as little fluent in English as though they had studied at Harvard. Captain Peter talked what he supposed to be English with excessive energy, but we could catch only the three words "now and again," repeated with frequency but in no apparent connection. "Now and again" something was to happen; meanwhile he beat up under the shore into quieter water, and presently, in a downpour of rain, we cast anchor in a bay, with mountains above, but a sand-beach within the coral reef, and native huts half hidden among the cocoa-nut palms. I insisted on going ashore straightway without respect for H. M.'s mail, and Captain Peter seemed not un-

[2] Harold Marsh Sewall (1860–1924).

willing. A splendid naked savage carried La Farge, in an
india-rubber water-proof, mildly kicking, from the boat to
the shore, and returned for me. I embraced his neck with
effusive gratitude, and so landed on the island of Tutuila,
which does not resemble the picture on the Oceanic Steam-
ship Company's colored advertisement. I found it densely
covered with tropical mountains and vegetation, but glad
as I was to set foot on mountains and see vegetation, I was
soon more interested in the refined hospitality of the cultured inhabitants. We entered the nearest hut, and put on
our best manners, which were none too good, for the natives had manners that made me feel withered prematurely
in association with the occupants of pig-sties. Grave, courteous, with quiet voices and a sort of benevolence beyond
the utmost expressiveness of Benjamin Franklin, they received us and made us at home. The cabin was charming
when one looked about it. Nearly circular, with a diameter
of some forty feet, its thatched roof, beautifully built up,
came within about five feet of the ground, ending there on
posts, and leaving the whole house open to the air. Within,
mats covered a floor of white corals, smooth and almost
soft like coarse sand. Fire was made in the middle of the
hut. Only women and children were there. One was stain-
ing a tapa-cloth; another was lying down unwell; others
were sitting about, and one or two naked children, won-
derfully silent and well-behaved, sat and stared at us. We
dropped our umbrellas and water-proofs and sat down on
the mats to wait for Captain Peter to sail; but presently a
proud young woman entered and seated herself in silence
after shaking hands. Captain Peter succeeded in making us
understand that this was the chief's daughter. Other young
women dropped in, shook hands and sat down. Soon we
seemed to have a *matinée*. As no one could say more than
a word or two in the other's language, communication was
as hard as at a Washington party, but it was more successful. In a very short time we were all intimate. La Farge
began to draw the Princess, as we called her, and Wakea
—for that was her name—was pleased to drop her dress-
skirt, and sit for him in her native undress, with a dignity
and gravity quite indescribable. The other girls were less

imposing, but very amusing. One, Sivà, a younger sister of
the Princess, was fascinating. Of course I soon devoted my
attention to talking, and, as I could understand nothing,
talk was moderately easy; but through Captain Peter we
learned a little, and some of the touches of savagery were
perfect. I asked Sivà her name—mine was Hen-li—and her
age. She did not know her age; even her father, an old man,
could not say how many years old she was. I guessed fourteen, equivalent to our eighteen. All her motions were splendid, and she threw a plate on the floor, as Martha Braggiotti
would say, like a race-horse. Her lines were all antique,
and in face she recalled a little my niece Lulu, Molly's sister. Presently she brought a curious pan-shaped wooden
dish, standing on eight legs, all of one block; and sitting
down behind it, began to grate a dry root, like flagroot but
larger, on a grater, over the dish. This was rather hard work,
and took some time. Then another girl brought some cocoa-
nuts full of water, and she poured the water on the grated
root. Then she took a bundle of clean cocoa-nut fibre, and
seemed to wash her hands in the water which was already
muddy and dirty with the grated root. We divined that she
really strained out the grated particles, which were caught
on the fibre, and wrung out by another girl. When all the
grains were strained off, the drink was ready, and we re-
alised that we had got to swallow it, for this was the *kawa*,
and we were grateful that in our first experience the root
was grated, not chewed, as it ought to be, by the girls.
Please read Kingsley's account of it in the "Earl and the
Doctor,"[3] a book you will probably be able to borrow from
Herbert, as it was done for or by his brother Pembroke. A
cocoa-nut half full of it was handed to us, and as usual
La Farge, who had kicked at the idea more than I did,
took to it at once, and drank it rather freely. I found it
"not nice, papa, but funny"; a queer lingering, varying,
aromatic, arumatic, Polynesian, old-gold flavor, that clings
to the palate like creosote or coal-oil. I drank the milk of a
green cocoa-nut to wash it off, but all the green cocoa-nuts

[3] *South Sea Bubbles, by the Earl and the Doctor*—George
Robert Charles Herbert, Earl of Pembroke, and George Henry
Kingsley.

in the ocean could not wash out that little taste. After the
kawa we became still more intimate. Besides Wakea and
her sister Sivà, we made the acquaintance of Tuvale,
Amerika, Sitoa, and Faaiuro, which is no other than Faya-
way, I imagine. We showed them our writing, and found
that they could write very well, as they proved by writing
us letters on the spot, in choice Samoan, which we tried
to translate, with the usual result. So evening came on; we
had some supper; a kerosene lamp was lit; and La Farge
and I began to cry out for the *Siva*.

The *Siva*, we had learned to know at Hawaii, is the
Samoan dance, and the girl, Sivà, had already been unable
to resist giving us snatches of the songs and motions. Sivà
was fascinating. She danced all over, and seemed more
Greek in every new motion. I could not understand what
orders were given by the elders, but, once they were assured that we were not missionaries, all seemed right. The
girls disappeared; and after some delay, while I was rather
discouraged, thinking that the Siva was not to be, suddenly
out of the dark, five girls came into the light, with a dramatic effect that really I never felt before. Naked to the
waist, their rich skins glistened with cocoa-nut oil. Around
their heads and necks they wore garlands of green leaves
in strips, like seaweeds, and these too glistened with oil, as
though the girls had come out of the sea. Around their
waists, to the knee, they wore leaf-clothes, or *lavalavas*,
also of fresh leaves, green and red. Their faces and figures
varied in looks, some shading the negro too closely; but
Sivà was divine, and you can imagine that we found our
attention absorbed in watching her. The mysterious depths
of darkness behind, against which the skins and dresses of
the dancers mingled rather than contrasted; the sense of
remoteness and of genuineness in the stage-management;
the conviction that at last the kingdom of old-gold was ours,
and that we were as good Polynesiacs as our neighbors—
the whole scene and association gave so much freshness to
our fancy that no future experience, short of being eaten,
will ever make us feel so new again. La Farge's spectacles
quivered with emotion and gasped for sheer inability to note
everything at once. To me the dominant idea was that the

girls, with their dripping grasses and leaves, and their glistening breasts and arms, had actually come out of the sea a few steps away. They entered in file, and sat down opposite us. Then the so-called Siva dance began. The girls sat cross-legged, and the dance was as much song as motion, although the motion was incessant. As the song or chant, a rhythmical and rather pleasant, quick movement, began, the dancers swayed about; clapped their hands, shoulders, legs; stretched out their arms in every direction and with every possible action, always in harmony, and seldom repeating the same figure. We had dozens of these different motives until I thought the poor girls would be exhausted, for they made so much muscular effort, feet, thighs, hips and even ribs working as energetically as the arms, that they panted at the close of each figure; but they were evidently enjoying it as much as we, and kept it up with glances at us and laughter among themselves. All through this part of the performance, our Princess did not dance but sat before us on the mats, and beat time with a stick. At last she too got up, and after ten minutes' absence, reappeared, costumed like the rest, but taller and more splendid. La Farge exploded with enthusiasm for her, and expressed boundless contempt for Carmencita. You can imagine the best female figure you ever saw, on about a six foot scale, neck, breast, back, arms and legs, all absolutely Greek in modelling and action, with such freedom of muscle and motion as the Greeks themselves hardly knew, and you can appreciate La Farge's excitement. When she came in the other dancers rose, and then began what I supposed to be a war or sword dance, the Princess brandishing a stick and evidently destroying her enemies, one of whom was a comic character and expressed abject cowardice. With this performance the dance ended; Sivà got out the *kawa* dish; Wakea and the others went for our tobacco, and soon we were all sprawling over the mats, smoking, laughing, trying to talk, with a sense of shoulders, arms, legs, cocoa-nut oil, and general nudeness most strangely mixed with a sense of propriety. Anyone would naturally suppose such a scene to be an orgy of savage license. I don't pretend to know what it was, but I give you my affidavit that we could see nothing in the songs or dances that suggested impropriety, and that not a word or a sign during our whole stay could have brought a blush to the cheek of Senator H—— himself. Unusual as the experience is of half dressed or undressed women lying about the floor, in all sorts of attitudes, and as likely as not throwing their arms or their shoulders across one as one lies or sits near them, as far as we could see the girls were perfectly good, and except occasionally for hinting that they would like a present of a handkerchief, or for giving us perhaps a ring, there was no approach to familiarity with us. Indeed at last we were extinguished by dropping a big mosquito netting over us, so that we were enclosed in a private room; the girls went off to their houses; our household sank into perfect quiet, and we slept in our clothes on the floor as comfortably as we knew how, while the kerosene lamp burned all night in the centre of the floor.

The next morning we very unwillingly tumbled into our boat, after a surf bath, and then, for the next four or five hours, we were pitching about, in a head wind and sea, trying to round the western point of Tutuila. Nothing could be more lovely than the day, the blue sea, and the green island stretching away in different planes of color, till lost in the distance. At two o'clock that afternoon we rounded our point, and our boat went ashore to fetch off Consul Sewall and Lieut. Parker on their return from Pango Pango, where they had gone to settle on the new naval station. They came instantly on board, and we four Americans then lay on the deck of that cutter from two o'clock Monday afternoon, till two o'clock Wednesday morning, thirty-six hours, going sixty miles, in a calm, with a vertical sun overhead, and three of the four seasick. You can conceive that we were glad to reach Apia on any terms, and tumbled ashore, in a leaky boat, in the dead of night, only too glad to get shelter about the consulate. Our only excitement at sea was a huge shark that looked like a whale. Once ashore, supper and bed were paradise; but my brain and stomach went on turning somersaults, and I was not wholly happy.

October 12. Sunday here, when it should be Saturday, but Samoa is above astronomy. Time has already made us familiar with our surroundings. I find myself now and then regaining consciousness that I was once an American supposing himself real. The Samoan is so different from all my preconceived ideas, that my own identity becomes hazy, and yours alone remains tolerably clear. I took one day of entire rest, after arriving, and passed it in looking at the sea, and rejoicing to have escaped it. The second day we performed our visits of ceremony. First, we called on King Malietoa, and I assure you that I was not in the least inclined to joke about him. He is not *opéra bouffe,* or Kalakaua. The ceremony was simple as though we were in a democratic republic. We began by keeping his Majesty waiting half an hour while we lounged over our cigars after breakfast. When we arrived at the audience-house, we found Malietoa gone, but he was sent for, and came to receive us. The house was the ordinary native house, such as we were in at Tutuila. We sat on the floor. Malietoa was alone, without officers or attendants, and was dressed as usual with chiefs on state occasions, in an ordinary white linen jacket and trousers. He is an elderly man, with the usual rather pathetic expression of these islanders, and with the charming voice and manner which seem to belong to high chiefs. He talked slowly, with a little effort, but with a dignity and seriousness that quite overawed me. As the interpreter translated, I caught only the drift of his words, which were at first formal; then became warm in expressions of regard for Americans; and at last turned to an interesting and rather important discussion of the political dangers and uneasiness in these islands. He said nothing of his own sufferings or troubles, but seemed anxious for fear of disturbance here, and evidently dreads some outbreak against his own authority unless the three foreign powers execute their treaty promptly, which the three foreign powers seem, for reasons of their own, determined not to do. If you want a lecture on Samoan politics, I am in a fair way to be able to give you one; for though I loathe the very word, and of all kinds of politics detest most those of islands, I am just soaked with the stuff here, where the natives are children, full of little jealousies and intrigues, and the foreigners are rather worse than the natives. The

three foreign powers have made a mess, and the natives
are in it. Even in case they fight, I do not much expect
to be massacred, as Americans are very popular indeed; but
I am a great *ali*—nobleman—because all the natives knew
the frigate "Adams," and I am the first American who has
ever visited the country merely for pleasure; so I feel bound
to look grave and let Sewall do the talking. Malietoa was
sad and despondent; Mata-afa, the intermediary king, who
led the fighting after Malietoa's deportation, and was deposed by the treaty of Berlin, seemed also depressed, but
was even more earnest in his expressions of gratitude to
America. We made also a ceremonial call on Mata-afa, after
we had seen Malietoa, and while we were going through
the unavoidable *kawa*, which becomes a serious swallow
after many repetitions, Mata-afa talked of his gratitude to
America. I won't bore you by explaining why he is grateful. I don't much care myself; and was much more interested in watching the dignity of his face, the modulation
of his voice, the extraordinary restraint and refinement of
his rhetoric, and the exquisite art of the slight choking in
his voice as he told us that his only hope was in Christ
and in America. I felt more interest in the art of his civilisa-
tion, you understand, than I did in the detail that Bayard
and Sewall had saved the islanders from being killed or enslaved. As rhetoricians and men of manners, the great
Samoan chiefs, and, for that matter, the little ones too,
make me feel as though I were the son of a camel-driver
degraded to the position of stable-boy in Spokane West
Centre. Aristocracy can go no further, and any ordinary
aristocracy is vulgar by the side of the Samoan. For centuries these people have thought of nothing else. They have
no other arts worth mentioning. Some day I will tell you of
their straw mats, their chief artistic pride; their houses, too,
are artistic in their way, and their taste in colors is splendidly bold; but their real art is social, and they have done
what in theory every scientific society would like to do—
they have bred themselves systematically. Love marriages
are unknown. The old chiefs select the wives for the young
chiefs, and choose for strength and form rather than beauty
of face. Each village elects a girl to be the village maiden,

a sort of candidate for ambitious marriage, and she is the
tallest and best made girl of the good society of the place.
She is bound to behave herself, and marry a handsome
young chief. The consequence is that the chiefs are the
handsomest men you can imagine, physically Apollos, and
the women can all carry me in their arms as though I was
a baby.

The chief of Apia is Seumano, the hero of the hurricane,
who took his boat through the surf and saved the ship-
wrecked crews. Our government sent him a present of a
fancy whaleboat, very handsome though a little like a
man-of-war, requiring about fifty men to move it. Seumano
is a giant in strength; his wife, Fatolea, is quite a *grande
dame,* and their adopted daughter, Fanua, is the village
maiden, or Taupo, of Apia. Sewall got Seumano, who is
as warmly American as all the rest, to give us a big Siva
dance that we might see the thing properly, and the occasion was evidently one of general interest. In general the
scene was the same as at Nua in Tutuila, but instead of
an improvised affair, Seumano gave us a regular party, with
the whole village taking part or looking on. Fanua was the
centre girl, and had nine or ten companions. Fanua wore
an immensely high and heavy headdress that belongs to the
village maiden. The others were dressed in the Siva costume, but spoiled their effect by wearing banana leaves
round their breasts, in deference to missionary prejudices.
The figure is everything in the native dance, and the color
counts almost as much as dress with you creatures of civi-
lisation. The banana leaves were as little objectionable as
such symbols of a corrupt taste could be, but they reminded
one of the world and the devil. Our impromptu at Nua was
better, for though some of the girls were more or less gro-
tesque, the handsome ones, with fine figures, were tremen-
dously effective. You can imagine what would be the effect
of applying such a test to a New York ball-room, and how
unpopular the banana leaf would be with girls whose figures were better than their faces. Nevertheless the Siva was
a good one, especially in the singing and the drill. The older
women sat in the dark behind the girls, and acted as chorus.
Sewall, his vice Consul Blacklock, La Farge and I sat in

front, opposite the dancers. Towards the end, when the dancers got up and began their last figure, which grows more and more vivacious to the end, Fanua, who had mischief in her eyes, pranced up before me, and bending over, put her arms round my neck and kissed me. The kissing felt quite natural and was loudly applauded with much laughter, but I have been redolent of cocoa-nut oil ever since, and the more because Fanua afterwards gave me her wreaths, and put one over my neck, the other round my waist, dripping with cocoa-nut oil.

October 14. I am hazy on dates. This may be any day of the week or month. I only know time by its passage. The weather has been warm, about 88° at noon-day, though cool enough except from eleven till four. Yesterday morning I took my boat out fishing on the reef. By the bye, I have set up a boat, as one sets up a carriage. The Consulate had none, and I thought I could repay Sewall's civility no better than by giving him a boat; so we have a swell man-of-war's boat with five fine natives to row us, and an awning and a consular flag, fine as Fiji. These luxuries are not inexpensive. A boat here costs as much or more than a carriage at home; but here I must be a great *ali* or bust. So, as I had nothing for my boat to do, I took it out to see how the natives fished. My stroke oar, or coxswain, did the fishing, and succeeded in catching a squid, or octopus, about twelve or eighteen inches span in the tentacles. The process was curious, but the fun came afterwards. Sewall sent the squid to Mele Samsoni—in English, Mary Hamilton—a native woman, married to an elderly American, who lives near by—and asked her to make some squid soup for us. So at noon we had a lunch in Samsoni's hut in the banana grove hard by. There was old Hamilton—once a whaleman and pilot—his wife Mele or Mary—three girls who live with them, Sewall, Blacklock, La Farge and I, sitting on the mats with the lunch spread on banana leaves before us. The squid soup was first distributed, and I found it delicious; rather rich, but not so strong as either clams or oysters. The squid is cut up and boiled in cocoa-nut milk. I am certain that in French hands it could be made a great success. To my horror I was then given a large dish of the squid itself. I had seen it for sale, dried, as an article of food in Japan, and had even tried to eat it in Honolulu where our American friends regarded it as they do oysters or truffles; but this was my first meeting with it face to face, and I attacked it with the shudder of desperate courage. In the end I eat nearly the whole beast, refused to eat anything else, and afterwards sucked half a dozen oranges, drank a green cocoa-nut, smoked a cigar and dropped off asleep, while Mele Samsoni fanned the flies from me with a banana leaf.

October 16. Yesterday I moved into my native house. We sleep and eat at the Consulate, but I have set up a native house as a studio and reception room. It is a large, handsome hut, commonly used as the guest-house of the village. The native church stands between it and the sea which is fifty yards away. Mata-afa's house is a few rods to the right, across the village green. Native houses are scattered round the green. Bread-fruit trees and cocoa-nut palms surround us. Just now half a dozen girls in costumes varying between the ordinary missionary nightgowns and the native waist-cloth, are chattering about the place, doing so-called work for us. Yesterday Mata-afa sent us a chief with a big green turtle as a gift, which is a present only made to great people. We are engaged for no end of feasts and dances, and I fear that the missionaries are deeply disgusted because we have caused their best parishioners to violate church discipline by our grand Siva at Seumano's, which turns out to have been a political event and demonstration of Samoan nationality. As we avow without disguise our preference for old Samoan customs over the European innovations, we must expect to give offence; but a just fear of ridicule restrains me from the only truly comfortable step of adopting the native want of costume. Possibly the mosquitoes and fleas have something to do with the ridicule too. Yesterday afternoon we took the boat to town, which is a mile or more away, and a heavy rain drove us to shelter in Seumano's where we were entertained with a pineapple and the infernal *kawa* which I swallow only by compulsion. I asked Seumano to show us his fine mats, so the women took down the bundle from the cross-beams where their valuables are stored, and untied it, producing half a dozen mats, about the texture of the finest Panama straw, some five or six feet square. These are the Samoan jewels and heirlooms, which give distinction and power to their owner, and are the dowry of the women. The gift of a fine mat will pay for a life, and the last war was caused by an attempt to confiscate mats. If possible I will buy one and send it to you, but you can do nothing with it, for it is too rare for use, and not showy enough for ornament. You will have to put it into a coarser mat, tie it with cords in a bundle, and put it up in the attic, if you wish to be appreciative and Samoan. Fine mats are rarely made now; the whole number of them in existence is small and diminishing; they are more highly prized than ever by the chiefs, and I am almost ashamed to take any out of the country. Just as I am writing, a woman has come in from a neighboring village with four fine mats for sale, and I have bought the oldest and most worn, but the best, for a little more than thirty dollars. If I send it to you, it must go to Martha as a dowry to secure her a handsome young chief for a husband. Three or four such would secure her the swellest match in Samoa.

October 17. Yesterday afternoon Sewall took La Farge and me to call on Robert Louis Stevenson. We mounted some gawky horses and rode up the hills about an hour on the native road or path which leads across the island. The forest is not especially exciting; not nearly so beautiful as that above Hilo in Hawaii, but every now and again, as Captain Peter, or Pito, used to say, we came on some little touch of tropical effect that had charm, especially a party of three girls in their dress of green leaves, or *titi,* which La Farge became glowing about. The afternoon was lowering, with drops of rain, and misty in the distance. At last we came out on a clearing dotted with burned stumps exactly like a clearing in our backwoods. In the middle stood a two-story Irish shanty with steps outside to the upper floor, and a galvanised iron roof. A pervasive atmosphere of dirt seemed to hang around it, and the squalor like a railroad navvy's board hut. As we reached the steps a figure came out that I cannot do justice to. Imagine a man so thin and emaciated that he looked like a bundle of sticks in a bag, with a head and eyes morbidly intelligent and restless. He was costumed in a dirty striped cotton pyjamas, the baggy legs tucked into coarse knit woollen stockings, one of which was bright brown in color, the other a purplish dark tone. With him was a woman who retired for a moment into the house to reappear a moment afterwards, probably in some change of costume, but, as far as I could see, the change could have consisted only in putting shoes on her bare feet. She wore the usual missionary nightgown which was no cleaner than her husband's shirt and drawers, but she omitted the stockings. Her complexion and eyes were dark and strong, like a half-breed Mexican. They received us cordially enough, and as soon as Stevenson heard La Farge's name and learned who he was, they became very friendly, while I sat by, nervously conscious that my eyes could not help glaring at Stevenson's stockings, and wondering, as La Farge said, which color he would have chosen if he had been obliged to wear a pair that matched. We sat an hour or more, perched on his verandah, looking down over his field of black stumps, and the forest beyond, to the misty line of distant ocean to the northward. He has bought a hundred acres or more of mountain and forest so dense that he says it costs him a dollar for every foot he walks in it. To me the place seemed oppressively shut in by forest and mountain, but the weather may have caused that impression. When conversation fairly began, though I could not forget the dirt and discomfort, I found Stevenson extremely entertaining. He has the nervous restlessness of his disease, and, although he said he was unusually well, I half expected to see him drop with a hemorrhage at any moment, for he cannot be quiet, but sits down, jumps up, darts off and flies back, at every sentence he utters, and his eyes and features gleam with a hectic glow. He seems weak, and complains that the ride of an hour up to his place costs him a day's work; but, as he describes his travels and life in the South Seas, he has been through what would have broken me into a miserable rag. For months he has sailed about the islands in wretched trading schooners and stray steamers almost worse than sailing vessels, with such food as he could get, or lived on coral atolls eating bread-fruit and yams, all the time working hard with his pen, and of course always dirty, uncomfortable and poorly served, not to speak of being ill-clothed, which matters little in these parts. He has seen more of the islands than any literary or scientific man ever did before, and knows all he has seen. His talk is most entertaining, and of course interested us peculiarly. He says that the Tahitians are by far finer men than the Samoans, and that he does not regard the Samoans as an especially fine race, or the islands here as specially beautiful. I am not surprised at the last opinion, for I do not think this island of Upolo very beautiful as these islands go; certainly not so beautiful as the Hilo district of Hawaii; but I shall wait for our own judgment about the men and women. Tahiti and Nukuheva are his ideals, which encourages us with something to look forward to. He had much to say about his experiences, and about atolls, French *gens d'armes*, beach-combers, natives and Chinamen; about the island of Flatterers where the natives surrounded him and stroked him down, saying "Alofa," "love," and "You handsome man," "You all same as my father"; and about islands where the girls took away all his plug tobacco and picked his pocket of his matchbox, and then with the utmost dignity gave him one match to light his cigarette. But the natives, he says, are always respectable, while some of the whites are degraded beyond description. Pembroke, in his "South Sea Bubbles" has scandalised all Polynesia by libelling the chieftainess of one island where he was very hospitably treated, and is said to have behaved very ill. I can easily understand getting very mixed up about Polynesian morals, for I feel that the subject is a deep one, and the best informed whites seem perplexed about it; but I remember how much poor Okakura was perplexed by the same subject in America, and how frankly La Farge and I avowed our own ignorance even among our own people. Stevenson is about to build a house, and says he shall never leave the island again, and cannot understand how any man who is able to live in the South Seas, should consent to live elsewhere.

October 22. Time runs on, bringing no great variety, but

every day a little novelty to amuse us. I have taken to my water-colors again, because I find that La Farge will not paint unless I make-believe to do so. We sit in our native house, receiving visits; watching what goes on among the natives of the village; firing off our Kodaks at everything worth taking; and sketching the most commonplace object we can find, because the objects worth sketching are un-sketchable. Every day I pick up more queer knowledge of the people about me—knowledge that would have made a great Professor of me twenty years ago, but now has no other value than to amuse me for the moment, and perhaps to amuse you some day when my wanderings end. Our great neighbor Mata-afa comes over to see us often, and sends us many fruits and eatables; but the most entertaining of his attentions is the *tafalo* which he sends every day. Usually at eleven o'clock we hear shouts from the further side of the village green, and instantly two splendid young men, dressed only in their waist-cloths—lavalavas—of green leaves, with garlands of green leaves round their heads, come running and jumping and shouting across the green towards our house. As they come near we see that their faces are blackened; sometimes one whole side is black, sometimes only a square or wedge-shaped patch at the corner of the mouth; and their look is ferocity itself; but they arrive in a broad laugh, and one of them carries a wooden trough, full of baked bread-fruit kneaded with cocoa-nut milk and generally a little salt-water, which he sets on the ground under our eaves, and then ladles out with his hands into large bread-fruit leaves, after which they bound away again. I can do no more than taste it, for it is a rich, pasty stuff, like corn-starch or batter; but the natives consider it a great treat; and yesterday Mele Samsoni and Fangalo and various other guests came to share Mata-afa's generosity. La Farge and I photographed the two men as they ladled out their *tafalo;* but I fear it will be a long time before I know how my photograph succeeded. . . . Remember that the photograph takes all the color, life and charm out of the tropics, and leaves nothing but a conventional hardness that might as well be Scotch or Yankee for all the truth it has. The women especially suffer, for they pose stiffly, and lose the freedom of movement and the play of feature that most attract us. The bare back of a Samoan woman, when she is in motion, is a joy forever. I never tire of watching the swing of their arms, and the play of light over the great round curves of their bodies. At this moment two of them are sitting on the mats by my side, Tagata—or Kanaka, as she calls it—is a giantess who lives with Mata-afa, either as his daughter or niece or wife, I cannot decide which; for Mata-afa is believed to have had so many wives that the world never knows which is the last. Tagata is as jolly as she is big, and talks a little English. Today her hair is powdered with lime to give it a proper red tone for a picnic we all attend tomorrow; she looks like a *marquise,* but instead of jewels in her hair, she has tied round her head a single reddish-purple ti-leaf, as classical as any Greek coin. Her face is not classic, but broad, good-natured and in its way rather fine. I have photographed her half a dozen times. On the whole the jolliest girl is Fangalo whose photograph I send to Hay. Fangalo and the two other girls at Samsoni's supply our house with flowers every morning, and generally the whole foreign population—English or American—is to be seen lounging on Samsoni's porch, or sprawling on mats in his enclosure, laughing with Mrs. Samsoni or Fangalo or the others. . . . Fanua is not handsome, but the photograph is peculiarly hard on her. When excited she is not without effectiveness, witness her Siva. . . .

Day after tomorrow we start on a boat-journey along the coast to visit the chief towns. Seumano, our chief at Apia, escorts us in his boat, and is certain to make a great affair of it. He has already written ahead to prepare for our reception. We shall have *kawa,* roast pig, *tafalo,* Sivas and gifts wherever we go. Consul-General Sewall goes with us. Tonight we dine with the German Consul Stuebel. Tomorrow a big feast *chez* Papalii, the Samoan native chief justice.

Mediaevalist

Chapters II, VII, and XI sample the world that Henry Adams created anew in Mont-St.-Michel and Chartres. *From the beginning, the middle, and the end of the remarkable book come sections concerned with the verse, the architecture, and the character of the people who lived a life equal to their arts and their beliefs.*

There was nothing static in Adams' re-creation of the great mediaeval age of northern France. The twentieth century was involved as well as the eleventh, twelfth, and thirteenth. Therefore, the long-lasting interest of the book is not antiquarian, but dynamic. Adams confronted a chosen past with an unavoidable present, and made them both mean more.

La Chanson de Roland[1]

Molz pelerins qui vunt al Munt

Most pilgrims who come to the Mount

Enquierent molt e grant dreit unt

Enquire much and are quite right,

Comment l'igliese fut fundee

How the church was founded

Premierement et estoree

At first, and established.

Cil qui lor dient de l'estoire

Those who tell them the story

Que cil demandent en memoire

That they ask, in memory

Ne l'unt pas bien ainz vunt faillant

Have it not well, but fall in error

En plusors leus e mespernant

In many places, and misapprehension.

Por faire la apertement

In order to make it clearly

Entendre a cels qui escient

Intelligible to those who have

N'unt de clerzie l'a tornee

No knowledge of letters, it has been turned

De latin tote et ordenee

From the Latin, and wholly rendered

Pars veirs romieus novelement

In Romanesque verses, newly,

Molt en segrei por son convent

Much in secret, for his convent,

Uns jovencels moine est del Munt

By a youth; a monk he is of the Mount.

Deus en son reigne part li dunt

God in his kingdom grant him part!

Guillaume a non de Saint Paier

William is his name, of Saint-Pair

Cen vei escrit en cest quaier

As is seen written in this book.

El tens Robeirt de Torignie

In the time of Robert of Torigny

Fut cil romanz fait e trove

Was this roman made and invented.

[1] Chapter II of *Mont-St.-Michel and Chartres*, privately printed in 1904, published by Houghton Mifflin Co., in 1913 under the sponsorship of the American Institute of Architects.

These verses begin the 'Roman du Mont-Saint-Michel,' and if the spelling is corrected, they still read almost as easily as Voltaire; more easily than Verlaine; and much like a nursery rhyme; but as tourists cannot stop to clear their path, or smooth away the pebbles, they must be lifted over the rough spots, even when roughness is beauty. Translation is an evil, chiefly because every one who cares for mediaeval architecture cares for mediaeval French, and ought to care still more for mediaeval English. The language of this 'Roman' was the literary language of England. William of Saint-Pair was a subject of Henry II, King of England and Normandy; his verses, like those of Richard Coeur-de-Lion, are monuments of English literature. To this day their ballad measure is better suited to English than to French; even the words and idioms are more English than French. Any one who attacks them boldly will find that the 'vers romieus' run along like a ballad, singing their own meaning, and troubling themselves very little whether the meaning is exact or not. One's translation is sure to be full of gross blunders, but the supreme blunder is that of translating at all when one is trying to catch not a fact but a feeling. If translate one must, we had best begin by trying to be literal, under protest that it matters not a straw whether we succeed. Twelfth-century art was not precise; still less 'précieuse,' like Molière's famous seventeenth-century prudes.

The verses of the young monk, William, who came from the little Norman village of Saint-Pair, near Granville, within sight of the Mount, were verses not meant to be brilliant. Simple human beings like rhyme better than prose, though both may say the same thing, as they like a curved line better than a straight one, or a blue better than a grey; but, apart from the sensual appetite, they chose rhyme in creating their literature for the practical reason that they remembered it better than prose. Men had to carry their libraries in their heads.

These lines of William, beginning his story, are valuable because for once they give a name and a date. Abbot Robert of Torigny ruled at the Mount from 1154 to 1186. We have got to travel again and again between Mont-Saint-

Michel and Chartres during these years, but for the moment we must hurry to get back to William the Conqueror and the 'Chanson de Roland.' William of Saint-Pair comes in here, out of place, only on account of a pretty description he gave of the annual pilgrimage to the Mount, which is commonly taken to be more or less like what he saw every year on the Archangel's Day, and what had existed ever since the Normans became Christian in 912:

Li jorz iert clers e sanz grant vent.	The day was clear, without much wind.
Les meschines e les vallez	The maidens and the varlets
Chascuns d'els dist verz ou sonnez.	Each of them said verse or song;
Neis li viellart revunt chantant	Even the old people go singing;
De leece funt tuit semblant.	All have a look of joy.
Qui plus ne seit si chante *outree*	Who knows no more sings *Hurrah*,
E *Dex aie* u *Asusee.*	Or *God help*, or *Up and On!*
Cil jugleor la u il vunt	The minstrels there where they go
Tuit lor vieles traites unt	Have all brought their viols;
Laiz et sonnez vunt vielant.	Lays and songs playing as they go.
Li tens est beals la joie est grant.	The weather is fine: the joy is great:
Cil palefrei e cil destrier	The palfreys and the chargers,
E cil roncin e cil sommier	And the hackneys and the packhorses
Qui errouent par le chemin	Which wander along the road
Que menouent cil pelerin	That the pilgrims follow,
De totes parz henissant vunt	On all sides neighing go,
Por la grant joie que il unt.	For the great joy they feel.
Neis par les bois chantouent tuit	Even in the woods sing all
Li oiselet grant et petit.	The little birds, big and small.
Li buef les vaches vunt muant	The oxen and the cows go lowing
Par les forez e repaissant.	Through the forests as they feed.
Cors e boisines e fresteals	Horns and trumpets and shepherd's pipes
E fleutes e chalemeals	And flutes and pipes of reed
Sonnoent si que les montaignes	Sound so that the mountains

En retintoent et les pleignes.	Echo to them, and the plains.
Que esteit donc les plaiseiz	How was it then with the glades
E des forez e des larriz.	And with the forests and the pastures?
En cels par a tel sonneiz	In these there was such sound
Com si ce fust cers acolliz.	As though it were a stag at bay.
Entor le mont el bois follu	About the Mount, in the leafy wood,
Cil travetier unt tres tendu	The workmen have tents set up:
Rues unt fait par les chemins.	Streets have made along the roads.
Plentei i out de divers vins	Plenty there was of divers wines,
Pain e pastez fruit e poissons	Bread and pasties, fruit and fish,
Oisels obleies veneisons	Birds, cakes, venison,
De totes parz aveit a vendre	Everywhere there was for sale.
Assez en out qui ad que tendre.	Enough he had who has the means to pay.

If you are not satisfied with this translation, any scholar of French will easily help to make a better, for we are not studying grammar or archaeology, and would rather be inaccurate in such matters than not, if, at that price, a freer feeling of the art could be caught. Better still, you can turn to Chaucer, who wrote his Canterbury Pilgrimage two hundred years afterwards:

> Whanne that April with his shoures sote
> The droughte of March hath perced to the rote . . .
> Than longen folk to gon on pilgrimages
> And palmeres for to seken strange strondes . . .
> And especially, from every shires ende
> Of Englelonde, to Canterbury they wende
> The holy blisful martyr for to seke,
> That hem hath holpen whan that they were seke.

The passion for pilgrimages was universal among our ancestors as far back as we can trace them. For at least a thousand years it was their chief delight, and is not yet extinct. To feel the art of Mont-Saint-Michel and Chartres we have got to become pilgrims again: but, just now, the point of most interest is not the pilgrim so much as the minstrel who sang to amuse him—the *jugleor* or *jongleur*—who was at home in every abbey, castle or cottage, as well as at every shrine. The jugleor became a jongleur and degenerated into the street-juggler; the minstrel, or *menestrier*, became very early a word of abuse, equivalent to blackguard; and from the beginning the profession seems to have been socially decried, like that of a music-hall singer or dancer in later times; but in the eleventh century, or perhaps earlier still, the jongleur seems to have been a poet, and to have composed the songs he sang. The immense mass of poetry known as the 'Chansons de Geste' seems to have been composed as well as sung by the un-named Homers of France, and of all spots in the many provinces where the French language in its many dialects prevailed, Mont-Saint-Michel should have been the favourite with the jongleur, not only because the swarms of pilgrims assured him food and an occasional small piece of silver, but also because Saint Michael was the saint militant of all the warriors whose exploits in war were the subject of the 'Chansons de Geste.' William of Saint-Pair was a priest-poet; he was not a minstrel, and his 'Roman' was not a *chanson;* it was made to read, not to recite; but the 'Chanson de Roland' was a different affair.

So it was, too, with William's contemporaries and rivals or predecessors, the monumental poets of Norman-English literature. Wace, whose rhymed history of the Norman dukes, which he called the 'Roman de Rou,' or 'Rollo,' is an English classic of the first rank, was a canon of Bayeux when William of Saint-Pair was writing at Mont-Saint-Michel. His rival Benoist, who wrote another famous chronicle on the same subject, was also a historian, and not a singer. In that day literature meant verse; elegance in French prose did not yet exist; but the elegancies of poetry in the twelfth century were as different, in kind, from the grand style of the eleventh, as Virgil was different from Homer.

William of Saint-Pair introduces us to the pilgrimage and to the jongleur, as they had existed at least two hundred years before his time, and were to exist two hundred years after him. Of all our two hundred and fifty million arithmetical ancestors who were going on pilgrimages in the middle of the eleventh century, the two who would probably most interest every one, after eight hundred years have passed, would be William the Norman and Harold the Saxon. Through William of Saint-Pair and Wace and Benoist, and the most charming literary monument of all, the Bayeux tapestry of Queen Matilda, we can build up the story of such a pilgrimage which shall be as historically exact as the battle of Hastings, and as artistically true as the Abbey Church.

According to Wace's 'Roman de Rou,' when Harold's father, Earl Godwin, died, April 15, 1053, Harold wished to obtain the release of certain hostages, a brother and a cousin, whom Godwin had given to Edward the Confessor as security for his good behaviour, and whom Edward had sent to Duke William for safe-keeping. Wace took the story from other and older sources, and its accuracy is much disputed, but the fact that Harold went to Normandy seems to be certain, and you will see at Bayeux the picture of Harold asking permission of King Edward to make the journey, and departing on horseback, with his hawk and hounds and followers, to take ship at Bosham, near Chichester and Portsmouth. The date alone is doubtful. Common sense seems to suggest that the earliest possible date could not be too early to explain the rash youth of the aspirant to a throne who put himself in the power of a rival in the eleventh century. When that rival chanced to be William the Bastard, not even boyhood could excuse the folly; but Mr. Freeman, the chief authority on this delicate subject, inclined to think that Harold was forty years old when he committed his blunder, and that the year was about 1064. Between 1054 and 1064 the historian is free to choose what year he likes, and the tourist is still freer. To save trouble for the memory, the year 1058 will serve, since this is the date of the triumphal arches of the Abbey Church on the Mount. Harold, in sailing from the neighbourhood of Portsmouth, must have been bound for Caen or Rouen, but the usual west winds drove him eastward till he was thrown ashore on the coast of Ponthieu, between Abbéville and Boulogne, where he fell into the hands of the Count of

Ponthieu, from whom he was rescued or ransomed by Duke
William of Normandy and taken to Rouen. According to
Wace and the 'Roman de Rou':

Guillaume tint Heraut maint jour	William kept Harold many a day,
Si com il dut a grant enor.	As was his due in great honour.
A maint riche torneiement	To many a rich tournament
Le fist aller mult noblement.	Made him go very nobly.
Chevals e armes li dona	Horses and arms gave him
Et en Bretaigne le mena	And into Brittany led him
Ne sai de veir treiz faiz ou quatre	I know not truly whether three or four times
Quant as Bretons se dut combattre.	When he had to make war on the Bretons.

Perhaps the allusion to rich tournaments belongs to the
time of Wace rather than to that of Harold a century
earlier, before the first crusade, but certainly Harold did
go with William on at least one raid into Brittany, and the
charming tapestry of Bayeux, which tradition calls by the
name of Queen Matilda, shows William's men-at-arms
crossing the sands beneath Mont-Saint-Michel, with the
Latin legend: 'Et venerunt ad Montem Michaelis. Hic
Harold dux trahebat eos de arena. Venerunt ad flumen
Cononis.' They came to Mont-Saint-Michel, and Harold
dragged them out of the quicksands. They came to the
river Couesnon. Harold must have got great fame by saving
life on the sands, to be remembered and recorded by the
Normans themselves after they had killed him; but this is
the affair of historians. Tourists note only that Harold and
William came to the Mount: 'Venerunt ad Montem.' They
would never have dared to pass it, on such an errand, without stopping to ask the help of Saint Michael.

If William and Harold came to the Mount, they certainly
dined or supped in the old refectory, which is where we
have lain in wait for them. Where Duke William was, his
jongleur—jugleor—was not far, and Wace knew, as every
one in Normandy seemed to know, who this favourite was
—his name, his character, and his song. To him Wace owed
one of the most famous passages in his story of the assault
at Hastings, where Duke William and his battle began their
advance against the English lines:

Taillefer qui mult bien chantout	Taillefer who was famed for song,
Sor un cheval qui tost alout	Mounted on a charger strong,
Devant le duc alout chantant	Rode on before the Duke, and sang
De Karlemaigne e de Rollant	Of Roland and of Charlemagne,
E d'Oliver e des vassals	Oliver and the vassals all
Qui morurent en Rencevals.	Who fell in fight at Roncesvals.
Quant il orent chevalchie tant	When they had ridden till they saw
Qu'as Engleis vindrent apreismant:	The English battle close before:
'Sire,' dist Taillefer, 'merci!	'Sire,' said Taillefer, 'a grace!
Io vos ai longuement servi.	I have served you long and well;
Tot mon servise me devez.	All reward you owe me still;
Hui se vos plaist le me rendez.	Today repay me if you please.
Por tot guerredon vos requier	For all guerdon I require,
E si vos voil forment preier	And ask of you in formal prayer,
Otreiez mei que io ni faille	Grant to me as mine of right
Le premier colp de la bataille.'	The first blow struck in the fight.'
Li dus respondi: 'Io l'otrei.'	The Duke answered: 'I grant.'

Of course, critics doubt the story, as they very properly doubt everything. They maintain that the 'Chanson de Roland' was not as old as the battle of Hastings, and certainly Wace gave no sufficient proof of it. Poetry was not usually written to prove facts. Wace wrote a hundred years after the battle of Hastings. One is not morally required to be pedantic to the point of knowing more than Wace knew, but the feeling of scepticism, before so serious a monument as Mont-Saint-Michel, is annoying. The 'Chanson de Roland' ought not to be trifled with, at least by tourists in search of art. One is shocked at the possibility of being deceived about the starting-point of American genealogy. Taillefer and the song rest on the same evidence that Duke William and Harold and the battle itself rest upon, and to doubt the 'Chanson' is to call the very roll of Battle Abbey in question. The whole fabric of society totters; the British peerage turns pale.

Wace did not invent all his facts. William of Malmesbury

is supposed to have written his prose chronicle about 1120 when many of the men who fought at Hastings must have been alive, and William expressly said: 'Tunc cantilena Rollandi inchoata ut martium viri exemplum pugnaturos accenderet, inclamatoque dei auxilio, praelium consertum.' Starting the 'Chanson de Roland' to inflame the fighting temper of the men, battle was joined. This seems enough proof to satisfy any sceptic, yet critics still suggest that the 'cantilena Rollandi' must have been a Norman 'Chanson de Rou,' or 'Rollo,' or at best an earlier version of the 'Chanson de Roland'; but no Norman chanson would have inflamed the martial spirit of William's army, which was largely French; and as for the age of the version, it is quite immaterial for Mont-Saint-Michel; the actual version is old enough.

Taillefer himself is more vital to the interest of the dinner in the refectory, and his name was not mentioned by William of Malmesbury. If the song was started by the Duke's order, it was certainly started by the Duke's jongleur, and the name of this jongleur happens to be known on still better authority than that of William of Malmesbury. Guy of Amiens went to England in 1068 as almoner of Queen Matilda, and there wrote a Latin poem on the battle of Hastings which must have been complete within ten years after the battle was fought, for Guy died in 1076. Taillefer, he said, led the Duke's battle:

> Incisor-ferri mimus cognomine dictus.

'Taillefer, a jongleur known by that name.' A mime was a singer, but Taillefer was also an actor:

> Histrio cor audax nimium quem nobilitabat.

'A jongleur whom a very brave heart ennobled.' The jongleur was not noble by birth, but was ennobled by his bravery.

> Hortatur Gallos verbis et territat Anglos
> Alte projiciens ludit et ense suo.

Like a drum-major with his staff, he threw his sword high in the air and caught it, while he chanted his song to the

French, and terrified the English. The rhymed chronicle
of Geoffroy Gaimer who wrote about 1150, and that of
Benoist who was Wace's rival, added the story that Taillefer died in the mêlée.

The most unlikely part of the tale was, after all, not the
singing of the 'Chanson,' but the prayer of Taillefer to the
Duke:

> 'Otreiez mei que io ni faille
> Le premier colp de la bataille.'

Legally translated, Taillefer asked to be ennobled, and offered to pay for it with his life. The request of a jongleur
to lead the Duke's battle seems incredible. In early French
'bataille' meant battalion—the column of attack. The Duke's
grant: 'Io l'otreil' seems still more fanciful. Yet Guy of
Amiens distinctly confirmed the story: 'Histrio cor audax
nimium quem nobilitabat'; a stage-player—a juggler—the
Duke's singer—whose bravery ennobled him. The Duke
granted him—*octroya*—his patent of nobility on the field.

All this preamble leads only to unite the 'Chanson' with
the architecture of the Mount, by means of Duke William
and his Breton campaign of 1058. The poem and the
church are akin; they go together, and explain each other.
Their common trait is their military character, peculiar to
the eleventh century. The round arch is masculine. The
'Chanson' is so masculine that, in all its four thousand lines,
the only Christian woman so much as mentioned was Alda,
the sister of Oliver and the betrothed of Roland, to whom
one stanza, exceedingly like a later insertion, was given, toward the end. Never after the first crusade did any great
poem rise to such heroism as to sustain itself without a
heroine. Even Dante attempted no such feat.

Duke William's party, then, is to be considered as assembled at supper in the old refectory, in the year 1058, while
the triumphal piers of the church above are rising. The
Abbot, Ralph of Beaumont, is host; Duke William sits with
him on a daïs; Harold is by his side 'a grant enor'; the Duke's
brother, Odo, Bishop of Bayeux, with the other chief vassals, are present; and the Duke's jongleur Taillefer is at his
elbow. The room is crowded with soldiers and monks, but

all are equally anxious to hear Taillefer sing. As soon as dinner is over, at a nod from the Duke, Taillefer begins:

Carles li reis nostre emperere magnes	Charles the king, our emperor, the great,
Set anz tuz pleins ad estet en Espaigne	Seven years complete has been in Spain,
Cunquist la tere tresque en la mer altaigne	Conquered the land as far as the high seas,
Ni ad castel ki devant lui remaigne	Nor is there castle that holds against him,
Murs ne citez ni est remes a fraindre.	Nor wall or city left to capture.

The 'Chanson' opened with these lines, which had such a direct and personal bearing on every one who heard them as to sound like prophecy. Within ten years William was to stand in England where Charlemagne stood in Spain. His mind was full of it, and of the means to attain it; and Harold was even more absorbed than he by the anxiety of the position. Harold had been obliged to take oath that he would support William's claim to the English throne, but he was still undecided, and William knew men too well to feel much confidence in an oath. As Taillefer sang on, he reached the part of Ganelon, the typical traitor, the invariable figure of mediaeval society. No feudal lord was without a Ganelon. Duke William saw them all about him. He might have felt that Harold would play the part, but if Harold should choose rather to be Roland, Duke William could have foretold that his own brother, Bishop Odo, after gorging himself on the plunder of half England, would turn into a Ganelon so dangerous as to require a prison for life. When Taillefer reached the battle-scenes, there was no further need of imagination to realize them. They were scenes of yesterday and tomorrow. For that matter, Charlemagne or his successor was still at Aix, and the Moors were still in Spain. Archbishop Turpin of Rheims had fought with sword and mace in Spain, while Bishop Odo of Bayeux was to marshal his men at Hastings, like a modern general, with a staff, but both were equally at home on the field of battle. Verse by verse, the song was a literal mirror of the Mount. The battle of Hastings was to be fought on the Archangel's

Day. What happened to Roland at Roncesvalles was to
happen to Harold at Hastings, and Harold, as he was dying
like Roland, was to see his brother Gyrth die like Oliver.
Even Taillefer was to be a part, and a distinguished part,
of his chanson. Sooner or later, all were to die in the large
and simple way of the eleventh century. Duke William himself, twenty years later, was to meet a violent death at
Mantes in the same spirit, and if Bishop Odo did not die
in battle, he died, at least, like an eleventh-century hero,
on the first crusade. First or last, the whole company died
in fight, or in prison, or on crusade, while the monks shrived
them and prayed.

Then Taillefer certainly sang the great death-scenes.
Even to this day every French school-boy, if he knows no
other poetry, knows these verses by heart. In the eleventh
century they wrung the heart of every man-at-arms in Europe, whose school was the field of battle and the hand-to-
hand fight. No modern singer ever enjoys such power over
an audience as Taillefer exercised over these men who were
actors as well as listeners. In the mêlée at Roncesvalles,
overborne by innumerable Saracens, Oliver at last calls for
help:

Munjoie escriet e haltement e cler.	'Montjoie!' he cries, loud and clear.
Rollant apelet sun ami e sun per;	Roland he calls, his friend and peer:
'Sire compainz a mei kar vus justez.	'Sir Friend! ride now to help me here!
A grant dulur ermes hoi de-serveret.' Aoi.	Parted today, great pity were.'

Of course the full value of the verse cannot be regained.
One knows neither how it was sung nor even how it was
pronounced. The assonances are beyond recovering; the
'laisse' or leash of verses or assonances with the concluding
cry, 'Aoi,' has long ago vanished from verse or song. The
sense is as simple as the 'Ballad of Chevy Chase,' but one
must imagine the voice and acting. Doubtless Taillefer
acted each motive; when Oliver called loud and clear,
Taillefer's voice rose; when Roland spoke 'doulcement et

suef,' the singer must have sung gently and soft; and when the two friends, with the singular courtesy of knighthood and dignity of soldiers, bowed to each other in parting and turned to face their deaths, Taillefer may have indicated the movement as he sang. The verses gave room for great acting. Hearing Oliver's cry for help, Roland rode up, and at sight of the desperate field, lost for a moment his consciousness:

As vus Rollant sur sun cheval pasmet
E Olivier ki est a mort nafrez!

Tant ad sainiet li oil li sunt trublet
Ne luinz ne pres ne poet veeir si cler
Que reconuisset nisun hume mortel.
Sun cumpaignun cum il l'ad encuntret
Sil fiert amunt sur l'elme a or gemmet
Tut li detrenchet d'ici que al nasel
Mais en la teste ne l'ad mie adeset.
A icel colp l'ad Rollanz reguardet
Si li demandet dulcement et suef
'Sire cumpainz, faites le vus de gred?
Ja est ço Rollanz ki tant vus soelt amer.
Par nule guise ne m'aviez desfiet,'
Dist Oliviers: 'Or vus oi jo parler
Io ne vus vei. Veied vus damnedeus!
Ferut vus ai. Kar le me pardunez!'
Rollanz respunt: 'Jo n'ai nient de mel.
Jol vus parduins ici e devant deu.'

There Roland sits unconscious on his horse,
And Oliver who wounded is to death,
So much has bled, his eyes grow dark to him,
Nor far nor near can see so clear
As to recognize any mortal man.
His friend, when he has encountered him,
He strikes upon the helmet of gemmed gold,
Splits it from the crown to the nosepiece,
But to the head he has not reached at all.
At this blow Roland looks at him,
Asks him gently and softly:
'Sir Friend, do you it in earnest?
You know 't is Roland who has so loved you.
In no way have you sent to me defiance.'
Says Oliver: 'Indeed I hear you speak,
I do not see you. May God see and save you!
Strike you I did. I pray you pardon me.'
Roland replies: 'I have no harm at all.
I pardon you here and before God!'

| A icel mot l'uns al altre ad clinet. | At this word, one to the other bends himself. |
| Par tel amur as les vus desev-rez! | With such affection, there they separate. |

No one should try to render this into English—or, indeed, into modern French—verse, but any one who will take the trouble to catch the metre and will remember that each verse in the 'leash' ends in the same sound—*aimer, parler, cler, mortel, damnedé, mel, deu, suef, nasel*—however the terminal syllables may be spelled, can follow the feeling of the poetry as well as though it were Greek hexameter. He will feel the simple force of the words and action, as he feels Homer. It is the grand style—the eleventh century:

> Ferut vus ail Kar le me pardunez!

Not a syllable is lost, and always the strongest syllable is chosen. Even the sentiment is monosyllabic and curt:

> Ja est ço Rollanz ki tant vus soelt amer!

Taillefer had, in such a libretto, the means of producing dramatic effects that the French comedy or the grand opera never approached, and such as made Bayreuth seem thin and feeble. Duke William's barons must have clung to his voice and action as though they were in the very mêlée, striking at the helmets of gemmed gold. They had all been there, and were to be there again. As the climax approached, they saw the scene itself; probably they had seen it every year, more or less, since they could swing a sword. Taillefer chanted the death of Oliver and of Archbishop Turpin and all the other barons of the rear guard, except Roland, who was left for dead by the Saracens when they fled on hearing the horns of Charlemagne's returning host. Roland came back to consciousness on feeling a Saracen marauder tugging at his sword Durendal. With a blow of his ivory horn—*oliphant*—he killed the pagan; then feeling death near, he prepared for it. His first thought was for Durendal, his sword, which he could not leave to infidels. In the singular triple repetition which gives more of the same solidity and architectural weight to the verse, he made three attempts to break the sword, with a lament—a *plaint*

—for each. Three times he struck with all his force against the rock; each time the sword rebounded without breaking. The third time—

Rollanz ferit en une pierre bise	Roland strikes on a grey stone,
Plus en abat que jo ne vus sai dire.	More of it cuts off than I can tell you.
L'espee cruist ne fruisset ne ne briset	The sword grinds, but shatters not nor breaks,
Cuntre le ciel amunt est resortie.	Upward against the sky it rebounds.
Quant veit li quens que ne la fraindrat mie	When the Count sees that he can never break it,
Mult dulcement la plainst a sei meisme.	Very gently he mourns it to himself:
'El Durendal cum ies bele e saintisme!	'Ah, Durendal, how fair you are and sacred!
En l'oret punt asez i ad reliques.	In your golden guard are many relics,
La dent saint Pierre e del sanc seint Basilie	The tooth of Saint Peter and blood of Saint Basil,
E des chevels mun seignur seint Denisie	And hair of my seigneur Saint Denis,
Del vestment i ad seinte Marie.	Of the garment too of Saint Mary.
Il nen est dreiz que paien te baillisent.	It is not right that pagans should own you.
De chrestiens devez estre servie.	By Christians you should be served,
Ne vus ait hum ki vacet cuardie!	Nor should man have you who does cowardice.
Mult larges terres de vus averai cunquises	Many wide lands by you I have conquered
Que Carles tient ki la barbe ad flurie.	That Charles holds, who has the white beard,
E li emperere en est e ber e riches.'	And emperor of them is noble and rich.'

This 'laisse' is even more eleventh-century than the other, but it appealed no longer to the warriors; it spoke rather to the monks. To the warriors, the sword itself was the religion, and the relics were details of ornament or strength. To the priest, the list of relics was more eloquent than the Regent diamond on the hilt and the Kohinoor on the scabbard. Even to us it is interesting if it is understood. Roland had gone on pilgrimage to the Holy Land. He had stopped at Rome and won the friendship of Saint Peter, as the tooth proved; he had passed through Constantinople and secured the help of Saint Basil; he had reached Jerusalem and gained the affection of the Virgin; he had come home to France and secured the support of his 'Seigneur' Saint Denis; for Roland, like Hugh Capet, was a liege-man of Saint Denis and French to the heart. France, to him, was Saint Denis, and at most the Île de France, but not Anjou or even Maine. These were countries he had conquered with Durendal:

> Jo l'en cunquis e Anjou e Bretaigne
> Si l'en cunquis e Peitou e le Maine
> Jo l'en cunquis Normendie la franche
> Si l'en cunquis Provence e Equitaigne.

He had conquered these for his emperor Charlemagne with the help of his immediate spiritual lord or seigneur Saint Denis, but the monks knew that he could never have done these feats without the help of Saint Peter, Saint Basil, and Saint Mary the Blessed Virgin, whose relics, in the hilt of his sword, were worth more than any king's ransom. To this day a tunic of the Virgin is the most precious property of the cathedral at Chartres. Either one of Roland's relics would have made the glory of any shrine in Europe, and every monk knew their enormous value and power better than he knew the value of Roland's conquests.

Yet even the religion is martial, as though it were meant for the fighting Archangel and Odo of Bayeux. The relics serve the sword; the sword is not in service of the relics. As the death-scene approaches, the song becomes even more military:

Ço sent Rollanz que la mort le tresprent	Then Roland feels that death is taking him;
Devers la teste sur le quer li descent.	Down from the head upon the heart it falls.
Desuz un pin i est alez curanz	Beneath a pine he hastens running;
Sur l'erbe verte si est culchiez adenz	On the green grass he throws himself down;
Desuz lui met s'espee e l'olifant	Beneath him puts his sword and oliphant,
Turnat sa teste vers la paiene gent.	Turns his face toward the pagan army.

Pur ço l'ad fait que il voelt veirement
Que Carles diet et trestute sa gent
Li gentils quens quil fut morz cunqueranz.

For this he does it, that he wishes greatly
That Charles should say and all his men,
The gentle Count has died a conqueror.

Thus far, not a thought or a word strays from the field of war. With a childlike intensity, every syllable bends toward the single idea—

Li gentils quens quil fut morz cunqueranz.

Only then the singer allowed the Church to assert some of its rights:

Ço sent Rollanz de sun tens ni ad plus
Devers Espaigne gist en un pui agut
A l'une main si ad sun piz batut.
'Deus meie culpe vers les tues vertuz
De mes pecchiez des granz e des menuz
Que jo ai fait des l'ure que nez fui
Tresqu'a cest jur que ci sui consouz.'
Sun destre guant en ad vers deu tendut
Angle del ciel i descendent a lui. Aoi.
Li quens Rollanz se jut desuz un pin
Envers Espaigne en ad turnet sun vis
De plusurs choses a remembrer li prist
De tantes terres cume li bers cunquist
De dulce France des humes de sun lign
De Carlemagne sun seignur kil nurrit
Ne poet muer men plurt e ne suspirt

Then Roland feels that his last hour has come
Facing toward Spain he lies on a steep hill,
While with one hand he beats upon his breast:
'Mea culpa, God! through force of thy miracles
Pardon my sins, the great as well as small,
That I have done from the hour I was born
Down to this day that I have now attained.'
His right glove toward God he lifted up.
Angels from heaven descend on him. Aoi.
Count Roland throws himself beneath a pine
And toward Spain has turned his face away.
Of many things he called the memory back,
Of many lands that he, the brave, had conquered,
Of gentle France, the men of his lineage,
Of Charlemagne his lord, who nurtured him;
He cannot help but weep and sigh for these,

Mais lui meisme ne voelt metre en ubli	But for himself will not forget to care;
Claimet sa culpe si priet deu mercit.	He cries his Culpe, he prays to God for grace.
'Veire paterne ki unkes ne mentis	'O God the Father who has never lied,
Seint Lazarun de mort resur-rexis	Who raised up Saint Lazarus from death,
E Daniel des liuns guaresis	And Daniel from the lions saved,
Guaris de mei l'anme de tuz perils	Save my soul from all the perils
Pur les pecchiez que en ma vie fis.'	For the sins that in my life I did!'
Sun destre guant a deu en pur-offrit	His right-hand glove to God he proffered;
E de sa main seinz Gabriel lad pris	Saint Gabriel from his hand took it;
Desur sun braz teneit le chief enclin	Upon his arm he held his head inclined,
Juintes ses mains est alez a sa fin.	Folding his hands he passed to his end.
Deus li tramist sun angle cheru-bin	God sent to him his angel cherubim
E Seint Michiel de la mer del peril	And Saint Michael of the Sea in Peril,
Ensemble od els Seinz Gabriels i vint	Together with them came Saint Gabriel.
L'anme del cunte portent en pareis.	The soul of the Count they bear to Paradise.

Our age has lost much of its ear for poetry, as it has its eye for colour and line, and its taste for war and worship, wine and women. Not one man in a hundred thousand could now feel what the eleventh century felt in these verses of the 'Chanson,' and there is no reason for trying to do so, but there is a certain use in trying for once to understand not so much the feeling as the meaning. The naïveté of the poetry is that of the society. God the Father was the feudal seigneur, who raised Lazarus—his baron or vassal—from the grave, and freed Daniel, as an evidence of his power and loyalty; a seigneur who never lied, or was false to his word. God the Father, as feudal seigneur, absorbs the Trinity, and, what is more significant, absorbs or excludes also the Virgin, who is not mentioned in the prayer. To this seigneur, Roland in dying, proffered (puroffrit) his right-hand gauntlet. Death was an act of homage. God sent down his Archangel Gabriel as his representative to accept the homage and receive the glove. To Duke William and his barons nothing could seem more natural and correct. God was not farther away than Charlemagne.

Correct as the law may have been, the religion even at that time must have seemed to the monks to need professional advice. Roland's life was not exemplary. The 'Chanson' had taken pains to show that the disaster at Roncesvalles was due to Roland's headstrong folly and temper. In dying, Roland had not once thought of these faults, or repented of his worldly ambitions, or mentioned the name of Alda, his betrothed. He had clung to the memory of his wars and conquests, his lineage, his earthly seigneur Charlemagne, and of 'douce France.' He had forgotten to give so much as an allusion to Christ. The poet regarded all these matters as the affair of the Church; all the warrior cared for was courage, loyalty, and prowess.

The interest of these details lies not in the scholarship or the historical truth or even the local colour, so much as in the art. The naïveté of the thought is repeated by the simplicity of the verse. Word and thought are equally monosyllabic. Nothing ever matched it. The words bubble like a stream in the woods:

> Ço sent Rollanz de sun tens ni ad plus.

Try and put them into modern French, and see what will happen:

> Que jo ai fait des l'ure que nez fui.

The words may remain exactly the same, but the poetry will have gone out of them. Five hundred years later, even the English critics had so far lost their sense for military poetry that they professed to be shocked by Milton's monosyllables:

> Whereat he inly raged, and, as they talked,
> Smote him into the midriff with a stone
> That beat out life.

Milton's language was indeed more or less archaic and Biblical; it was a Puritan affectation; but the 'Chanson' in the refectory actually reflected, repeated, echoed, the piers and arches of the Abbey Church just rising above. The verse is built up. The qualities of the architecture reproduce themselves in the song: the same directness, simplicity, absence of self-consciousness; the same intensity of purpose; even the same material; the prayer is granite:

> Guaris de mei l'anme de tuz perils
> Pur les pecchiez que en ma vie fis!

The action of dying is felt, like the dropping of a keystone into the vault, and if the Romanesque arches in the church, which are within hearing, could speak, they would describe what they are doing in the precise words of the poem:

Desur sun braz teneit le chief enclin	Upon their shoulders have their heads inclined,
Juintes ses mains est alez a sa fin.	Folded their hands, and sunken to their rest.

Many thousands of times these verses must have been sung at the Mount and echoed in every castle and on every battlefield from the Welsh Marches to the shores of the Dead Sea. No modern opera or play ever approached the popularity of the 'Chanson.' None has ever expressed with anything like the same completeness the society that produced it. Chanted by every minstrel—known by heart, from beginning to end, by every man and woman and child, lay or clerical—translated into every tongue—more intensely felt, if possible, in Italy and Spain than in Normandy and England—perhaps most effective, as a work of art, when sung by the Templars in their great castles in the Holy Land —it is now best felt at Mont-Saint-Michel, and from the first must have been there at home. The proof is the line, evidently inserted for the sake of its local effect, which invoked Saint Michael in Peril of the Sea at the climax of Roland's death, and one needs no original documents or contemporary authorities to prove that, when Taillefer came to this invocation, not only Duke William and his

barons, but still more Abbot Ranulf and his monks, broke
into a frenzy of sympathy which expressed the masculine
and military passions of the Archangel better than it accorded with the rules of Saint Benedict.

Roses and Apses[1]

Like all great churches, that are not mere storehouses of
theology, Chartres expressed, besides whatever else it
meant, an emotion, the deepest man ever felt—the struggle
of his own littleness to grasp the infinite. You may, if you
like, figure in it a mathematic formula of infinity—the
broken arch, our finite idea of space; the spire, pointing,
with its converging lines, to unity beyond space; the sleep-
less, restless thrust of the vaults, telling the unsatisfied, in-
complete, overstrained effort of man to rival the energy,
intelligence, and purpose of God. Thomas Aquinas and the
schoolmen tried to put it in words, but their Church is another chapter. In act, all man's work ends there;—mathematics, physics, chemistry, dynamics, optics, every sort of
machinery science may invent—to this favour come at last,
as religion and philosophy did before science was born. All
that the centuries can do is to express the idea differently:
a miracle or a dynamo; a dome or a coal-pit; a cathedral
or a world's fair; and sometimes to confuse the two expressions together. The world's fair tends more and more vigorously to express the thought of infinite energy; the great
cathedrals of the Middle Ages always reflected the industries and interests of a world's fair. Chartres showed it less
than Laon or Paris, for Chartres was never a manufacturing
town, but a shrine, such as Lourdes, where the Virgin was
known to have done miracles, and had been seen in person;
but still the shrine turned itself into a market and created
valuable industries. Indeed, this was the chief objection
which Saint Paul made to Ephesus and Saint Bernard to
the cathedrals. They were in some ways more industrial

[1] Chapter VII of *Mont-St.-Michel and Chartres*.

than religious. The mere masonry and structure made a vast market for labour; the fixed metalwork and woodwork were another; but the decoration was by far the greatest. The wood-carving, the glass windows, the sculpture, inside and out, were done mostly in workshops on the spot, but besides these fixed objects, precious works of the highest perfection filled the church treasuries. Their money value was great then; it is greater now. No world's fair is likely to do better today. After five hundred years of spoliation, these objects fill museums still, and are bought with avidity at every auction, at prices continually rising and quality steadily falling, until a bit of twelfth-century glass would be a trouvaille like an emerald; a tapestry earlier than 1600 is not for mere tourists to hope; an enamel, a missal, a crystal, a cup, an embroidery of the Middle Ages belongs only to our betters, and almost invariably, if not to the State, to the rich Jews, whose instinctive taste has seized the whole field of art which rested on their degradation. Royalty and feudality spent their money rather on arms and clothes. The Church alone was universal patron, and the Virgin was the dictator of taste.

With the Virgin's taste, during her regency, critics never find fault. One cannot know its whole magnificence, but one can accept it as a matter of faith and trust, as one accepts all her other miracles without cavilling over small details of fact. The period of eighteenth-century scepticism about such matters and the bourgeois taste of Voltaire and Diderot have long since passed, with the advent of a scientific taste still more miraculous; the whole world of the Virgin's art, catalogued in the 'Dictionnaire du Mobilier Français' in six volumes by Viollet-le-Duc; narrated as history by M. Labarte, M. Molinier, M. Paul Lacroix; catalogued in museums by M. du Sommerard and a score of others, in works almost as costly as the subjects—all the vast variety of bric-à-brac, useful or ornamental, belonging to the Church, increased enormously by the insatiable, universal, private demands for imagery, in ivory, wood, metal, stone, for every room in every house, or hung about every neck, or stuck on every hat, made a market such as artists never knew before or since, and such as instantly explains to the practical American not only the reason for the Church's tenacity of life, but also the inducements for its plunder. The Virgin especially required all the resources of art, and the highest. Notre Dame of Chartres would have laughed at Notre Dame of Paris if she had detected an economy in her robes; Notre Dame of Rheims or Rouen would have derided Notre Dame of Amiens if she had shown a feminine, domestic, maternal turn toward cheapness. The Virgin was never cheap. Her great ceremonies were as splendid as her rank of Queen in Heaven and on Earth required; and as her procession wound its way along the aisles, through the crowd of her subjects, up to the high altar, it was impossible then, and not altogether easy now, to resist the rapture of her radiant presence. Many a young person, and now and then one who is not in first youth, witnessing the sight in the religious atmosphere of such a church as this, without a suspicion of susceptibility, has suddenly seen what Paul saw on the road to Damascus, and has fallen on his face with the crowd, grovelling at the foot of the Cross, which, for the first time in his life, he feels.

If you want to know what churches were made for, come down here on some great festival of the Virgin, and give yourself up to it; but come alone! That kind of knowledge cannot be taught and can seldom be shared. We are not now seeking religion; indeed, true religion generally comes unsought. We are trying only to feel Gothic art. For us, the world is not a schoolroom or a pulpit, but a stage, and the stage is the highest yet seen on earth. In this church the old Romanesque leaps into the Gothic under our eyes; of a sudden, between the portal and the shrine, the infinite rises into a new expression, always a rare and excellent miracle in thought. The two expressions are nowhere far apart; not further than the Mother from the Son. The new artist drops unwillingly the hand of his father or his grandfather; he looks back, from every corner of his own work, to see whether it goes with the old. He will not part with the western portal or the lancet windows; he holds close to the round columns of the choir; he would have kept the round arch if he could, but the round arch was unable to do the work; it could not rise; so he broke it, lifted the vaulting, threw out flying buttresses, and satisfied the Virgin's wish.

The matter of Gothic vaulting, with its two weak points, the flying buttress and the false, wooden shelter-roof, is the bête noire of the Beaux Arts. The duty of defence does not lie on tourists, who are at best hardly able to understand what it matters whether a wall is buttressed without or within, and whether a roof is single or double. No one objects to the dome of Saint Peter's. No one finds fault with the Pont Neuf. Yet it is true that the Gothic architect showed contempt for facts. Since he could not support a heavy stone vault on his light columns, he built the lightest possible stone vault and protected it with a wooden shelter-roof which constantly burned. The lightened vaults were still too heavy for the walls and columns, so the architect threw out buttress beyond buttress resting on separate foundations, exposed to extreme inequalities of weather, and liable to multiplied chances of accident. The results were certainly disastrous. The roofs burned; the walls yielded.

Flying buttresses were not a necessity. The Merveille had none; the Angevin school rather affected to do without them; Albi had none; Assisi stands up independent; but they did give support wherever the architect wanted it and nowhere else; they were probably cheap; and they were graceful. Whatever expression they gave to a church, at least it was not that of a fortress. Amiens and Albi are different religions. The expression concerns us; the construction concerns the Beaux Arts. The problem of permanent equilibrium which distresses the builder of arches is a technical matter which does not worry, but only amuses, us who sit in the audience and look with delight at the theatrical stage-decoration of the Gothic vault; the astonishing feat of building up a skeleton of stone ribs and vertebrae, on which every pound of weight is adjusted, divided, and carried down from level to level till it touches ground at a distance as a bird would alight. If any stone in any part, from apex to foundation, weathers or gives way, the whole must yield, and the charge for repairs is probably great, but, on the best building the École des Beaux Arts can build, the charge for repairs is not to be wholly ignored, and at least the Cathedral of Chartres, in spite of terribly hard usage, is as solid today as when it was built, and as plumb, without crack or crevice. Even the towering fragment at Beauvais, poorly built from the first, which has broken down oftener than most Gothic structures, and seems ready to crumble again whenever the wind blows over its windy plains, has managed to survive, after a fashion, six or seven hundred years, which is all that our generation had a right to ask.

The vault of Beauvais is nearly one hundred and sixty feet high (48 metres), and was cheaply built. The vault of Saint Peter's at Rome is nearly one hundred and fifty feet (45 metres). That of Amiens is one hundred and forty-four feet (44 metres). Rheims, Bourges, and Chartres are nearly the same height; at the entrance, one hundred and twenty-two feet. Paris is one hundred and ten feet. The Abbé Bulteau is responsible for these measurements; but at Chartres, as in several very old churches, the nave slopes down to the entrance, because—as is said—pilgrims came in such swarms that they were obliged to sleep in the church, and the nave had to be sluiced with water to clean it. The true height of Chartres, at the croisée of nave and transept, is as near as possible one hundred and twenty feet (36.55 metres).

The measured height is the least interest of a church. The architect's business is to make a small building look large, and his failures are in large buildings which he makes to look small. One chief beauty of the Gothic is to exaggerate height, and one of its most curious qualities is its success in imposing an illusion of size. Without leaving the heart of Paris any one can study this illusion in the two great churches of Notre Dame and Saint-Sulpice; for Saint-Sulpice is as lofty as Notre Dame in vaulting, and larger in its other dimensions, besides being, in its style, a fine building; yet its Roman arches show, as if they were of the eleventh century, why the long, clean, unbroken, refined lines of the Gothic, curving to points, and leading the eye with a sort of compulsion to the culminating point above, should have made an architectural triumph that carried all Europe off its feet with delight. The world had seen nothing to approach it except, perhaps, in the dome of Sancta Sophia in Constantinople; and the discovery came at a moment when Europe was making its most united and desperate struggle to attain the kingdom of Heaven.

According to Viollet-le-Duc, Chartres was the final triumph of the experiment on a very great scale, for Chartres has never been altered and never needed to be strengthened. The flying buttresses of Chartres answered their purpose, and if it were not a matter of pure construction it would be worth while to read what Viollet-le-Duc says about them (article, 'Arcs-boutants'). The vaulting above is heavy, about fifteen inches thick; the buttressing had also to be heavy; and to lighten it, the architect devised an amusing sort of arcades, applied on his outside buttresses. Throughout the church, everything was solid beyond all later custom, so that architects would have to begin by a study of the crypt which came down from the eleventh century so strongly built that it still carries the church without a crack in its walls; but if we went down into it, we should understand nothing; so we will begin, as we did outside, at the front.

A single glance shows what trouble the architect had with the old façade and towers, and what temptation to pull them all down. One cannot quite say that he has spoiled his own church in trying to save what he could of the old, but if he did not quite spoil it, he saved it only by the exercise of an amount of intelligence that we shall never learn enough to feel our incapacity to understand. True ignorance approaches the infinite more nearly than any amount of knowledge can do, and, in our case, ignorance is fortified by a certain element of nineteenth-century indifference which refuses to be interested in what it cannot understand; a violent reaction from the thirteenth century which cared little to comprehend anything except the incomprehensible. The architect at Chartres was required by the Virgin to provide more space for her worshippers within the church, without destroying the old portal and flèche which she loved. That this order came directly from the Virgin, may be taken for granted. At Chartres, one sees everywhere the Virgin, and nowhere any rival authority;

one sees her give orders, and architects obey them; but very rarely a hesitation as though the architect were deciding for himself. In his western front, the architect has obeyed orders so literally that he has not even taken the trouble to apologize for leaving unfinished the details which, if he had been responsible for them, would have been his anxious care. He has gone to the trouble of moving the heavy door-ways forward, so that the chapels in the towers, which were meant to open on a porch, now open into the nave, and the nave itself has, in appearance, two more spans than in the old church; but the work shows blind obedience, as though he were doing his best to please the Virgin without trying to please himself. Probably he could in no case have done much to help the side aisles in their abrupt collision with the solid walls of the two towers, but he might at least have brought the vaulting of his two new bays, in the nave, down to the ground, and finished it. The vaulting is awkward in these two bays, and yet he has taken great trouble to effect what seems at first a small matter. Whether the great rose window was an afterthought or not can never be known, but any one can see with a glass, and better on the architectural plan, that the vaulting of the main church was not high enough to admit the great rose, and that the architect has had to slope his two tower-spans upward. So great is the height that you cannot see this difference of level very plainly even with a glass, but on the plans it seems to amount to several feet; perhaps a metre. The archi-tect has managed to deceive our eyes, in order to enlarge the rose; but you can see as plainly as though he were here to tell you, that, like a great general, he has concentrated his whole energy on the rose, because the Virgin has told him that the rose symbolized herself, and that the light and splendour of her appearance in the west were to redeem all his awkwardnesses.

Of course this idea of the Virgin's interference sounds to you a mere bit of fancy, and that is an account which may be settled between the Virgin and you; but even twentieth-century eyes can see that the rose redeems ev-erything, dominates everything, and gives character to the whole church.

In view of the difficulties which faced the artist, the rose is inspired genius—the kind of genius which Shakespeare showed when he took some other man's play, and adapted it. Thus far, it shows its power chiefly by the way it comes forward and takes possession of the west front, but if you want a foot-rule to measure by, you may mark that the old, twelfth-century lancet-windows below it are not exactly in its axis. At the outset, in the original plan of 1090, or thereabouts, the old tower—the southern tower—was given greater width than the northern. Such inequalities were common in the early churches, and so is a great deal of dispute in modern books whether they were accidental or intentional, while no one denies that they are amusing. In these towers the difference is not great—perhaps fourteen or fifteen inches—but it caused the architect to correct it, in order to fit his front to the axis of the church, by throwing his entrance six or seven inches to the south, and narrowing to that extent the south door and south lancet. The effect was bad, even then, and went far to ruin the south window; but when, after the fire of 1194, the architect inserted his great rose, filling every inch of possible space between the lancet and the arch of the vault, he made another correction which threw his rose six or seven inches out of axis with the lancets. Not one person in a hundred thousand would notice it, here in the interior, so completely are we under the control of the artist and the Virgin; but it is a measure of the power of the rose.

Looking farther, one sees that the rose-motive, which so dominates the west front, is carried round the church, and comes to another outburst of splendour in the transepts. This leads back to fenestration on a great scale, which is a terribly ambitious flight for tourists; all the more, because here the tourist gets little help from the architect, who, in modern times, has seldom the opportunity to study the subject at all, and accepts as solved the problems of early Gothic fenestration. One becomes pedantic and pretentious at the very sound of the word, which is an intolerable piece of pedantry in itself; but Chartres is all windows, and its windows were as triumphant as its Virgin, and were one of her miracles. One can no more overlook the windows of

Chartres than the glass which is in them. We have already
looked at the windows of Mantes; we have seen what happened to the windows at Paris. Paris had at one leap risen
twenty-five feet higher than Noyon, and even at Noyon,
the architect, about 1150, had been obliged to invent new
fenestration. Paris and Mantes, twenty years later, made
another effort, which proved a failure. Then the architect
of Chartres, in 1195, added ten feet more to his vault, and
undertook, once for all, to show how a great cathedral
should be lighted. As an architectural problem, it passes far
beyond our powers of understanding, even when solved; but
we can always turn to see what the inevitable Viollet-le-
Duc says about its solution at Chartres:

> Toward the beginning of the thirteenth century, the
> architect of the Cathedral of Chartres sought out en-
> tirely new window combinations to light the nave from
> above. Below, in the side aisles he kept to the customs
> of the times; that is, he opened pointed windows which
> did not wholly fill the spaces between the piers; he
> wanted, or was willing to leave here below, the effect
> of a wall. But in the upper part of his building we see
> that he changed the system; he throws a round arch di-
> rectly across from one pier to the next; then, in the enor-
> mous space which remains within each span, he inserts
> two large pointed windows surmounted by a great rose.
> . . . We recognize in this construction of Notre Dame
> de Chartres a boldness, a force, which contrast with
> the fumbling of the architects in the Île de France and
> Champagne. For the first time one sees at Chartres the
> builder deal frankly with the clerestory, or upper fenes-
> tration, occupying the whole width of the arches, and
> taking the arch of the vault as the arch of the window.
> Simplicity of construction, beauty in form, strong work-
> manship, structure true and solid, judicious choice of
> material, all the characteristics of good work, unite in
> this magnificent specimen of architecture at the begin-
> ning of the thirteenth century.

Viollet-le-Duc does not call attention to a score of other
matters which the architect must have had in his mind,

such as the distribution of light, and the relations of one arrangement with another: the nave with the aisles, and both with the transepts, and all with the choir. Following him, we must take the choir separately, and the aisles and chapels of the apse also. One cannot hope to understand all the experiments and refinements of the artist, either in their successes or their failures, but, with diffidence, one may ask one's self whether the beauty of the arrangement, as compared with the original arrangement in Paris, did not consist in retaining the rose-motive throughout, while throwing the whole upper wall into window. Triumphant as the clerestory windows are, they owe their charm largely to their roses, as you see by looking at the same scheme applied on a larger scale on the transept fronts; and then, by taking stand under the croisée, and looking at all in succession as a whole.

The rose window was not Gothic but Romanesque, and needed a great deal of coaxing to feel at home within the pointed arch. At first, the architects felt the awkwardness so strongly that they avoided it wherever they could. In the beautiful façade of Laon, one of the chief beauties is the setting of the rose under a deep round arch. The western roses of Mantes and Paris are treated in the same way, although a captious critic might complain that their treatment is not so effective or so logical. Rheims boldly imprisoned the roses within the pointed arch; but Amiens, toward 1240, took refuge in the same square exterior setting that was preferred, in 1200, here at Chartres; and in the interior of Amiens the round arch of the rose is the last vault of the nave, seen through a vista of pointed vaults, as it is here. All these are supposed to be among the chief beauties of the Gothic façade, although the Gothic architect, if he had been a man of logic, would have clung to his lines, and put a pointed window in his front, as in fact he did at Coutances. He felt the value of the rose in art, and perhaps still more in religion, for the rose was Mary's emblem. One is fairly sure that the great Chartres rose of the west front was put there to please her, since it was to be always before her eyes, the most conspicuous object she would see from the high altar, and therefore the most carefully considered ornament in the whole church outside the choir. The mere size proves the importance she gave it. The exterior diameter is nearly forty-four feet (13.36 metres). The nave of Chartres is, next perhaps to the nave of Angers, the widest of all Gothic naves; about fifty-three feet (16.31 metres); and the rose takes every inch it can get of this enormous span. The value of the rose, among architects of the time, was great, since it was the only part of the church that Villard de Honnecourt sketched; and since his time, it has been drawn and redrawn, described and commented by generations of architects till it has become as classic as the Parthenon.

Yet this Chartres rose is solid, serious, sedate, to a degree unusual in its own age; it is even more Romanesque than the pure Romanesque roses. At Beauvais you must stop a moment to look at a Romanesque rose on the transept of the Church of Saint-Étienne; Viollet-le-Duc mentions it, with a drawing (article, 'Pignon'), as not earlier than the year 1100, therefore about a century earlier than the rose of Chartres; it is not properly a rose, but a wheel of fortune, with figures climbing up and falling over. Another supposed twelfth-century rose is at Étampes, which goes with that of Laon and Saint-Leu-d'Esserent and Mantes. The rose of Chartres is so much the most serious of them all that Viollet-le-Duc has explained it by its material—the heavy stone of Berchères;—but the material was not allowed to affect the great transept roses, and the architect made his material yield to his object wherever he thought it worth while. Standing under the central croisée, you can see all three roses by simply turning your head. That on the north, the Rose de France, was built, or planned, between 1200 and 1210, in the reign of Philip Augustus, since the porch outside, which would be a later construction, was begun by 1212. The Rose de France is the same in diameter as the western rose, but lighter, and built of lighter stone. Opposite the Rose de France stands, on the south front, Pierre Mauclerc's Rose de Dreux, of the same date, with the same motive, but even lighter; more like a rose and less like a wheel. All three roses must have been planned at about the same time, perhaps by the same architect, within the same workshop; yet the western rose stands quite apart, as though it had been especially designed to suit the twelfth-century façade and portal which it rules. Whether this was really the artist's idea is a question that needs the artist to answer; but that this is the effect, needs no expert to prove; it stares one in the face. Within and without, one feels that the twelfth-century spirit is respected and preserved with the same religious feeling which obliged the architect to injure his own work by sparing that of his grandfathers.

Conspicuous, then, in the west front are two feelings: respect for the twelfth-century work, and passion for the rose fenestration; both subordinated to the demand for light. If it worries you to have to believe that these three things are in fact one; that the architect is listening, like the stone Abraham, for orders from the Virgin, while he caresses and sacrifices his child; that Mary and not her architects built this façade; if the divine intention seems to you a needless impertinence, you can soon get free from it by going to any of the later churches, where you will not be forced to see any work but that of the architect's compasses. According to Viollet-le-Duc, the inspiration ceased about 1250, or, as the Virgin would have dated it, on the death of Blanche of Castile in 1252. The work of Chartres, where her own hand is plainly shown, belongs in feeling, if not in execution, to the last years of the twelfth century (1195–1200). The great western rose which gives the motive for the whole decoration and is repeated in the great roses of the transepts, marks the Virgin's will—the taste and knowledge of 'cele qui la rose est des roses,' or, if you prefer the Latin of Adam de Saint-Victor, the hand of her who is 'Super rosam rosida.'

All this is easy; but if you really cannot see the hand of Mary herself in these broad and public courts, which were intended, not for her personal presence, but for the use of her common people, you had better stop here, and not venture into the choir. Great halls seem to have been easy architecture. Naves and transepts were not often failures; façades and even towers and flèches are invariably more or less successful because they are more or less balanced, mathematical, calculable products of reason and thought. The most serious difficulties began only with the choir, and even then did not become desperate until the architect reached the curve of the apse, with its impossible vaultings, its complicated lines, its cross-thrusts, its double problems, internal and external, its defective roofing and unequal lighting. A perfect Gothic apse was impossible; an apse that satisfied perfectly its principal objects was rare; the simplest and cheapest solution was to have no apse at all, and that was the English scheme, which was tried also at Laon; a square, flat wall and window. If the hunt for Norman towers offered a summer's amusement, a hunt for apses would offer an education, but it would lead far out of France. Indeed, it would be simpler to begin at once with Sancta Sophia at Constantinople, San Vitale at Ravenna and Monreale at Palermo, and the churches at Torcello and Murano, and San Marco at Venice; and admit that no device has ever equalled the startling and mystical majesty of the Byzantine half-dome, with its marvellous mosaic Madonna dominating the church, from the entrance, with her imperial and divine presence. Unfortunately, the northern churches needed light, and the northern architects turned their minds to a desperate effort for a new apse.

The scheme of the cathedral at Laon seems to have been rejected unanimously; the bare, flat wall at the end of the choir was an eyesore; it was quite bad enough at the end of the nave, and became annoying at the end of the transepts, so that at Noyon and Soissons the architect, with a keen sense of interior form, had rounded the transept ends; but, though external needs might require a square transept, the unintelligence of the flat wall became insufferable at the east end. Neither did the square choir suit the church ceremonies and processions, or offer the same advantages of arrangement, as the French understood them. With one voice, the French architects seem to have rejected the Laon experiment, and turned back to a solution taken directly from the Romanesque.

Quite early—in the eleventh century—a whole group of churches had been built in Auvergne—at Clermont and

Issoire, for example—possibly by one architect, with a circular apse, breaking out into five apsidal chapels. Tourists who get down as far south as Toulouse see another example of this Romanesque apse in the famous Church of Saint-Sernin, of the twelfth century; and few critics take offence at one's liking it. Indeed, as far as concerns the exterior, one might even risk thinking it more charming than the

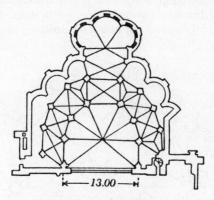

Saint-Martin-des-Champs

exterior of any Gothic apse ever built. Many of these Romanesque apses of the eleventh and twelfth centuries still remain in France, showing themselves in unsuspected parish churches, here and there, but always a surprise for their quiet, unobtrusive grace, making a harmony with the Romanesque tower, if there is one, into which they rise, as at Saint-Sernin; but all these churches had only one aisle, and, in the interior, there came invariable trouble when the vaults rose in height. The architect of Chartres, in 1200, could get no direct help from these, or even from Paris which was a beautifully perfect apse, but had no apsidal chapels. The earliest apse that could have served as a suggestion for Chartres—or, at least, as a point of observation for us—was that of the Abbey Church of Saint-Martin-des-Champs, which we went to see in Paris, and which is said to date from about 1150. Here is a circular choir, surrounded by two rows of columns, irregularly spaced, with

circular chapels outside, which seems to have been more
or less what the architect of Chartres, for the Virgin's purposes, had set his heart on obtaining. Closely following the
scheme of Saint-Martin-des-Champs came the scheme of
the Abbey Church at Vézelay, built about 1160–80. Here
the vaulting sprang directly from the last arch of the choir,
as is shown on the plan, and bearing first on the light columns of the choir, which were evenly spaced, then fell on
a row of heavier columns outside, which were also evenly
spaced, and came to rest at last on massive piers, between

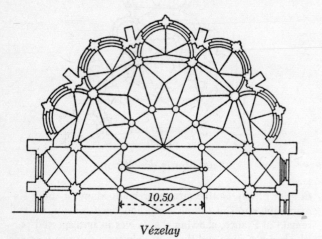

10.50

Vézelay

which were five circular chapels. The plan shows at a
glance that this arrangement stretched the second row of
columns far apart, and that a church much larger than
Vézelay would need to space them so much farther apart
that the arch uniting them would have to rise indefinitely;
while, if beyond this, another aisle were added outside, the
piers finally would require impossible vaulting.

The problem stood thus when the great cathedrals were
undertaken, and the architect of Paris boldly grappled with
the double aisle on a scale requiring a new scheme. Here,
in spite of the most virtuous resolutions not to be technical,
we must attempt a technicality, because without it, one of

the most interesting eccentricities of Chartres would be lost. Once more, Viollet-le-Duc:

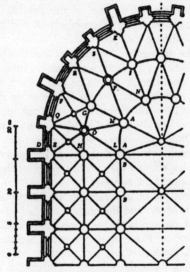

Notre Dame de Paris

As the architect did not want to give the interior bays of the apse spaces between the columns (AA) less than that of the parallel bays (BB), it followed that the first radiating bay gave a first space (LMGH) which was difficult to vault, and a second space (HGEF) which was impossible; for how establish an arch from F to E? Even if round, its key would have risen much higher than the key of the pointed archivolt LM. As the second radiating bay opened out still wider, the difficulty was increased. The builder therefore inserted the two intermediate pillars O and P between the columns of the second aisle (H, G, and I); which he supported, in the outside wall of the church, by one corresponding pier (Q) in the first bay of the apse, and by two similar piers (R and S) in the second bay.

'There is no need to point out,' continued Viollet-le-Duc,

as though he much suspected that there might be need of pointing out, 'what skill this system showed and how much the art of architecture had already been developed in the Île de France toward the end of the twelfth century; to what an extent the unity of arrangement and style preoccupied the artists of that province.'

In fact, the arrangement seems mathematically and technically perfect. At all events, we know too little to criticize it. Yet one would much like to be told why it was not repeated by any other architect or in any other church. Apparently the Parisians themselves were not quite satisfied with it, since they altered it a hundred years later, in 1296, in order to build out chapels between the piers. As the architects of each new cathedral had, in the interval, insisted on apsidal chapels, one may venture to guess that the Paris scheme hampered the services.

At Chartres the church services are Mary's own tastes; the church is Mary; and the chapels are her private rooms. She was not pleased with the arrangements made for her in her palace at Paris; they were too architectural; too regular and mathematical; too popular; too impersonal; and she rather abruptly ordered her architect at Chartres to go back to the old arrangement. The apse at Paris was hardly covered with its leading before the architect of Chartres adopted a totally new plan, which, according to Viollet-le-Duc, does him little credit, but which was plainly imposed on him, like the twelfth-century portal. Not only had it nothing of the mathematical correctness and precision of the Paris scheme, easy to understand and imitate, but it carried even a sort of violence—a wrench—in its system, as though the Virgin had said, with her grand Byzantine air: I will it!

'At Chartres,' said Viollet-le-Duc, 'the choir of the Cathedral presents a plan which does no great honour to its architect. There is want of accord between the circular apse and the parallel sides of the sanctuary; the spacings of the columns of the second collateral are loose (*lâches*); the vaults quite poorly combined; and in spite of the great width of the spaces between the columns of the second aisle, the architect had still to narrow those between the interior columns.'

The plan shows that, from the first, the architect must have deliberately rejected the Paris scheme; he must have begun by narrowing the spaces between his inner columns; then, with a sort of violence, he fitted on his second row of columns; and, finally, he showed his motive by constructing an outer wall of an original or unusual shape.

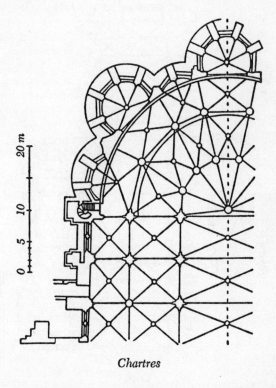

Chartres

Any woman would see at once the secret of all this ingenuity and effort. The Chartres apse, enormous in size and width, is exquisitely lighted. Here, as everywhere throughout the church, the windows give the law, but here they actually take place of law. The Virgin herself saw to the lighting of her own boudoir. According to Viollet-le-Duc, Chartres differs from all the other great cathedrals by be-

ing built not for its nave or even for its choir, but for its
apse; it was planned not for the people or the court, but
for the Queen; not a church but a shrine; and the shrine
is the apse where the Queen arranged her light to please
herself and not her architect, who had already been sac-

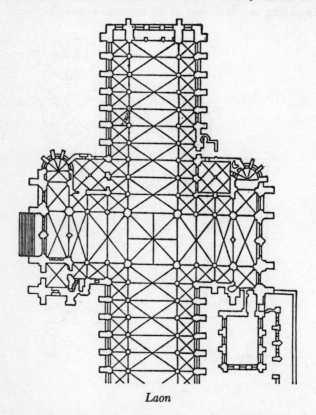

Laon

rificed at the western portal and who had a free hand only
in the nave and transepts where the Queen never went, and
which, from her own apartment, she did not even see.

This is, in effect, what Viollet-le-Duc says in his professional language, which is perhaps—or sounds—more reasonable to tourists, whose imaginations are hardly equal to

the effort of fancying a real deity. Perhaps, indeed, one
might get so high as to imagine a real Bishop of Laon, who
should have ordered his architect to build an enormous hall
of religion, to rival the immense abbeys of the day, and to
attract the people, as though it were a clubroom. There
they were to see all the great sights; church ceremonies;

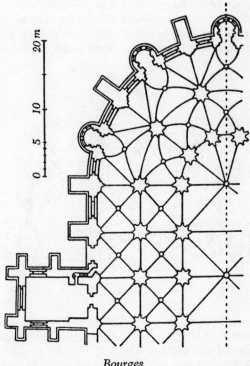

Bourges

theatricals; political functions; there they were to do business, and frequent society. They were to feel at home
in their church because it was theirs, and did not belong
to a priesthood or to Rome. Jealousy of Rome was a leading motive of Gothic architecture, and Rome repaid it in
full. The Bishop of Laon conceded at least a transept to

custom or tradition, but the Archbishop of Bourges abolished even the transept, and the great hall had no special religious expression except in the circular apse with its chapels which Laon had abandoned. One can hardly decide whether Laon or Bourges is the more popular, industrial, political, or, in other words, the less religious; but the Parisians, as the plan of Viollet-le-Duc has shown, were quite as advanced as either, and only later altered their scheme into one that provided chapels for religious service.

Amiens and Beauvais have each seven chapels, but only one aisle, so that they do not belong in the same class with

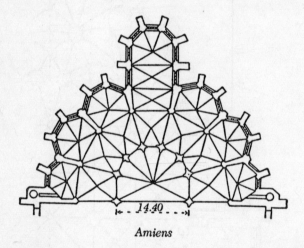

Amiens

the apses of Paris, Bourges, and Chartres, though the plans are worth studying for comparison, since they show how many-sided the problem was, and how far from satisfied the architects were with their own schemes. The most interesting of all, for comparison with Chartres, is Le Mans, where the apsidal chapels are carried to fanaticism, while the vaulting seems to be reasonable enough, and the double aisle successfully managed, if Viollet-le-Duc permits ignorant people to form an opinion on architectural dogma. For our purposes, the architectural dogma may stand, and the Paris scheme may be taken for granted, as alone correct and orthodox; all that Viollet-le-Duc teaches is that the Chartres scheme is unorthodox, not to say heretical; and this is the point on which his words are most interesting.

The church at Chartres belonged not to the people, not to the priesthood, and not even to Rome; it belonged to

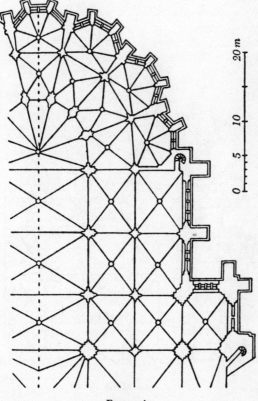

Beauvais

the Virgin. 'Here the religious influence appears wholly; three large chapels in the apse; four others less pronounced; double aisles of great width round the choir; vast transepts! Here the church ceremonial could display all its pomp; the choir, more than at Paris, more than at Bourges, more than at Soissons, and especially more than at Laon, is the principal object; for it, the church is built.'

One who is painfully conscious of ignorance, and who never would dream of suggesting a correction to anybody,

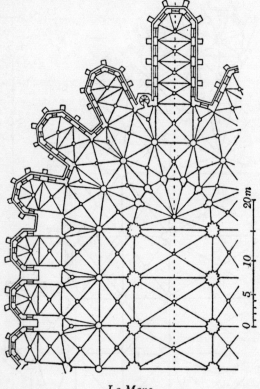

Le Mans

may not venture to suggest an idea of any sort to an architect; but if it were allowed to paraphrase Viollet-le-Duc's words into a more or less emotional or twelfth-century form, one might say, after him, that, compared with Paris or Laon, the Chartres apse shows the same genius that is

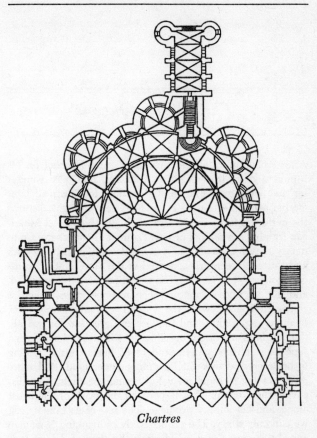

Chartres

shown in the Chartres rose; the same large mind that over-rules—the same strong will that defies difficulties. The Chartres apse is as entertaining as all the other Gothic apses to-gether, because it overrides the architect. You may, if you really have no imagination whatever, reject the idea that the Virgin herself made the plan; the feebleness of our fancy is now congenital, organic, beyond stimulant or strychnine, and we shrink like sensitive-plants from the touch of a vision or spirit; but at least one can still some-times feel a woman's taste, and in the apse of Chartres one feels nothing else.

The Three Queens[1]

After worshipping at the shrines of Saint Michael on his
Mount and of the Virgin at Chartres, one may wander
far and wide over France, and seldom feel lost; all later
Gothic art comes naturally, and no new thought disturbs
the perfected form. Yet tourists of English blood and American training are seldom or never quite at home there. Commonly they feel it only as a stage-decoration. The twelfth
and thirteenth centuries, studied in the pure light of political economy, are insane. The scientific mind is atrophied,
and suffers under inherited cerebral weakness, when it
comes in contact with the eternal woman—Astarte, Isis,
Demeter, Aphrodite, and the last and greatest deity of all,
the Virgin. Very rarely one lingers, with a mild sympathy,
such as suits the patient student of human error, willing
to be interested in what he cannot understand. Still more
rarely, owing to some revival of archaic instincts, he redis-
covers the woman. This is perhaps the mark of the artist
alone, and his solitary privilege. The rest of us cannot feel;
we can only study. The proper study of mankind is woman
and, by common agreement since the time of Adam, it is
the most complex and arduous. The study of Our Lady,
as shown by the art of Chartres, leads directly back to
Eve, and lays bare the whole subject of sex.

If it were worth while to argue a paradox, one might
maintain that Nature regards the female as the essential,
the male as the superfluity of her world. Perhaps the best
starting-point for study of the Virgin would be a practical
acquaintance with bees, and especially with queen bees.
Precisely where the French man may come in, on the gene-

[1] Chapter XI of *Mont-St.-Michel and Chartres*.

alogical tree of parthenogenesis, one hesitates to say; but certain it is that the French woman, from very early times, has shown qualities peculiar to herself, and that the French woman of the Middle Ages was a masculine character. Almost any book which deals with the social side of the twelfth century has something to say on this subject, like the following page from M. Garreau's volume published in 1899, on the 'Social State of France during the Crusades':

A trait peculiar to this epoch is the close resemblance between the manners of men and women. The rule that such and such feelings or acts are permitted to one sex and forbidden to the other was not fairly settled. Men had the right to dissolve in tears, and women that of talking without prudery. . . . If we look at their intellectual level, the women appear distinctly superior. They are more serious; more subtle. With them we do not seem dealing with the rude state of civilization that their husbands belong to. . . . As a rule, the women seem to have the habit of weighing their acts; of not yielding to momentary impressions. While the sense of Christianity is more developed in them than in their husbands, on the other hand they show more perfidy and art in crime. . . . One might doubtless prove by a series of examples that the maternal influence when it predominated in the education of a son gave him a marked superiority over his contemporaries. Richard Coeur-de-Lion the crowned poet, artist, the king whose noble manners and refined mind in spite of his cruelty exercised so strong an impression on his age, was formed by that brilliant Eleanor of Guienne who, in her struggle with her husband, retained her sons as much as possible within her sphere of influence in order to make party chiefs of them. Our great Saint Louis, as all know, was brought up exclusively by Blanche of Castile; and Joinville, the charming writer so worthy of Saint Louis's friendship, and apparently so superior to his surroundings, was also the pupil of a widowed and regent mother.

The superiority of the woman was not a fancy, but a fact. Man's business was to fight or hunt or feast or make love. The man was also the travelling partner in commerce, commonly absent from home for months together, while the woman carried on the business. The woman ruled the household and the workshop; cared for the economy; supplied the intelligence, and dictated the taste. Her ascendancy was secured by her alliance with the Church, into which she sent her most intelligent children; and a priest or clerk, for the most part, counted socially as a woman. Both physically and mentally the woman was robust, as the men often complained, and she did not greatly resent being treated as a man. Sometimes the husband beat her, dragged her about by the hair, locked her up in the house; but he was quite conscious that she always got even with him in the end. As a matter of fact, probably she got more than even. On this point, history, legend, poetry, romance, and especially the popular fabliaux—invented to amuse the gross tastes of the coarser class—are all agreed, and one could give scores of volumes illustrating it. The greatest men illustrate it best, as one might show almost at hazard. The greatest men of the eleventh, twelfth, and thirteenth centuries were William the Norman; his great-grandson Henry II Plantagenet; Saint Louis of France; and, if a fourth be needed, Richard Coeur-de-Lion. Notoriously all these men had as much difficulty as Louis XIV himself with the women of their family. Tradition exaggerates everything it touches, but shows, at the same time, what is passing in the minds of the society which *tradites*. In Normandy, the people of Caen have kept a tradition, told elsewhere in other forms, that one day, Duke William—the Conqueror—exasperated by having his bastardy constantly thrown in his face by the Duchess Matilda, dragged her by the hair, tied to his horse's tail, as far as the suburb of Vaucelles; and this legend accounts for the splendour of the Abbaye-aux-Dames, because William, the common people believed, afterwards regretted the impropriety, and atoned for it by giving her money to build the abbey. The story betrays the man's weakness. The Abbaye-aux-Dames stands in the same relation to the Abbaye-aux-Hommes that Matilda took towards William. Inferiority there was none; on the contrary, the woman was socially the superior, and William was probably more afraid of her than she of him, if Mr. Freeman is right in insisting that he married her in spite of her having a husband living, and certainly two children. If William was the strongest man in the eleventh century, his great-grandson, Henry II of England, was the strongest man of the twelfth; but the history of the time resounds with the noise of his battles with Queen Eleanor whom he, at last, held in prison for fourteen years. Prisoner as she was, she broke him down in the end. One is tempted to suspect that, had her husband and children been guided by her, and by her policy as peacemaker for the good of Guienne, most of the disasters of England and France might have been postponed for the time; but we can never know the truth, for monks and historians abhor emancipated women—with good reason, since such women are apt to abhor them—and the quarrel can never be pacified. Historians have commonly shown fear of women without admitting it, but the man of the Middle Ages knew at least why he feared the woman, and told it openly, not to say brutally. Long after Eleanor and Blanche were dead, Chaucer brought the Wife of Bath on his Shakespearean stage, to explain the woman, and as usual he touched masculine frailty with caustic, while seeming to laugh at woman and man alike:

> 'My liege lady! generally,' quoth he,
> 'Women desiren to have soverainetee.'

The point was that the Wife of Bath, like Queen Blanche and Queen Eleanor, not only wanted sovereignty, but won and held it.

That Saint Louis, even when a grown man and king, stood in awe of his mother, Blanche of Castile, was not only notorious but seemed to be thought natural. Joinville recorded it not so much to mark the King's weakness, as the woman's strength; for his Queen, Margaret of Provence, showed the courage which the King had not. Blanche and Margaret were exceedingly jealous of each other. 'One day,' said Joinville, 'Queen Blanche went to the Queen's [Margaret] chamber where her son [Louis IX] had gone before to comfort her, for she was in great danger of death from a bad delivery; and he hid himself behind the Queen [Margaret] to avoid being seen; but his mother perceived him, and taking him by the hand said: "Come along! you will do no good here!" and put him out of the chamber. Queen Margaret, observing this, and that she was to be separated from her husband, cried aloud: "Alas! will you not allow me to see my lord either living or dying?"' According to Joinville, King Louis always hid himself when, in his wife's chamber, he heard his mother coming.

The great period of Gothic architecture begins with the coming of Eleanor (1137) and ends with the passing of Blanche (1252). Eleanor's long life was full of energy and passion of which next to nothing is known; the woman was always too slippery for monks or soldiers to grasp.

Eleanor came to Paris, a Queen of fifteen years old, in 1137, bringing Poitiers and Guienne as the greatest dowry ever offered to the French Crown. She brought also the tastes and manners of the South, little in harmony with the tastes and manners of Saint Bernard whose authority at court rivalled her own. The Abbé Suger supported her, but the King leaned toward the Abbé Bernard. What this puritan reaction meant is a matter to be studied by itself, if one can find a cloister to study in; but it bore the mark of most puritan reactions in its hostility to women. As long as the woman remained docile, she ruled, through the Church; but the man feared her and was jealous of her, and she of him. Bernard specially adored the Virgin because she was an example of docile obedience to the Trinity who atoned for the indocility of Eve, but Eve herself remained the instrument of Satan, and French society as a whole showed a taste for Eves.

Eleanor could hardly be called docile. Whatever else she loved, she certainly loved rule. She shared this passion to the full with her only great successor and rival on the English throne, Queen Elizabeth, and she happened to become Queen of France at the moment when society was turning from worship of its military ideal, Saint Michael, to worship of its social ideal, the Virgin. According to the monk Orderic, men had begun to throw aside their old military dress and manners even before the first crusade, in the days

THE THREE QUEENS

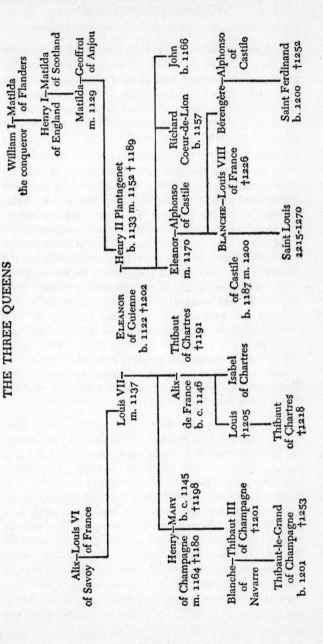

William I—Matilda
the conqueror | of Flanders

Henry I—Matilda
of England | of Scotland

Matilda—Geoffroi
m. 1129 | of Anjou

Alix—Louis VI
of Savoy | of France

Louis VII—
m. 1137

ELEANOR
of Guienne
b. 1122 †1202

Henry II Plantagenet
b. 1133 m. 1152 †1189

Eleanor—Alphonso
m. 1170 | of Castile

Richard
Coeur-de-Lion
b. 1157

John
b. 1166

Alix—
de France
b. c. 1146

Thibaut
of Chartres
†1191

BLANCHE—Louis VIII
of Castile | of France
b. 1187 m. 1200 | †1226

Bérengère—Alphonso
| of
| Castile

Henry—MARY
of Champagne | b. c. 1145
m. 1164 †1180 | †1198

Isabel
of Chartres

Louis
†1205

Thibaut
of Chartres
†1218

Saint Louis
1215-1270

Saint Ferdinand
b. 1200 †1252

Blanche—Thibaut III
of | of Champagne
Navarre | †1201

Thibaut-le-Grand
of Champagne
b. 1201 †1253

of William Rufus (1087–1100), and to affect feminine fashions. In all ages, priests and monks have denounced the growing vices of society, with more or less reason; but there seems to have been a real outbreak of display at about the time of the first crusade, which set a deep mark on every sort of social expression, even down to the shoes of the statues on the western portal of Chartres:

> A debauched fellow named Robert [said Orderic] was the first, about the time of William Rufus, who introduced the practice of filling the long points of the shoes with tow, and of turning them up like a ram's horn. Hence he got the surname of Cornard; and this absurd fashion was speedily adopted by great numbers of the nobility as a proud distinction and sign of merit. At this time effeminacy was the prevailing vice throughout the world. . . . They parted their hair from the crown of the head on each side of the forehead, and their locks grew long like women, and wore long shirts and tunics, closely tied with points. . . . In our days, ancient customs are almost all changed for new fashions. Our wanton youths are sunk in effeminacy. . . . They insert their toes in things like serpents' tails which present to view the shape of scorpions. Sweeping the dusty ground with the prodigious trains of their robes and mantles, they cover their hands with gloves . . .

If you are curious to follow these monkish criticisms on your ancestors' habits, you can read Orderic at your leisure; but you want only to carry in mind the fact that the generation of warriors who fought at Hastings and captured Jerusalem were regarded by themselves as effeminate, and plunged in luxury. 'Their locks are curled with hot irons, and instead of wearing caps, they bind their heads with fillets. A knight seldom appears in public with his head uncovered and properly shaved according to the apostolic precept.' The effeminacy of the first crusade took artistic shape in the west portal of Chartres and the glass of Saint Denis, and led instantly to the puritan reaction of Saint Bernard, followed by the gentle asceticism of Queen Blanche and Saint Louis. Whether the pilgrimages to Jerusalem and

contact with the East were the cause or only a consequence
of this revolution, or whether it was all one—a result of
converting the Northern pagans to peaceful habits and the
consequent enrichment of northern Europe—is indifferent;
the fact and the date are enough. The art is French, but
the ideas may have come from anywhere, like the game
of chess which the pilgrims or crusaders brought home
from Syria. In the Oriental game, the King was followed
step by step by a *Minister* whose functions were personal.
The crusaders freed the piece from control; gave it liberty
to move up or down or diagonally, forwards and backwards; made it the most arbitrary and formidable cham-
pion on the board, while the King and the Knight were
the most restricted in movement; and this piece they named
Queen, and called the Virgin:

> Li Baudrains traist sa *fierge* por son paon sauver,
> E cele son aufin qui cuida conquester
> La *firge* ou le paon, ou faire reculer.

The *aufin* or *dauphin* became the *Fou* of the French game,
and the bishop of the English. Baldwin played his Virgin to
save his pawn; his opponent played the bishop to threaten
either the Virgin or the pawn.

For a hundred and fifty years, the Virgin and Queens
ruled French taste and thought so successfully that the
French man has never yet quite decided whether to be
more proud or ashamed of it. Life has ever since seemed
a little flat to him, and art a little cheap. He saw that the
woman, in elevating herself, had made him appear ridiculous, and he tried to retaliate with a wit not always sparkling, and too often at his own expense. Sometimes in
museums or collections of bric-à-brac, you will see, in an illuminated manuscript, or carved on stone, or cast in bronze,
the figure of a man on his hands and knees, bestridden
by another figure holding a bridle and a whip; it is Aris-
totle, symbol of masculine wisdom, bridled and driven by
woman. Six hundred years afterwards, Tennyson revived
the same motive in Merlin, enslaved not for a time but forever. In both cases the satire justly punished the man. Another version of the same story—perhaps the original—was

the Mystery of Adam, one of the earliest Church plays. Gaston Paris says 'it was written in England in the twelfth century, and its author had real poetic talent; the scene of the seduction of Eve by the serpent is one of the best pieces of Christian dramaturgy. . . . This remarkable work seems to have been played no longer inside the church, but under the porch':

Diabolus.
   Jo vi Adam mais trop est fols.

Eva.
   Un poi est durs.
Diabolus.
           Il serra mols.
   Il est plus durs qui n'est enfers.
Eva.
   Il est mult francs.
Diabolus.
           Ainz est mult sers.
   Cure ne volt prendre de sei

   Car la prenge sevals de tei.

   Tu es fieblette et tendre chose
   E es plus fresche que n'est rose.
   Tu es plus blanche que cristal
   Que neif que chiet sor glace en val.
   Mal cuple en fist li Criatur.

   Tu es trop tendre e il trop dur.
   Mais neporquant tu es plus sage
   En grant sens as mis tun corrage
   Por co fait bon traire a tei.
   Parler te voil.
Eva.
           Ore ja fai.

Devil.
   Adam I've seen, but he's too rough.

Eve.
   A little hard!
Devil.
       He'll soon be soft enough!
   Harder than hell he is till now.
Eve.
   He's very frank!
Devil.
           Say very low!
   To help himself he does not care;
   The helping you shall be my share;
   For you are tender, gentle, true,
   The rose is not so fresh as you;
   Whiter than crystal, or than snow
   That falls from heaven on ice below.
   A sorry mixture God has brewed,
   You too tender, he too rude.

   But you have much the greater sense.
   Your will is all intelligence.

   Therefore it is I turn to you.
   I want to tell you—
Eve.
           Do it now!

The woman's greater intelligence was to blame for Adam's fall. Eve was justly punished because she should have known better, while Adam, as the Devil truly said, was a dull animal, hardly worth the trouble of deceiving. Adam was disloyal, too, untrue to his wife after being untrue to his Creator:

La femme que tu me donas	The woman that you made me take
Ele fist prime icest trespas	First led me into this mistake.
Donat le mei e jo mangai.	She gave the apple that I ate
Or mest vis tornez est a gwai	And brought me to this evil state.
Mal acontai icest manger.	Badly for me it turned, I own,
Jo ai mesfait par ma moiller.	But all the fault is hers alone.

The audience accepted this as natural and proper. They recognized the man as, of course, stupid, cowardly, and traitorous. The men of the baser sort revenged themselves by boorishness that passed with them for wit in the taverns of Arras, but the poets of the higher class commonly took sides with the women. Even Chaucer, who lived after the glamour had faded, and who satirized women to satiety, told their tale in his 'Legend of Good Women,' with evident sympathy. To him, also, the ordinary man was inferior —stupid, brutal, and untrue. 'Full brittle is the truest,' he said:

> For well I wote that Christ himself telleth
> That in Israel, as wide as is the lond,
> That so great faith in all the lond he ne fond
> As in a woman, and this is no lie;
> And as for men, look ye, such tyrannie
> They doen all day, assay hem who so list,
> The truest is full brotell for to trist.

Neither brutality nor wit helped the man much. Even Bluebeard in the end fell a victim to the superior qualities of his last wife, and Scheherazade's wit alone has preserved the memory of her royal husband. The tradition of thirteenth-century society still rules the French stage. The struggle between two strong-willed women to control one weak-willed man is the usual motive of the French drama in the nineteenth century, as it was the whole motive of Partenopeus of Blois, one of the best twelfth-century romans; and Joinville described it, in the middle of the thirteenth, as the leading motive in the court of Saint Louis, with Queen Blanche and Queen Margaret for players, and Saint Louis himself for pawn.

One has only to look at the common, so-called Elzevirian, volume of thirteenth-century nouvelles to see the Frenchman as he saw himself. The story of 'La Comtesse de Ponthieu' is the more Shakespearean, but 'La Belle Jehanne' is the more natural and lifelike. The plot is the common masculine intrigue against the woman, which was used over and over again before Shakespeare appropriated it in 'Much Ado'; but its French development is rather in the line of 'All's Well.' The fair Jeanne, married to a penniless knight, not at all by her choice, but only because he was a favourite of her father's, was a woman of the true twelfth-century type. She broke the head of the traitor, and when he, with his masculine falseness, caused her husband to desert her, she disguised herself as a squire and followed Sir Robert to Marseilles in search of service in war, for the poor knight could get no other means of livelihood. Robert was the husband, and the wife, in entering his service as squire without pay, called herself John:

Molt fu mesire Robiers dolans cant il vint a Marselle de çou k'il n'oï parler de nulle chose ki fust ou païs; si dist a Jehan:

—Ke ferons nous? Vous m'aves preste de vos deniers la vostre mierchi; si les vos renderai car je venderai mon palefroi et m'acuiterai a vous.

—Sire, dist Jehans, crees moi se il vous plaist je vous dirai ke nous ferons; jou ai bien enchore .c. sous de tournois; s'il vous plaist je venderai nos .ii. chevaus et en ferai deniers; et je suis li miousdres boulengiers ke vous sacies; si ferai pain françois et je ne douc mie ke je ne gaagne bien et largement mon depens.

Much was Sir Robert grieved when he came to Marseilles and found that there was no talk of anything doing in the country; and he said to John: 'What shall we do? You have lent me your money; I thank you, and will repay you, for I will sell my palfrey and discharge the debt to you.'

'Sir,' said John, 'trust to me, if you please, I will tell you what we will do; I have still a hundred sous; if you please I will sell our two horses and turn them into money; and I am the best baker you ever knew; I will make French bread, and I've no doubt I shall pay my expenses well and make money.'

—Jehans, dist mesire Robiers, je m'otroi del tout a faire votre volente.

Et lendemain vendi Jehans ses .ii. chevaux .X. livres de tornois, et achata son ble et le fist muire, et achata des corbelles et coumencha a faire pain françois si bon et si bien fait k'il en vendoit plus ke li doi melleur boulengier de la ville; et fist tant dedens les .ii. ans k'il ot bien .c. livres de katel. Lors dist Jehans a son segnour:

—Je lo bien que nous louons une tres grant mason et jou akaterai del vin et hierbegerai la bonne gent.

—Jehan, dist mesire Robiers, faites a vo volente kar je l'otroi et si me loc molt de vous.

Jehans loua une mason grant et bielle, et si hierbrega la bonne gent et gaegnoit ases a plente, et viestoit son segnour biellement et richement; et avoit mesire Robiers son palefroi et aloit boire et mengier aveukes les plus vallans de la ville; et Jehans li envoioit vins et viandes ke tout cil ki o lui conpagnoient s'en esmervelloient. Si gaegna tant ke dedens .iiii. ans il gaegna plus de .ccc. livres de meuble sains son harnois qui valoit bien .L. livres.

'John,' said Sir Robert, 'I agree wholly to do whatever you like.'

And the next day John sold their two horses for ten pounds, and bought his wheat and had it ground, and bought baskets, and began to make French bread so good and so well made that he sold more of it than the two best bakers in the city; and made so much within two years that he had a good hundred pounds property.

Then he said to his lord: 'I advise our hiring a very large house, and I will buy wine and will keep lodgings for good society.'

'John,' said Sir Robert, 'do what you please, for I grant it, and am greatly pleased with you.'

John hired a large and fine house and lodged the best people and gained a great plenty, and dressed his master handsomely and richly; and Sir Robert kept his palfrey and went out to eat and drink with the best people of the city; and John sent them such wines and food that all his companions marvelled at it. He made so much that within four years he gained more than three hundred pounds in money besides clothes, etc., well worth fifty.

The docile obedience of the man to the woman seemed as reasonable to the thirteenth century as the devotion of the woman to the man, not because she loved him, for there was no question of love, but because he was *her* man, and she owned him as though he were her child. The tale went on to develop her character always in the same sense. When she was ready, Jeanne broke up the establishment at Marseilles, brought her husband back to Hainault, and made him, without knowing her object, kill the traitor and redress her wrongs. Then after seven years' patient waiting, she revealed herself and resumed her place.

If you care to see the same type developed to its highest capacity, go to the theatre the first time some ambitious actress attempts the part of Lady Macbeth. Shakespeare realized the thirteenth-century woman more vividly than the thirteenth-century poets ever did; but that is no new thing to say of Shakespeare. The author of 'La Comtesse de Ponthieu' made no bad sketch of the character. These are fictions, but the Chronicles contain the names of women by scores who were the originals of the sketch. The society which Orderic described in Normandy—the generation of the first crusade—produced a great variety of Lady Macbeths. In the country of Evreux, about 1100, Orderic says that 'a worse than civil war was waged between two powerful brothers, and the mischief was fomented by the spiteful jealousy of their haughty wives. The Countess Havise of Evreux took offence at some taunts uttered by Isabel de Conches—wife of Ralph, the Seigneur of Conches, some ten miles from Evreux—and used all her influence with her husband, Count William, and his barons, to make trouble. . . . Both the ladies who stirred up these fierce enmities were great talkers and spirited as well as handsome; they ruled their husbands, oppressed their vassals, and inspired terror in various ways. But still their characters were very different. Havise had wit and eloquence, but she was cruel and avaricious. Isabel was generous, enterprising, and gay, so that she was beloved and esteemed by those about her. She rode in knight's armour when her vassals were called to war, and showed as much daring among men-at-arms and mounted knights as Camilla. . . .' More than three hundred years afterwards, far off in the Vosges, from a village never heard of, appeared a common peasant of seventeen years old, a girl without birth, education, wealth, or claim of any sort to consideration, who made her way to Chinon and claimed from Charles VII a commission to lead his army against the English. Neither the king nor the court had faith in her, and yet the commission was given, and the rank-and-file showed again that the true Frenchman had more confidence in the woman than in the man, no matter what the gossips might say. No one was surprised when Jeanne did what she promised, or when the men burned her for doing it. There were Jeannes in every village. Ridicule was powerless against them. Even Voltaire became what the French call frankly 'bête,' in trying it.

Eleanor of Guienne was the greatest of all Frenchwomen. Her decision was law, whether in Bordeaux or Poitiers, in Paris or in Palestine, in London or in Normandy; in the court of Louis VII, or in that of Henry II, or in her own Court of Love. For fifteen years she was Queen of France; for fifty she was Queen in England; for eighty or thereabouts she was equivalent to Queen over Guienne. No other Frenchwoman ever had such rule. Unfortunately, as Queen of France, she struck against an authority greater than her own, that of Saint Bernard, and after combating it, with Suger's help, from 1137 until 1152, the monk at last gained such mastery that Eleanor quitted the country and Suger died. She was not a person to accept defeat. She royally divorced her husband and went back to her own kingdom of Guienne. Neither Louis nor Bernard dared to stop her, or to hold her territories from her, but they put the best face they could on their defeat by proclaiming her as a person of irregular conduct. The irregularity would not have stood in their way, if they had dared to stand in hers, but Louis was much the weaker, and made himself weaker still by allowing her to leave him for the sake of Henry of Anjou, a story of a sort that rarely raised the respect in which French kings were held by French society. Probably politics had more to do with the matter than personal attachments, for Eleanor was a great ruler, the equal of any ordinary king, and more powerful than most kings living in 1152. If she deserted France in order to join the enemies of France, she had serious reasons besides love for young Henry of Anjou; but in any case she did, as usual, what pleased her, and forced Louis to pronounce the divorce at a council held at Beaugency, March 18, 1152, on the usual pretext of relationship. The humours of the twelfth century were Shakespearean. Eleanor, having obtained her divorce at Beaugency, to the deep regret of all Frenchmen, started at once for Poitiers, knowing how unsafe she was in any territory but her own. Beaugency is on the Loire, between Orléans and Blois, and Eleanor's first night was at Blois, or should have been; but she was told, on arriving, that Count Thibaut of Blois, undeterred by King Louis's experience, was making plans to detain her, with perfectly honourable views of marriage; and, as she seems at least not to have been in love with Thibaut, she was obliged to depart at once, in the night, to Tours. A night journey on horseback from Blois to Tours in the middle of March can have been no pleasure-trip, even in 1152; but, on arriving at Tours in the morning, Eleanor found that her lovers were still so dangerously near that she set forward at once on the road to Poitiers. As she approached her own territory she learned that Geoffrey of Anjou, the younger brother of her intended husband, was waiting for her at the border, with views of marriage as strictly honourable as those of all the others. She was driven to take another road, and at last got safe to Poitiers.

About no figure in the Middle Ages, man or woman, did so many legends grow, and with such freedom, as about Eleanor, whose strength appealed to French sympathies and whose adventures appealed to their imagination. They never forgave Louis for letting her go. They delighted to be told that in Palestine she had carried on relations of the most improper character, now with a Saracen slave of great beauty; now with Raymond of Poitiers, her uncle, the handsomest man of his time; now with Saladin himself; and, as all this occurred at Antioch in 1147 or 1148, they could not explain why her husband should have waited until 1152 in order to express his unwilling disapproval; but they quoted with evident sympathy a remark attributed to her that she thought she had married a king, and found she had married a monk. To the Frenchman, Eleanor remained always sympathetic, which is the more significant because, in English tradition, her character suffered a violent and incredible change. Although English history has lavished on Eleanor somewhat more than her due share of conventional moral reproof, considering that, from the moment she married Henry of Anjou, May 18, 1152, she was never charged with a breath of scandal, it atoned for her want of wickedness by French standards, in the usual manner of historians, by inventing traits which reflected the moral standards of England. Tradition converted her into the fairy-book type of feminine jealousy and invented for her the legend of the Fair Rosamund and the poison of toads.

For us, both legends are true. They reflected, not perhaps the character of Eleanor, but what the society liked to see acted on its theatre of life. Eleanor's real nature in no way concerns us. The single fact worth remembering was that she had two daughters by Louis VII, as shown in the table; who, in due time, married—Mary, in 1164, married Henry, the great Count of Champagne; Alix, at the same time, became Countess of Chartres by marriage with Thibaut, who had driven her mother from Blois in 1152 by his marital intentions. Henry and Thibaut were brothers whose sister Alix had married Louis VII in 1160, eight years after the divorce. The relations thus created were fantastic, especially for Queen Eleanor, who, besides her two French daughters, had eight children as Queen of England. Her second son, Richard Coeur-de-Lion, born in 1157, was affianced in 1174 to a daughter of Louis VII and Alix, a child only six years old, who was sent to England to be brought up as future queen. This was certainly Eleanor's doing, and equally certain was it that the child came to no good in the English court. The historians, by exception, have not charged this crime to Queen Eleanor; they charged it to Eleanor's husband, who passed most of his life in crossing his wife's political plans; but with politics we want as little as possible to do. We are concerned with the artistic and social side of life, and have only to notice the coincidence that while the Virgin was miraculously using the power of spiritual love to elevate and purify the people, Eleanor and her daughters were using the power of earthly love to discipline and refine the courts. Side by side with the crude realities about them, they insisted on teaching and enforcing an ideal that contradicted the realities, and had no value for them or for us except in the contradiction.

The ideals of Eleanor and her daughter Mary of Champagne were a form of religion, and if you care to see its evangels, you had best go directly to Dante and Petrarch, or, if you like it better, to Don Quixote de la Mancha. The religion is dead as Demeter, and its art alone survives as, on the whole, the highest expression of man's thought or emotion; but in its day it was almost as practical as it now is fanciful. Eleanor and her daughter Mary and her granddaughter Blanche knew as well as Saint Bernard did, or Saint Francis, what a brute the emancipated man could be; and as though they foresaw the society of the sixteenth and eighteenth centuries, they used every terror they could invent, as well as every tenderness they could invoke, to tame the beasts around them. Their charge was of manners, and, to teach manners, they made a school which they called their Court of Love, with a code of law to which they gave the name of 'courteous love.' The decisions of this court were recorded, like the decisions of a modern bench, under the names of the great ladies who made them, and were enforced by the ladies of good society for whose guidance they were made. They are worth reading, and any one who likes may read them to this day, with considerable scepticism about their genuineness. The doubt is only ignorance. We do not, and never can, know the twelfth-century woman, or, for that matter, any other woman, but we do know the literature she created; we know the art she lived in, and the religion she professed. We can collect from them some idea why the Virgin Mary ruled, and what she was taken to be, by the world which worshipped her.

Mary of Champagne created the literature of courteous love. She must have been about twenty years old when she married Count Henry and went to live at Troyes, not actually a queen in title, but certainly a queen in social influence. In 1164, Champagne was a powerful country, and Troyes a centre of taste. In Normandy, at the same date, William of Saint-Pair and Wace were writing the poetry we know. In Champagne the court poet was Christian of Troyes, whose poems were new when the churches of

Noyon and Senlis and Saint-Leu-d'Esserent, and the flèche of Chartres, and the Leaning Tower of Pisa, were building, at the same time with the Abbey of Vézelay, and before the church at Mantes. Christian died not long after 1175, leaving a great mass of verse, much of which has survived, and which you can read more easily than you can read Dante or Petrarch, although both are almost modern compared with Christian. The quality of this verse is something like the quality of the glass windows—conventional decoration; colours in conventional harmonies; refinement, restraint, and feminine delicacy of taste. Christian has not the grand manner of the eleventh century, and never recalls the masculine strength of the 'Chanson de Roland' or 'Raoul de Cambrai.' Even his most charming story, 'Erec et Enide,' carries chiefly a moral of courtesy. His is poet-laureate's work, says M. Gaston Paris; the flower of a twelfth-century court and of twelfth-century French; the best example of an admirable language; but not lyric; neither strong, nor deep, nor deeply felt. What we call tragedy is unknown to it. Christian's world is sky-blue and rose, with only enough red to give it warmth, and so flooded with light that even its mysteries count only by the clearness with which they are shown.

Among other great works, before Mary of France came to Troyes, Christian had, toward 1160, written a 'Tristan,' which is lost. Mary herself, he says, gave him the subject of 'Lancelot,' with the request or order to make it a lesson of 'courteous love,' which he obeyed. Courtesy has lost its meaning as well as its charm, and you might find the 'Chevalier de la Charette' even more unintelligible than tiresome; but its influence was great in its day, and the lesson of courteous love, under the authority of Mary of Champagne, lasted for centuries as the standard of taste. 'Lancelot' was never finished, but later, not long after 1174, Christian wrote a 'Perceval,' or 'Conte du Graal,' which must also have been intended to please Mary, and which is interesting because, while the 'Lancelot' gave the twelfth-century idea of courteous love, the 'Perceval' gave the twelfth-century idea of religious mystery. Mary was certainly concerned with both. 'It is for this same Mary,' says Gaston Paris, 'that Walter of Arras undertook his poem of "Eracle"; she was the object of the songs of the troubadours as well as of their French imitators; for her use also she caused the translations of books of piety like Genesis, or the paraphrase at great length, in verse, of the psalm "Eructavit."'

With her theories of courteous love, every one is more or less familiar if only from the ridicule of Cervantes and the follies of Quixote, who, though four hundred years younger, was Lancelot's child; but we never can know how far she took herself and her laws of love seriously, and to speculate on so deep a subject as her seriousness is worse than useless, since she would herself have been as uncertain as her lovers were. Visionary as the courtesy was, the Holy Grail was as practical as any bric-à-brac that has survived of the time. The mystery of Perceval is like that of the Gothic cathedral, illuminated by floods of light, and enlivened by rivers of colour. Unfortunately Christian never told what he meant by the fragment, itself a mystery, in which he narrated the story of the knight who saw the Holy Grail, because the knight, who was warned, as usual, to ask no questions, for once, unlike most knights, obeyed the warning when he should have disregarded it. As knights-errant necessarily did the wrong thing in order to make their adventures possible, Perceval's error cannot be in itself mysterious, nor was the castle in any way mysterious where the miracle occurred. It appeared to him to be the usual castle, and he saw nothing unusual in the manner of his reception by the usual old lord, or in the fact that both seated themselves quite simply before the hall-fire with the usual household. Then, as though it were an everyday habit, the Holy Grail was brought in (Bartsch, 'Chrestomathie,' 183–85, ed. 1895):

Et leans avait luminaire	And, within, the hall was bright
Si grant con l'an le porrait faire	As any hall could be with light
De chandoiles a un ostel.	Of candles in a house at night.
Que qu'il parloient d'un et d'el,	So, while of this and that they talked,
Uns vallez d'une chambre vint	A squire from a chamber walked,

Qui une blanche lance tint

Ampoigniee par le mi lieu.

Si passa par endroit le feu

Et cil qui al feu se seoient,
Et tuit cil de leans veoient

La lance blanche et le fer
    blanc.
S'issoit une gote de sang
Del fer de la lance au sommet,

Et jusqu'a la main au vaslet

Coroit cele gote vermoille....
A tant dui autre vaslet vindrent

Qui chandeliers an lors mains
    tindrent
De fin or ovrez a neel.
Li vaslet estoient moult bel
Qui les chandeliers aportoient.

An chacun chandelier ardoient
Dous chandoiles a tot le mains.

Un graal antre ses dous mains

Une demoiselle tenoit,

Qui avec les vaslets venoit,

Bele et gente et bien acesmee.

Quant ele fu leans antree
Atot le graal qu'ele tint

Une si granz clartez i vint
Qu'ausi perdirent les chan-
    doiles
Lor clarte come les estoiles

Qant li solauz luist et la lune.
Apres celi an revint une
Qui tint un tailleor d'argent.

Bearing a white lance in his
    hand,

Grasped by the middle, like a
    wand;

And, as he passed the chim-
    ney wide,

Those seated by the fireside,
And all the others, caught a
    glance

Of the white steel and the
    white lance.
As they looked, a drop of blood
Down the lance's handle
    flowed;

Down to where the youth's
    hand stood,

From the lance-head at the top
They saw run that crimson
    drop....

Presently came two more
    squires,

In their hands two chandeliers,
Of fine gold in enamel wrought.
Each squire that the candle
    brought

Was a handsome chevalier.
There burned in every chande-
    lier

Two lighted candles at the
    least.

A damsel, graceful and well
    dressed,

Behind the squires followed
    fast

Who carried in her hands a
    graal;

And as she came within the hall
With the graal there came a
    light

So brilliant that the candles all
Lost clearness, as the stars at
    night

When moon shines, or in day
    the sun.

After her there followed one
Who a dish of silver bore.

[291]

Le graal qui aloit devant	The graal, which had gone before,
De fin or esmere estoit,	Of gold the finest had been made,
Pierres precieuses avoit	With precious stones had been inlaid,
El graal de maintes menieres	Richest and rarest of each kind
Des plus riches et des plus chieres	That man in sea or earth could find.
Qui en mer ne en terre soient.	All other jewels far surpassed
Totes autres pierres passoient	Those which the holy graal enchased.
Celes del graal sanz dotance.	
Tot ainsi con passa la lance	Just as before had passed the lance
Par devant le lit trespasserent	They all before the bed advance,
Et d'une chambre a l'autre alerent.	Passing straightway through the hall,
Et li vaslet les vit passer,	And the knight who saw them pass
Ni n'osa mire demander	Never ventured once to ask
Del graal cui l'an an servoit.	For the meaning of the graal.

The simplicity of this narration gives a certain dramatic effect to the mystery, like seeing a ghost in full daylight, but Christian carried simplicity further still. He seemed either to feel, or to want others to feel, the reality of the adventure and the miracle, and he followed up the appearance of the graal by a solid meal in the style of the twelfth century, such as one expects to find in 'Ivanhoe' or the 'Talisman.' The knight sat down with his host to the best dinner that the county of Champagne afforded, and they ate their haunch of venison with the graal in full view. They drank their Champagne wine of various sorts, out of gold cups:

> Vins clers ne raspez ne lor faut
> A copes dorees a boivre;

they sat before the fire and talked till bedtime, when the squires made up the beds in the hall, and brought in supper—dates, figs, nutmegs, spices, pomegranates, and at last lectuaries, suspiciously like what we call jams; and 'alexandrine gingerbread'; after which they drank various drinks, with or without spice or honey or pepper; and old moret, which is thought to be mulberry wine, but which generally went with claret, a colourless grape-juice, or piment. At least, here are the lines, and one may translate them to suit one's self:

> Et li vaslet aparellierent
> Les lis et le fruit au colchier
> Que il en i ot de moult chier,
> Dates, figues, et nois mugates,
> Girofles et pomes de grenates,
> Et leituaires an la fin,
> Et gingenbret alixandrin.
> Apres ce burent de maint boivre,
> Piment ou n'ot ne miel ne poivre
> Et viez more et cler sirop.

The twelfth century had the child's love of sweets and spices and preserved fruits, and drinks sweetened or spiced, whether they were taken for supper or for poetry; the true knight's palate was fresh and his appetite excellent either for sweets or verses or love; the world was young then; Robin Hoods lived in every forest, and Richard Coeur-de-Lion was not yet twenty years old. The pleasant adventures of Robin Hood were real, as you can read in the stories of a dozen outlaws, and men troubled themselves about pain and death much as healthy bears did, in the mountains. Life had miseries enough, but few shadows deeper than those of the imaginative lover, or the terrors of ghosts at night. Men's imaginations ran riot, but did not keep them awake; at least, neither the preserved fruits nor the mulberry wine nor the clear syrup nor the gingerbread nor the Holy Graal kept Perceval awake, but he slept the sound and healthy sleep of youth, and when he woke the next morning, he felt only a mild surprise to find that his host and household had disappeared, leaving him to ride away without farewell, breakfast, or Graal.

Christian wrote about Perceval in 1174 in the same spirit in which the workmen in glass, thirty years later, told the story of Charlemagne. One artist worked for Mary of Champagne; the others for Mary of Chartres, commonly known as the Virgin; but all did their work in good faith,

with the first, fresh, easy instinct of colour, light, and line.
Neither of the two Maries was mystical, in a modern sense;
none of the artists was oppressed by the burden of doubt;
their scepticism was as childlike as faith. If one has to make
an exception, perhaps the passion of love was more serious
than that of religion, and gave to religion the deepest emotion, and the most complicated one, which society knew.
Love was certainly a passion; and even more certainly it
was, as seen in poets like Dante and Petrarch—in romans
like 'Lancelot' and 'Aucassin'—in ideals like the Virgin—
complicated beyond modern conception. For this reason
the loss of Christian's 'Tristan' makes a terrible gap in art,
for Christian's poem would have given the first and best
idea of what led to courteous love. The 'Tristan' was written before 1160, and belonged to the cycle of Queen Eleanor of England rather than to that of her daughter Mary
of Troyes; but the subject was one neither of courtesy nor
of France; it belonged to an age far behind the eleventh
century, or even the tenth, or indeed any century within
the range of French history; and it was as little fitted for
Christian's way of treatment as for any avowed burlesque.
The original Tristan—critics say—was not French, and neither Tristan nor Isolde had ever a drop of French blood
in their veins. In their form as Christian received it, they
were Celts or Scots; they came from Brittany, Wales, Ireland, the northern ocean, or farther still. Behind the Welsh
Tristan, which passed probably through England to Normandy and thence to France and Champagne, critics detect a far more ancient figure living in a form of society
that France could not remember ever to have known. King
Marc was a tribal chief of the Stone Age whose subjects
loved the forest and lived on the sea or in caves; King
Marc's royal hall was a common shelter on the banks of
a stream, where every one was at home, and king, queen,
knights, attendants, and dwarf slept on the floor, on beds
laid down where they pleased; Tristan's weapons were the
bow and stone knife; he never saw a horse or a spear; his
ideas of loyalty and Isolde's ideas of marriage were as
vague as Marc's royal authority; and all were alike unconscious of law, chivalry, or church. The note they sang was

more unlike the note of Christian, if possible, than that of Richard Wagner; it was the simplest expression of rude and primitive love, as one could perhaps find it among North American Indians, though hardly so defiant even there, and certainly in the Icelandic Sagas hardly so lawless; but it was a note of real passion, and touched the deepest chords of sympathy in the artificial society of the twelfth century, as it did in that of the nineteenth. The task of the French poet was to tone it down and give it the fashionable dress, the pointed shoes and long sleeves, of the time. 'The Frenchman,' says Gaston Paris, 'is specially interested in making his story entertaining for the society it is meant for; he is "social"; that is, of the world; he smiles at the adventures he tells, and delicately lets you see that he is not their dupe; he exerts himself to give to his style a constant elegance, a uniform polish, in which a few neatly turned, clever phrases sparkle here and there; above all, he wants to please, and thinks of his audience more than of his subject.'

In the twelfth century he wanted chiefly to please women, as Orderic complained; Isolde came out of Brittany to meet Eleanor coming up from Guienne, and the Virgin from the east; and all united in giving law to society. In each case it was the woman, not the man, who gave the law;—it was Mary, not the Trinity; Eleanor, not Louis VII; Isolde, not Tristan. No doubt, the original Tristan had given the law like Roland or Achilles, but the twelfth-century Tristan was a comparatively poor creature. He was in his way a secondary figure in the romance, as Louis VII was to Eleanor and Abélard to Héloïse. Every one knows how, about twenty years before Eleanor came to Paris, the poet-professor Abélard, the hero of the Latin Quarter, had sung to Héloïse those songs which—he tells us—resounded through Europe as widely as his scholastic fame, and probably to more effect for his renown. In popular notions Héloïse was Isolde, and would in a moment have done what Isolde did (Bartsch, 107–08):

Quaint reis Marcs nus out conjeies	When King Marc had banned us both,

E de sa curt nus out chascez,	And from his court had chased us forth,
As mains ensemble nus preismes	Hand in hand each clasping fast
E hors de la sale en eissimes,	Straight from out the hall we passed;
A la forest puis en alasmes	To the forest turned our face;
E un mult bel liu i trouvames	Found in it a perfect place,
E une roche, fu cavee,	Where the rock that made a cave
Devant ert estraite la entree,	Hardly more than passage gave;
Dedans fu voesse ben faite,	Spacious within and fit for use,
Tante bel cum se fust purtraite.	As though it had been planned for us.

At any time of her life, Héloïse would have defied society or church, and would—at least in the public's fancy —have taken Abélard by the hand and gone off to the forest much more readily than she went to the cloister; but Abélard would have made a poor figure as Tristan. Abélard and Christian of Troyes were as remote as we are from the legendary Tristan; but Isolde and Héloïse, Eleanor and Mary were the immortal and eternal woman. The legend of Isolde, both in the earlier and the later version, seems to have served as a sacred book to the women of the twelfth and thirteenth centuries, and Christian's Isolde surely helped Mary in giving law to the Court of Troyes and decisions in the Court of Love.

Countess Mary's authority lasted from 1164 to 1198, thirty-four years, during which, at uncertain intervals, glimpses of her influence flash out in poetry rather than in prose. Christian began his 'Roman de la Charette' by invoking her:

> Puisque ma dame de Chanpaigne
> Vialt que romans a faire anpraigne
>
> . . . .
> Si deist et jel tesmoignasse
> Que ce est la dame qui passe
> Totes celes qui sont vivanz
> Si con li funs passe les vanz
> Qui vante en Mai ou en Avril
>
> . . . .
> Dirai je: tant com une jame

> Vaut de pailes et de sardines
> Vaut la contesse de reïnes?

Christian chose curious similes. His dame surpassed all living rivals as smoke passes the winds that blow in May; or as much as a gem would buy of straws and sardines is the Countess worth in queens. Louis XIV would have thought that Christian might be laughing at him, but court styles changed with their masters. Louis XIV would scarcely have written a prison-song to his sister such as Richard Coeur-de-Lion wrote to Mary of Champagne:

Ja nus hons pris ne dirat sa raison
   Adroitement s'ansi com dolans non;
   Mais par confort puet il faire chanson.
Moult ai d'amins, mais povre sont li don;
Honte en avront se por ma rëançon
   Suix ces deus yvers pris.
	No prisoner can tell his honest thought
	   Unless he speaks as one who suffers wrong;
	   But for his comfort he may make a song.
	My friends are many, but their gifts are naught.
	Shame will be theirs, if, for my ransom, here
	   I lie another year.

Ceu sevent bien mi home et mi baron,
   Englois, Normant, Poitevin et Gascon,
   Ke je n'avoie si povre compaingnon
Cui je laissasse por avoir an prixon.
Je nel di pas por nulle retraison,
 	
   Mais ancor suix je pris.
	They know this well, my barons and my men,
	   Normandy, England, Gascony, Poitou,
	   That I had never follower so low
	Whom I would leave in prison to my gain.
	I say it not for a reproach to them,
	   But prisoner I am!

Or sai ge bien de voir certainement
   Ke mors ne pris n'ait amin ne parent,
   Cant on me lait por or ne por argent.
Moult m'est de moi, mais plus m'est de ma gent
C'apres ma mort avront reprochier grant
   Se longement suix pris.
	The ancient proverb now I know for sure:
	   Death and a prison know nor kin nor tie,
	   Since for mere lack of gold they let me lie.
	Much for myself I grieve; for them still more.
	After my death they will have grievous wrong
	   If I am prisoner long.

N'est pas mervelle se j'ai lo
  cuer dolent
Cant li miens sires tient ma
  terre en torment.
S'or li menbroit de nostre
  sairement
Ke nos fëismes andui com-
  munament,
Bien sai de voir ke ceans longe-
  ment
  Ne seroie pas pris.

What marvel that my heart is
  sad and sore
When my own lord torments
  my helpless lands!
Well do I know that, if he
  held his hands,
Remembering the common
  oath we swore,
I should not here imprisoned
  with my song,
  Remain a prisoner long.

Ce sevent bien Angevin et To-
  rain,
  Cil bacheler ki or sont fort et
  sain,
C'ancombreis suix long d'aus
  en autrui main.
Forment m'amoient, mais or ne
  m'aimment grain.
De belles armes sont ores veut
  cil plain,
  Por tant ke je suix pris.

They know this well who now
  are rich and strong
  Young gentlemen of Anjou
  and Touraine,
That far from them, on hostile bonds I strain.
They loved me much, but have
  not loved me long.
Their plains will see no more
  fair lists arrayed,
  While I lie here betrayed.

Mes compaingnons cui j'amoie
  et cui j'aim,
  Ces dou Caheu et ces dou
  Percherain,
Me di, chanson, kil ne sont
  pas certain,
C'onques vers aus n'en oi cuer
  faus ne vain.
S'il me guerroient, il font moult
  que vilain
  Tant com je serai pris.

Companions whom I loved,
  and still do love,
  Geoffroi du Perche and Ansel
  de Caïeux,
Tell them, my song, that
  they are friends untrue.
Never to them did I false-
  hearted prove;
But they do villainy if they war
  on me,
  While I lie here, unfree.

Comtesse suer, vostre pris sov-
  erain
Vos saut et gart cil a cui je me
  claim
  Et par cui je suix pris.
Je n'ou di pas de celi de Char-
  tain
  Le meire Lowëis.

Countess sister! your sovereign
  fame
May he preserve whose help I
  claim,
  Victim for whom am I!
I say not this of Chartres' dame,
  Mother of Louis!

Richard's prison-song, one of the chief monuments of
English literature, sounds to every ear, accustomed to

twelfth-century verse, as charming as when it was household rhyme to

mi ome et mi baron
Englois, Normant, Poitevin et Gascon.

Not only was Richard a far greater king than any Louis ever was, but he also composed better poetry than any other king who is known to tourists, and, when he spoke to his sister in this cry of the heart altogether singular among monarchs, he made law and style, above discussion. Whether he meant to reproach his other sister, Alix of Chartres, historians may tell, if they know. If he did, the reproach answered its purpose, for the song was written in 1193; Richard was ransomed and released in 1194; and in 1198 the young Count 'Loweis' of Chartres and Blois leagued with the Counts of Flanders, Le Perche, Guines, and Toulouse, against Philip Augustus, in favor of Coeur-de-Lion to whom they rendered homage. In any case, neither Mary nor Alice in 1193 was reigning Countess. Mary was a widow since 1181, and her son Henry was Count in Champagne, apparently a great favourite with his uncle Richard Coeur-de-Lion. The life of this Henry of Champagne was another twelfth-century romance, but can serve no purpose here except to recall the story that his mother, the great Countess Mary, died in 1198 of sorrow for the death of this son, who was then King of Jerusalem, and was killed, in 1197, by a fall from the window of his palace at Acre. Coeur-de-Lion died in 1199. In 1201, Mary's other son, who succeeded Henry—Count Thibaut III—died, leaving a posthumous heir, famous in the thirteenth century as Thibaut-le-Grand —the Thibaut of Queen Blanche.

They were all astonishing—men and women—and filled the world, for two hundred years, with their extraordinary energy and genius; but the greatest of all was old Queen Eleanor, who survived her son Coeur-de-Lion, as well as her two husbands—Louis-le-Jeune and Henry II Plantagenet—and was left in 1200 still struggling to repair the evils and fend off the dangers they caused. 'Queen by the wrath of God,' she called herself, and she knew what just claim she had to the rank. Of her two husbands and ten children,

little remained except her son John, who, by the unanimous
voice of his family, his friends, his enemies, and even his
admirers, achieved a reputation for excelling in every form
of twelfth-century crime. He was a liar and a traitor, as was
not uncommon, but he was thought to be also a coward,
which, in that family, was singular. Some redeeming quality
he must have had, but none is recorded. His mother saw
him running, in his masculine, twelfth-century recklessness,
to destruction, and she made a last and a characteristic
effort to save him and Guienne by a treaty of amity with
the French king, to be secured by the marriage of the heir
of France, Louis, to Eleanor's granddaughter, John's niece,
Blanche of Castile, then twelve or thirteen years old. Eleanor herself was eighty, and yet she made the journey to
Spain, brought back the child to Bordeaux, affianced her to
Louis VIII as she had herself been affianced in 1137 to
Louis VII, and in May, 1200, saw her married. The French
had then given up their conventional trick of attributing
Eleanor's acts to her want of morals; and France gave her
—as to most women after sixty years old—the benefit of the
convention which made women respectable after they had
lost the opportunity to be vicious. In French eyes, Eleanor
played out the drama according to the rules. She could not
save John, but she died in 1202, before his ruin, and you
can still see her lying with her husband and her son Richard
at Fontevrault in her twelfth-century tomb.

In 1223, Blanche became Queen of France. She was
thirty-six years old. Her husband, Louis VIII, was ambitious
to rival his father, Philip Augustus, who had seized Normandy in 1203. Louis undertook to seize Toulouse and
Avignon. In 1225, he set out with a large army in which,
among the chief vassals, his cousin Thibaut of Champagne
led a contingent. Thibaut was five-and-twenty years old,
and, like Pierre de Dreux, then Duke of Brittany, was one
of the most brilliant and versatile men of his time, and one
of the greatest rulers. As royal vassal Thibaut owed forty
days' service in the field; but his interests were at variance
with the King's, and at the end of the term he marched
home with his men, leaving the King to fall ill and die in

Auvergne, November 8, 1226, and a child of ten years old
to carry on the government as Louis IX.

Chartres Cathedral has already told the story twice, in
stone and glass; but Thibaut does not appear there, although he saved the Queen. Some member of the royal
family must be regent. Queen Blanche took the place, and
of course the princes of the blood, who thought it was
their right, united against her. At first, Blanche turned violently on Thibaut and forbade him to appear at the corona-
tion at Rheims in his own territory, on November 29, as
though she held him guilty of treason; but when the league
of great vassals united to deprive her of the regency, she
had no choice but to detach at any cost any member of
the league, and Thibaut alone offered help. What price she
paid him was best known to her; but what price she would
be believed to have paid him was as well known to her as
what had been said of her grandmother Eleanor when she
changed her allegiance in 1152. If the scandal had concerned Thibaut alone, she might have been well content,
but Blanche was obliged also to pay desperate court to
the papal legate. Every member of her husband's family
united against her and libelled her character with the freedom which enlivened and envenomed royal tongues.

> Maintes paroles en dit en
> Comme d'Iseult et de Tristan.

Had this been all, she would have cared no more than
Eleanor or any other queen had cared, for in French drama,
real or imaginary, such charges were not very serious and
hardly uncomplimentary; but Iseult had never been accused, over and above her arbitrary views on the marriage-
contract, of acting as an accomplice with Tristan in poison-
ing King Marc. French convention required that Thibaut
should have poisoned Louis VIII for love of the Queen, and
that this secret reciprocal love should control their lives.
Fortunately for Blanche she was a devout ally of the
Church, and the Church believed evil only of enemies. The
legate and the prelates rallied to her support and after eight
years of desperate struggle they crushed Pierre Mauclerc
and saved Thibaut and Blanche.

For us the poetry is history, and the facts are false. French art starts not from facts, but from certain assumptions as conventional as a legendary window, and the commonest convention is the Woman. The fact, then as now, was Power, or its equivalent in exchange, but Frenchmen, while struggling for the Power, expressed it in terms of Art. They looked on life as a drama—and on drama as a phase of life—in which the bystanders were bound to assume and accept the regular stage-plot. That the plot might be altogether untrue to real life affected in no way its interest. To them Thibaut and Blanche were bound to act Tristan and Isolde. Whatever they were when off the stage, they were lovers on it. Their loves were as real and as reasonable as the worship of the Virgin. Courteous love was avowedly a form of drama, but not the less a force of society. Illusion for illusion, courteous love, in Thibaut's hands, or in the hands of Dante and Petrarch, was as substantial as any other convention;—the balance of trade, the rights of man, or the Athanasian Creed. In that sense the illusions alone were real; if the Middle Ages had reflected only what was practical, nothing would have survived for us.

Thibaut was Tristan, and is said to have painted his verses on the walls of his château. If he did, he painted there, in the opinion of M. Gaston Paris, better poetry than any that was written on paper or parchment, for Thibaut was a great prince and great poet who did in both characters whatever he pleased. In modern equivalents, one would give much to see the château again with the poetry on its walls. Provins has lost the verses, but Troyes still keeps some churches and glass of Thibaut's time which hold their own with the best. Even of Thibaut himself, something survives, and though it were only the memories of his seneschal, the famous Sire de Joinville, history and France would be poor without him. With Joinville in hand, you may still pass an hour in the company of these astonishing thirteenth-century men and women: crusaders who fight, hunt, make love, build churches, put up glass windows to the Virgin, buy missals, talk scholastic philosophy, compose poetry; Blanche, Thibaut, Perron, Joinville, Saint Louis, Saint Thomas, Saint Dominic, Saint Francis—you may know them as intimately as you can ever know a world that is lost; and in the case of Thibaut you may know more, for he is still alive in his poems; he even vibrates with life. One might try a few verses, to see what he meant by courtesy. Perhaps he wrote them for Queen Blanche, but, to whomever he sent them, the French were right in thinking that she ought to have returned his love (edition of 1742):

Nus hom ne puet ami recon-   There is no comfort to be found
    forter   for pain
Se cele non ou il a son cuer mis.   Save only where the heart has
                               made its home.

Pour ce m'estuet sovent plain-   Therefore I can but murmur
    dre et plourer   and complain
Que nus confors ne me vient,   Because no comfort to my pain
    ce m'est vis,   has come
De la ou j'ai tote ma remem-   From where I garnered all my
    brance.   happiness.
Pour bien amer ai sovent esmai-   From true love have I only
    ance   earned distress
    A dire voir.   The truth to say.
Dame, merci! donez moi espe-   Grace, lady! give me comfort to
    rance   possess
    De joie avoir.   A hope, one day.

Je ne puis pas sovent a li parler   Seldom the music of her voice
                              I hear
Ne remirer les biaus iex de son   Or wonder at the beauty of her
    vis.   eyes.
Ce pois moi que je n'i puis aler   It grieves me that I may not
                              follow there
Car ades est mes cuers ententis.   Where at her feet my heart
                              attentive lies.
Ho! bele riens, douce sans con-   Oh, gentle Beauty without
    oissance,   consciousness,
Car me mettez en millor atten-   Let me once feel a moment's
    dance   hopefulness,
    De bon espoir!   If but one ray!
Dame, merci! donez moi espe-   Grace, lady! give me comfort
    rance   to possess
    De joie avoir.   A hope, one day.

Aucuns si sont qui me vuelent   Certain there are who blame
    blamer   upon me throw
Quant je ne di a qui je suis   Because I will not tell whose
    amis;   love I seek;
Mais ja, dame, ne saura mon   But truly, lady, none my
    penser   thought shall know,

Nus qui soit nes fors vous cui
  je le dis
Couardement a pavours a dou-
  tance
Dont puestes vous lors bien a
  ma semblance

  Mon cuer savoir.
Dame, merci! donez moi espe-
  rance
  De joie avoir.

None that is born, save you to
  whom I speak
In cowardice and awe and
  doubtfulness,
That you may happily with
  fearlessness

  My heart essay.
Grace, lady! give me comfort
  to possess
  A hope, one day.

Does Thibaut's verse sound simple? It is the simplicity
of the thirteenth-century glass—so refined and complicated
that sensible people are mostly satisfied to feel, and not to
understand. Any blunderer in verse, who will merely look
at the rhymes of these three stanzas, will see that simplicity
is about as much concerned there as it is with the windows
of Chartres; the verses are as perfect as the colours, and
the versification as elaborate. These stanzas might have
been addressed to Queen Blanche; now see how Thibaut
kept the same tone of courteous love in addressing the
Queen of Heaven!

De grant travail et de petit
  esploit
  Voi ce siegle cargie et en-
    combre
  Que tant somes plain de
    maleurte
Ke nus ne pens a faire ce
  qu'il doit,
  Ains avons si le Deauble
    trouve
Qu'a lui servir chascuns paine
  et essaie
Et Diex ki ot pour nos ja cruel
  plaie
  Metons arrier et sa grant
    dignite;
Molt est hardis qui pour mort
  ne s'esmaie.

Diex que tout set et tout puet
  et tout voit
  Nous auroit tost en entre-
    deus giete

With travail great, and little
  cargo fraught,
  See how our world is labour-
    ing in pain;
  So filled we are with love of
    evil gain
That no one thinks of doing
  what he ought,
  But we all hustle in the
    Devil's train,
And only in his service toil
  and pray;
And God, who suffered for us
  agony,
  We set behind, and treat him
    with disdain;
Hardy is he whom death does
  not dismay.

God who rules all, from whom
  we can hide nought,
  Had quickly flung us back
    to nought ag*ⁱⁿ*

Se la Dame plaine de grant
bonte
Pardelez lui pour nos ne li
prioit
Si tres douc mot plaisant et
savoure
Le grant courous dou grant
Signour apaie;
Molt par est fox ki autre amor
essai
K'en cestui n'a barat ne
fausete
Ne es autres n'a ne merci ne
manaie.

La souris quiert pour son cors
garandir
Contre l'yver la noif et le
forment
Et nous chaitif nous n'alons
rien querant
Quant nous morrons ou nous
puissions garir.
Nous ne cherchons fors
k'infer le puant;
Or esgardes come beste sau-
vage
Pourvoit de loin encontre son
domage
Et nous n'avons ne sens ne
hardement;
Il est avis que plain somes de
rage.

Li Deable a getey por nos ravir

Quatre ameçons aeschies de
torment;
Covoitise lance premiere-
ment
Et puis Orguel por sa grant
rois emplir
Et Luxure va le batel train-
ant
Felonie les governe et les nage.

Ensi peschant s'en viegnent au
rivage

But that our gentle, gra-
cious, Lady Queen
Begged him to spare us, and
our pardon wrought;
Striving with words of
sweetness to restrain
Our angry Lord, and his great
wrath allay.
Felon is he who shall her love
betray
Which is pure truth, and
falsehood cannot feign,
While all the rest is lie and
cheating play.

The feeble mouse, against the
winter's cold,
Garners the nuts and grain
within his cell,
While man goes groping,
without sense to tell
Where to seek refuge against
growing old.
We seek it in the smoking
mouth of Hell.
With the poor beast our impotence compare!
See him protect his life with
utmost care,
While us nor wit nor courage can compel
To save our souls, so foolish
mad we are.

The Devil doth in snares our
life enfold;
Four hooks has he with tor-
ments baited well;
And first with Greed he casts
a mighty spell,
And then, to fill his nets, has
Pride enrolled,
And Luxury steers the boat,
and fills the sail,
And Perfidy controls and sets
the snare;
Thus the poor fish are brought
to land, and there

Dont Diex nous gart par son
    commandement
En qui sains fons nous feismes
    homage.

May God preserve us and
    the foe repel!
Homage to him who saves us
    from despair!

————

————

A la Dame qui tous les biens
    avance
  T'en va, chançon s'el te vielt
    escouter
Onques ne fu nus de millor
    chaunce.

To Mary Queen, who passes all
    compare,
  Go, little song! to her your
    sorrows tell!
Nor Heaven nor Earth holds
    happiness so rare.

Autobiographer

Where he had come from; where he was going; an early chapter and a late chapter of The Education of Henry Adams, taken together, suggest the monstrous gulf between the beginning and the end of the life. When he came to write The Education he still believed—gay in the midst of gloom—that a good question was better than an easy answer.

It has turned out that Adams asked the right questions. He is more read now, and more graspingly read, than ever. Of all his books, the difficult, teasing Education seems the most pertinent to the atomic age. Adams will continue to be pertinent because he never fooled himself into believing that any one of his several theories of history was absolutely or literally true; it was only suggestibly and analogically so.

He opened his Chapter XXXIV, "A Law of Acceleration," with these significant words:

> Images are not arguments, rarely even lead to proof, but the mind craves them, and, of late more than ever, the keenest experimenters find twenty images better than one, especially if contradictory; since the human mind has already learned to deal in contradictions.

Quincy [1]

Under the shadow of Boston State House, turning its back
on the house of John Hancock, the little passage called Hancock Avenue runs, or ran, from Beacon Street, skirting the
State House grounds, to Mount Vernon Street, on the summit of Beacon Hill; and there, in the third house below
Mount Vernon Place, February 16, 1838, a child was born,
and christened later by his uncle, the minister of the First
Church after the tenets of Boston Unitarianism, as Henry
Brooks Adams.

Had he been born in Jerusalem under the shadow of the
Temple and circumcised in the Synagogue by his uncle the
high priest, under the name of Israel Cohen, he would
scarcely have been more distinctly branded, and not much
more heavily handicapped in the races of the coming century, in running for such stakes as the century was to offer;
but, on the other hand, the ordinary traveller, who does not
enter the field of racing, finds advantage in being, so to
speak, ticketed through life, with the safeguards of an old,
established traffic. Safeguards are often irksome, but sometimes convenient, and if one needs them at all, one is apt
to need them badly. A hundred years earlier, such safeguards as his would have secured any young man's success;
and although in 1838 their value was not very great compared with what they would have had in 1738, yet the
mere accident of starting a twentieth-century career from
a nest of associations so colonial—so troglodytic—as the First
Church, the Boston State House, Beacon Hill, John Hancock and John Adams, Mount Vernon Street and Quincy,

[1] Chapter I of *The Education of Henry Adams,* privately
printed in 1907, published in 1918 by Houghton Mifflin Co.

all crowding on ten pounds of unconscious babyhood, was so queer as to offer a subject of curious speculation to the baby long after he had witnessed the solution. What could become of such a child of the seventeenth and eighteenth centuries, when he should wake up to find himself required to play the game of the twentieth? Had he been consulted, would he have cared to play the game at all, holding such cards as he held, and suspecting that the game was to be one of which neither he nor any one else back to the beginning of time knew the rules or the risks or the stakes? He was not consulted and was not responsible, but had he been taken into the confidence of his parents, he would certainly have told them to change nothing as far as concerned him. He would have been astounded by his own luck. Probably no child, born in the year, held better cards than he. Whether life was an honest game of chance, or whether the cards were marked and forced, he could not refuse to play his excellent hand. He could never make the usual plea of irresponsibility. He accepted the situation as though he had been a party to it, and under the same circumstances would do it again, the more readily for knowing the exact values. To his life as a whole he was a consenting, contracting party and partner from the moment he was born to the moment he died. Only with that understanding—as a consciously assenting member in full partnership with the society of his age—had his education an interest to himself or to others.

As it happened, he never got to the point of playing the game at all; he lost himself in the study of it, watching the errors of the players; but this is the only interest in the story, which otherwise has no moral and little incident. A story of education—seventy years of it—the practical value remains to the end in doubt, like other values about which men have disputed since the birth of Cain and Abel; but the practical value of the universe has never been stated in dollars. Although every one cannot be a Gargantua-Napoleon-Bismarck and walk off with the great bells of Notre Dame, every one must bear his own universe, and most persons are moderately interested in learning how their neighbors have managed to carry theirs.

This problem of education, started in 1838, went on for three years, while the baby grew, like other babies, unconsciously, as a vegetable, the outside world working as it never had worked before, to get his new universe ready for him. Often in old age he puzzled over the question whether, on the doctrine of chances, he was at liberty to accept himself or his world as an accident. No such accident had ever happened before in human experience. For him, alone, the old universe was thrown into the ash-heap and a new one created. He and his eighteenth-century, troglodytic Boston were suddenly cut apart—separated forever—in act if not in sentiment, by the opening of the Boston and Albany Railroad; the appearance of the first Cunard steamers in the bay; and the telegraphic messages which carried from Baltimore to Washington the news that Henry Clay and James K. Polk were nominated for the Presidency. This was in May, 1844; he was six years old; his new world was ready for use, and only fragments of the old met his eyes.

Of all this that was being done to complicate his education, he knew only the color of yellow. He first found himself sitting on a yellow kitchen floor in strong sunlight. He was three years old when he took this earliest step in education; a lesson of color. The second followed soon; a lesson of taste. On December 3, 1841, he developed scarlet fever. For several days he was as good as dead, reviving only under the careful nursing of his family. When he began to recover strength, about January 1, 1842, his hunger must have been stronger than any other pleasure or pain, for while in afterlife he retained not the faintest recollection of his illness, he remembered quite clearly his aunt entering the sickroom bearing in her hand a saucer with a baked apple.

The order of impressions retained by memory might naturally be that of color and taste, although one would rather suppose that the sense of pain would be first to educate. In fact, the third recollection of the child was that of discomfort. The moment he could be removed, he was bundled up in blankets and carried from the little house in Hancock Avenue to a larger one which his parents were to occupy for the rest of their lives in the neighboring

Mount Vernon Street. The season was midwinter, January 10, 1842, and he never forgot his acute distress for want of air under his blankets, or the noises of moving furniture.

As a means of variation from a normal type, sickness in childhood ought to have a certain value not to be classed under any fitness or unfitness of natural selection; and especially scarlet fever affected boys seriously, both physically and in character, though they might through life puzzle themselves to decide whether it had fitted or unfitted them for success; but this fever of Henry Adams took greater and greater importance in his eyes, from the point of view of education, the longer he lived. At first, the effect was physical. He fell behind his brothers two or three inches in height, and proportionally in bone and weight. His character and processes of mind seemed to share in this fining-down process of scale. He was not good in a fight, and his nerves were more delicate than boys' nerves ought to be. He exaggerated these weaknesses as he grew older. The habit of doubt; of distrusting his own judgment and of totally rejecting the judgment of the world; the tendency to regard every question as open; the hesitation to act except as a choice of evils; the shirking of responsibility; the love of line, form, quality; the horror of ennui; the passion for companionship and the antipathy to society—all these are well-known qualities of New England character in no way peculiar to individuals but in this instance they seemed to be stimulated by the fever, and Henry Adams could never make up his mind whether, on the whole, the change of character was morbid or healthy, good or bad for his purpose. His brothers were the type; he was the variation.

As far as the boy knew, the sickness did not affect him at all, and he grew up in excellent health, bodily and mentally, taking life as it was given; accepting its local standards without a difficulty, and enjoying much of it as keenly as any other boy of his age. He seemed to himself quite normal, and his companions seemed always to think him so. Whatever was peculiar about him was education, not character, and came to him, directly and indirectly, as the result of that eighteenth-century inheritance which he took with his name.

The atmosphere of education in which he lived was colonial, revolutionary, almost Cromwellian, as though he were steeped, from his greatest grandmother's birth, in the odor of political crime. Resistance to something was the law of New England nature; the boy looked out on the world with the instinct of resistance; for numberless generations his predecessors had viewed the world chiefly as a thing to be reformed, filled with evil forces to be abolished, and they saw no reason to suppose that they had wholly succeeded in the abolition; the duty was unchanged. That duty implied not only resistance to evil, but hatred of it. Boys naturally look on all force as an enemy, and generally find it so, but the New Englander, whether boy or man, in his long struggle with a stingy or hostile universe, had learned also to love the pleasure of hating; his joys were few.

Politics, as a practice, whatever its professions, had always been the systematic organization of hatreds, and Massachusetts politics had been as harsh as the climate. The chief charm of New England was harshness of contrasts and extremes of sensibility—a cold that froze the blood, and a heat that boiled it—so that the pleasure of hating—one's self if no better victim offered—was not its rarest amusement; but the charm was a true and natural child of the soil, not a cultivated weed of the ancients. The violence of the contrast was real and made the strongest motive of education. The double exterior nature gave life its relative values. Winter and summer, cold and heat, town and country, force and freedom, marked two modes of life and thought, balanced like lobes of the brain. Town was winter confinement, school, rule, discipline; straight, gloomy streets, piled with six feet of snow in the middle; frosts that made the snow sing under wheels or runners; thaws when the streets became dangerous to cross; society of uncles, aunts, and cousins who expected children to behave themselves, and who were not always gratified; above all else, winter represented the desire to escape and go free. Town was restraint, law, unity. Country, only seven miles away, was liberty, diversity, outlawry, the endless delight of mere sense impressions given by nature for nothing, and breathed by boys without knowing it.

Boys are wild animals, rich in the treasures of sense, but the New England boy had a wider range of emotions than boys of more equable climates. He felt his nature crudely, as it was meant. To the boy Henry Adams, summer was drunken. Among senses, smell was the strongest—smell of hot pine-woods and sweet-fern in the scorching summer noon; of new-mown hay; of ploughed earth; of box hedges; of peaches, lilacs, syringas; of stables, barns, cow-yards; of salt water and low tide on the marshes; nothing came amiss. Next to smell came taste, and the children knew the taste of everything they saw or touched, from pennyroyal and flagroot to the shell of a pignut and the letters of a spelling-book—the taste of A-B, AB, suddenly revived on the boy's tongue sixty years afterwards. Light, line, and color as sensual pleasures, came later and were as crude as the rest. The New England light is glare, and the atmosphere harshens color. The boy was a full man before he ever knew what was meant by atmosphere; his idea of pleasure in light was the blaze of a New England sun. His idea of color was a peony, with the dew of early morning on its petals. The intense blue of the sea, as he saw it a mile or two away, from the Quincy hills; the cumuli in a June afternoon sky; the strong reds and greens and purples of colored prints and children's picture-books, as the American colors then ran; these were ideals. The opposites or antipathies, were the cold grays of November evenings, and the thick, muddy thaws of Boston winter. With such standards, the Bostonian could not but develop a double nature. Life was a double thing. After a January blizzard, the boy who could look with pleasure into the violent snow-glare of the cold white sunshine, with its intense light and shade, scarcely knew what was meant by tone. He could reach it only by education.

Winter and summer, then, were two hostile lives, and bred two separate natures. Winter was always the effort to live; summer was tropical license. Whether the children rolled in the grass, or waded in the brook, or swam in the salt ocean, or sailed in the bay, or fished for smelts in the

creeks, or netted minnows in the salt-marshes, or took to
the pine-woods and the granite quarries, or chased musk-
rats and hunted snapping-turtles in the swamps, or mush-
rooms or nuts on the autumn hills, summer and country
were always sensual living, while winter was always com-
pulsory learning. Summer was the multiplicity of nature;
winter was school.

The bearing of the two seasons on the education of Henry
Adams was no fancy; it was the most decisive force he ever
knew; it ran through life, and made the division between
its perplexing, warring, irreconcilable problems, irreducible
opposites, with growing emphasis to the last year of study.
From earliest childhood the boy was accustomed to feel
that, for him, life was double. Winter and summer, town
and country, law and liberty, were hostile, and the man
who pretended they were not, was in his eyes a schoolmaster—that is, a man employed to tell lies to little boys. Though
Quincy was but two hours' walk from Beacon Hill, it belonged in a different world. For two hundred years, every
Adams, from father to son, had lived within sight of State
Street, and sometimes had lived in it, yet none had ever
taken kindly to the town, or been taken kindly by it. The
boy inherited his double nature. He knew as yet nothing
about his great-grandfather, who had died a dozen years
before his own birth: he took for granted that any great-
grandfather of his must have always been good, and his
enemies wicked; but he divined his great-grandfather's
character from his own. Never for a moment did he connect the two ideas of Boston and John Adams; they were
separate and antagonistic; the idea of John Adams went
with Quincy. He knew his grandfather John Quincy Adams
only as an old man of seventy-five or eighty who was
friendly and gentle with him, but except that he heard his
grandfather always called "the President," and his grandmother "the Madam," he had no reason to suppose that his
Adams grandfather differed in character from his Brooks
grandfather who was equally kind and benevolent. He
liked the Adams side best, but for no other reason than that
it reminded him of the country, the summer, and the absence of restraint. Yet he felt also that Quincy was in a way

inferior to Boston, and that socially Boston looked down on Quincy. The reason was clear enough even to a five-year-old child. Quincy had no Boston style. Little enough style had either; a simpler manner of life and thought could hardly exist, short of cave-dwelling. The flint-and-steel with which his grandfather Adams used to light his own fires in the early morning was still on the mantelpiece of his study. The idea of a livery or even a dress for servants, or of an evening toilette, was next to blasphemy. Bathrooms, water-supplies, lighting, heating, and the whole array of domestic comforts, were unknown at Quincy. Boston had already a bathroom, a water-supply, a furnace, and gas. The superiority of Boston was evident, but a child liked it no better for that.

The magnificence of his grandfather Brooks's house in Pearl Street or South Street has long ago disappeared, but perhaps his country house at Medford may still remain to show what impressed the mind of a boy in 1845 with the idea of city splendor. The President's place at Quincy was the larger and older and far the more interesting of the two; but a boy felt at once its inferiority in fashion. It showed plainly enough its want of wealth. It smacked of colonial age, but not of Boston style or plush curtains. To the end of his life he never quite overcame the prejudice thus drawn in with his childish breath. He never could compel himself to care for nineteenth-century style. He was never able to adopt it, any more than his father or grandfather or great-grandfather had done. Not that he felt it as particularly hostile, for he reconciled himself to much that was worse; but because, for some remote reason, he was born an eighteenth-century child. The old house at Quincy was eighteenth century. What style it had was in its Queen Anne mahogany panels and its Louis Seize chairs and sofas. The panels belonged to an old colonial Vassall who built the house; the furniture had been brought back from Paris in 1789 or 1801 or 1817, along with porcelain and books and much else of old diplomatic remnants; and neither of the two eighteenth-century styles—neither English Queen Anne nor French Louis Seize—was comfortable for a boy, or for anyone else. The dark mahogany had been painted white to suit daily life in winter gloom. Nothing seemed to favor, for a child's objects, the older forms. On the contrary, most boys, as well as grown-up people, preferred the new, with good reason, and the child felt himself distinctly at a disadvantage for the taste.

Nor had personal preference any share in his bias. The Brooks grandfather was as amiable and as sympathetic as the Adams grandfather. Both were born in 1767, and both died in 1848. Both were kind to children, and both belonged rather to the eighteenth than to the nineteenth centuries. The child knew no difference between them except that one was associated with winter and the other with summer; one with Boston, the other with Quincy. Even with Medford, the association was hardly easier. Once as a very young boy he was taken to pass a few days with his grandfather Brooks under charge of his aunt, but became so violently homesick that within twenty-four hours he was brought back in disgrace. Yet he could not remember ever being seriously homesick again.

The attachment to Quincy was not altogether sentimental or wholly sympathetic. Quincy was not a bed of thornless roses. Even there the curse of Cain set its mark. There as elsewhere a cruel universe combined to crush a child. As though three or four vigorous brothers and sisters, with the best will, were not enough to crush any child, every one else conspired towards an education which he hated. From cradle to grave this problem of running order through chaos, direction through space, discipline through freedom, unity through multiplicity, has always been, and must always be, the task of education, as it is the moral of religion, philosophy, science, art, politics, and economy; but a boy's will is his life, and he dies when it is broken, as the colt dies in harness, taking a new nature in becoming tame. Rarely has the boy felt kindly towards his tamers. Between him and his master has always been war. Henry Adams never knew a boy of his generation to like a master, and the task of remaining on friendly terms with one's own family, in such a relation, was never easy.

All the more singular it seemed afterwards to him that his first serious contact with the President should have been a struggle of will, in which the old man almost necessarily defeated the boy, but instead of leaving, as usual in such defeats, a lifelong sting, left rather an impression of as fair treatment as could be expected from a natural enemy. The boy met seldom with such restraint. He could not have been much more than six years old at the time—seven at the utmost—and his mother had taken him to Quincy for a long stay with the President during the summer. What became of the rest of the family he quite forgot; but he distinctly remembered standing at the house door one summer morning in a passionate outburst of rebellion against going to school. Naturally his mother was the immediate victim of his rage; that is what mothers are for, and boys also; but in this case the boy had his mother at unfair disadvantage, for she was a guest, and had no means of enforcing obedience. Henry showed a certain tactical ability by refusing to start, and he met all efforts at compulsion by successful, though too vehement protest. He was in fair way to win, and was holding his own, with sufficient energy, at the bottom of the long staircase which led up to the door of the President's library, when the door opened, and the old man slowly came down. Putting on his hat, he took the boy's hand without a word, and walked with him, paralyzed by awe, up the road to the town. After the first moments of consternation at this interference in a domestic dispute, the boy reflected that an old gentleman close on eighty would never trouble himself to walk near a mile on a hot summer morning over a shadeless road to take a boy to school, and that it would be strange if a lad imbued with the passion of freedom could not find a corner to dodge around, somewhere before reaching the school door. Then and always, the boy insisted that this reasoning justified his apparent submission; but the old man did not stop, and the boy saw all his strategical points turned, one after another, until he found himself seated inside the school, and obviously the centre of curious if not malevolent criticism. Not till then did the President release his hand and depart.

The point was that this act, contrary to the inalienable rights of boys, and nullifying the social compact, ought to have made him dislike his grandfather for life. He could not recall that it had this effect even for a moment. With a certain maturity of mind, the child must have recognized that the President, though a tool of tyranny, had done his disreputable work with a certain intelligence. He had shown no temper, no irritation, no personal feeling, and had made no display of force. Above all, he had held his tongue. During their long walk he had said nothing; he had uttered no syllable of revolting cant about the duty of obedience and the wickedness of resistance to law; he had shown no concern in the matter; hardly even a consciousness of the boy's existence. Probably his mind at that moment was actually troubling itself little about his grandson's iniquities, and much about the iniquities of President Polk, but the boy could scarcely at that age feel the whole satisfaction of thinking that President Polk was to be the vicarious victim of his own sins, and he gave his grandfather credit for intelligent silence. For this forbearance he felt instinctive respect. He admitted force as a form of right; he admitted even temper, under protest; but the seeds of a moral education would at that moment have fallen on the stoniest soil in Quincy, which is, as every one knows, the stoniest glacial and tidal drift known in any Puritan land.

Neither party to this momentary disagreement can have felt rancor, for during these three or four summers the old President's relations with the boy were friendly and almost intimate. Whether his older brothers and sisters were still more favored he failed to remember, but he was himself admitted to a sort of familiarity which, when in his turn he had reached old age, rather shocked him, for it must have sometimes tried the President's patience. He hung about the library; handled the books; deranged the papers; ransacked the drawers; searched the old purses and pocketbooks for foreign coins; drew the sword-cane; snapped the travelling-pistols; upset everything in the corners, and penetrated the President's dressing-closet where a row of tumblers, inverted on the shelf, covered caterpillars which were supposed to become moths or butterflies, but never did. The Madam bore with fortitude the loss of the tumblers which her husband purloined for these hatcheries; but she made protest when he carried off her best cut-glass bowls to plant with acorns or peachstones that he might see the roots grow, but which, she said, he commonly forgot like the caterpillars.

At that time the President rode the hobby of tree-culture, and some fine old trees should still remain to witness it, unless they have been improved off the ground; but his was a restless mind, and although he took his hobbies seriously and would have been annoyed had his grandchild asked whether he was bored like an English duke, he probably cared more for the processes than for the results, so that his grandson was saddened by the sight and smell of peaches and pears, the best of their kind, which he brought up from the garden to rot on his shelves for seed. With the inherited virtues of his Puritan ancestors, the little boy Henry conscientiously brought up to him in his study the finest peaches he found in the garden, and ate only the less perfect. Naturally he ate more by way of compensation, but the act showed that he bore no grudge. As for his grandfather, it is even possible that he may have felt a certain self-reproach for his temporary rôle of schoolmaster—seeing that his own career did not offer proof of the worldly advantages of docile obedience—for there still exists somewhere a little volume of critically edited Nursery Rhymes with the boy's name in full written in the President's trembling hand on the fly-leaf. Of course there was also the Bible, given to each child at birth, with the proper inscription in the President's hand on the fly-leaf; while their grandfather Brooks supplied the silver mugs.

So many Bibles and silver mugs had to be supplied, that a new house, or cottage, was built to hold them. It was "on the hill," five minutes' walk above "the old house," with a far view eastward over Quincy Bay, and northward over Boston. Till his twelfth year, the child passed his summers there, and his pleasures of childhood mostly centered in it. Of education he had as yet little to complain. Country schools were not very serious. Nothing stuck to the mind except home impressions, and the sharpest were those of kindred children; but as influences that warped a mind, none compared with the mere effect of the back of the President's bald head, as he sat in his pew on Sundays, in line with that of President Quincy, who, though some ten years younger, seemed to children about the same age. Before railways entered the New England town, every parish church showed half-a-dozen of these leading citizens, with gray hair, who sat on the main aisle in the best pews, and had sat there, or in some equivalent dignity, since the time of St. Augustine, if not since the glacial epoch. It was unusual for boys to sit behind a President grandfather, and to read over his head the tablet in memory of a President great-grandfather, who had "pledged his life, his fortune, and his sacred honor" to secure the independence of his country and so forth; but boys naturally supposed, without much reasoning, that other boys had the equivalent of President grandfathers, and that churches would always go on, with the bald-headed leading citizens on the main aisle, and Presidents or their equivalents on the walls. The Irish gardener once said to the child: "You'll be thinkin' you'll be President too!" The casualty of the remark made so strong an impression on his mind that he never forgot it. He could not remember ever to have thought on the subject; to him, that there should be a doubt of his being President was a new idea. What had been would continue to be. He doubted neither about Presidents nor about Churches, and no one suggested at that time a doubt whether a system of society which had lasted since Adam would outlast one Adams more.

The Madam was a little more remote than the President, but more decorative. She stayed much in her own room with the Dutch tiles, looking out on her garden with the box walks, and seemed a fragile creature to a boy who sometimes brought her a note or a message, and took distinct pleasure in looking at her delicate face under what seemed to him very becoming caps. He liked her refined figure; her gentle voice and manner; her vague effect of not belonging there, but to Washington or to Europe, like her furniture, and writing-desk with little glass doors above and little eighteenth-century volumes in old binding, labelled "Peregrine Pickle" or "Tom Jones" or "Hannah More." Try as she might, the Madam could never be Bostonian, and it was her cross in life, but to the boy it was her charm. Even at that age, he felt drawn to it. The Madam's life had been in truth far from Boston. She was born in London in 1775, daughter of Joshua Johnson, an American merchant, brother of Governor Thomas Johnson of Maryland; and Catherine Nuth, of an English family in London. Driven from England by the Revolutionary War, Joshua Johnson took his family to Nantes, where they remained till the peace. The girl Louisa Catherine was nearly ten years old when brought back to London, and her sense of nationality must have been confused; but the influence of the Johnsons and the services of Joshua obtained for him from President Washington the appointment of Consul in London on the organization of the Government in 1790. In 1794 President Washington appointed John Quincy Adams Minister to The Hague. He was twenty-seven years old when he returned to London, and found the Consul's house a very agreeable haunt. Louisa was then twenty.

At that time, and long afterwards, the Consul's house, far more than the Minister's, was the centre of contact for travelling Americans, either official or other. The Legation was a shifting point, between 1785 and 1815; but the Consulate, far down in the City, near the Tower, was convenient and inviting; so inviting that it proved fatal to young Adams. Louisa was charming, like a Romney portrait, but among her many charms that of being a New England woman was not one. The defect was serious. Her future mother-in-law, Abigail, a famous New England woman whose authority over her turbulent husband, the second President, was hardly so great as that which she exercised over her son, the sixth to be, was troubled by the fear that Louisa might not be made of stuff stern enough, or brought up in conditions severe enough, to suit a New England climate, or to make an efficient wife for her paragon son, and Abigail was right on that point, as on most others where sound judgment was involved; but sound judgment is sometimes a source of weakness rather than of force, and John Quincy already had reason to think that his mother held sound judgments on the subject of daughters-in-law which human nature, since the fall of Eve, made Adams helpless to realize. Being three thousand miles away from his mother, and equally far in love, he married Louisa in London, July 26, 1797, and took her to Berlin to be the head of the United States Legation. During three or four exciting years, the young bride lived in Berlin; whether she was happy or not, whether she was content or not, whether she was socially successful or not, her descendants did not surely know; but in any case she could by no chance have become educated there for a life in Quincy or Boston. In 1801 the overthrow of the Federalist Party drove her and her husband to America, and she became at last a member of the Quincy household, but by that time her children needed all her attention, and she remained there with occasional winters in Boston and Washington, till 1809. Her husband was made Senator in 1803, and in 1809 was appointed Minister to Russia. She went with him to St. Petersburg, taking her baby, Charles Francis, born in 1807; but broken-hearted at having to leave her two older boys behind. The life at St. Petersburg was hardly gay for her; they were far too poor to shine in that extravagant society; but she survived it, though her little girl baby did not, and in the winter of 1814–15, alone with the boy of seven years old, crossed Europe from St. Petersburg to Paris, in her travelling-carriage, passing through the armies, and reaching Paris in the *Cent Jours* after Napoleon's return from Elba. Her husband next went to England as Minister, and she was for two years at the Court of the Regent. In 1817 her husband came home to be Secretary of State, and she lived for eight years in F Street, doing her work of entertainer for President Monroe's administration. Next she lived four miserable years in the White House. When that chapter was closed in 1829, she had earned the right to be tired and delicate, but she still had fifteen years to serve as wife of a Member of the House, after her husband went back to Congress in 1833. Then it was that the little Henry, her grandson, first remembered her, from 1843 to 1848, sitting in her panelled room, at breakfast, with her heavy silver teapot and sugar-bowl and cream-jug, which still exist somewhere as an heir-loom of the modern safety-vault. By that time she was seventy years old or more, and thoroughly weary of being beaten about a stormy world. To the boy she seemed singularly peaceful, a vision of silver gray, presiding over her old President and her Queen Anne mahogany; an exotic, like her Sèvres china; an object of deference to every one, and of great affection to her son Charles; but hardly more Bostonian than she had been fifty years before, on her wedding-day, in the shadow of the Tower of London.

Such a figure was even less fitted than that of her old husband, the President, to impress on a boy's mind, the standards of the coming century. She was Louis Seize, like the furniture. The boy knew nothing of her interior life, which had been, as the venerable Abigail, long since at peace, foresaw, one of severe stress and little pure satisfaction. He never dreamed that from her might come some of those doubts and self-questionings, those hesitations, those rebellions against law and discipline, which marked more than one of her descendants; but he might even then have felt some vague instinctive suspicion that he was to inherit from her the seeds of the primal sin, the fall from grace, the curse of Abel, that he was not of pure New England stock, but half exotic. As a child of Quincy he was not a true Bostonian, but even as a child of Quincy he inherited a quarter taint of Maryland blood. Charles Francis, half Marylander by birth, had hardly seen Boston till he was ten years old, when his parents left him there at school in 1817, and he never forgot the experience. He was to be nearly as old as his mother had been in 1845, before he quite accepted Boston, or Boston quite accepted him.

A boy who began his education in these surroundings, with physical strength inferior to that of his brothers, and with a certain delicacy of mind and bone, ought rightly to have felt at home in the eighteenth century and should, in proper self-respect, have rebelled against the standards of the nineteenth. The atmosphere of his first ten years must have been very like that of his grandfather at the same age, from 1767 till 1776, barring the battle of Bunker Hill, and even as late as 1846, the battle of Bunker Hill remained actual. The tone of Boston society was colonial. The true Bostonian always knelt in self-abasement before the majesty of English standards; far from concealing it as a weakness, he was proud of it as his strength. The eighteenth century ruled society long after 1850. Perhaps the boy began to shake it off rather earlier than most of his mates.

Indeed this prehistoric stage of education ended rather abruptly with his tenth year. One winter morning he was conscious of a certain confusion in the house in Mount Vernon Street, and gathered, from such words as he could catch, that the President, who happened to be then staying there, on his way to Washington had fallen and hurt himself. Then he heard the word paralysis. After that day he came to associate the word with the figure of his grandfather, in a tall-backed, invalid armchair, on one side of the spare bedroom fireplace, and one of his old friends, Dr. Parkman or P. P. F. Degrand, on the other side, both dozing.

The end of this first, or ancestral and Revolutionary, chapter came on February 21, 1848—and the month of February brought life and death as a family habit—when the eighteenth century, as an actual and living companion, vanished. If the scene on the floor of the House, when the old President fell, struck the still simple-minded American public with a sensation unusually dramatic, its effect on a ten-year-old boy, whose boy-life was fading away with the life of his grandfather, could not be slight. One had to pay for Revolutionary patriots; grandfathers and grandmothers; Presidents; diplomats; Queen Anne mahogany and Louis Seize chairs, as well as for Stuart portraits. Such things warp young life. Americans commonly believed that they ruined it, and perhaps the practical common-sense of the American mind judged right. Many a boy might be ruined by much less than the emotions of the funeral service in the Quincy church, with its surroundings of national respect and family pride. By another dramatic chance it happened that the clergyman of the parish, Dr. Lunt, was an unusual pulpit orator, the ideal of a somewhat austere intellectual type, such as the school of Buckminster and Channing inherited from the old Congregational clergy. His extraordinarily refined appearance, his dignity of manner, his deeply cadenced voice, his remarkable English and his fine appreciation, gave to the funeral service a character that left an overwhelming impression on the boy's mind. He was to see many great functions—funerals and festivals—in afterlife, till his only thought was to see no more, but he never again witnessed anything nearly so impressive to him as the last services at Quincy over the body of one President and the ashes of another.

The effect of the Quincy service was deepened by the official ceremony which afterwards took place in Faneuil Hall, when the boy was taken to hear his uncle, Edward Everett, deliver a Eulogy. Like all Mr. Everett's orations, it was an admirable piece of oratory, such as only an admirable orator and scholar could create; too good for a ten-year-old boy to appreciate at its value; but already the boy knew that the dead President could not be in it, and had even learned why he would have been out of place there; for knowledge was beginning to come fast. The shadow of the War of 1812 still hung over State Street; the shadow of the Civil War to come had already begun to darken Faneuil Hall. No rhetoric could have reconciled Mr. Everett's audience to his subject. How could he say there, to an assemblage of Bostonians in the heart of mercantile Boston, that the only distinctive mark of all the Adamses, since old Sam Adams's father a hundred and fifty years before, had been their inherited quarrel with State Street, which had again and again broken out into riot, bloodshed, personal feuds, foreign and civil war, wholesale banishments and confiscations, until the history of Florence was hardly more turbulent than that of Boston? How could he whisper the word Hartford Convention before the men who had made it? What would have been said had he suggested the chance of Secession and Civil War?

Thus already, at ten years old, the boy found himself standing face to face with a dilemma that might have puzzled an early Christian. What was he?—where was he going? Even then he felt that something was wrong, but he concluded that it must be Boston. Quincy had always been right, for Quincy represented a moral principle—the principle of resistance to Boston. His Adams ancestors must have been right, since they were always hostile to State Street. If State Street was wrong, Quincy must be right! Turn the dilemma as he pleased, he still came back on the eighteenth century and the law of Resistance; of Truth; of Duty, and of Freedom. He was a ten-year-old priest and politician. He could under no circumstances have guessed what the next fifty years had in store, and no one could teach him; but sometimes, in his old age, he wondered—and could never decide—whether the most clear and certain knowledge would have helped him. Supposing he had seen a New York stock-list of 1900, and had studied the statistics of railways, telegraphs, coal, and steel—would he have quitted his eighteenth-century, his ancestral prejudices, his abstract ideals, his semi-clerical training, and the rest, in order to perform an expiatory pilgrimage to State Street, and ask for the fatted calf of his grandfather Brooks and a clerkship in the Suffolk Bank?

Sixty years afterwards he was still unable to make up his mind. Each course had its advantages, but the material advantages, looking back, seemed to lie wholly in State Street.

A Law of Acceleration[1]

Images are not arguments, rarely even lead to proof, but the mind craves them, and, of late more than ever, the keenest experimenters find twenty images better than one, especially if contradictory; since the human mind has already learned to deal in contradictions.

The image needed here is that of a new centre, or preponderating mass, artificially introduced on earth in the midst of a system of attractive forces that previously made their own equilibrium, and constantly induced to accelerate its motion till it shall establish a new equilibrium. A dynamic theory would begin by assuming that all history, terrestrial or cosmic, mechanical or intellectual, would be reducible to this formula if we knew the facts.

For convenience, the most familiar image should come first; and this is probably that of the comet, or meteoric streams, like the Leonids and Perseids; a complex of minute mechanical agencies, reacting within and without, and guided by the sum of forces attracting or deflecting it. Nothing forbids one to assume that the man-meteorite might grow, as an acorn does, absorbing light, heat, electricity—or thought; for, in recent times, such transference of energy has become a familiar idea; but the simplest figure, at first, is that of a perfect comet—say that of 1843—which drops from space, in a straight line, at the regular acceleration of speed, directly into the sun, and after wheeling sharply about it, in heat that ought to dissipate any known substance, turns back unharmed, in defiance of law, by the path on which it came. The mind, by analogy,

[1] Chapter XXXIV of *The Education*.

may figure as such a comet, the better because it also defies law.

Motion is the ultimate object of science, and measures of motion are many; but with thought as with matter, the true measure is mass in its astronomic sense—the sum or difference of attractive forces. Science has quite enough trouble in measuring its material motions without volunteering help to the historian, but the historian needs not much help to measure some kinds of social movement; and especially in the nineteenth century, society by common accord agreed in measuring its progress by the coal-output. The ratio of increase in the volume of coal-power may serve as dynamometer.

The coal-output of the world, speaking roughly, doubled every ten years between 1840 and 1900, in the form of utilized power, for the ton of coal yielded three or four times as much power in 1900 as in 1840. Rapid as this rate of acceleration in volume seems, it may be tested in a thousand ways without greatly reducing it. Perhaps the ocean steamer is nearest unity and easiest to measure, for any one might hire, in 1905, for a small sum of money, the use of 30,000 steam-horse-power to cross the ocean, and by halving this figure every ten years, he got back to 234 horse-power for 1835, which was accuracy enough for his purposes. In truth, his chief trouble came not from the ratio in volume of heat, but from the intensity, since he could get no basis for a ratio there. All ages of history have known high intensities, like the iron-furnace, the burning-glass, the blow-pipe; but no society has ever used high intensities on any large scale till now, nor can a mere bystander decide what range of temperature is now in common use. Loosely guessing that science controls habitually the whole range from absolute zero to 3000° Centigrade, one might assume, for convenience, that the ten-year ratio for volume could be used temporarily for intensity; and still there remained a ratio to be guessed for other forces than heat. Since 1800 scores of new forces had been discovered; old forces had been raised to higher powers, as could be measured in the navy-gun; great regions of chemistry had been opened up, and connected with other regions of physics. Within ten years a new universe of force had been revealed in radiation. Complexity had extended itself on immense horizons, and arithmetical ratios were useless for any attempt at accuracy. The force evolved seemed more like explosion than gravitation, and followed closely the curve of steam; but, at all events, the ten-year ratio seemed carefully conservative. Unless the calculator was prepared to be instantly overwhelmed by physical force and mental complexity, he must stop there.

Thus, taking the year 1900 as the starting point for carrying back the series, nothing was easier than to assume a ten-year period of retardation as far back as 1820, but beyond that point the statistician failed, and only the mathematician could help. Laplace would have found it child's-play to fix a ratio of progression in mathematical science between Descartes, Leibnitz, Newton, and himself. Watt could have given in pounds the increase of power between Newcomen's engines and his own. Volta and Benjamin Franklin would have stated their progress as absolute creation of power. Dalton could have measured minutely his advance on Boerhaave. Napoleon I must have had a distinct notion of his own numerical relation to Louis XIV. No one in 1789 doubted the progress of force, least of all those who were to lose their heads by it.

Pending agreement between these authorities, theory may assume what it likes—say a fifty, or even a five-and-twenty-year period of reduplication for the eighteenth century, for the period matters little until the acceleration itself is admitted. The subject is even more amusing in the seventeenth than in the eighteenth century, because Galileo and Kepler, Descartes, Huygens, and Isaac Newton took vast pains to fix the laws of acceleration for moving bodies, while Lord Bacon and William Harvey were content with showing experimentally the fact of acceleration in knowledge; but from their combined results a historian might be tempted to maintain a similar rate of movement back to 1600, subject to correction from the historians of mathematics.

The mathematicians might carry their calculations back as far as the fourteenth century when algebra seems to have become for the first time the standard measure of mechanical progress in western Europe; for not only Copernicus and Tycho Brahe, but even artists like Leonardo, Michael Angelo, and Albert Dürer worked by mathematical processes, and their testimony would probably give results more exact than that of Montaigne or Shakespeare; but, to save trouble, one might tentatively carry back the same ratio of acceleration, or retardation, to the year 1400, with the help of Columbus and Gutenberg, so taking a uniform rate during the whole four centuries (1400–1800), and leaving to statisticians the task of correcting it.

Or better, one might, for convenience, use the formula of squares to serve for a law of mind. Any other formula would do as well, either of chemical explosion, or electrolysis, or vegetable growth, or of expansion or contraction in innumerable forms; but this happens to be simple and convenient. Its force increases in the direct ratio of its squares. As the human meteoroid approached the sun or centre of attractive force, the attraction of one century squared itself to give the measure of attraction in the next.

Behind the year 1400, the process certainly went on, but the progress became so slight as to be hardly measurable. What was gained in the east or elsewhere, cannot be known; but forces, called loosely Greek fire and gunpowder, came into use in the west in the thirteenth century, as well as instruments like the compass, the blow-pipe, clocks and spectacles, and materials like paper; Arabic notation and algebra were introduced, while metaphysics and theology acted as violent stimulants to mind. An architect might detect a sequence between the Church of St. Peter's at Rome, the Amiens Cathedral, the Duomo at Pisa, San Marco at Venice, Sancta Sofia at Constantinople and the churches at Ravenna. All the historian dares affirm is that a sequence is manifestly there, and he has a right to carry back his ratio, to represent the fact, without assuming its numerical correctness. On the human mind as a moving body, the break in acceleration in the Middle Ages is only apparent; the attraction worked through shifting forms of force, as the sun works by light or heat, electricity, gravitation, or what not, on different organs with different sensibilities, but with invariable law.

The science of prehistoric man has no value except to prove that the law went back into indefinite antiquity. A stone arrowhead is as convincing as a steam-engine. The values were as clear a hundred thousand years ago as now, and extended equally over the whole world. The motion at last became infinitely slight, but cannot be proved to have stopped. The motion of Newton's comet at aphelion may be equally slight. To evolutionists may be left the processes of evolution; to historians the single interest is the law of reaction between force and force—between mind and nature —the law of progress.

The great division of history into phases by Turgot and Comte first affirmed this law in its outlines by asserting the unity of progress, for a mere phase interrupts no growth, and nature shows innumerable such phases. The development of coal-power in the nineteenth century furnished the first means of assigning closer values to the elements; and the appearance of supersensual forces towards 1900 made this calculation a pressing necessity; since the next step became infinitely serious.

A law of acceleration, definite and constant as any law of mechanics, cannot be supposed to relax its energy to suit the convenience of man. No one is likely to suggest a theory that man's convenience had been consulted by Nature at any time, or that Nature has consulted the convenience of any of her creations, except perhaps the *Terebratula*. In every age man has bitterly and justly complained that Nature hurried and hustled him, for inertia almost invariably has ended in tragedy. Resistance is its law, and resistance to superior mass is futile and fatal.

Fifty years ago, science took for granted that the rate of acceleration could not last. The world forgets quickly, but even today the habit remains of founding statistics on the faith that consumption will continue nearly stationary. Two generations, with John Stuart Mill, talked of this stationary period, which was to follow the explosion of new power. All the men who were elderly in the forties died in this faith, and other men grew old nursing the same conviction, and happy in it; while science, for fifty years, permitted, or encouraged, society to think that force would prove to be limited in supply. This mental inertia of science lasted through the eighties before showing signs of breaking up; and nothing short of radium fairly wakened men to the fact, long since evident, that force was inexhaustible. Even then the scientific authorities vehemently resisted.

Nothing so revolutionary had happened since the year 300. Thought had more than once been upset, but never caught and whirled about in the vortex of infinite forces. Power leaped from every atom, and enough of it to supply the stellar universe showed itself running to waste at every pore of matter. Man could no longer hold it off. Forces grasped his wrists and flung him about as though he had hold of a live wire or a runaway automobile; which was very nearly the exact truth for the purposes of an elderly and timid single gentleman in Paris, who never drove down the Champs Élysées without expecting an accident, and commonly witnessing one; or found himself in the neighborhood of an official without calculating the chances of a bomb. So long as the rates of progress held good, these bombs would double in force and number every ten years.

Impossibilities no longer stood in the way. One's life had fattened on impossibilities. Before the boy was six years old, he had seen four impossibilities made actual—the ocean-steamer, the railway, the electric telegraph, and the Daguerreotype; nor could he ever learn which of the four had most hurried others to come. He had seen the coal-output of the United States grow from nothing to three hundred million tons or more. What was far more serious, he had seen the number of minds, engaged in pursuing force—the truest measure of its attraction—increase from a few scores or hundreds, in 1838, to many thousands in 1905, trained to sharpness never before reached, and armed with instruments amounting to new senses of indefinite power and accuracy, while they chased force into hiding-places where Nature herself had never known it to be, making analyses that contradicted being, and syntheses that endangered the elements. No one could say that the social mind now failed to respond to new force, even when the new force annoyed it horribly. Every day Nature violently revolted, causing so-called accidents with enormous destruction of property and life, while plainly laughing at man, who helplessly groaned and shrieked and shuddered, but never for a single instant could stop. The railways alone approached the carnage of war; automobiles and fire-arms ravaged society, until an earthquake became almost a nervous relaxation. An immense volume of force had detached itself from the unknown universe of energy, while still vaster reservoirs, supposed to be infinite, steadily revealed themselves, attracting mankind with more compulsive course than all the Pontic Seas or Gods or Gold that ever existed, and feeling still less of retiring ebb.

In 1850, science would have smiled at such a romance as this, but, in 1900, as far as history could learn, few men of science thought it a laughing matter. If a perplexed but laborious follower could venture to guess their drift, it seemed in their minds a toss-up between anarchy and order. Unless they should be more honest with themselves in the future than ever they were in the past, they would be more astonished than their followers when they reached the end. If Karl Pearson's notions of the universe were sound, men like Galileo, Descartes, Leibnitz, and Newton should have stopped the progress of science before 1700, supposing them to have been honest in the religious convictions they expressed. In 1900 they were plainly forced back on faith in a unity unproved and an order they had themselves disproved. They had reduced their universe to a series of relations to themselves. They had reduced themselves to motion in a universe of motions, with an acceleration, in their own case, of vertiginous violence. With the correctness of their science, history had no right to meddle, since their science now lay in a plane where scarcely one or two hundred minds in the world could follow its mathematical processes; but bombs educate vigorously, and even wireless telegraphy or airships might require the reconstruction of society. If any analogy whatever existed between the human mind, on one side, and the laws of motion, on the other, the mind had already entered a field of attraction so violent that it must immediately pass beyond, into new equilibrium, like the Comet of Newton, to suffer dissipation altogether, like meteoroids in the earth's atmosphere. If it behaved like an explosive, it must rapidly recover equilibrium; if it behaved like a vegetable, it must reach its limits of growth; and even if it acted like the earlier creations of energy—the saurians and sharks—it must have nearly reached the limits of its expansion. If science were to go on doubling or quadrupling its complexities every ten years, even mathematics would soon succumb. An average mind had succumbed already in 1850; it could no longer understand the problem in 1900.

Fortunately, a student of history had no responsibility for the problem; he took it as science gave it, and waited only to be taught. With science or with society, he had no quarrel and claimed no share of authority. He had never been able to acquire knowledge, still less to impart it; and if he had, at times, felt serious differences with the American of the nineteenth century, he felt none with the American of the twentieth. For this new creation, born since 1900, a historian asked no longer to be teacher or even friend; he asked only to be a pupil, and promised to be docile, for once, even though trodden under foot; for he could see that the new American—the child of incalculable coal-power, chemical power, electric power, and radiating energy, as well as of new forces yet undetermined—must be a sort of God compared with any former creation of nature. At the rate of progress since 1800, every American who lived into the year 2000 would know how to control unlimited power. He would think in complexities unimaginable to an earlier mind. He would deal with problems altogether beyond the range of earlier society. To him the nineteenth century would stand on the same plane with the fourth—equally childlike—and he would only wonder how both of them, knowing so little, and so weak in force, should have done so much. Perhaps even he might go back, in 1964, to sit with Gibbon on the steps of Ara Cœli.

Meanwhile he was getting education. With that, a teacher who had failed to educate even the generation of 1870, dared not interfere. The new forces would educate. History saw few lessons in the past that would be useful

in the future; but one, at least, it did see. The attempt of
the American of 1800 to educate the American of 1900
had not often been surpassed for folly; and since 1800 the
forces and their complications had increased a thousand
times or more. The attempt of the American of 1900 to
educate the American of 2000, must be even blinder than
that of the Congressman of 1800, except so far as he had
learned his ignorance. During a million or two of years, every generation in turn had toiled with endless agony to attain and apply power, all the while betraying the deepest
alarm and horror at the power they created. The teacher
of 1900, if foolhardy, might stimulate; if foolish, might resist; if intelligent, might balance, as wise and foolish have
often tried to do from the beginning; but the forces would
continue to educate, and the mind would continue to react.
All the teacher could hope was to teach it reaction.

Even there his difficulty was extreme. The most elemen-
tary books of science betrayed the inadequacy of old im-
plements of thought. Chapter after chapter closed with
phrases such as one never met in older literature: "The
cause of this phenomenon is not understood"; "science no
longer ventures to explain causes"; "the first step towards a
causal explanation still remains to be taken"; "opinions are
very much divided"; "in spite of the contradictions involved"; "science gets on only by adopting different theories, sometimes contradictory." Evidently the new American would need to think in contradictions, and instead of
Kant's famous four antinomies, the new universe would
know no law that could not be proved by its anti-law.

To educate—one's self to begin with—had been the effort
of one's life for sixty years; and the difficulties of education had gone on doubling with the coal-output, until the
prospect of waiting another ten years, in order to face a
seventh doubling of complexities, allured one's imagination
but slightly. The law of acceleration was definite, and did
not require ten years more study except to show whether
it held good. No scheme could be suggested to the new
American, and no fault needed to be found, or complaint
made; but the next great influx of new forces seemed near
at hand, and its style of education promised to be violently

coercive. The movement from unity into multiplicity, between 1200 and 1900, was unbroken in sequence, and rapid in acceleration. Prolonged one generation longer, it would require a new social mind. As though thought were common salt in indefinite solution it must enter a new phase subject to new laws. Thus far, since five or ten thousand years, the mind had successfully reacted, and nothing yet proved that it would fail to react—but it would need to jump.

Verse Writer

In Japan in 1886, and coming home from the Pacific in 1891, skirting the shores of Asia, Adams felt the strong pull on him of Buddhism and other related Eastern beliefs. These others had found a way to shake off the passions of action and find peace in passionlessness. Even act, in their systems, might be pure and lead to peace. In this unemphatic meditation in verse Adams established a sympathetic and unorthodox relation between his own outlook and the eastern one. His raising up of a monument to his wife was a parallel act. St. Gaudens' notes and Adams' own musings disclose the Eastern flavor of the project.

It is Adams who speaks, and not the Rajah:

> But we, who cannot fly the world, must seek
> To live two separate lives; one, in the world
> Which we must seem to treat as real;
> The other in ourselves, behind a veil
> Not to be raised without disturbing both.

His own life had not seemed real to him since his wife's death. He stated a personal psychological reality as well as a proposition that was perhaps religious too.

His "Buddhism" was a valid element of his later thought, but no more a creed than the "Stoicism" he later admired, or the "Conservative Christian Anarchism" he sardonically espoused.

Buddha and Brahma[1]

The Buddha, known to men by many names—
Siddartha, Sakya Muni, Blessed One,—
Sat in the forest, as had been his wont
These many years since he attained perfection;
In silent thought, abstraction, purity,
His eyes fixed on the Lotus in his hand,
He meditated on the perfect Life,
While his disciples, sitting round him, waited
His words of teaching, every syllable
More and more precious as the Master gently
Warned them how near was come his day of parting.
In silence, as the Master gave example,
They meditated on the Path and Law,
Till one, Malunka, looking up and speaking,
Said to the Buddha: "O Omniscient One,
Teach us, if such be in the Perfect Way,
Whether the World exists eternally."

The Buddha made no answer, and in silence
All the disciples bent their contemplation
On the perfection of the Eight-fold Way,
Until Malunka spoke again: "O Master,
What answer shall we offer to the Brahman
Who asks us if our Master holds the World
To be, or not, Eternal?"
                              Still the Buddha sat
As though he heard not, contemplating

[1] A poem sent to John Hay in a letter dated April 26, 1895, published in October 1915 in the *Yale Review*.

The pure white Lotus in his sacred hand,
Till a third time Malunka questioned him:
"Lord of the World, we know not what we ask;
We fear to teach what thou hast not made pure."

Then gently, still in silence, lost in thought,
The Buddha raised the Lotus in his hand,
His eyes bent downward, fixed upon the flower.
No more! A moment so he held it only,
Then his hand sank into its former rest.

Long the disciples pondered on the lesson.
Much they discussed its mystery and meaning,
Each finding something he could make his own,
Some hope or danger in the Noble Way,
Some guide or warning to the Perfect Life.
Among them sat the last of the disciples,
Listening and pondering, silently and still;
And when the scholars found no certain meaning
In Buddha's answer to Malunka's prayer,
The young man pondered: I will seek my father,
The wisest man of all men in the world,
And he with one word will reveal this secret,
And make me in an instant reach the light
Which these in many years have not attained
Though guided by the Buddha and the Law.

So the boy sought his father—an old man
Famous for human wisdom, subtle counsel,
Boldness in action, recklessness in war—
Gautama's friend, the Rajah of Mogadha.
No follower of Buddha, but a Brahman,
Devoted first to Vishnu, then to caste,
He made no sign of anger or remonstrance
When his son left him at Siddartha's bidding
To take the vows of poverty and prayer—
If Vishnu willed it, let his will be done!

The Rajah sat at evening in his palace,
Deep in the solitude of his own thought,
When silently the young man entering
Crouched at a distance, waiting till his father

Should give some sign of favor. Then he spoke:
"Father, you are wise! I come to ask you
A secret meaning none of us can read;
For, when Malunka three times asked the Master
Whether the world was or was not eternal,
Siddartha for a moment lifted up
The Lotus, and kept silence."

The Rajah pondered long, with darkened features,
As though in doubt increasing. Then he said:
"Reflect, my son! The Master had not meant
This last and deepest lesson to be learned
From any but himself—by any means
But silent thought, abstraction, purity,
The living spirit of his Eight-fold Way,
The jewels of his Lotus. Least of all
Had he, whose first and easiest lesson taught
The nothingness of caste, intended you
To seek out me, a Warrior, Kshatriya,
Knowing no duties but to caste and sword,
To teach the Buddha and unveil his shrine.
My teaching is not his; mine not his way;
You quit your Master when you question me."

Silent they sat, and long. Then slowly spoke
The younger: "Father, you are wise.
I must have Wisdom." "Not so, my son.
Old men are often fools, but young men always.
Your duty is to act; leave thought to us."
The younger sat in patience, eyes cast down,
Voice low and gentle as the Master taught;
But still repeated the same prayer: "You are wise;
I must have wisdom. Life for me is thought,
But, were it action, how, in youth or age,
Can man act wisely, leaving thought aside?"

The Rajah made no answer, but almost
His mouth seemed curving to a sudden smile
That hardened to a frown: and then he spoke:
"If Vishnu wills it, let his will be done!
The child sees jewels on his father's sword,

[343]

And cries until he gets it for a plaything.
He cannot use it but to wound himself;
Its perfect workmanship wakes no delight;
Its jewels are for him but common glass;
The sword means nothing that the child can know;
But when at last the child has grown to man,
Has learned the beauty of the weapon's art,
And proved its purpose on the necks of men,
Still must he tell himself, as I tell you:
Use it, but ask no questions! *Think not! Strike!*
This counsel you reject, for you want wisdom.
So be it! Yet I swear to you in truth
That all my wisdom lies in these three words.
"You ask Gautama's meaning, for you know
That since his birth, his thoughts and acts alike
Have been to me a mirror, clearer far
Than to himself, for no man sees himself.
With the solemnity of youth, you ask
Of me, on whom the charm of childhood still
Works greater miracles than magicians know,
To tell, as though it were a juggler's trick
The secret meaning which himself but now
Could tell you only by a mystic sign,
The symbol of a symbol—so far-thought,
So vague and vast and intricate its scope.
And I, whom you compel to speak for him,
Must give his thought through mine, for his
Passes your powers—yours and all your school.

"Your Master, Sakya Muni, Gautama,
Is, like myself and you, a Kshatriya,
And in our youths we both, like you, rebelled
Against the priesthood and their laws of caste.
We sought new paths, desperate to find escape
Out of the jungle that the priests had made.
Gautama found a path. You follow it.
I found none, and I stay here, in the jungle,
Content to tolerate what I cannot mend.
I blame not him or you, but would you know
Gautama's meaning, you must fathom mine.

He failed to cope with life; renounced its cares;
Fled to the forest, and attained the End,
Reaching the End by sacrificing life.
You know both End and Path. You, too, attain.
I could not. Ten years older, I;
Already trained to rule, to fight, to scheme,
To strive for objects that I dared not tell,
Not for myself alone, but for us all;
Had I thrown down my sword, and fled my throne,
Not all the hermits, priests, and saints of Ind,
Buddhist or Brahman, could have saved our heads
From rolling in the dirt; for Rajahs know
A quicker than the Eight-fold Noble Way
To help their scholars to attain the End.
Renounce I could not, and could not reform.
How could I battle with the Brahman priests,
Or free the people from the yoke of caste,
When, with the utmost aid that priests could give,
And willing service from each caste in turn,
I saved but barely both my throne and them.

"So came it that our paths were separate,
And his led up to so supreme a height
That from its summit he can now look down
And see where still the jungle stifles me.
Yet was our starting-point the same, and though
We now seem worlds apart—hold fast to this!—
The Starting-point must be the End-point too!
You know the Veda, and need not be taught
The first and last idea of all true knowledge:
One single spirit from which all things spring;
One thought containing all thoughts possible;
Not merely those that we, in our thin reason,
Hold to be true, but all their opposites;
For Brahma is Beginning, Middle, End,
Matter and Mind, Time, Space, Form, Life and Death.
The Universal has no limit. Thought
Travelling in constant circles, round and round,
Must ever pass through endless contradictions,

Returning on itself at last, till lost
In silence.

    "This is the Veda, as you know,
The alphabet of all philosophy,
For he who cannot or who dares not grasp
And follow this necessity of Brahma,
Is but a fool and weakling; and must perish
Among the follies of his own reflection.

"Your Master, you, and I, and all wise men,
Have one sole purpose which we never lose:
Through different paths we each seek to attain,
Sooner or later, as our paths allow,
A perfect union with the single Spirit.
Gautama's way is best, but all are good.
He breaks a path at once to what he seeks.
By silence and absorption he unites
His soul with the great soul from which it started.
But we, who cannot fly the world, must seek
To live two separate lives; one, in the world
Which we must ever seem to treat as real;
The other in ourselves, behind a veil
Not to be raised without disturbing both.

"The Rajah is an instrument of Brahma,
No more, no less, than sunshine, lightning, rain;
And when he meets resistance in his path,
And when his sword falls on a victim's neck,
It strikes as strikes the lightning—as it must;
Rending its way through darkness to the point
It needs must seek, by no choice of its own.
Thus in the life of Ruler, Warrior, Master,
The wise man knows his wisdom has no place,
And when most wise, we act by rule and law,
Talk to conceal our thought, and think
Only within the range of daily need,
Ruling our subjects while ourselves rebel,
Death always on our lips and in our act.

"This is the jungle in which we must stay,
According to the teachings of the Master,

Never can we attain the Perfect Life.
Yet in this world of selfishness and striving
The wise man lives as deeply sunk in silence,
As conscious of the Perfect Life he covets,
As any recluse in his forest shadows,
As any Yogi in his mystic trances.
We need no Noble Way to teach us Freedom
Amid the clamor of a world of slaves.
We need no Lotus to love purity
Where life is else corruption.

"So read Siddartha's secret! He has taught
A certain pathway to attain the End;
And best and simplest yet devised by man,
Yet still so hard that every energy
Must be devoted to its sacred law.
Then, when Malunka turns to ask for knowledge,
Would seek what lies beyond the Path he teaches,
What distant horizon transcends his own,
He bids you look in silence on the Lotus.
For you, he means no more. For me, this meaning
Points back and forward to that common goal
From which all paths diverge; to which,
All paths must tend—Brahma, the only Truth!

"Gautama tells me my way too is good;
Life, Time, Space, Thought, the World, the Universe
End where they first begin, in one sole Thought
Of Purity in Silence."

Prayer to
the Virgin of Chartres

Most important of the faiths Adams admired but did not profess (only metaphorically, imaginatively practiced) was the habit of devotion to the Virgin. It was the Virgin who was the creator of the energy of the high Middle Ages. It was she who had raised up the cathedrals and caused poets to sing and philosophers to build structures of majestic thought. Who or what, then, raised up our railroad stations, or set evolutionists or pragmatists to thinking?

The best symbol Adams could find in answer to his own question was that of the dynamo. Power could be religious, or economic, or political, or could be naked and unmotivated. He believed the beautiful, efficient dynamo to be the best symbol of his own century's allegiance to undirected, purposeless power. He might have used the atomic reactor as his symbol if he had lived fifty years later; the thought would have been the same, but only sardonically justified.

The Prayer *unites the two worlds of* Mont-St.-Michel and Chartres *and* The Education of Henry Adams. *It is a bridge between them.*

PRAYER TO THE VIRGIN OF CHARTRES[1]

Gracious Lady:—

Simple as when I asked your aid before;

[1] Published by the Houghton Mifflin Co., in 1920 in *Letters to a Niece and Prayer to the Virgin of Chartres*, edited by Mabel La Farge.

Prayer to the Virgin of Chartres

Humble as when I prayed for grace in vain
Seven hundred years ago; weak, weary, sore
   In heart and hope, I ask your help again.

You, who remember all, remember me;
   An English scholar of a Norman name,
I was a thousand who then crossed the sea
   To wrangle in the Paris schools for fame.

When your Byzantine portal was still young
   I prayed there with my master Abailard;
When Ave Maris Stella was first sung,
   I helped to sing it here with Saint Bernard.

When Blanche set up your gorgeous Rose of France
   I stood among the servants of the Queen;
And when Saint Louis made his penitence,
   I followed barefoot where the King had been.

For centuries I brought you all my cares,
   And vexed you with the murmurs of a child;
You heard the tedious burden of my prayers;
   You could not grant them, but at least you smiled.

If then I left you, it was not my crime,
   Or if a crime, it was not mine alone.
All children wander with the truant Time.
   Pardon me too! You pardoned once your Son!

For He said to you:—"Wist ye not that I
   Must be about my Father's business?" So,
Seeking his Father he pursued his way
   Straight to the Cross towards which we all must go.

So I too wandered off among the host
   That racked the earth to find the father's clue.
I did not find the Father, but I lost
   What now I value more, the Mother,—You!

I thought the fault was yours that foiled my search;
   I turned and broke your image on its throne,
Cast down my idol, and resumed my march
   To claim the father's empire for my own.

Crossing the hostile sea, our greedy band
   Saw rising hills and forests in the blue;
Our father's kingdom in the promised land!
   —We seized it, and dethroned the father too.

And now we are the Father, with our brood,
   Ruling the Infinite, not Three but One;
We made our world and saw that it was good;
   Ourselves we worship, and we have no Son.

Yet we have Gods, for even our strong nerve
   Falters before the Energy we own.
Which shall be master? Which of us shall serve?
   Which wears the fetters? Which shall bear the crown?

Brave though we be, we dread to face the Sphinx,
   Or answer the old riddle she still asks.
Strong as we are, our reckless courage shrinks
   To look beyond the piece-work of our tasks.

But when we must, we pray, as in the past
   Before the Cross on which your Son was nailed.
Listen, dear lady! You shall hear the last
   Of the strange prayers Humanity has wailed.

PRAYER TO THE DYNAMO

Mysterious Power! Gentle Friend!
   Despotic Master! Tireless Force!
You and We are near the End.
Either You or We must bend
   To bear the martyrs' Cross.

We know ourselves, what we can bear
   As men; our strength and weakness too;
Down to the fraction of a hair;
And know that we, with all our care
   And knowledge, know not you.

You come in silence, Primal Force,
   We know not whence, or when, or why;
You stay a moment in your course

[350]

Prayer to the Virgin of Chartres

To play; and, lo! you leap across
  To Alpha Centauri!

We know not whether you are kind,
  Or cruel in your fiercer mood;
But be you Matter, be you Mind,
We think we know that you are blind,
  And we alone are good.

We know that prayer is thrown away,
  For you are only force and light;
A shifting current; night and day;
We know this well, and yet we pray,
  For prayer is infinite,

Like you! Within the finite sphere
  That bounds the impotence of thought,
We search an outlet everywhere
But only find that we are here
  And that you are—are not!

What are we then? the lords of space?
  The master-mind whose tasks you do?
Jockey who rides you in the race?
Or are we atoms whirled apace,
  Shaped and controlled by you?

Still silence! Still no end in sight!
  No sound in answer to our cry!
Then, by the God we now hold tight,
Though we destroy soul, life and light,
  Answer you shall—or die!

We are no beggars! What care we
  For hopes or terrors, love or hate?
What for the universe? We see
Only our certain destiny
  And the last word of Fate.

Seize, then, the Atom! rack his joints!
  Tear out of him his secret spring!
Grind him to nothing!—though he points
To us, and his life-blood anoints
  Me—the dead Atom-King!

A curious prayer, dear lady! is it not?
    Strangely unlike the prayers I prayed to you!
Stranger because you find me at this spot,
    Here, at your feet, asking your help anew.

Strangest of all, that I have ceased to strive,
    Ceased even care what new coin fate shall strike.
In truth it does not matter. Fate will give
    Some answer; and all answers are alike.

So, while we slowly rack and torture death
    And wait for what the final void will show,
Waiting I feel the energy of faith
    Not in the future science, but in you!

The man who solves the Infinite, and needs
    The force of solar systems for his play,
Will not need me, nor greatly care what deeds
    Made me illustrious in the dawn of day.

He will send me, dethroned, to claim my rights,
    Fossil survival of an age of stone,
Among the cave-men and the troglodytes
    Who carved the mammoth on the mammoth's bone.

He will forget my thought, my acts, my fame,
    As we forget the shadows of the dusk,
Or catalogue the echo of a name
    As we the scratches on the mammoth's tusk.

But when, like me, he too has trod the track
    Which leads him up to power above control,
He too will have no choice but wander back
    And sink in helpless hopelessness of soul,

Before your majesty of grace and love,
    The purity, the beauty and the faith;
The depth of tenderness beneath; above,
    The glory of the life and of the death.

When your Byzantine portal still was young,
    I came here with my master Abailard;
When Ave Maris Stella was first sung,
    I joined to sing it here with Saint Bernard.

When Blanche set up your glorious Rose of France,
   In scholar's robes I waited on the Queen;
When good Saint Louis did his penitence,
   My prayer was deep like his: my faith as keen.

What loftier prize seven hundred years shall bring,
   What deadlier struggles for a larger air,
What immortality our strength shall wring
   From Time and Space, we may—or may not—care;

But years, or ages, or eternity,
   Will find me still in thought before your throne,
Pondering the mystery of Maternity,
   Soul within Soul,—Mother and Child in One!

Help me to see! not with my mimic sight—
   With yours! which carried radiance, like the sun,
Giving the rays you saw with—light in light—
   Tying all suns and stars and worlds in one.

Help me to know! not with my mocking art—
   With you, who knew yourself unbound by laws;
Gave God your strength, your life, your sight, your heart,
   And took from him the Thought that Is—the Cause.

Help me to feel! not with my insect sense,—
   With yours that felt all life alive in you;
Infinite heart beating at your expense;
   Infinite passion breathing the breath you drew!

Help me to bear! not my own baby load,
   But yours; who bore the failure of the light,
The strength, the knowledge and the thought of God,—
   The futile folly of the Infinite!

Speculative Essayist

Adams wanted fervently to locate a system of thought that would explain life to him. He searched expectantly but fruitlessly. His later essays were carriers of the anxiety and interest of this search. They were smaller in scope than his books but were filled with an undiminished wit and verve, and a kind of delight in skating elegantly over thin ice.

In 1894, ducking the public responsibility of his unsought job as president of the American Historical Association, he silently declined to address his colleagues in person but sent them a written message, which was later given the title The Tendency of History. Pleasantly but firmly he hoaxed them by affixing a Mexican dateline to his message while remaining safely hidden away at 1603 H Street.

The Rule of Phase Applied to History is the most interesting of his attempts to use scientific theories to image historical trends, a remarkable performance, even for a jaunty Henry Adams at seventy. In it he invented, or rather borrowed from the physicist Willard Gibbs, a new theory to explain the direction and momentum of human development.

The Tendency of History[1]

Guada'-c-Jara, December 12, 1894.

Dear Sir: I regret extremely that constant absence has prevented me from attending the meetings of the Historical Association. On the date which your letter mentions as that of its first decennial I shall not be within reach. I have to ask you to offer my apology to the members, and the assurance that at that moment I am believed to be somewhere beyond the Isthmus of Panama. Perhaps this absence runs in some of the mysterious ways of nature's law, for you will not forget that when you did me the honor to make me your president I was still farther away—in Tahiti or Fiji, I believe—and never even had an opportunity to thank you. Evidently I am fitted only to be an absent president, and you will pardon a defect which is clearly not official, but a condition of the man.

I regret this fault the more because I would have liked to be of service, and perhaps there is service that might be usefully performed. Even the effort to hold together the persons interested in history is worth making. That we should ever act on public opinion with the weight of one compact and one energetic conviction is hardly to be expected, but that one day or another we shall be compelled to act individually or in groups I cannot doubt. With more anxiety than confidence, I should have liked to do something, however trifling, to hold the association together and unite it on some common ground, with a full understanding

[1] From Henry Adams' *The Degradation of the Democratic Dogma*, copyright 1919 by The Macmillan Co. Sent as a message to a meeting of the American Historical Association from Adams as president of the Association.

of the course which history seems destined to take and with a good-natured willingness to accept or reject the result, but in any case not to quarrel over it.

No one who has watched the course of history during the last generation can have felt doubt of its tendency. Those of us who read Buckle's first volume when it appeared in 1857, and almost immediately afterwards, in 1859, read the Origin of Species and felt the violent impulse which Darwin gave to the study of natural laws, never doubted that historians would follow until they had exhausted every possible hypothesis to create a science of history. Year after year passed, and little progress has been made. Perhaps the mass of students are more skeptical now than they were thirty years ago of the possibility that such a science can be created. Yet almost every successful historian has been busy with it, adding here a new analysis, a new generalization there; a clear and definite connection where before the rupture of idea was absolute; and, above all, extending the field of study until it shall include all races, all countries, and all times. Like other branches of science, history is now encumbered and hampered by its own mass, but its tendency is always the same, and cannot be other than what it is. That the effort to make history a science may fail is possible, and perhaps probable; but that it should cease, unless for reasons that would cause all science to cease, is not within the range of experience. Historians will not, and even if they would they can not, abandon the attempt. Science itself would admit its own failure if it admitted that man, the most important of all its subjects, could not be brought within its range.

You may be sure that four out of five serious students of history who are living to-day have, in the course of their work, felt that they stood on the brink of a great generalization that would reduce all history under a law as clear as the laws which govern the material world. As the great writers of our time have touched one by one the separate fragments of admitted law by which society betrays its character as a subject for science, not one of them can have failed to feel an instant's hope that he might find the secret which would transform these odds and ends of philosophy into one self-evident, harmonious, and complete system. He has seemed to have it, as the Spanish say, in his inkstand. Scores of times he must have dropped his pen to think how one short step, one sudden inspiration, would show all human knowledge; how, in these thickset forests of history, one corner turned, one faint trail struck, would bring him on the highroad of science. Every professor who has tried to teach the doubtful facts which we now call history must have felt that sooner or later he or another would put order in the chaos and bring light into darkness. Not so much genius or favor was needed as patience and good luck. The law was certainly there, and as certainly was in places actually visible, to be touched and handled, as though it were a law of chemistry or physics. No teacher with a spark of imagination or with an idea of scientific method can have helped dreaming of the immortality that would be achieved by the man who should successfully apply Darwin's method to the facts of human history.

Those of us who have had occasion to keep abreast of the rapid progress which has been made in history during the last fifty years must be convinced that the same rate of progress during another half century would necessarily raise history to the rank of a science. Our only doubt is whether the same rate can possibly be maintained. If not, our situation is simple. In that case, we shall remain more or less where we are. But we have reached a point where we ought to face the possibility of a great and perhaps a sudden change in the importance of our profession. We cannot help asking ourselves what would happen if some new Darwin were to demonstrate the laws of historical evolution.

I admit that the mere idea of such an event fills my mind with anxiety. When I remember the astonishing influence exerted by a mere theorist like Rousseau; by a reasoner like Adam Smith; by a philosopher, beyond contact with material interests, like Darwin, I cannot imagine the limits of the shock that might follow the establishment of a fixed science of history. Hitherto our profession has been encouraged, or, at all events, tolerated by governments and by society as an amusing or instructive and, at any rate, a safe and harmless branch of inquiry. But what will be the attitude of government or of society toward any conceivable science of history? We know what followed Rousseau; what industrial and political struggles have resulted from the teachings of Adam Smith; what a revolution and what vehement opposition has been and still is caused by the ideas of Darwin. Can we imagine any science of history that would not be vastly more violent in its effects than the dissensions roused by any one or by all three of these great men?

I ask myself, What shape can be given to any science of history that will not shake to its foundations some prodigious interest? The world is made up of a few immense forces, each with an organization that corresponds with its strength. The church stands first; and at the outset we must assume that the church will not and cannot accept any science of history, because science, by its definition, must exclude the idea of a personal and active providence. The state stands next; and the hostility of the state would be assured toward any system or science that might not strengthen its arm. Property is growing more and more timid and looks with extreme jealousy on any new idea that may weaken vested rights. Labor is growing more and more self-confident and looks with contempt on all theories that do not support its own. Yet we cannot conceive of a science of history that would not, directly or indirectly, affect all these vast social forces.

Any science assumes a necessary sequence of cause and effect, a force resulting in motion which cannot be other than what it is. Any science of history must be absolute, like other sciences, and must fix with mathematical certainty the path which human society has got to follow. That path can hardly lead toward the interests of all the great social organizations. We cannot conceive that it should help at the same time the church and the state, property and communism, capital and poverty, science and religion, trade and art. Whatever may be its orbit, it must, at least for a time, point away from some of these forces toward others which are regarded as hostile. Conceivably, it might lead off in eccentric lines away from them all, but by no power of our imagination can we conceive that it should lead toward them all.

Although I distrust my own judgment and look earnestly for guidance to those who are younger than I and closer to the movement of the time, I cannot be wholly wrong in thinking that a change has come over the tendency of liberal thought since the middle of the century. Darwin led an intellectual revival much more hopeful than any movement that can now be seen in Europe, except among the socialists. Had history been converted into a science at that time it would perhaps have taken the form of cheerful optimism which gave to Darwin's conclusions the charm of a possible human perfectibility. Of late years the tone of European thought has been distinctly despondent among the classes which were formerly most hopeful. If a science of history were established to-day on the lines of its recent development I greatly fear it would take its tone from the pessimism of Paris, Berlin, London, and St. Petersburg, unless it brought into sight some new and hitherto unsuspected path for civilization to pursue.

If it pointed to a socialistic triumph it would place us in an attitude of hostility toward existing institutions. Even supposing that our universities would permit their professors in this country to announce the scientific certainty of communistic triumphs, could Europe be equally liberal? Would property, on which the universities depend, allow such freedom of instruction? Would the state suffer its foundation to be destroyed? Would society as now constituted tolerate the open assertion of a necessity which should affirm its approaching overthrow?

If, on the other hand, the new science required us to announce that the present evils of the world—its huge armaments, its vast accumulations of capital, its advancing materialism, and declining arts—were to be continued, exaggerated, over another thousand years, no one would listen to us with satisfaction. Society would shut its eyes and ears. If we proved the certainty of our results we should prove it without a sympathetic audience and without good effect. No one except artists and socialists would listen, and the conviction which we should produce on them could lead only to despair and attempts at anarchy in art, in thought, and in society.

If, finally, the science should prove that society must at a given time revert to the church and recover its old foundation of absolute faith in a personal providence and a revealed religion, it commits suicide.

In whatever direction we look we can see no possibility of converting history into a science without bringing it into hostility toward one or more of the most powerful organizations of the era. If the world is to continue moving toward the point which it has so energetically pursued during the last fifty years, it will destroy the hopes of the vast organizations of labor. If it is to change its course and become communistic, it places us in direct hostility to the entire fabric of our social and political system. If it goes on, we must preach despair. If it goes back, it must deny and repudiate science. If it goes forward, round a circle which leads through communism, we must declare ourselves hostile to the property that pays us and the institutions we are bound in duty to support.

A science cannot be played with. If an hypothesis is advanced that obviously brings into a direct sequence of cause and effect all the phenomena of human history, we must accept it, and if we accept we must teach it. The mere fact that it overthrows social organizations cannot affect our attitude. The rest of society can reject or ignore, but we must follow the new light no matter where it leads. Only about two hundred and fifty years ago the common sense of mankind, supported by the authority of revealed religion, affirmed the undoubted and self-evident fact that the sun moved round the earth. Galileo suddenly asserted and proved that the earth moved round the sun. You know what followed, and the famous "E pur si muove." Even if we, like Galileo, should be obliged by the religious or secular authority to recant and repudiate our science, we should still have to say as he did in secret if not in public, "E pur si muove."

Those of us who have reached or passed middle age need not trouble ourselves very much about the future. We have seen one or two great revolutions in thought and we have had enough. We are not likely to accept any new theory that shall threaten to disturb our repose. We should reject at once, and probably by a large majority, a hypothetical science that must obviously be incapable of proof. We should take the same attitude that our fathers took toward the theories and hypotheses of Darwin. We may meantime reply to such conundrums by the formula that has smoothed our path in life over many disasters and cataclysms: "Perhaps the crisis will never occur; and even if it does occur, we shall probably be dead." To us who have already gone as far as we set out to go, this answer is good and sufficient, but those who are to be the professors and historians of the future have got duties and responsibilities of a heavier kind than we older ones ever have had to carry. They cannot afford to deal with such a question in such a spirit. They would have to rejoin in Heine's words:

> Also fragen wir beständig,
> Bis man uns mit einer Handvoll
> Erde endlich stopft die Maüler,
> Aber is das eine Antwort?

They may at any time in the next fifty years be compelled to find an answer, "Yes" or "No," under the pressure of the most powerful organizations the world has ever known for the suppression of influences hostile to its safety. If this association should be gifted with the length of life that we all wish for it, a span of a century at least, it can hardly fail to be torn by some such dilemma. Our universities, at all events, must be prepared to meet it. If such a crisis should come, the universities throughout the world will have done most to create it, and are under most obligation to find a solution for it. I will not deny that the shadow of this coming event has cast itself on me, both as a teacher and a writer; or that, in the last ten years, it has often kept me silent where I should once have spoken with confidence, or has caused me to think long and anxiously before expressing in public any opinion at all. Beyond a doubt, silence is best. In these remarks, which are only casual and offered in the paradoxical spirit of private conversation, I have not ventured to express any opinion of my own; or, if I have expressed it, pray consider it as withdrawn. The situation seems to call for no opinion, unless we have some scientific theory to offer; but to me it seems so interesting that, in taking leave of the association, I feel inclined to invite them, as individuals, to consider the matter in a spirit that will enable us, should the crisis arise, to deal with it in a kindly temper, and a full understanding of its serious dangers and responsibilities.

   Ever truly yours,

            Henry Adams.

Herbert B. Adams, Esq.,
Secretary, etc., American Historical Association.

The Rule of Phase
Applied to History[1]

In 1876–1878 Willard Gibbs, Professor of Mathematical Physics at Yale, published in the Transactions of the Connecticut Academy his famous memoir on the "Equilibrium of Heterogeneous Substances," containing the short chapter "On Existent Phases of Matter," which, in the hands of the Dutch chemists, became, some ten years afterwards, a means of greatly extending the science of Static Chemistry. Although the name of Willard Gibbs is probably to-day the highest in scientific fame of all Americans since Benjamin Franklin, his Rule of Phases defies translation into literary language. The mathematical formulas in which he hid it were with difficulty intelligible to the chemists themselves, and are quite unintelligible to an unmathematical public, while the sense in which the word Phase was used, confused its meaning to a degree that alters its values, and reduces it to a chemical relation. Willard Gibbs helped to change the face of science, but his Phase was not the Phase of History.

As he used it, the word meant Equilibrium, which is in fact the ordinary sense attached to it, but his equilibrium was limited to a few component parts. Ice, water, and water-vapor were three phases of a single substance, under different conditions of temperature and pressure; but if another element were added,—if one took sea-water, for instance,—the number of phases was increased according to

[1] From Henry Adams' *The Degradation of the Democratic Dogma*, copyright 1919 by The Macmillan Co. Written in 1908, dated by Adams January 1, 1909, not published during Adams' lifetime.

the nature of the components. The chemical phase thus became a distinct physical section of a solution, and as many sections existed as there were independent components.

The common idea of phase is that of the solution itself, as when salt is dissolved in water. It is the whole equilibrium or state of apparent rest. It means, perhaps, when used of movement, a variance of direction, but it seems not to have been so much employed to indicate a mere change in speed. Yet the word would apply in literature as well as it does in physical chemistry to the three stages of equilibrium: ice, water, and steam. Where only one component is concerned, the Rule of Phase is the same for chemistry as for general usage. A change of phase, in all cases, means a change of equilibrium.

Whether the equilibrium or phase is temporary or permanent,—whether the change is rapid or slow,—whether the force at work for the purpose is a liquid solvent, or heat, or a physical attraction or repulsion,—the interest of the equilibrium lies in its relations, and the object of study is the behavior of each group under new relations. Chemists and physicists have turned their studies, for twenty or thirty years past, to these relations, and the various conditions of temperature, pressure, and volume have become more important than the atoms and molecules themselves, while new processes,—osmosis, electrolysis, magnetic action,—have made a new world that is slowly taking the place of the world as it existed fifty years ago; though as yet the old curriculum of thought has been hardly touched by the change.

The new field can be entered only by timid groping for its limits, and with certainty of constant error; but in order to enter it at all, one must begin by following the lines given by physical science. If the Rule of Phase is to serve for clue, the first analogy which imposes itself as the starting-point for experiment is the law of solutions, which seems to lie on the horizon of science as the latest and largest of possible generalizations. As science touches every material or immaterial substance, each in its turn dissolves, until the ether itself becomes an ocean of discontinuous particles.

A solution is defined as a homogeneous mixture, which

can pass through continuous variations of composition within the limits that define its existence. Solids, as we all know, may be dissolved, but we do not all realize that liquids and gases may also be dissolved, or that a change in composition must accompany a change of phase. As early as 1662, Isaac Voss, in his work, "De Lucis Natura," on the Nature of Light, defined Heat as "actus dissolvens corpora," the solvent of material bodies; and in 1870, the French chemist Rosenstiehl published a paper in the Comptes Rendues of the French Academy (vol. LXX) suggesting that any gas might be likened to a body dissolved in the medium of the universal solvent, the ether. Reversing the theory, the English and Dutch physicists have solidified every gas, including even helium. The solvent has been suggested or found for every form of matter, even the most subtle, until it trembles on the verge of the ether itself; and a by-stander, who is interested in watching the extension of this new synthesis, cannot help asking himself where it can find a limit. If every solid is soluble into a liquid, and every liquid into a gas, and every gas into corpuscles which vanish in an ocean of ether,—if nothing remains of energy itself except potential motion in absolute space,— where can science stop in the application of this fecund idea?

Where it can stop is its own affair, dependent on its own will or convenience; but where it must stop is a larger question that interests philosophy. There seems to be no reason for insisting that it must necessarily stop anywhere within the region of experience. Certainly it cannot stop with static electricity, which is itself more obviously a mere phase than water-vapor. The physicists cannot conceive it without conceiving something more universal behind or above it. The logic of former thought, in its classic simplicity, would have taken for granted that electricity must be capable of reduction to a solid,—that it can be frozen,—and that it must also be soluble in ether. One has learned to distrust logic, and to expect contradiction from nature, but we cannot easily prevent thought from behaving as though sequence were probable until the contrary becomes still more probable; and the mind insists on asking what would happen if, in the absence of known limit, every substance that falls within human experience should be soluble successively in a more volatile substance, or under more volatile conditions. Supposing the mechanical theories of matter to be carried out as far as experience warrants,—supposing each centre of motion capable of solution in a less condensed motion,—supposing every vortex-centre treated as a phase or state of equilibirum which passes, more or less abruptly, into another phase, under changed conditions; must all motion merge at last into ultimate static energy existing only as potential force in absolute space?

The reply of the physicist is very simple as a formula of experiment; he can carry his theory no further than he can carry his experience; but how far does he, as a matter of fact, carry his habitual, ordinary experience? Time was when experiment stopped with matter perceptible to the senses; but the chemist long ago lost sight of matter so limited. Vehemently resisting, he had been dragged into regions where supersensual forces alone had play. Very unwillingly, after fifty years of struggle, chemists had been forced to admit the existence of inconceivable and incredible substances, and their convulsive efforts to make these substances appear comprehensible had measured the strain on their thought. Static electricity already lay beyond the legitimate domain of sensual science, while beyond static electricity lay a vast supersensual ocean roughly called the ether which the physicists and chemists, on their old principles, were debarred from entering at all, and had to be dragged into, by Faraday and his school. Beyond the ether, again, lay a vast region, known to them as the only substance which they knew or could know—their own thought, —which they positively refused to touch.

Yet the physicists here, too, were helpless to escape the step, for where they refused to go as experimenters, they had to go as mathematicians. Without the higher mathematics they could no longer move, but with the higher mathematics, metaphysics began. There the restraints of physics did not exist. In the mathematical order, infinity became the invariable field of action, and not only did the mathematician deal habitually and directly with all sorts of infinities, but he also built up hyper-infinites, if he liked, or hyper-spaces, or infinite hierarchies of hyper-space. The true mathematician drew breath only in the hyper-space of Thought; he could exist only by assuming that all phases of material motion merged in the last conceivable phase of immaterial motion—pure mathematical thought.

The physicist, in self-defence, though he may not deny, prefers to ignore this rigorous consequence of his own principles, as he refused for many years to admit the consequences of Faraday's experiments; but at least he can surely rely upon this admission being the last he will ever be called upon to make. No phase of hyper-substance more subtle than thought can ever be conceived, since it could exist only as his own thought returning into itself. Possibly, in the inconceivable domains of abstraction, the ultimate substance may show other sides or extensions, but to man it can be known only as hyper-thought,—the region of pure mathematics and metaphysics,—the last and universal solvent.

There even mathematics must stop. Motion itself ended; even thought became merely potential in this final solution. The hierarchy of phases was complete. Each phase, measured by its rapidity of vibration, arranged itself in the physical sequence familiar to physicists, such as that sketched by Stoney in his well-known memoirs of 1885, 1890, and 1899, and as reasonable as the solar spectrum. The hierarchy rose in an order more or less demonstrable, from:—

1. The *Solids,* among which the Rule of Phases offers ice as a convenient example of its first phase, because under a familiar change of temperature it passes instantly into its next phase:—

2. The *Fluid,* or water, which by a further change of temperature transforms itself suddenly into the third phase:—

3. *Vapor,* or gas, which has laws and habits of its own forming the chief subject of chemical study upon the molecule and the atom. Thus far, each phase falls within the range of human sense, but the gases, under new conditions, seem to resolve themselves into a fourth phase:—

4. The Electron or *Electricity,* which is not within the range of any sense except when set in motion. Another form

of the same phase is Magnetism; and some psychologists have tried to bring animal consciousness or thought into relation with electro-magnetism, which would be very convenient for scientific purposes. The most prolonged and painful effort of the greatest geniuses has not yet succeeded in uniting Electricity with Magnetism, much less with Mind, but all show the strongest signs of a common origin in the next phase of undifferentiated energy or energies called:—

5. The *Ether*, endowed with qualities which are not so much substantial or material as they are concepts of thought,—self-contradictions in experience. Very slowly and unwillingly have the scientists yielded to the necessity of admitting that this form of potential energy—this undifferentiated substance supporting matter and mind alike—exists, but it now forms the foundation of physics, and in it both mind and matter merge. Yet even this semi-sensual, semi-concrete, inconceivable complex of possibilities, the agent or home of infinite and instantaneous motion like gravitation,—infinitely rigid and infinitely elastic at once,— is solid and concrete compared with its following phase:—

6. *Space*, knowable only as a concept of extension, a thought, a mathematical field of speculation, and yet almost the only concrete certainty of man's consciousness. Space can be conceived as a phase of potential strains or disturbances of equilibrium, but whether studied as static substance or substance in motion, it must be endowed with an infinite possibility of strain. That which is infinitely formless must produce form. That which is only intelligible as a thought, must have a power of self-induction or disturbance that can generate motion.

7. Finally, the last phase conceivable is that which lies beyond motion altogether as Hyper-space, knowable only as Hyper-thought, or pure mathematics, which, whether a subjective idea or an objective theme, is the only phase that man can certainly know and about which he can be sure. Whether he can know it from more than one side, or otherwise than as his own self-consciousness, or whether he can ever reach higher phases by developing higher powers, is a matter for mathematicians to decide; but, even after re-

ducing it to pure negation, it must still possess, in the abstractions of ultimate and infinite equilibrium, the capacity for self-disturbance; it cannot be absolutely dead.

The Rule of Phases lends itself to mathematical treatment, and the rule of science which is best suited to mathematical treatment will always be favored by physicists, other merits being equal. Though the terms be as general as those of Willard Gibbs' formulas, if they hold good for every canonical system they will be adopted. The Rule itself assumes the general fact, ascertained by experiment or arbitrarily taken as starting point, that every equilibrium, or phase, begins and ends with what is called a critical point, at which, under a given change of temperature or pressure, a mutation occurs into another phase; and that this passage from one to the other can always be expressed mathematically. The time required for establishing a new equilibrium varies with the nature or conditions of the substance, and is sometimes very long in the case of solids, but the formula does not vary.

In chemistry the Rule of Phase applied only to material substances, but in physics no such restriction exists. Down to the moment of Hertz's experiments in 1887 and 1888, common-sense vigorously rejected the idea that material substance could be reduced to immaterial energy, but this resistance had to be abandoned with the acceptance of magneto-electricity and ether, both of which were as immaterial as thought itself; and the surrender became final with the discovery of radium, which brought the mutation of matter under the closest direct observation. Thenceforward nothing prevented the mathematical physicist from assuming the existence of as many phases, and calculating the values of as many mutations, as he liked, up to the last thinkable stage of hyper-thought and hyper-space which he knew as pure mathematics, and in which all motion, all relation, and all form, were merged.

The laws governing potential strains and stresses in an ideal equilibrium infinitely near perfection, or the volatility of an ideal substance infinitely near a perfect rest, or the possibilities of self-induction in an infinitely attenuated substance, may be left to mathematics for solution; but the ether, with its equally contradictory qualities, is admitted to exist; it is a real substance—or series of substances,—objective and undeniable as a granite rock. It is an equilibrium, a phase, with laws of its own which are not the laws of Newtonian mechanics; it requires new methods, perhaps new mind; but, as yet, the physicist has found no reason to exclude it from the sequence of substances. The dividing line between static electricity and ether is hardly so sharp as that between any of the earlier phases,—solid, fluid, gaseous, or electric.

The physicist has been reluctantly coerced into this concession, and if he had been also a psychologist he would have been equally driven, under the old laws of association formerly known as logic, to admit that what he conceded to motion in its phase as matter, he must concede to motion in its form as mind. Without this extension, any new theory of the universe based on mechanics must be as ill-balanced as the old. Whatever dogmatic confidence the mechanist had professed in his mechanical theory of the universe, his own mind had always betrayed an uneasy protest against being omitted from its own mechanical creation. This neglect involved not only a total indifference to its claim to exist as a material—or immaterial—vibration, although such mere kinetic movement was granted in theory to every other substance it knew; but it ignored also the higher claim, which was implied in its own definition, that it existed as the sole source of Direction, or Form, without which all mechanical systems must remain forever as chaotic as they show themselves in a thousand nebulae. The matter of Direction was more vital to science than all kinematics together. The question how order could have got into the universe at all was the chief object of human thought since thought existed; and order,—to use the expressive figure of Rudolph Goldscheid,—was but Direction regarded as stationary, like a frozen waterfall. The sum of motion without direction is zero, as in the motion of a kinetic gas where only Clerk Maxwell's demon of Thought could create a value. Possibly, in the chances of infinite time and space, the law of probabilities might assert that, sooner or later, some volume of kinetic motion must end in the accident of Direction, but no such accident has yet affected the gases, or imposed a general law on the visible universe. Down to our day Vibration and Direction remain as different as Matter and Mind. Lines of force go on vibrating, rotating, moving in waves, up and down, forward and back, indifferent to control and pure waste of energy,—forms of repulsion,—until their motion becomes guided by motive, as an electric current is induced by a dynamo.

History, so far as it recounts progress, deals only with such induction or direction, and therefore in history only the attractive or inductive mass, as Thought, helps to construct. Only attractive forces have a positive, permanent value for the advance of society on the path it has actually pursued. The processes of History being irreversible, the action of Pressure can be exerted only in one direction, and therefore the variable called Pressure in physics has its equivalent in the Attraction, which, in the historical rule of phase, gives to human society its forward movement. Thus in the historical formula, Attraction is equivalent to Pressure, and takes its place.

In physics, the second important variable is Temperature. Always a certain temperature must coincide with a certain pressure before the critical point of change in phase can be reached. In history, and possibly wherever the movement is one of translation in a medium, the Temperature is a result of acceleration, or its equivalent, and in the Rule of historical phase Acceleration takes its place.

The third important variable in the physico-chemical phase is Volume, and it reappears in the historical phase unchanged. Under the Rule of Phase, therefore, man's Thought, considered as a single substance passing through a series of historical phases, is assumed to follow the analogy of water, and to pass from one phase to another through a series of critical points which are determined by the three factors, Attraction, Acceleration, and Volume, for each change of equilibrium. Among the score of figures that might be used to illustrate the idea, that of a current is perhaps the nearest; but whether the current be conceived as a fluid, a gas, or as electricity,—whether it is drawn on by gravitation or induction,—whether it be governed by the laws of astronomical or electric mass,—it must always be conceived as a solvent, acting like heat or electricity, and increasing in volume by the law of squares.

This solvent, then,—this ultimate motion which absorbs all other forms of motion is an ultimate equilibrium,—this ethereal current of Thought,—is conceived as existing, like ice on a mountain range, and trickling from every pore of rock, in innumerable rills, uniting always into larger channels, and always dissolving whatever it meets, until at last it reaches equilibrium in the ocean of ultimate solution. Historically the current can be watched for only a brief time, at most ten thousand years. Inferentially it can be divined for perhaps a hundred thousand. Geologically it can be followed back perhaps a hundred million years, but however long the time, the origin of consciousness is lost in the rocks before we can reach more than a fraction of its career.

In this long and—for our purposes—infinite stretch of time, the substance called Thought has,—like the substance called water or gas,—passed through a variety of phases, or changes, or states of equilibrium, with which we are all, more or less, familiar. We live in a world of phases, so much more astonishing than the explosion of rockets, that we cannot, unless we are Gibbs or Watts, stop every moment to ask what becomes of the salt we put in our soup, or the water we boil in our teapot, and we are apt to remain stupidly stolid when a bulb bursts into a tulip, or a worm turns into a butterfly. No phase compares in wonder with the mere fact of our own existence, and this wonder has so completely exhausted the powers of Thought that mankind, except in a few laboratories, has ceased to wonder, or even to think. The Egyptians had infinite reason to bow down before a beetle; we have as much reason as they, for we know no more about it; but we have learned to accept our beetle Phase, and to recognize that everything, animate or inanimate, spiritual or material, exists in Phase; that all is equilibrium more or less unstable, and that our whole vision is limited to the bare possibility of calculating in mathematical form the degree of a given instability.

Thus results the plain assurance that the future of Thought, and therefore of History, lies in the hands of the physicists, and that the future historian must seek his education in the world of mathematical physics. Nothing can be expected from further study on the old lines. A new generation must be brought up to think by new methods, and if our historical department in the Universities cannot enter this next Phase, the physical department will have to assume the task alone.

Meanwhile, though quite without the necessary education, the historical inquirer or experimenter may be permitted to guess for a moment,—merely for the amusement of guessing,—what may perhaps turn out to be a possible term of the problem as the physicist will take it up. He may assume, as his starting-point, that Thought is a historical substance, analogous to an electric current, which has obeyed the laws,—whatever they are,—of Phase. The hypothesis is not extravagant. As a fact, we know only too well that our historical Thought has obeyed, and still obeys, some law of Inertia, since it has habitually and obstinately resisted deflection by new forces or motives; we know even that it acts as though it felt friction from resistance, since it is constantly stopped by all sorts of obstacles; we can apply to it, letter for letter, one of the capital laws of physical chemistry, that, where an equilibrium is subjected to conditions which tend to change, it reacts internally in ways that tend to resist the external constraint, and to preserve its established balance; often it is visibly set in motion by sympathetic forces which act upon it as a magnet acts on soft iron, by induction; the commonest school-history takes for granted that it has shown periods of unquestioned acceleration. If, then, society has in so many ways obeyed the ordinary laws of attraction and inertia, nothing can be more natural than to inquire whether it obeys them in all respects, and whether the rules that have been applied to fluids and gases in general, apply also to society as a current of Thought. Such a speculative inquiry is the source of almost all that is known of magnetism, electricity and ether, and all other possible immaterial substances, but in history the inquiry has the vast advantage that a Law of Phase has been long established for the stages of human thought.

No student of history is so ignorant as not to know that

fully fifty years before the chemists took up the study of
Phases, Auguste Comte laid down in sufficiently precise
terms a law of phase for history which received the warm
adhesion of two authorities,—the most eminent of that day,
—Émile Littré and John Stuart Mill. Nearly a hundred and
fifty years before Willard Gibbs announced his mathematical formulas of phase to the physicists and chemists, Turgot
stated the Rule of historical Phase as clearly as Franklin
stated the law of electricity. As far as concerns theory, we
are not much further advanced now than in 1750, and
know little better what electricity or thought is, as substance, than Franklin and Turgot knew it; but this failure
to penetrate the ultimate synthesis of nature is no excuse
for professors of history to abandon the field which is theirs
by prior right, and still less can they plead their ignorance
of the training in mathematics and physics which it was
their duty to seek. The theory of history is a much easier
study than the theory of light.

It was about 1830 that Comte began to teach the law
that the human mind, as studied in the current of human
thought, had passed through three stages or phases:—
theological, metaphysical, and what he called positive as
developed in his own teaching; and that this was the first
principle of social dynamics. His critics tacitly accepted in
principle the possibility of some such division, but they fell
to disputing Comte's succession of phases as though this
were essential to the law. Comte's idea of applying the rule
had nothing to do with the validity of the rule itself. Once
it was admitted that human thought had passed through
three known phases,—analogous to the chemical phases of
solid, liquid, and gaseous,—the standard of measurement
which was to be applied might vary with every experimenter until the most convenient should be agreed upon.
The commonest objection to Comte's rule,—the objection
that the three phases had always existed and still exist, together,—had still less to do with the validity of the law. The
residuum of every distillate contains all the original elements in equilibrium with the whole series, if the process
is not carried too far. The three phases always exist together in equilibrium; but their limits on either side are

fixed by changes of temperature and pressure, manifesting themselves in changes of Direction or Form.

Discarding, then, as unessential, the divisions of history suggested by Comte, the physicist-historian would assume that a change of phase was to be recognized by a change of Form; that is, by a change of Direction; and that it was caused by Acceleration, and increase of Volume or Concentration. In this sense the experimenter is restricted rigidly to the search for changes of Direction or Form of thought, but has no concern in its acceleration except as one of the three variables to which he has to assign mathematical values in order to fix the critical point of change. The first step in experiment is to decide upon some particular and unquestioned change of Direction or Form in human thought.

By common consent, one period of history has always been regarded, even by itself, as a Renaissance, and has boasted of its singular triumph in breaking the continuity of Thought. The exact date of this revolution varies within a margin of two hundred years or more, according as the student fancies the chief factor to have been the introduction of printing, the discovery of America, the invention of the telescope, the writings of Galileo, Descartes, and Bacon, or the mechanical laws perfected by Newton, Huyghens, and the mathematicians as late as 1700; but no one has ever doubted the fact of a distinct change in direction and form of thought during that period; which furnishes the necessary starting-point for any experimental study of historical Phase.

Any one who reads half a dozen pages of Descartes or Bacon sees that these great reformers expressly aimed at changing the Form of thought; that they had no idea but to give it new direction, as Columbus and Galileo had expressly intended to affect direction in space; and even had they all been unconscious of intent, the Church would have pointed it out to them, as it did with so much emphasis to Galileo in 1633. On this point there was no difference of opinion; the change of direction in Thought was not a mere acceleration; it was an angle or tangent so considerable that the Church in vain tried to ignore it. Galileo proved

it, and the Church agreed with him on that point if on no
other. Nothing could be more unanimously admitted than
the change of direction between the thought of St. Augus-
tine and that of Lord Bacon.

Since the Rule of historical Phase has got to rest on this
admission, theory cannot venture on the next step unless
this one is abundantly proved; but, in fact, no one as yet
has ever doubted it. The moment was altogether the most
vital that history ever recorded, and left the deepest impression on men's memory, but this popular impression
hardly expresses its scientific value. As a change of phase
it offered singular interest, because, in this case alone, the
process could be followed as though it were electrolytic,
and the path of each separate molecule were visible under
the microscope. Any school-boy could plot on a sheet of
paper in abscissae and ordinates the points through which
the curve of thought passed, as fixed by the values of the
men and their inventions or discoveries. History offers no
other demonstration to compare with it, and the more because the curve shows plainly that the new lines of Force
or Thought were induced lines, obeying the laws of mass,
and not those of self-induction. On this obedience Lord
Bacon dwelt with tireless persistence; "the true and legitimate object of science is only to endow human life with
new inventions and forces"; but he defined the attractive
power of this magnet as equal to the sum of nature's forces,
so far as they could serve man's needs or wishes; and he
followed that attraction precisely as Columbus followed the
attraction of a new world, or as Newton suffered the law
of gravitation on his mind as he did on his body. As each
newly appropriated force increased the attraction between
the sum of nature's forces and the volume of human mind,
by the usual law of squares, the acceleration hurried society
towards the critical point that marked the passage into a
new phase as though it were heat impelling water to ex-
plode as steam.

Only the electrolytic process permits us to watch such
movements in physics and chemistry, and the change of
phase in 1500–1700 is marvellously electrolytic, but the
more curious because we can even give names to the atoms

or molecules that passed over to the positive or negative electrode, and can watch the accumulation of force which ended at last by deflecting the whole current of Thought. The maximum movement possible in the old channel was exceeded; the acceleration and concentration, or volume, reached the point of sudden expansion, and the new phase began.

The history of the new phase has no direct relation with that which preceded it. The gap between theology and mathematics was so sharp in its rapid separation that history is much perplexed to maintain the connection. The earlier signs of the coming change,—before 1500,—were mostly small additions to the commoner mechanical resources of society; but when, after 1500, these additions assumed larger scope and higher aim, they still retained mechanical figure and form even in expanding the law of gravitation into astronomical space. If a direct connection between the two phases is more evident on one line than on another, it is in the curious point of view that society seemed to take of Newton's extension of the law of gravitation to include astronomical mass, which, for two hundred years, resembled an attribute of divinity, and grew into a mechanical theory of the universe amounting to a religion. The connection of thought lay in the human reflection of itself in the universe; yet the acceleration of the seventeenth century, as compared with that of any previous age, was rapid, and that of the eighteenth was startling. The acceleration became even measurable, for it took the form of utilizing heat as force, through the steam-engine, and this addition of power was measurable in the coal-output. Society followed the same lines of attraction with little change, down to 1840, when the new chemical energy of electricity began to deflect the thought of society again, and Faraday rivalled Newton in the vigor with which he marked out the path of changed attractions, but the purely mechanical theory of the universe typified by Newton and Dalton held its own, and reached its highest authority towards 1870, or about the time when the dynamo came into use.

Throughout these three hundred years, and especially in the nineteenth century, the acceleration suggests at once the old, familiar law of squares. The curve resembles that of the vaporization of water. The resemblance is too close to be disregarded, for nature loves the logarithm, and perpetually recurs to her inverse square. For convenience, if only as a momentary refuge, the physicist-historian will probably have to try the experiment of taking the law of

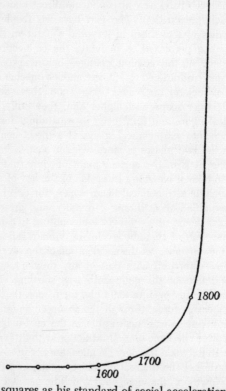

inverse squares as his standard of social acceleration for the nineteenth century, and consequently for the whole phase, which obliges him to accept it experimentally as a general law of history. Nature is rarely so simple as to act rigorously on the square, but History, like Mathematics, is obliged to assume that eccentricities more or less balance each other, so that something remains constant at last, and it is compelled to approach its problems by means of some fiction, —some infinitesimal calculus,—which may be left as general and undetermined as the formulas of our greatest master, Willard Gibbs, but which gives a hypothetical movement for an ideal substance that can be used for relation. Some experimental starting-point must always be assumed, and the mathematical historian will be at liberty to assume the most convenient, which is likely to be the rule of geometrical progression.

Thus the first step towards a Rule of Phase for history may be conceived as possible. In fact the Phase may be taken as admitted by all society and every authority since the condemnation of Galileo in 1633; it is only the law, or rule, that the mathematician and physicist would aim at establishing. Supposing, then, that he were to begin by the Phase of 1600–1900, which he might call the Mechanical Phase, and supposing that he assumes for the whole of it the observed acceleration of the nineteenth century, the law of squares, his next step would lead him backward to the far more difficult problem of fixing the limits of the Phase that preceded 1600.

Here was the point which Auguste Comte and all other authorities have failed to agree upon. Although no one denies that at some moment between 1500 and 1700 society passed from one form of thought to another, every one may reasonably hesitate to fix upon the upper limit to be put on the earlier. Comte felt the difficulty so strongly that he subdivided his scale into a fetish, polytheistic, monotheistic, and metaphysical series, before arriving at himself, or Positivism. Most historians would admit the change from polytheism to monotheism, about the year 500, between the establishment of Christianity and that of Mohammedanism as a distinct change in the form or direction of thought, and perhaps in truth society never performed a more remarkable feat than when it consciously unified its religious machinery as it had already concentrated its political and social organism. The concentration certainly marked an era; whether it marked a change of Direction may be disputed. The physicist may prefer to regard it as a refusal to change direction; an obedience to the physico-chemical law that when an equilibrium is subjected to conditions which tend towards change, it reacts internally in ways that tend to resist the external constraint; and, in fact, the establishment of monotheism was regarded by the philosophers even in its own day rather as a reaction than an advance. No doubt the Mohammedan or the Christian felt the change of deity as the essence of religion; but the mathematician might well think that the scope and nature of religion had little to do with the number of Gods. Religion is the recognition of unseen power which has control of man's destiny, and the power which man may, at different times or in different regions, recognize as controlling his destiny, in no way alters his attitude or the form of the thought. The physicist, who affects psychology, will regard religion as the self-projection of mind into nature in one direction, as science is the projection of mind into nature in another. Both are illusions, as the metaphysician conceives, and in neither case does—or can—the mind reach anything but a different reflection of its own features; but in changing from polytheism to monotheism the mind merely concentrated the image; it was an acceleration, not a direction that was changed. From first to last the fetish idea inhered in the thought; the idea of an occult power to which obedience was due,—a reflection of the human self from the unknown depths of nature—was as innate in the Allah of Mohammed as in the fetish serpent which Moses made of brass.

The reflection or projection of the mind in nature was the earliest and will no doubt be the last motive of man's mind, whether as religion or as science, and only the attraction will vary according to the value which the mind assigns to the image of the thing that moves it; but the mere concentration of the image need not change the direction of movement, any more than the concentration of converging paths into one single road need change the direction of travel or traffic. The direction of the social movement may be taken, for scientific purposes, as unchanged from the beginning of history to the condemnation of Galileo which marked the conscious recognition of break in continuity;

but in that case the physicist-historian will probably find nowhere the means of drawing any clean line of division across the current of thought, even if he follows it back to the lowest known archaic race. Notoriously, during this enormously long Religious Phase, the critical point seemed to be touched again and again,—by Greeks and Romans, in Athens, Alexandria, and Constantinople, long before it was finally passed in 1600; but so also, in following the stream backwards to its source, the historian will probably find suggestions of a critical point in ethnology long before such a critical point can be fixed. So far as he will see, man's thought began by projecting its own image, in this form, into the unknown of nature. Yet nothing in science is quite so firmly accepted as the fact that such a change of phase took place. Whether evolution was natural or supernatural, the leap of nature from the phase of instinct to the phase of thought was so immense as to impress itself on every imagination. No one denies that it must have been relatively ancient;—few anthropologists would be content with less than a hundred thousand years;—and no one need be troubled by admitting that it may have been relatively sudden, like many other mutations, since all the intermediate steps have vanished, and the line of connection is obliterated. Yet the anthropoid ape remains to guide the physical historian, and, what is more convincing than the ape, the whole phase of instinct survives, not merely as a force in actual evidence, but as the foundation of the whole geological record. As an immaterial force, Instinct was so strong as to overcome obstacles that Intellect has been helpless to affect. The bird, the beetle, the butterfly accomplished feats that still defy all the resources of human reason. The attractions that led instinct to pursue so many and such varied lines to such great distances, must have been intensely strong and indefinitely lasting. The quality that developed the eye and the wing of the bee and the condor has no known equivalent in man. The vast perspective of time opened by the most superficial study of this phase has always staggered belief; but geology itself breaks off abruptly in the middle of the story, when already the fishes and crustaceans astonish by their modern airs.

Yet the anthropoid ape is assumed to have potentially contained the future, as he actually epitomized the past; and to him, as to us, the phase to which he belonged was the last and briefest. Behind him and his so-called instinct or consciousness, stretched other phases of vegetable and mechanical motion,—more or less organic,—phases of semi-physical, semi-material, attractions and repulsions,—that could have, in the concept, no possible limitation of time. Neither bee, nor monkey, nor man, could conceive a time when stones could not fall. The anthropoid ape could look back, as certainly as the most scientific modern historian, to a critical point at which his own phase must have begun, when the rudimentary forces that had developed in the vegetables had acquired a volume and complexity which could no longer be enclosed in rigid forms, and had expanded into freer movement. The ape might have predicted his own expansion into new force, for, long before the first man was sketched, the monkeys and their companions in instinct had peopled every continent, and civilized—according to their standards—the whole world.

The problem to the anthropoid ape a hundred thousand years ago was the same as that addressed to the physicist-historian of 1900:—How long could he go on developing indefinite new phases in response to the occult attractions of an infinitely extended universe? What new direction could his genius take? To him, the past was a miraculous development, and, to perfect himself, he needed only to swim like a fish and soar like a bird; but probably he felt no conscious need of mind. His phase had lasted unbroken for millions of years, and had produced an absolutely miraculous triumph of instinct. Had he been so far gifted as to foresee his next mutation, he would have possibly found in it only a few meagre pages, telling of impoverished life, at the end of his own enormous library of records, the bulk of which had been lost. Had he studied these past records, he would probably have admitted that thus far, by some mechanism totally incomprehensible, the series of animated beings had in some directions responded to nature's call, and had thrown out tentacles on many sides; but he, as a creature of instinct, would have instinctively wished to develop in the old directions,—he could have felt no conscious wish to become a mathematician.

Thus the physicist-historian seems likely to be forced into admitting that an attractive force, like gravitation, drew these trickling rivulets of energy into new phases by an external influence which tended to concentrate and accelerate their motion by a law with which their supposed wishes or appetites had no conscious relation. At a certain point the electric corpuscle was obliged to become a gas, the gas a liquid, the liquid a solid. For material mass, only one law was known to hold good. Ice, water, and gas, all have weight; they obey the law of astronomical mass; they are guided by the attraction of matter. If the current of Thought has shown obedience to the law of gravitation it is material, and its phases should be easily calculated.

The physicist will, therefore, have to begin by trying the figure of the old Newtonian or Cartesian vortices, or gravitating group of heterogeneous substances moving in space as though in a closed receptacle. Any nebula or vortex-group would answer his purpose,—say the great nebula of Orion, which he would conceive as containing potentially every possible phase of substance. Here the various local centres of attraction would tend to arrange the diffused elements like iron-filings round a magnet in a phase of motion which, if the entire equilibrium were perfect, would last forever; but if, at any point, the equilibrium were disturbed, the whole volume would be set in new motion, until, under the rise in pressure and temperature, one phase after another must mechanically,—and more and more suddenly, —occur with the increasing velocity of movement.

That such sudden changes of phase do in fact occur is one of the articles of astronomical faith, but the reality of the fact has little to do with the convenience of the figure. The nebula is beyond human measurements. A simple figure is needed, and our solar system offers none. The nearest analogy would be that of a comet, not so much because it betrays marked phases, as because it resembles Thought in certain respects, since, in the first place, no one knows what it is, which is also true of Thought, and it seems in some cases to be immaterial, passing in a few hours from the cold of space to actual contact with the sun at a temperature some two thousand times that of incandescent iron, and so back to the cold of space, without apparent harm, while its tail sweeps round an inconceivable circle with almost the speed of thought,—certainly the speed of light,— and its body may show no nucleus at all. If not a Thought, the comet is a sort of brother of Thought, an early condensation of the ether itself, as the human mind may be

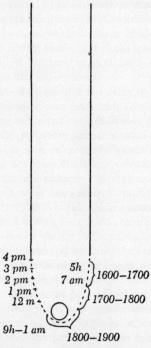

4 pm
3 pm
2 pm
1 pm
12 m   5h
7 am   }1600–1700
              }1700–1800
9h–1 am
            1800–1900

Passage of the Comet of 1843, February 27, twelve hours

another, traversing the infinite without origin or end, and attracted by a sudden object of curiosity that lies by chance near its path. If such elements are subject to the so-called law of gravitation, no good reason can exist for denying gravitation to the mind.

Such a typical comet is that of 1668, or 1843, or Newton's

comet of 1680; bodies which fall in a direct line,—itself a miracle,—from space, for some hundreds of years, with an acceleration given by the simple formula $k\frac{M}{r^2}$, where k is the constant of gravitation, M the mass of the sun and r the distance between the comet and the centre of the sun. If not deflected from its straight course by any of the planets, it penetrates at last within the orbit of Venus, and approaches the sun.

At five o'clock one winter morning in 1843, the comet began to show deflection at about two-and-a-half diameters distance from the sun; at ten o'clock it was abreast of the sun, and swung about at a right angle; at half past ten it passed perihelion at a speed of about 350 miles a second; and at noon, after having passed three hours in a temperature exceeding 5000° Centigrade, it appeared unharmed on its return course, until at five o'clock in the afternoon it was flying back to the space it came from, on the same straight line, parallel to that by which it came.

Nothing in the behavior of Thought is more paradoxical than that of these planets, or shows direction or purpose more flagrantly, and it happens that they furnish the only astronomical parallel for the calculated acceleration of the last Phase of Thought. No other heavenly body shows the same sharp curve or excessive speed. Yet, if the calculated curve of deflection of Thought in 1600–1900 were put on that of the planet, it would show that man's evolution had passed perihelion, and that his movement was already retrograde. To some minds, this objection might not seem fatal, and in fact another fifty years must elapse before the rate of human movement would sensibly relax; but another objection would be serious, if not for the theory, at least for the figure. The acceleration of the comet is much slower than that of society. The world did not double or treble its movement between 1800 and 1900, but, measured by any standard known to science—by horse-power, calories, volts, mass in any shape,—the tension and vibration and volume and so-called progression of society were fully a thousand times greater in 1900 than in 1800;—the force had doubled ten times over, and the speed, when measured by electrical standards as in telegraphy, approached infinity, and had annihilated both space and time. No law of material movement applied to it.

Some such result was to be expected. Nature is not so simple as to obey only one law, or to apply necessarily a law of material mass to immaterial substance. The result proves only that the comet is material, and that thought is less material than the comet. The figure serves the physicist only to introduce the problem. If the laws of material mass do not help him, he will seek for a law of immaterial mass, and here he has, as yet, but one analogy to follow,—that of electricity. If the comet, or the current of water, offers some suggestion for the current of human society, electricity offers one so much stronger that psychologists are apt instinctively to study the mind as a phase of electro-magnetism. Whether such a view is sound, or not, matters nothing to its convenience as a figure. Thought has always moved under the incumbrance of matter, like an electron in a solution, and, unless the conditions are extremely favorable, it does not move at all, as has happened in many solutions,—as in China,—or in some cases may become enfeebled and die out, without succession. Only by watching its motion on the enormous scale of historical and geological or biological time can one see,—across great gulfs of ignorance,—that the current has been constant as measured by its force and volume in the absorption of nature's resources, and that, within the last century, its acceleration has been far more rapid than before,—more rapid than can be accounted for by the laws of material mass; but only highly trained physicists could invent a model to represent such motion. The ignorant student can merely guess what the skilled experimenter would do; he can only imagine an ideal case.

This ideal case would offer to his imagination the figure of nature's power as an infinitely powerful dynamo, attracting or inducing a current of human thought according to the usual electric law of squares,—that is to say, that the average motion of one phase is the square of that which precedes it. The curve is thus:—

Assuming that the change of phase began in 1500, and

that the new Mechanical Phase dates in its finished form from Galileo, Bacon, and Descartes, with a certain lag in its announcement by them,—say from 1600,—the law of squares gives a curve like that of ice, water, and steam, running off to the infinite in almost straight lines at either end, like the comet, but at right angles. Supposing a value in numbers of any sort,—say 6, 36, 1296,—and assigning 1296 to the period 1600–1900, the preceding religious phase would have a value of only 36 as the average of many thousand years, representing therefore nearly a straight line, while the twentieth century would be represented by the square of 1296 or what is equivalent to a straight line to infinity.

Reversing the curve to try the time-sequence by the same rule, the Mechanical Phase being represented by 300 years, the Religious Phase would require not less than 90,000. Perhaps this result might not exactly suit a physicist's views, but if he accepts the sequence 90,000 and 300 for these two phases in time, he arrives at some curious results for the future, and in calculating the period of the fourth, or electric phase, he must be prepared for extreme figures.

No question in the series is so vital as that of fixing the limits of the Mechanical Phase. Assuming, as has been done, the year 1600 for its beginning, the question remains to decide the probable date of its close. Perhaps the physicist might regard it as already closed. He might say that the highest authority of the mechanical universe was reached about 1870, and that, just then, the invention of the dynamo turned society sharply into a new channel of electric thought as different from the mechanical as electric mass is different from astronomical mass. He might assert that Faraday, Clerk Maxwell, Hertz, Helmholz, and the whole electro-magnetic school, thought in terms quite unintelligible to the old chemists and mechanists. The average man, in 1850, could understand what Davy or Darwin had to say; he could not understand what Clerk Maxwell meant. The later terms were not translatable into the earlier; even the mathematics became hyper-mathematical. Possibly a physicist might go so far as to hold that the most arduous intellectual effort ever made by man with a distinct consciousness of needing new mental powers, was made after 1870 in the general effort to acquire habits of electro-magnetic thought,—the familiar use of formulas carrying in-definite self-contradiction into the conception of force. The physicist knows best his own difficulties, and perhaps to him the process of evolution may seem easy, but to the mere by-stander the gap between electric and astronomic mass seems greater than that between Descartes and St. Augus-tine, or Lord Bacon and Thomas Aquinas. The older ideas, though hostile, were intelligible; the idea of electro-magnetic-ether is not.

Thus it seems possible that another generation, trained after 1900 in the ideas and terms of electro-magnetism and radiant matter, may regard that date as marking the sharp-est change of direction, taken at the highest rate of speed, ever effected by the human mind; a change from the mate-rial to the immaterial,—from the law of gravitation to the law of squares. The Phases were real: the change of direc-tion was measured by the consternation of physicists and chemists at the discovery of radium which was quite as notorious as the consternation of the Church at the discov-ery of Galileo; but it is the affair of science, not of histo-rians, to give it a mathematical value.

Should the physicist reject the division, and insist on the experience of another fifty or a hundred years, the conse-quence would still be trifling for the fourth term of the series. Supposing the Mechanical Phase to have lasted 300 years, from 1600 to 1900, the next or Electric Phase would have a life equal to $\sqrt{300}$, or about seventeen years and a half, when—that is, in 1917—it would pass into an-other or Ethereal Phase, which, for half a century, science has been promising, and which would last only $\sqrt{17.5}$, or about four years, and bring Thought to the limit of its pos-sibilities in the year 1921. It may well be! Nothing what-ever is beyond the range of possibility; but even if the life of the previous phase, 1600–1900, were extended another hundred years, the difference to the last term of the series would be negligible. In that case, the Ethereal Phase would last till about 2025.

The mere fact that society should think in terms of Ether

or the higher mathematics might mean little or much. According to the Phase Rule, it lived from remote ages in terms of fetish force, and passed from that into terms of mechanical force, which again led to terms of electric force, without fairly realizing what had happened except in slow social and political revolutions. Thought in terms of Ether means only Thought in terms of itself, or, in other words, pure Mathematics and Metaphysics, a stage often reached by individuals. At the utmost it could mean only the subsidence of the current into an ocean of potential thought, or mere consciousness, which is also possible, like static electricity. The only consequence might be an indefinitely long stationary period, such as John Stuart Mill foresaw. In that case, the current would merely cease to flow.

But if, in the prodigiously rapid vibration of its last phases, Thought should continue to act as the universal solvent which it is, and should reduce the forces of the molecule, the atom, and the electron to that costless servitude to which it has reduced the old elements of earth and air, fire and water; if man should continue to set free the infinite forces of nature, and attain the control of cosmic forces on a cosmic scale, the consequences may be as surprising as the change of water to vapor, of the worm to the butterfly, of radium to electrons. At a given volume and velocity, the forces that are concentrated on his head must act.

Such seem to be, more or less probably, the lines on which any physical theory of the universe would affect the study of history, according to the latest direction of physics. Comte's Phases adapt themselves easily to some such treatment, and nothing in philosophy or metaphysics forbids it. The figure used for illustration is immaterial except so far as it limits the nature of the attractive force. In any case the theory will have to assume that the mind has always figured its motives as reflections of itself, and that this is as true in its conception of electricity as in its instinctive imitation of a God. Always and everywhere the mind creates its own universe, and pursues its own phantoms; but the force behind the image is always a reality,— the attractions of occult power. If values can be given to these attractions, a physical theory of history is a mere matter of physical formula, no more complicated than the formulas of Willard Gibbs or Clerk Maxwell; but the task of framing the formula and assigning the values belongs to the physicist, not to the historian; and if one such arrangement fails to accord with the facts, it is for him to try another, to assign new values to his variables, and to verify the results. The variables themselves can hardly suffer much change.

If the physicist-historian is satisfied with neither of the known laws of mass,—astronomical or electric,—and cannot arrange his variables in any combination that will conform with a phase-sequence, no resource seems to remain but that of waiting until his physical problems shall be solved, and he shall be able to explain what Force is. As yet he knows almost as little of material as of immaterial substance. He is as perplexed before the phenomena of Heat, Light, Magnetism, Electricity, Gravitation, Attraction, Repulsion, Pressure, and the whole schedule of names used to indicate unknown elements, as before the common, infinitely familiar fluctuations of his own Thought whose action is so astounding on the direction of his energies. Probably the solution of any one of the problems will give the solution for them all.

Washington, January 1, 1909.